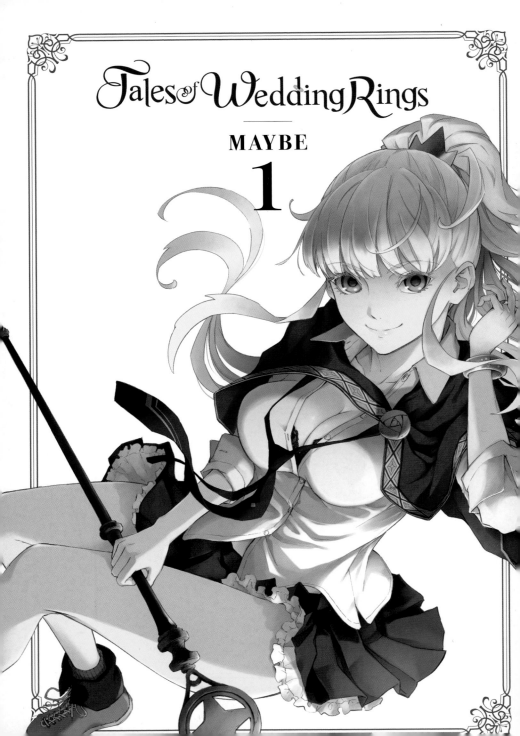

# Tales of Wedding Rings

## MAYBE

# 1

# Tales of Wedding Rings

## 1

## Contents

Chapter

### 1

003

Chapter

### 2

065

Chapter

### 3

101

Chapter

### 4

135

◯

*Presented by*
MAYBE

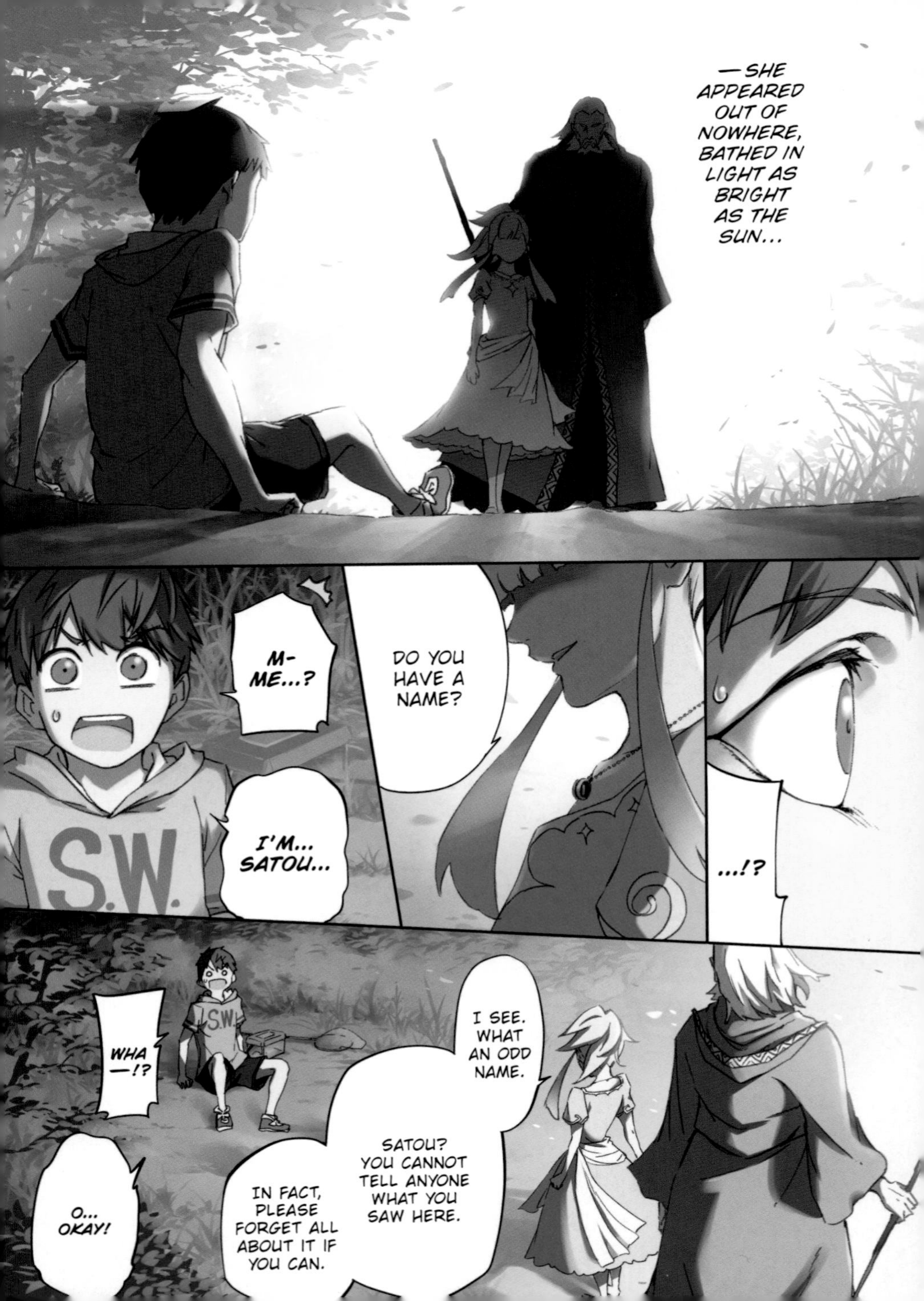
—SHE APPEARED OUT OF NOWHERE, BATHED IN LIGHT AS BRIGHT AS THE SUN...
...!?
DO YOU HAVE A NAME?
M-ME...?
I'M... SATOU...
I SEE. WHAT AN ODD NAME.
SATOU? YOU CANNOT TELL ANYONE WHAT YOU SAW HERE.
IN FACT, PLEASE FORGET ALL ABOUT IT IF YOU CAN.
WHA—!?
O... OKAY!

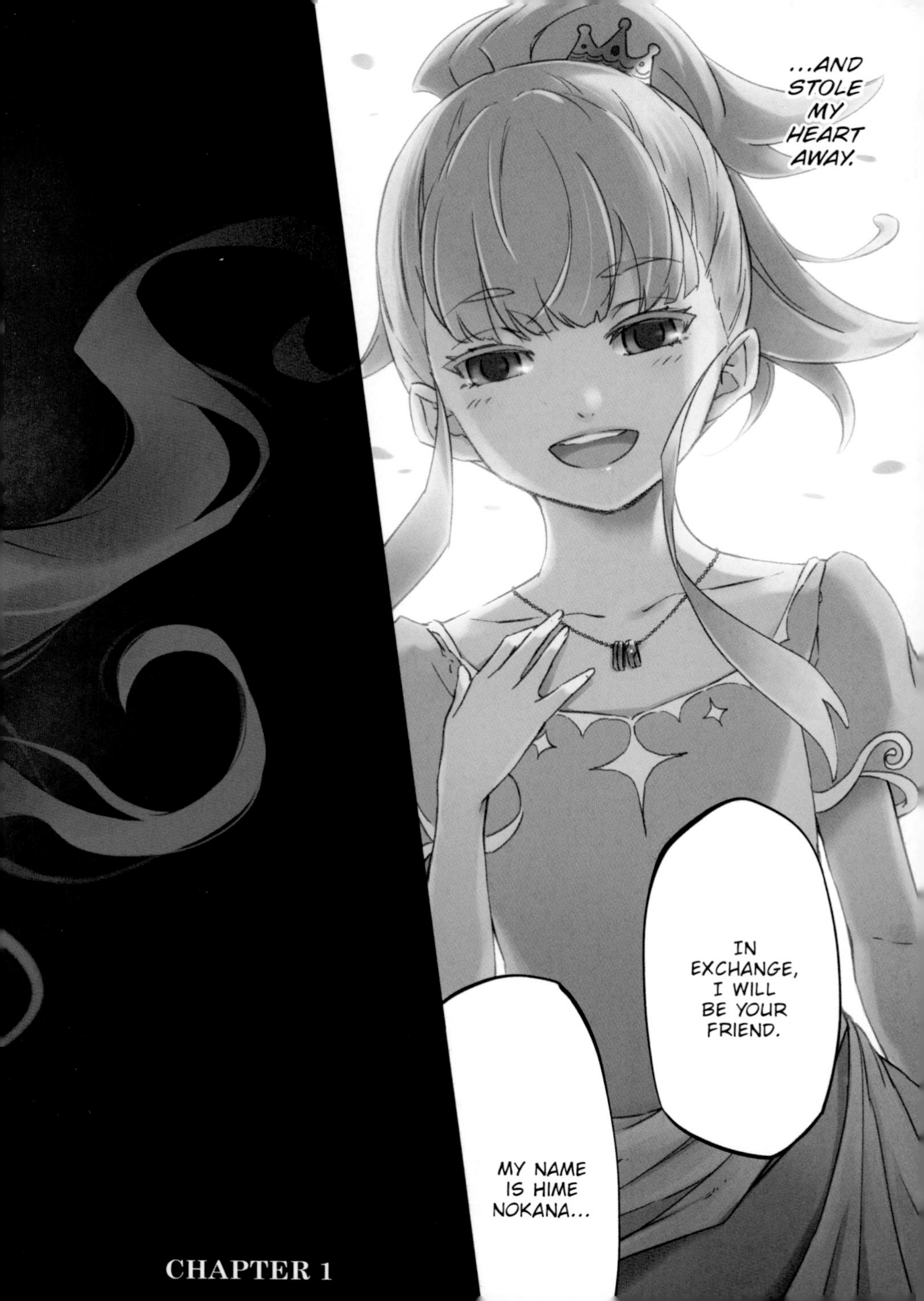
...AND STOLE MY HEART AWAY.
IN EXCHANGE, I WILL BE YOUR FRIEND.
MY NAME IS HIME NOKANA...
CHAPTER 1

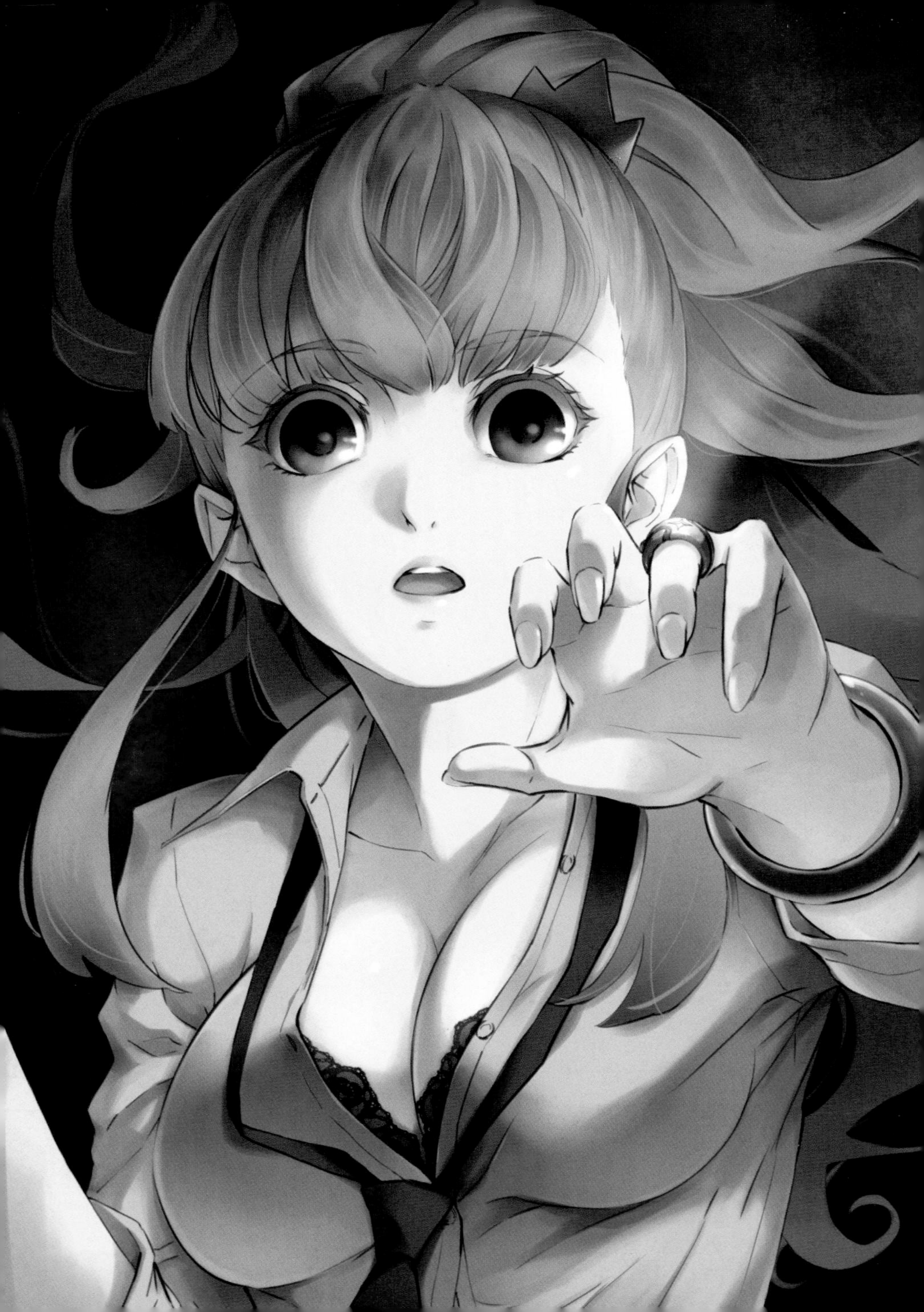

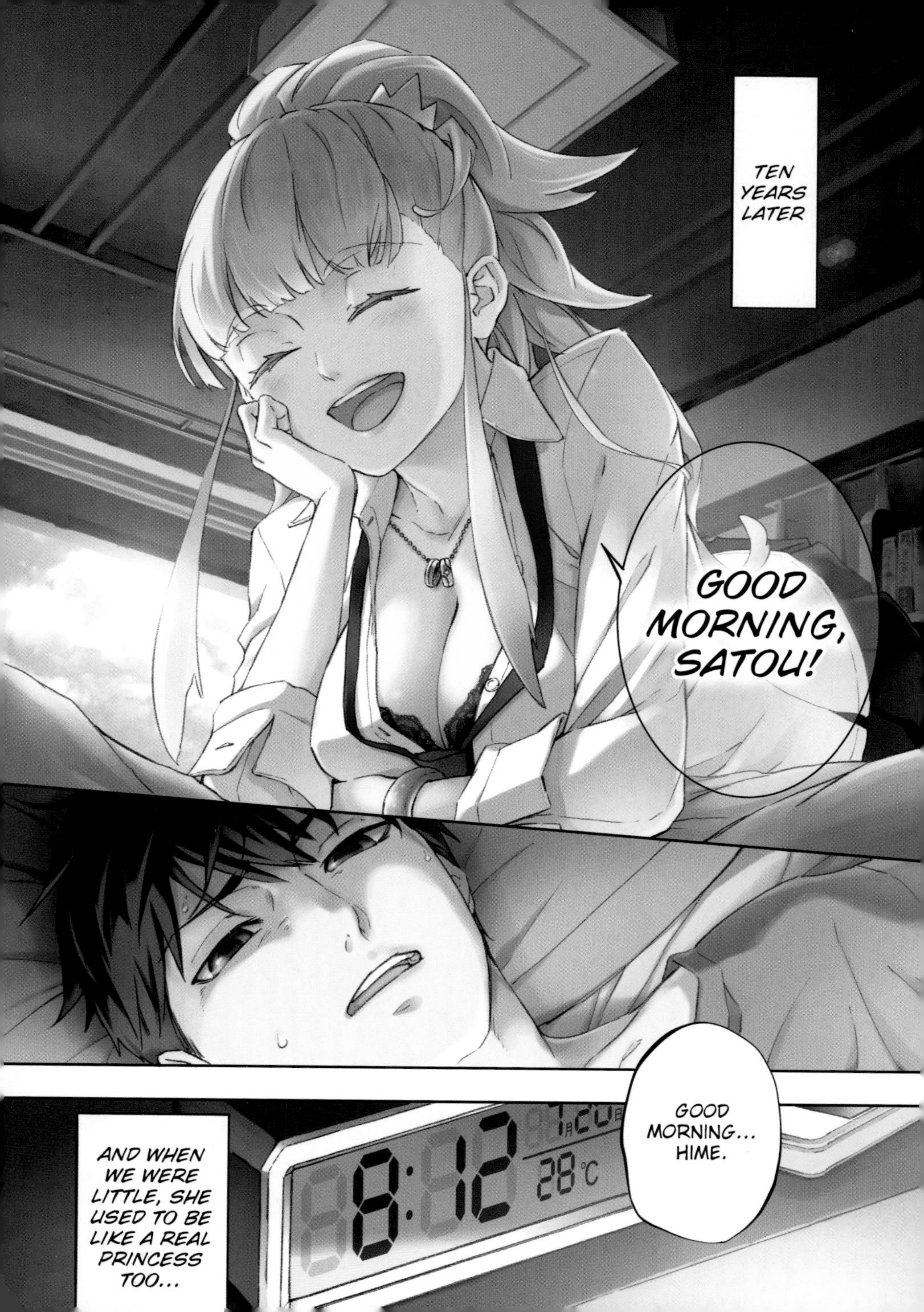
TEN YEARS LATER
GOOD MORNING, SATOU!
GOOD MORNING... HIME.
AND WHEN WE WERE LITTLE, SHE USED TO BE LIKE A REAL PRINCESS TOO...

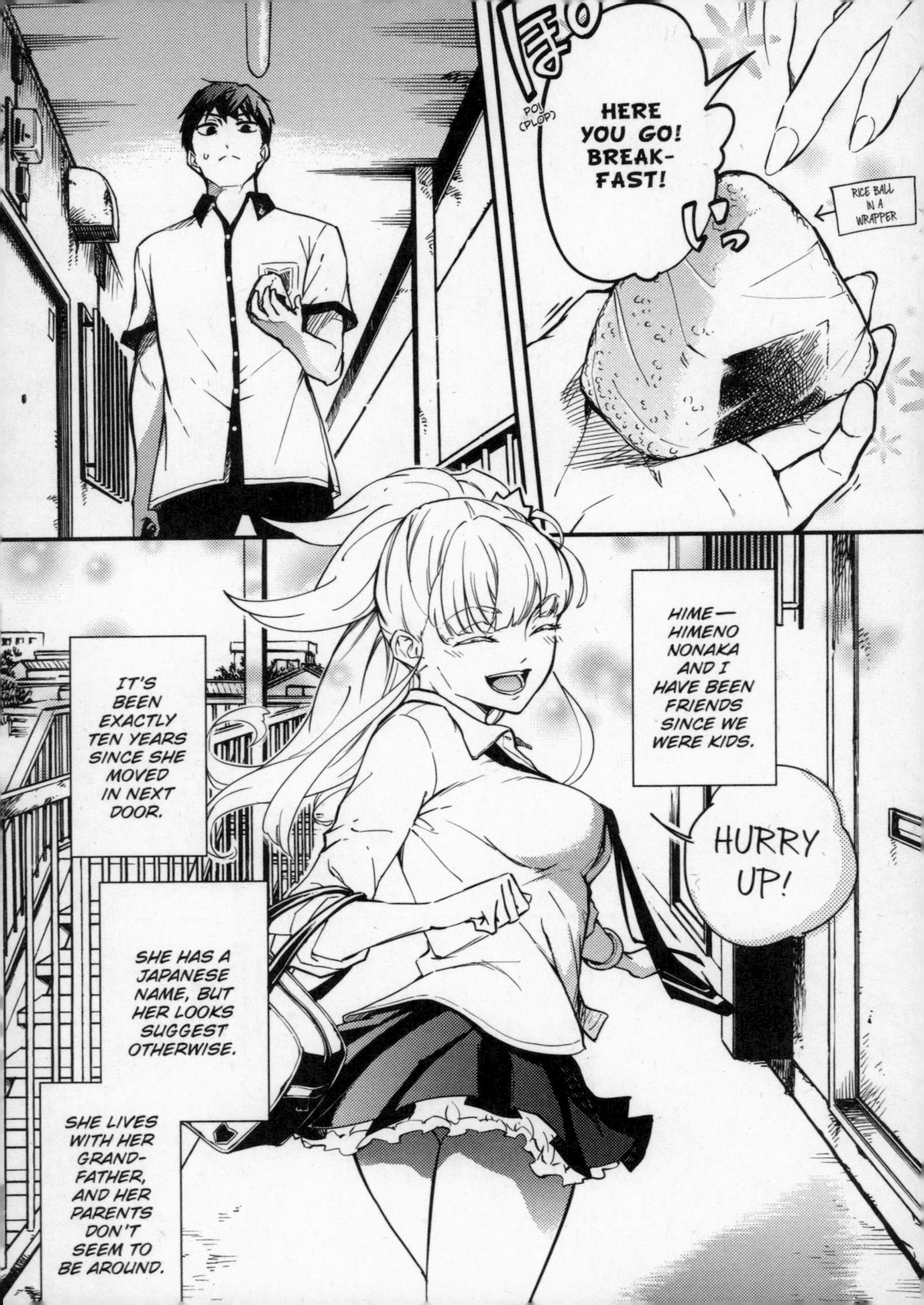
RICE BALL IN A WRAPPER
HERE YOU GO! BREAK-FAST!
POI (PLOP)
HIME— HIMENO NONAKA AND I HAVE BEEN FRIENDS SINCE WE WERE KIDS.
HURRY UP!
IT'S BEEN EXACTLY TEN YEARS SINCE SHE MOVED IN NEXT DOOR.
SHE HAS A JAPANESE NAME, BUT HER LOOKS SUGGEST OTHERWISE.
SHE LIVES WITH HER GRAND-FATHER, AND HER PARENTS DON'T SEEM TO BE AROUND.

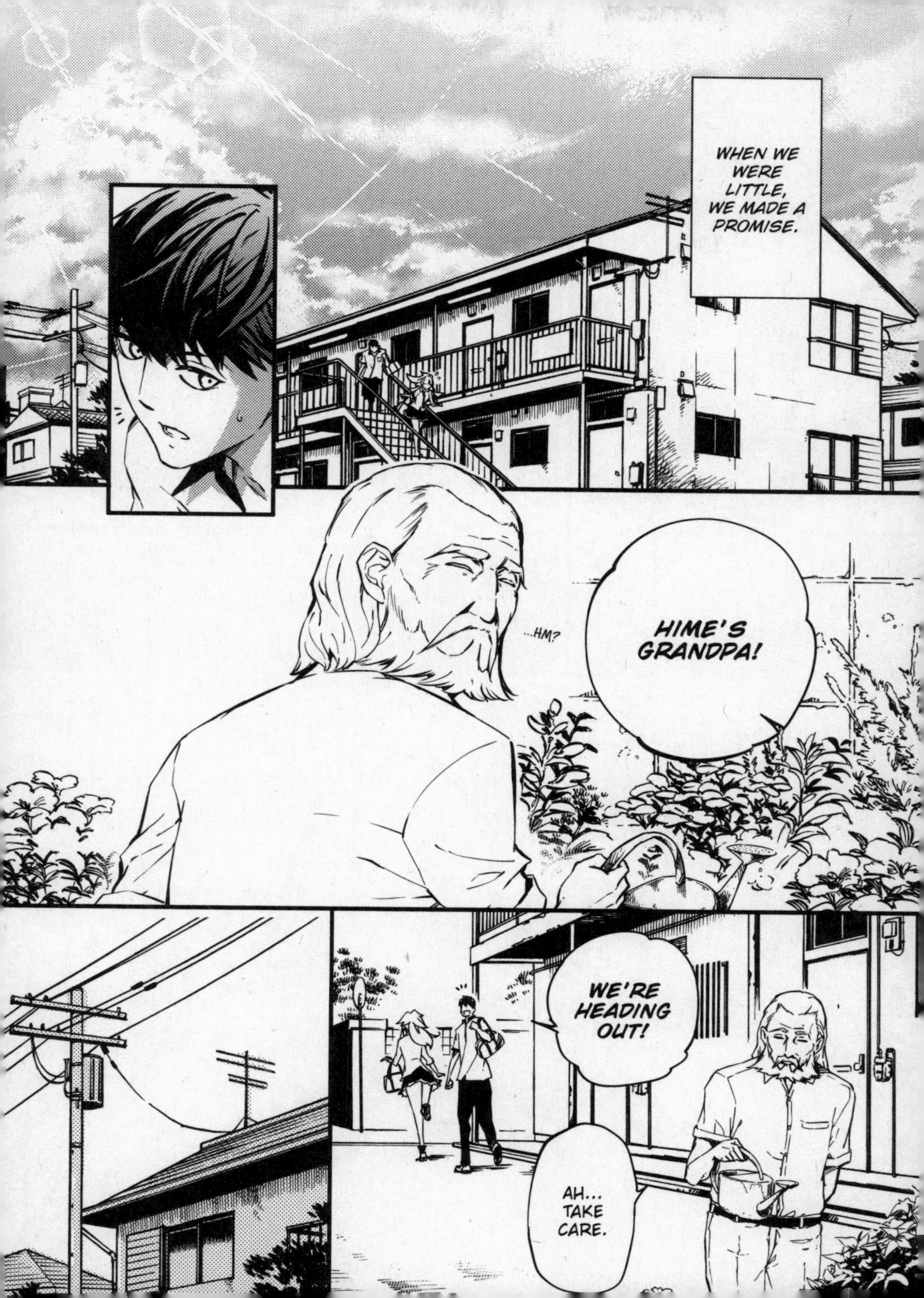
WHEN WE WERE LITTLE, WE MADE A PROMISE.
HIME'S GRANDPA!
...HM?
WE'RE HEADING OUT!
AH... TAKE CARE.

SATOU, YOUR DAD...

IS HE STILL NOT BACK YET?

IT'LL BE ANOTHER MONTH...I GUESS HE WON'T BE BACK UNTIL SUMMER VACATION'S OVER.

SOUNDS LIKE A ROUGH JOB.

HE'S GOTTEN USED TO IT.

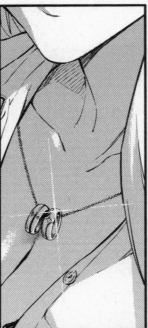

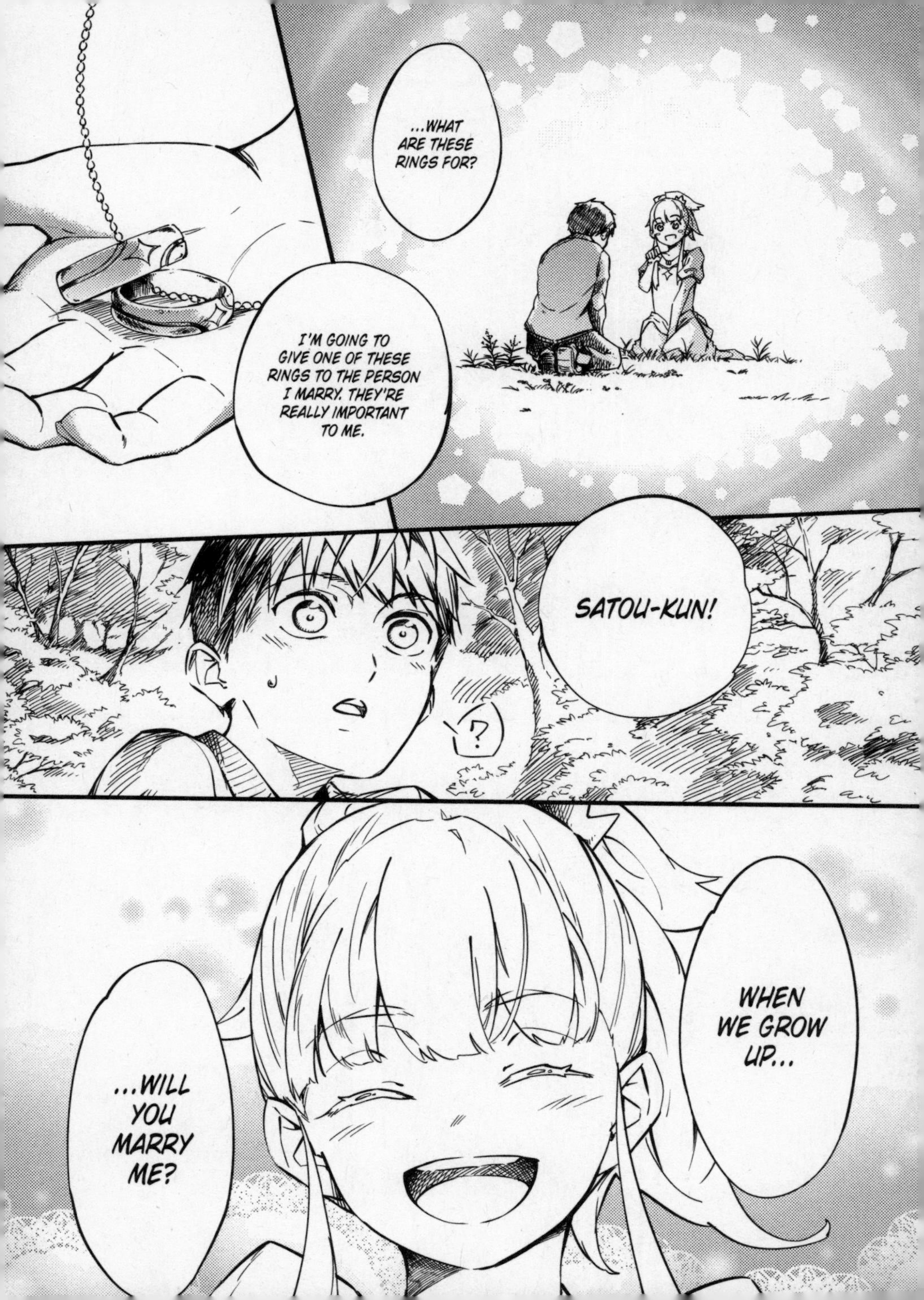
...WHAT ARE THESE RINGS FOR?
I'M GOING TO GIVE ONE OF THESE RINGS TO THE PERSON I MARRY. THEY'RE REALLY IMPORTANT TO ME.
SATOU-KUN!
!?
WHEN WE GROW UP...
...WILL YOU MARRY ME?

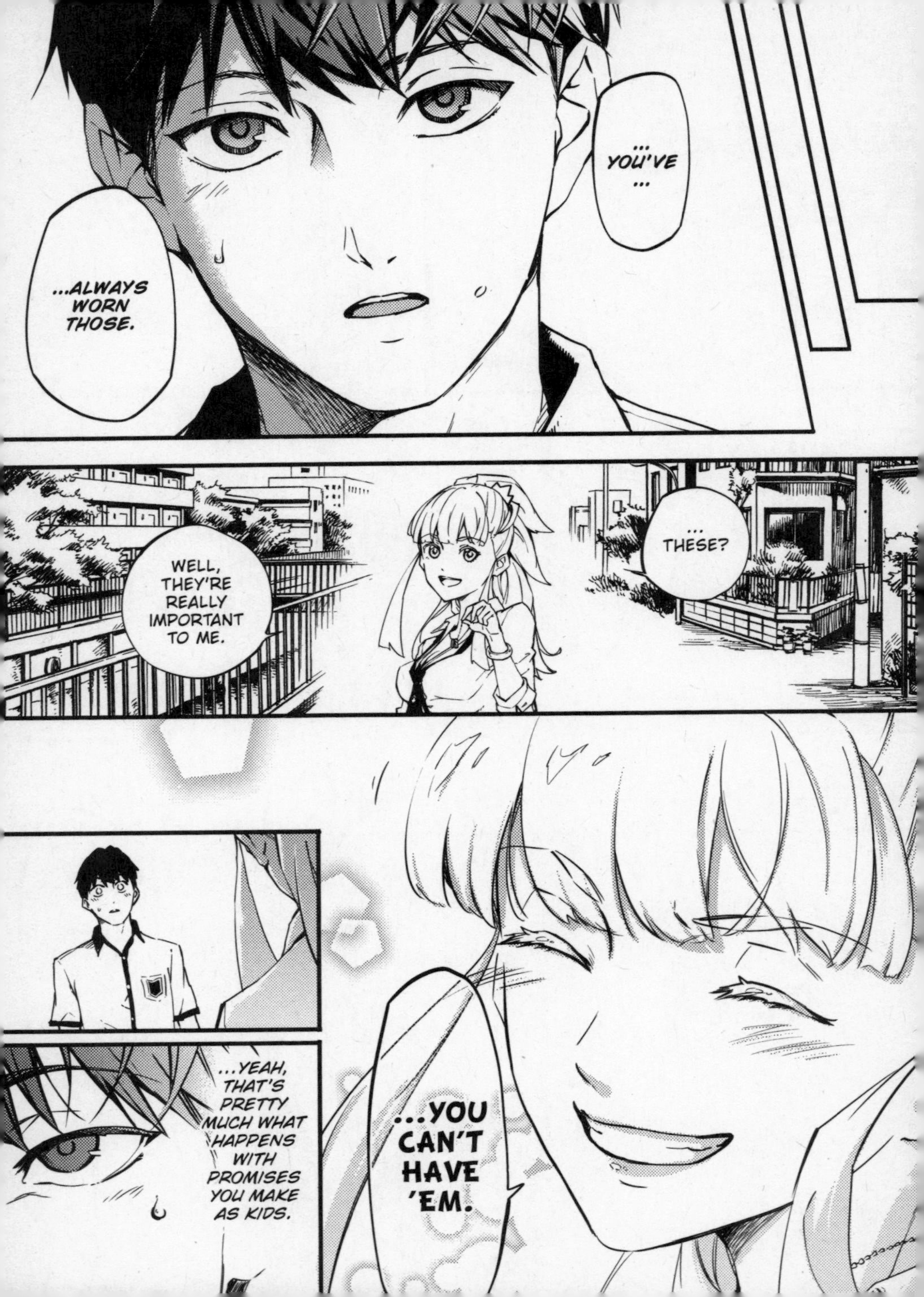
...YOU'VE...
...ALWAYS WORN THOSE.
...THESE?
WELL, THEY'RE REALLY IMPORTANT TO ME.
...YOU CAN'T HAVE 'EM.
...YEAH, THAT'S PRETTY MUCH WHAT HAPPENS WITH PROMISES YOU MAKE AS KIDS.

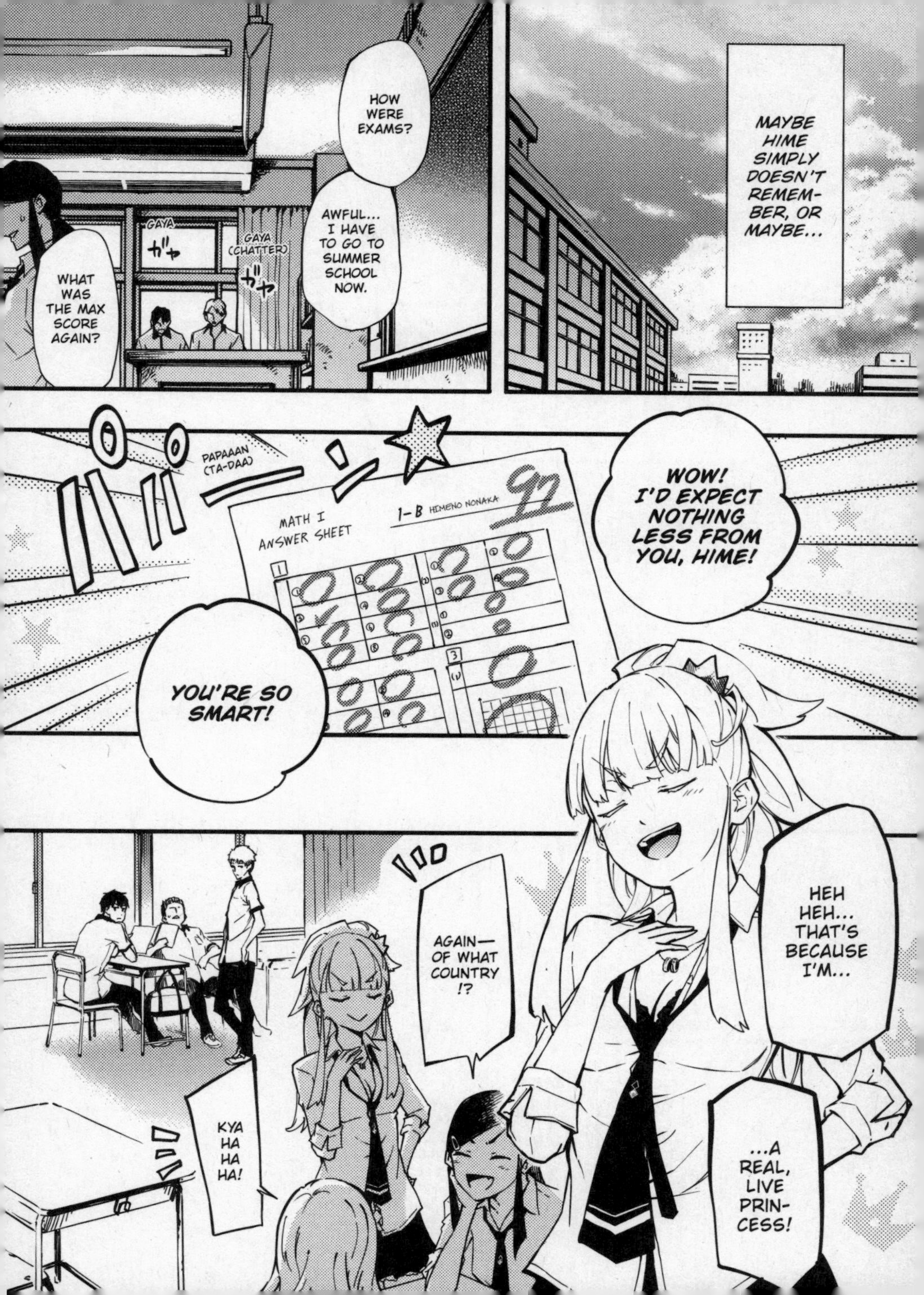
MAYBE HIME SIMPLY DOESN'T REMEMBER, OR MAYBE...
HOW WERE EXAMS?
AWFUL... I HAVE TO GO TO SUMMER SCHOOL NOW.
GAYA (CHATTER)
GAYA
WHAT WAS THE MAX SCORE AGAIN?
WOW! I'D EXPECT NOTHING LESS FROM YOU, HIME!
1-B HIMENO NONAKA
MATH I ANSWER SHEET
PAPAAAN (TA-DAA)
YOU'RE SO SMART!
HEH HEH... THAT'S BECAUSE I'M...
...A REAL, LIVE PRINCESS!
AGAIN— OF WHAT COUNTRY !?
KYA HA HA HA!

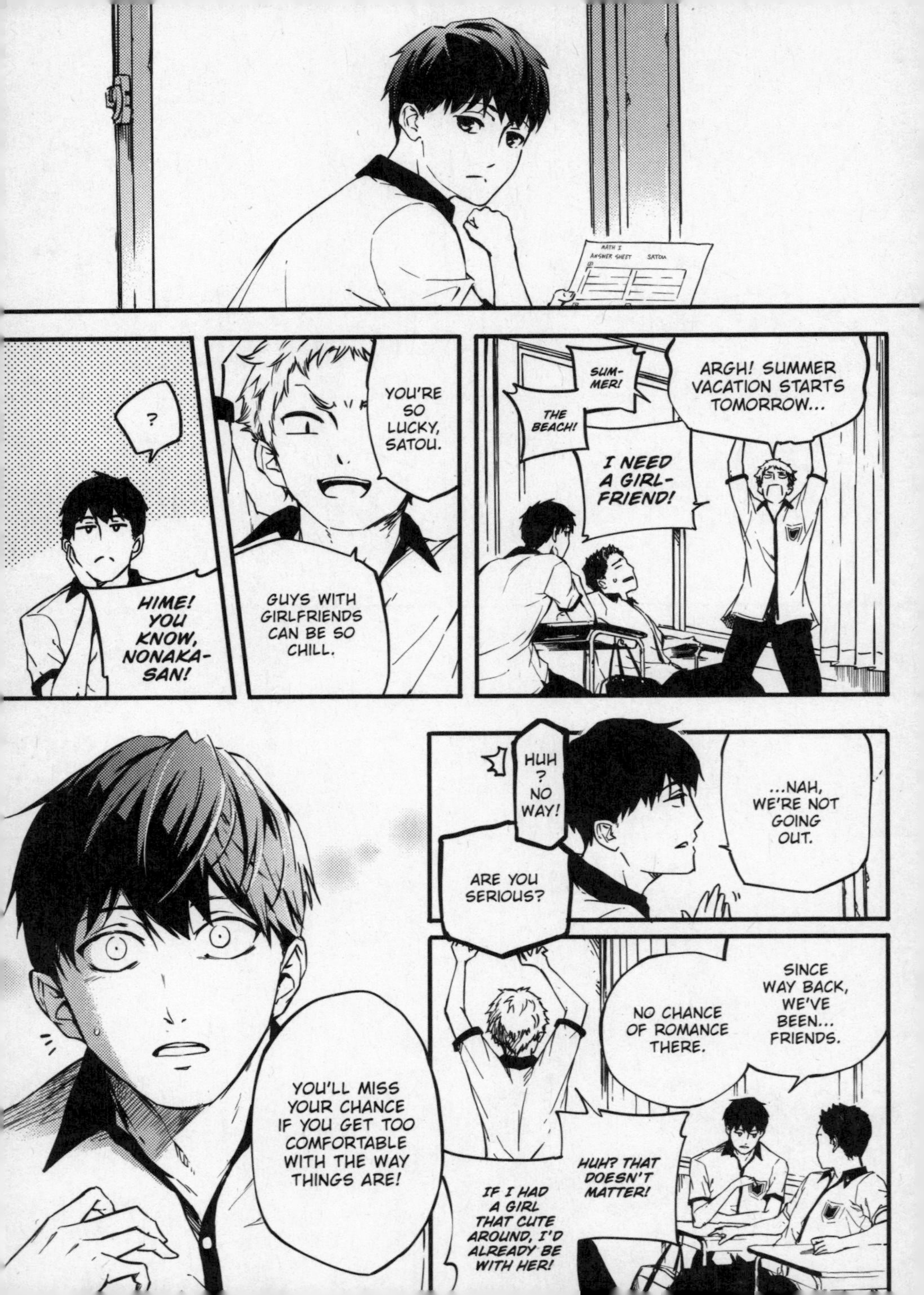
MATH I
ANSWER SHEET SATOU
ARGH! SUMMER VACATION STARTS TOMORROW...
SUMMER!
THE BEACH!
I NEED A GIRLFRIEND!
YOU'RE SO LUCKY, SATOU.
GUYS WITH GIRLFRIENDS CAN BE SO CHILL.
?
HIME! YOU KNOW, NONAKA-SAN!
...NAH, WE'RE NOT GOING OUT.
HUH? NO WAY!
ARE YOU SERIOUS?
SINCE WAY BACK, WE'VE BEEN... FRIENDS.
NO CHANCE OF ROMANCE THERE.
HUH? THAT DOESN'T MATTER!
IF I HAD A GIRL THAT CUTE AROUND, I'D ALREADY BE WITH HER!
YOU'LL MISS YOUR CHANCE IF YOU GET TOO COMFORTABLE WITH THE WAY THINGS ARE!

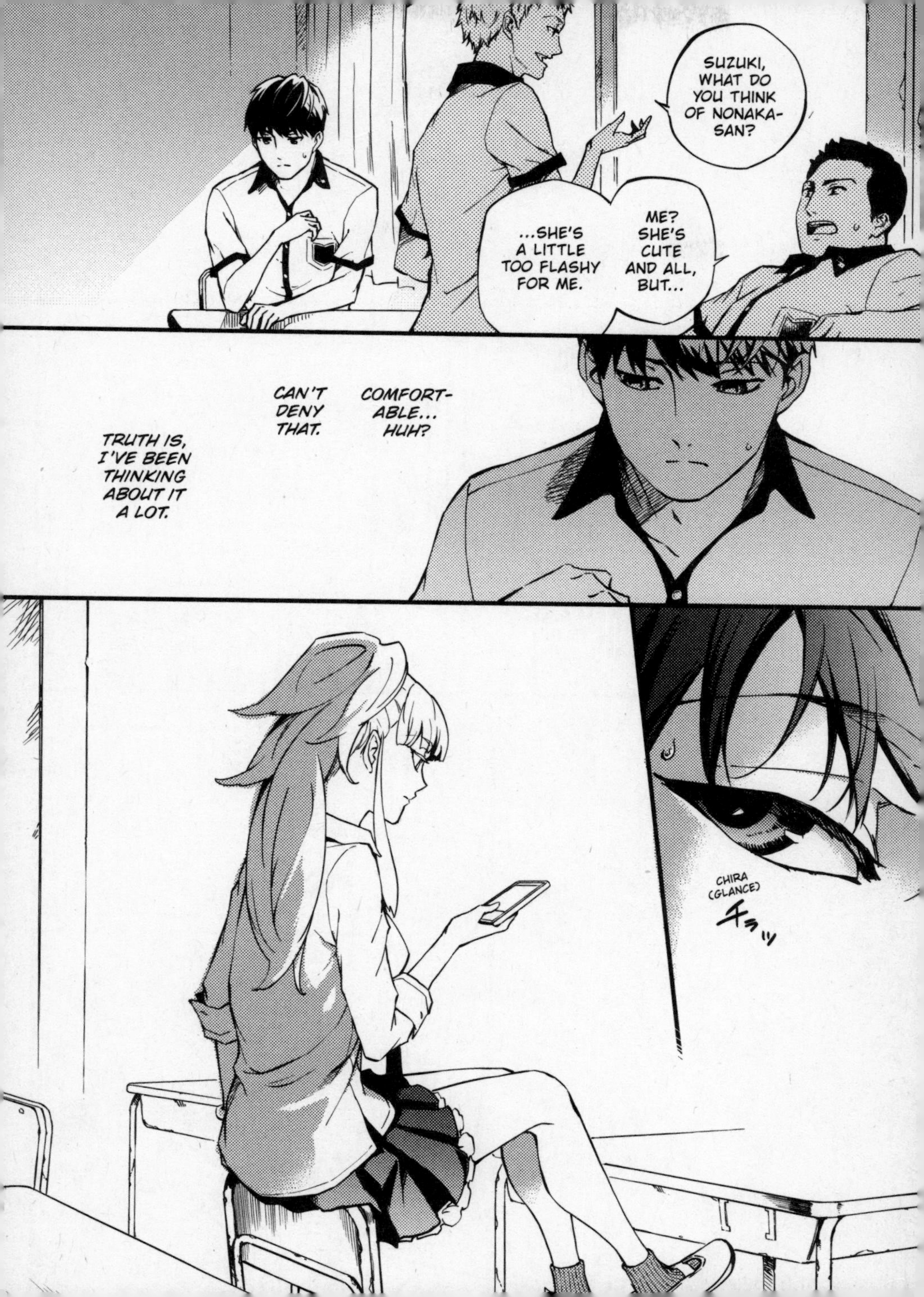
SUZUKI, WHAT DO YOU THINK OF NONAKA-SAN?
ME? SHE'S CUTE AND ALL, BUT...
...SHE'S A LITTLE TOO FLASHY FOR ME.
COMFORTABLE... HUH?
CAN'T DENY THAT.
TRUTH IS, I'VE BEEN THINKING ABOUT IT A LOT.
CHIRA (GLANCE)
チラッ

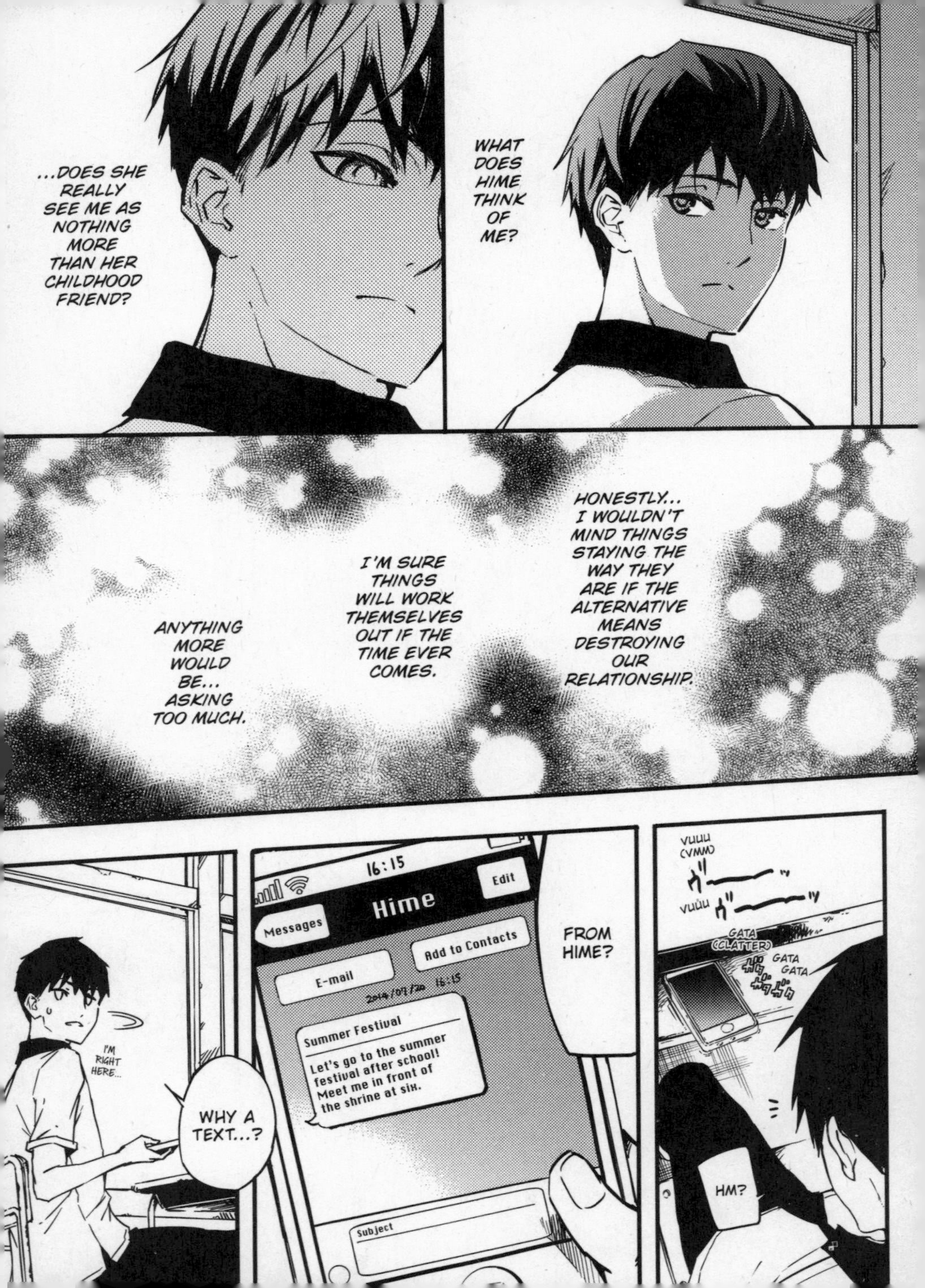
WHAT DOES HIME THINK OF ME?
...DOES SHE REALLY SEE ME AS NOTHING MORE THAN HER CHILDHOOD FRIEND?
HONESTLY... I WOULDN'T MIND THINGS STAYING THE WAY THEY ARE IF THE ALTERNATIVE MEANS DESTROYING OUR RELATIONSHIP.
I'M SURE THINGS WILL WORK THEMSELVES OUT IF THE TIME EVER COMES.
ANYTHING MORE WOULD BE... ASKING TOO MUCH.
VUUU (VMM)
ヴーーッ
VUUU
ヴーーッ
GATA (CLATTER)
GATA GATA
HM?
FROM HIME?
16:15
Edit
Hime
Messages
Add to Contacts
E-mail
2014/07/20 16:15
Summer Festival
Let's go to the summer festival after school! Meet me in front of the shrine at six.
Subject
WHY A TEXT...?
I'M RIGHT HERE...

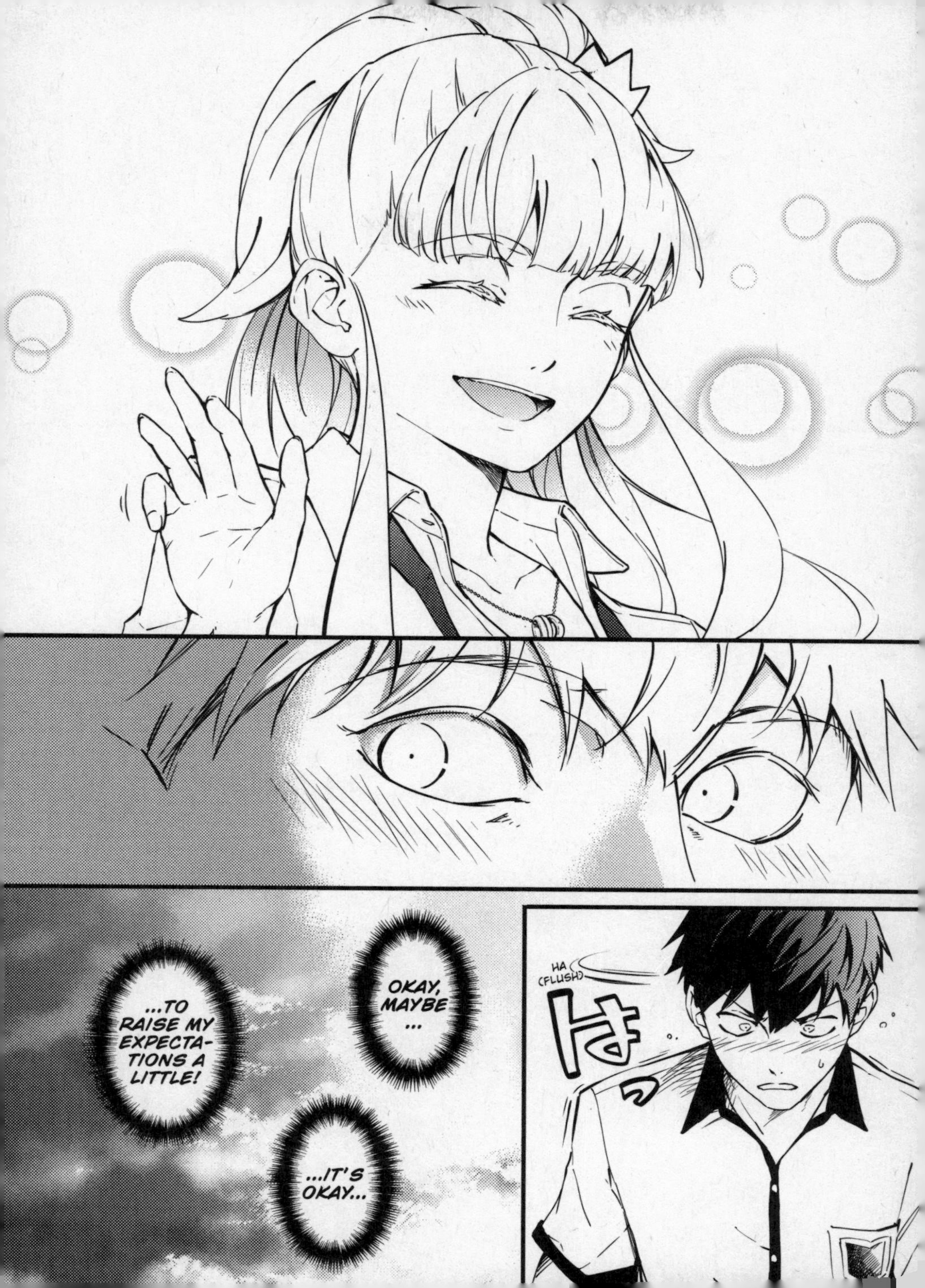
HA (FLUSH)
はっ
OKAY, MAYBE...
...IT'S OKAY...
...TO RAISE MY EXPECTATIONS A LITTLE!

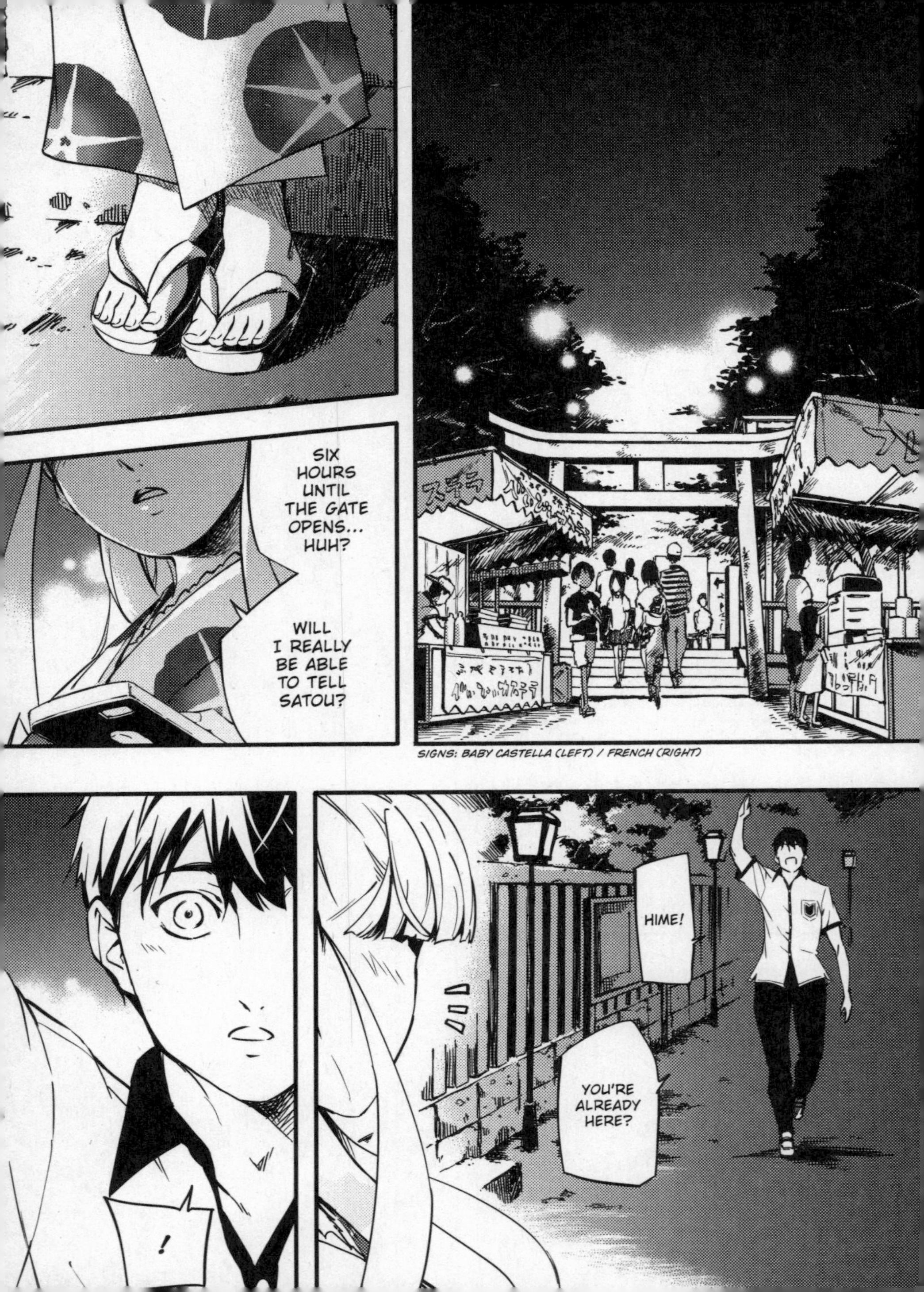
SIGNS: BABY CASTELLA (LEFT) / FRENCH (RIGHT)
SIX HOURS UNTIL THE GATE OPENS... HUH?
WILL I REALLY BE ABLE TO TELL SATOU?
HIME!
YOU'RE ALREADY HERE?
!

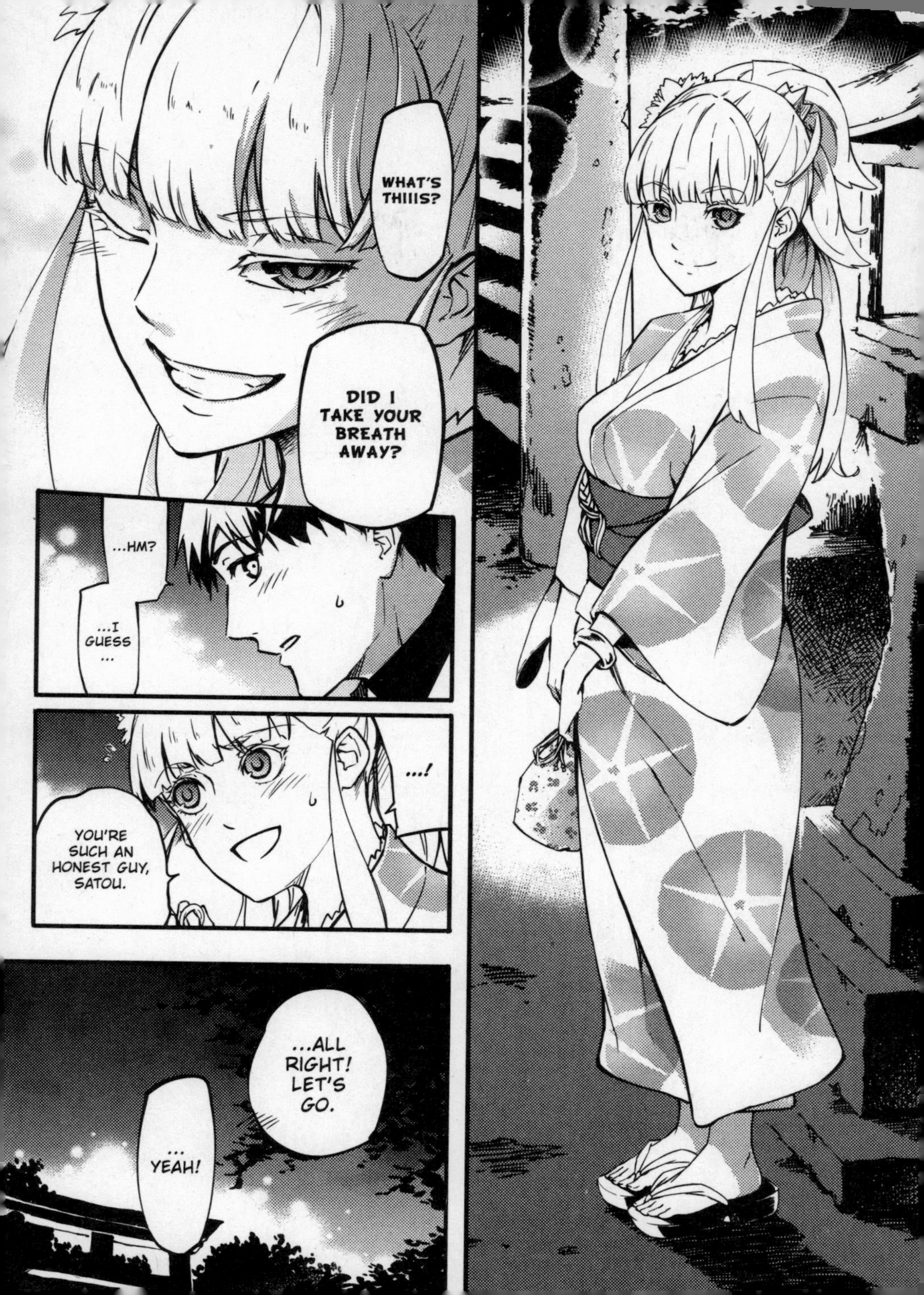
WHAT'S THIIIS?
DID I TAKE YOUR BREATH AWAY?
...HM?
...I GUESS ...
...!
YOU'RE SUCH AN HONEST GUY, SATOU.
...ALL RIGHT! LET'S GO.
... YEAH!

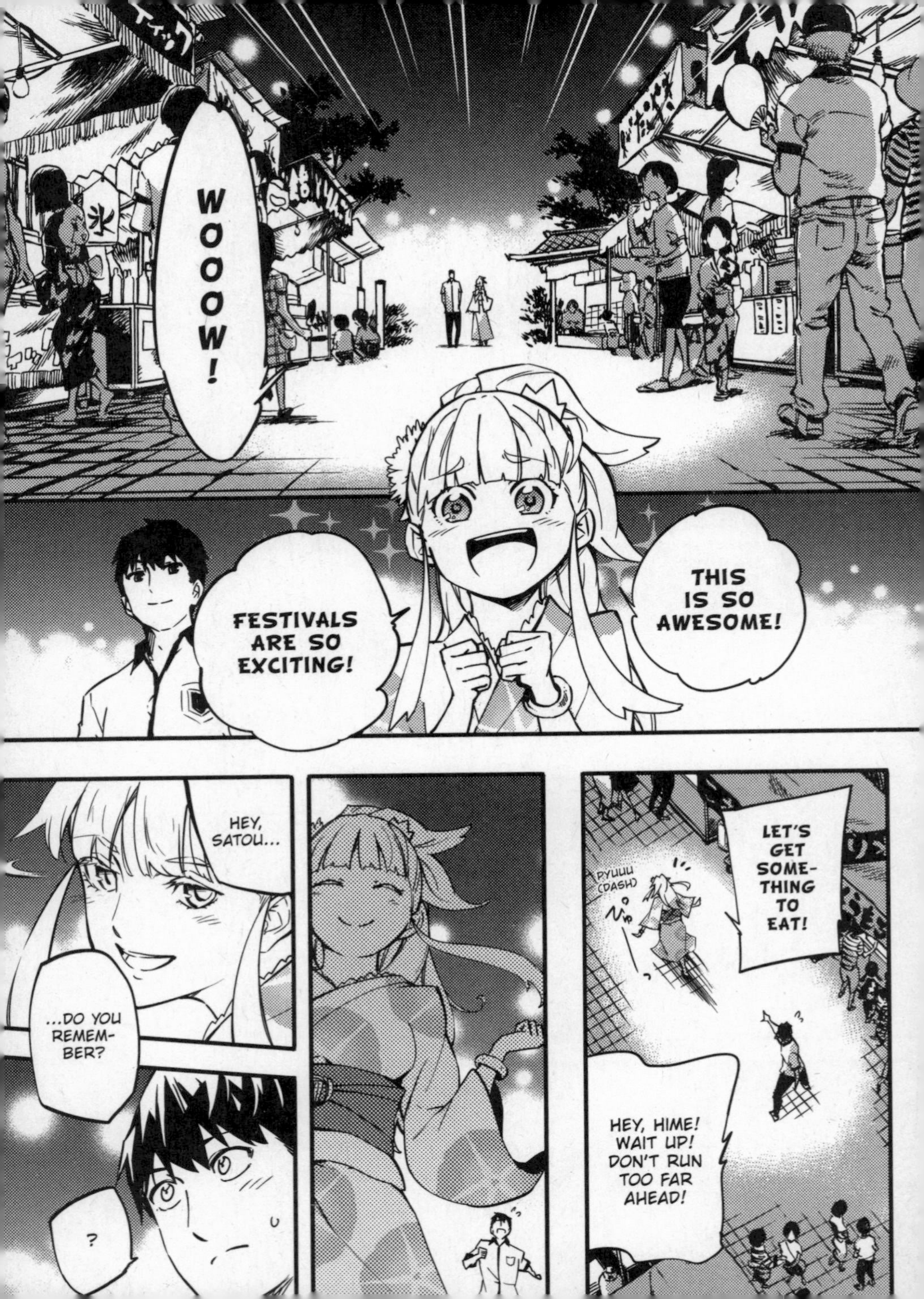
WOOOW!
THIS IS SO AWESOME!
FESTIVALS ARE SO EXCITING!
LET'S GET SOMETHING TO EAT!
PYUUU (DASH)
HEY, HIME! WAIT UP! DON'T RUN TOO FAR AHEAD!
HEY, SATOU...
...DO YOU REMEMBER?
?

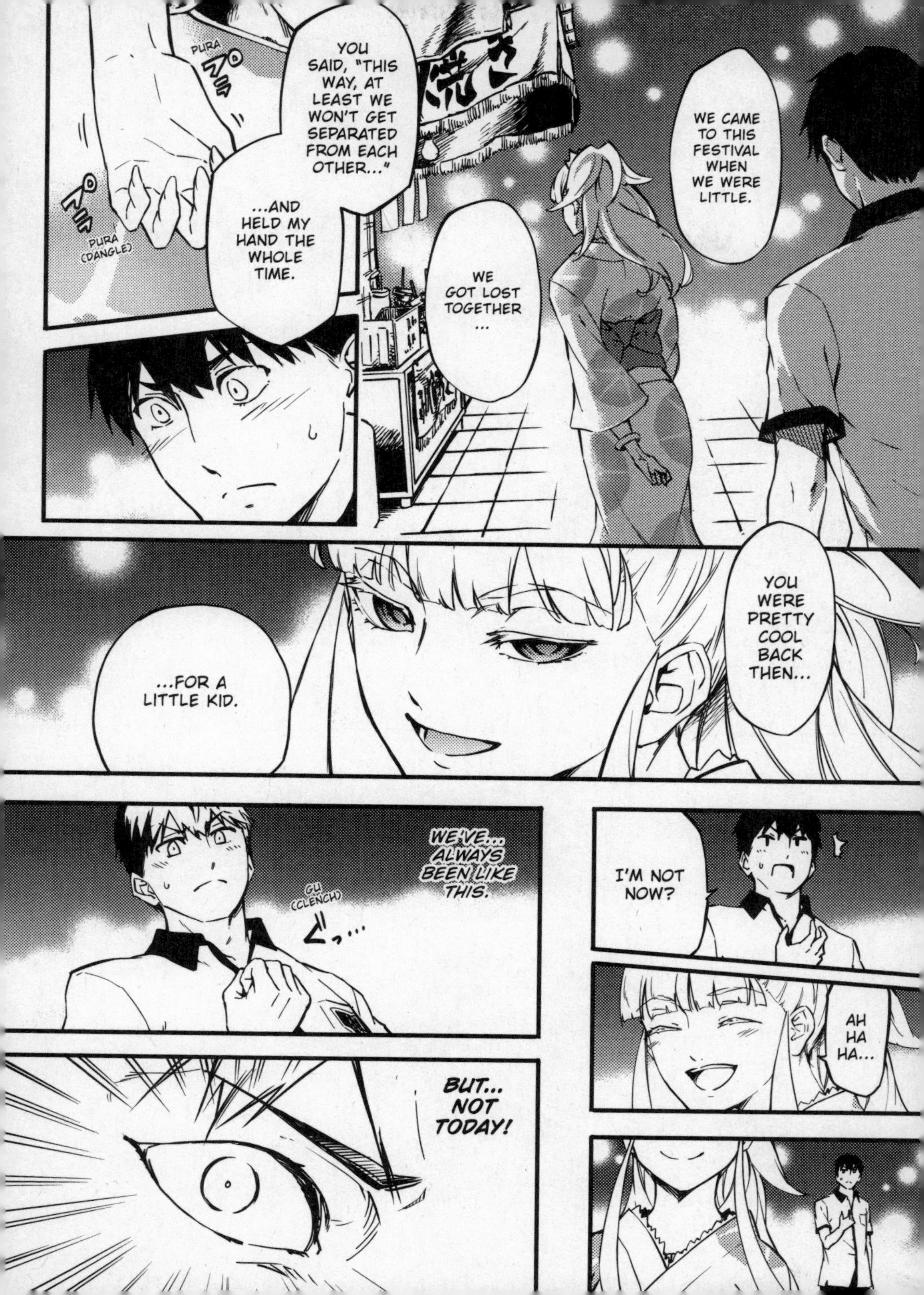
WE CAME TO THIS FESTIVAL WHEN WE WERE LITTLE.
WE GOT LOST TOGETHER...
PURA
YOU SAID, "THIS WAY, AT LEAST WE WON'T GET SEPARATED FROM EACH OTHER..."
PURA (DANGLE)
...AND HELD MY HAND THE WHOLE TIME.
YOU WERE PRETTY COOL BACK THEN...
...FOR A LITTLE KID.
I'M NOT NOW?
AH HA HA...
WE'VE... ALWAYS BEEN LIKE THIS.
GU (CLENCH)
BUT... NOT TODAY!

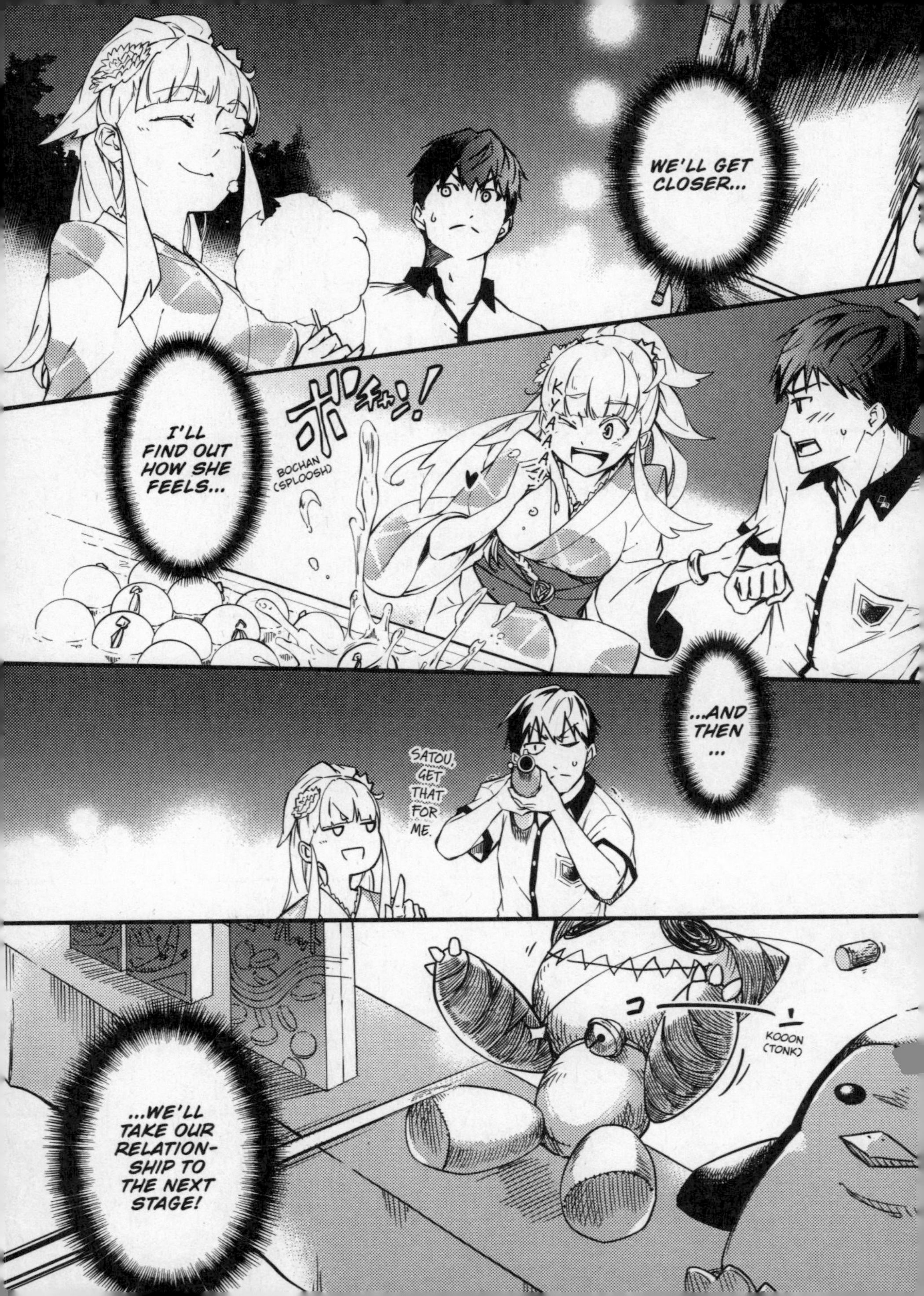
WE'LL GET CLOSER...
I'LL FIND OUT HOW SHE FEELS...
KYAAAA!
ボチャン!
BOCHAN (SPLOOSH)
...AND THEN...
SATOU, GET THAT FOR ME.
KOOON (TONK)
...WE'LL TAKE OUR RELATIONSHIP TO THE NEXT STAGE!

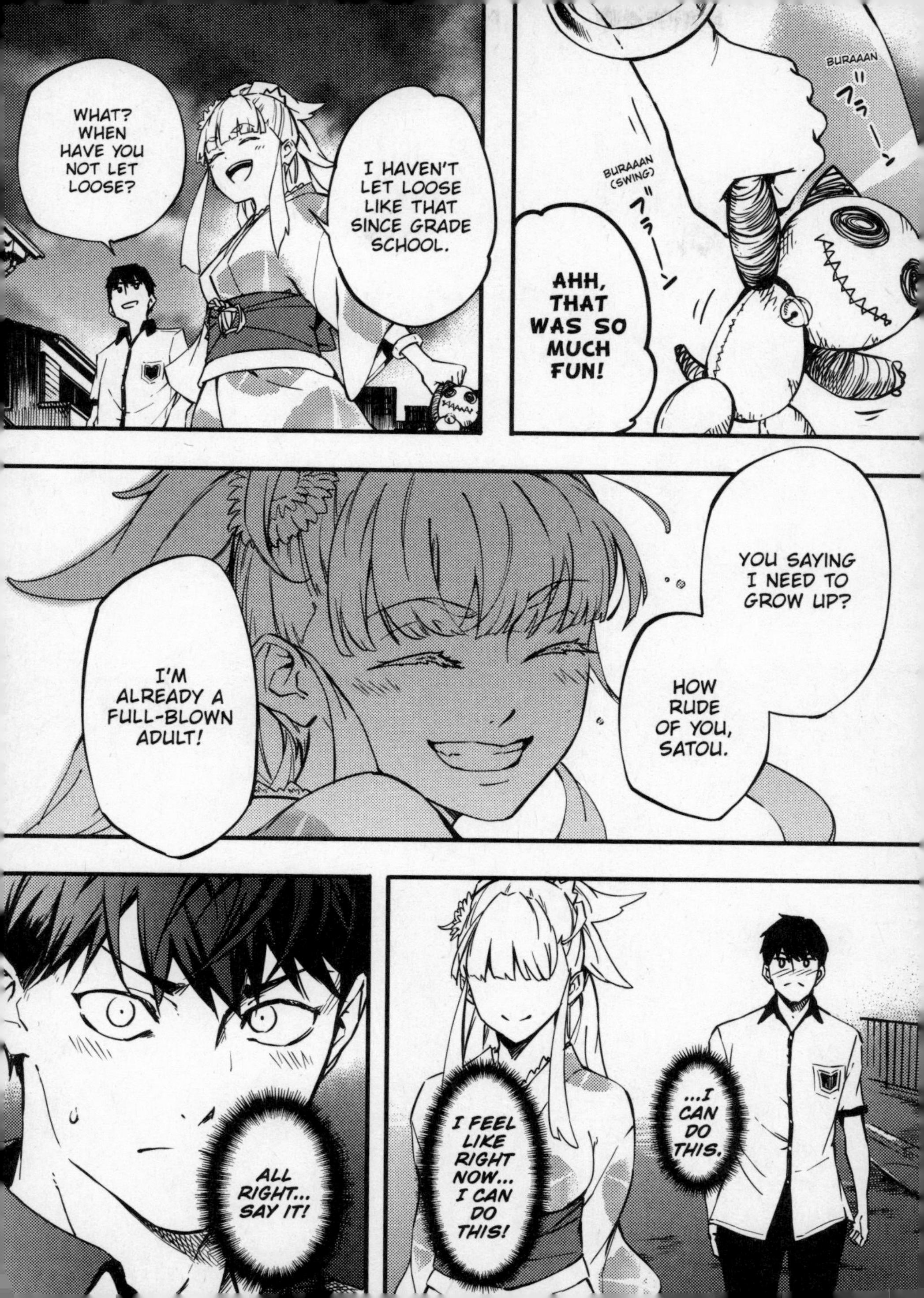
BURAAAN
ブラーン
BURAAAN (SWING)
ブラーン
AHH, THAT WAS SO MUCH FUN!
I HAVEN'T LET LOOSE LIKE THAT SINCE GRADE SCHOOL.
WHAT? WHEN HAVE YOU NOT LET LOOSE?
YOU SAYING I NEED TO GROW UP?
HOW RUDE OF YOU, SATOU.
I'M ALREADY A FULL-BLOWN ADULT!
...I CAN DO THIS.
I FEEL LIKE RIGHT NOW... I CAN DO THIS!
ALL RIGHT... SAY IT!

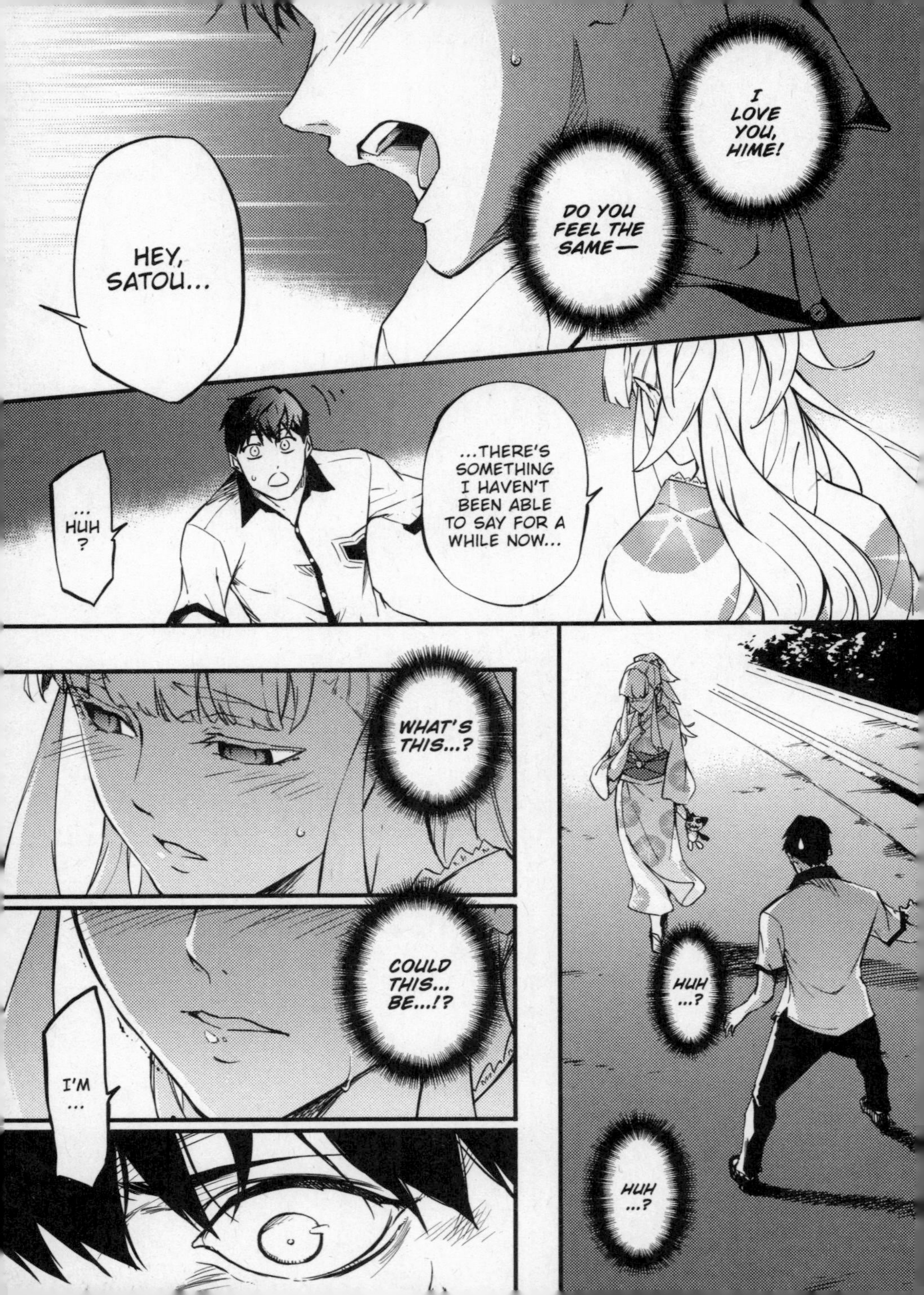
I LOVE YOU, HIME!
DO YOU FEEL THE SAME—
HEY, SATOU...
...THERE'S SOMETHING I HAVEN'T BEEN ABLE TO SAY FOR A WHILE NOW...
...HUH?
HUH...?
HUH...?
WHAT'S THIS...?
COULD THIS... BE...!?
I'M...

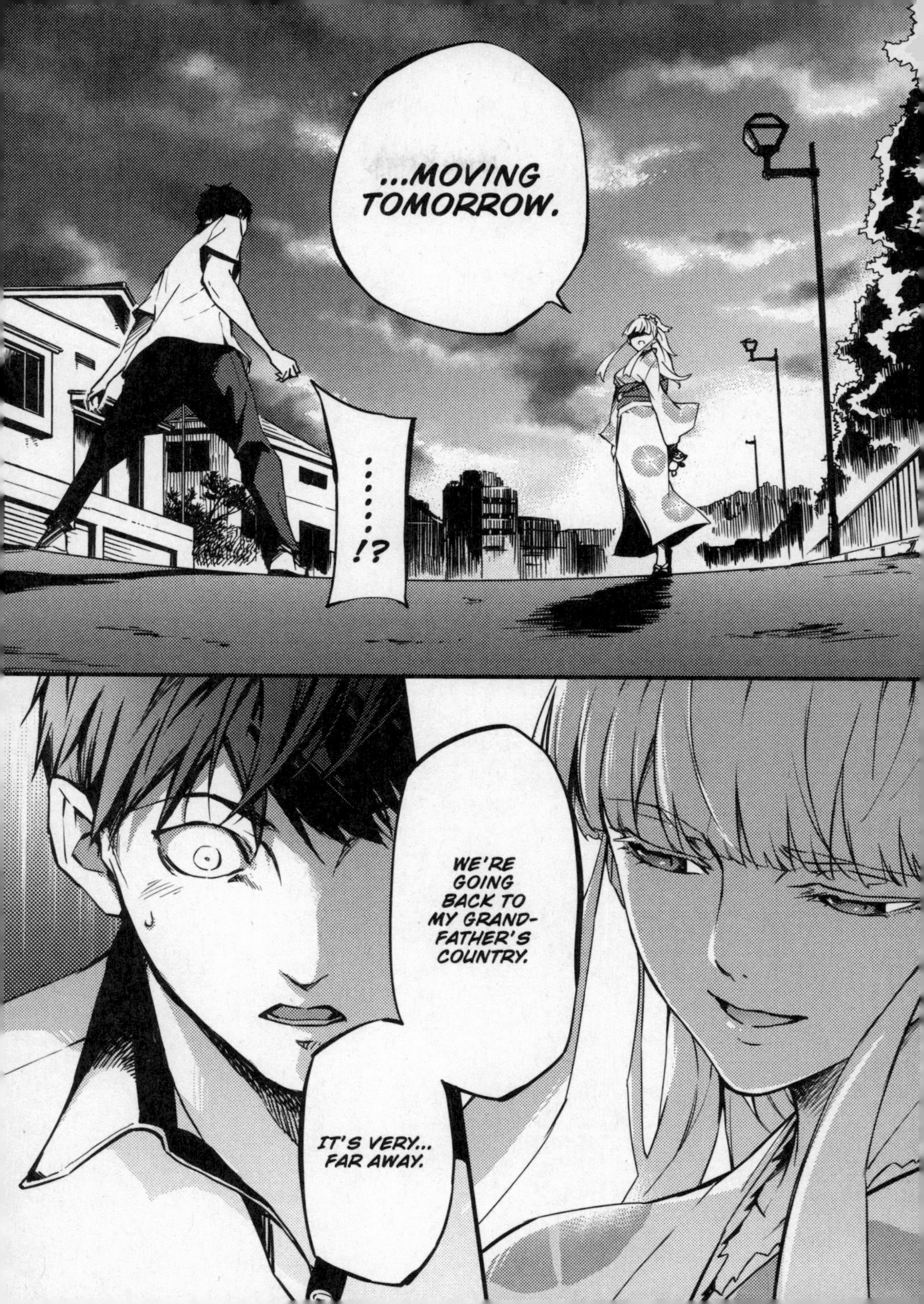
...MOVING TOMORROW.
......!?
WE'RE GOING BACK TO MY GRAND-FATHER'S COUNTRY.
IT'S VERY... FAR AWAY.

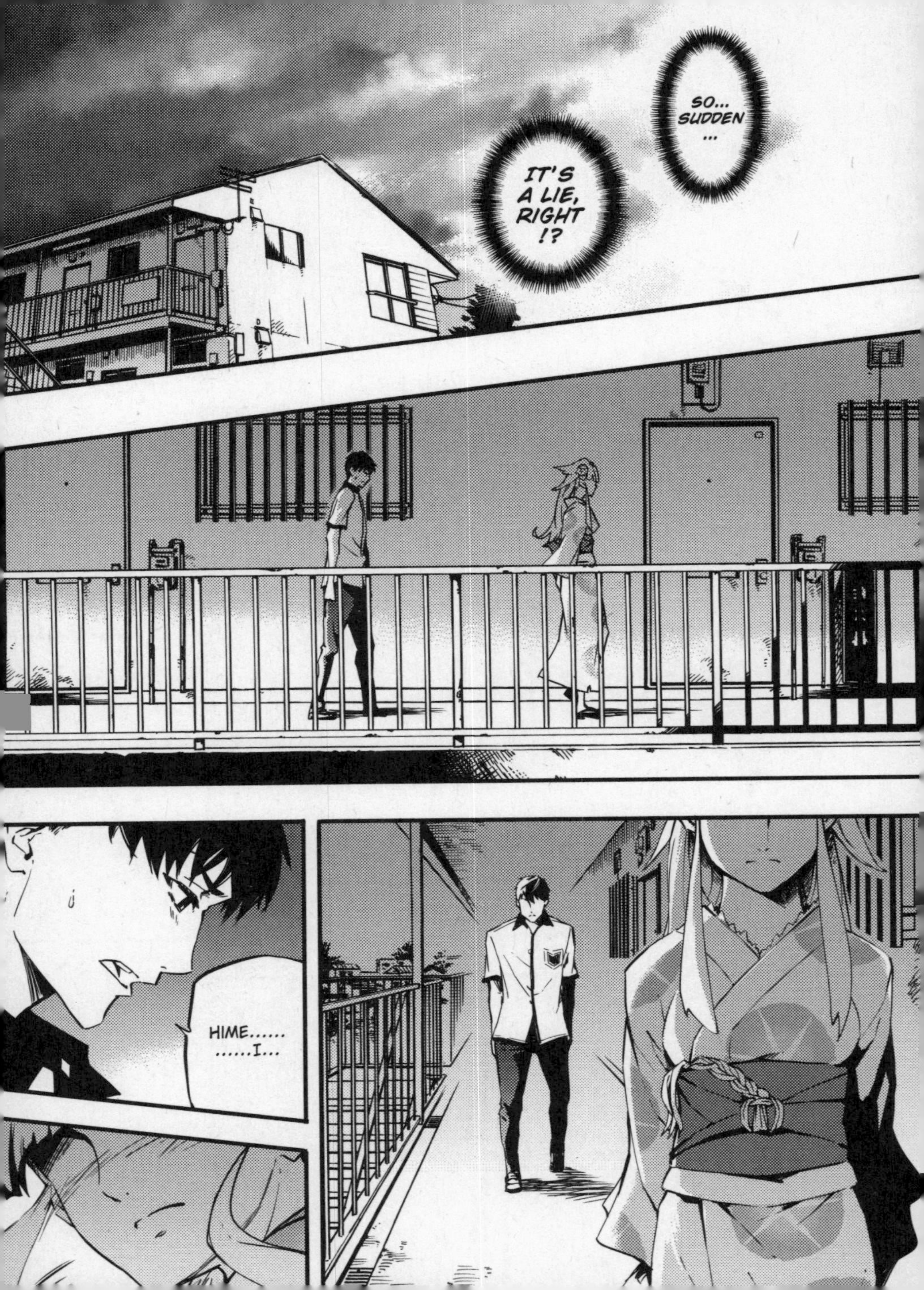
SO... SUDDEN ...
IT'S A LIE, RIGHT !?
HIME...... ......I...

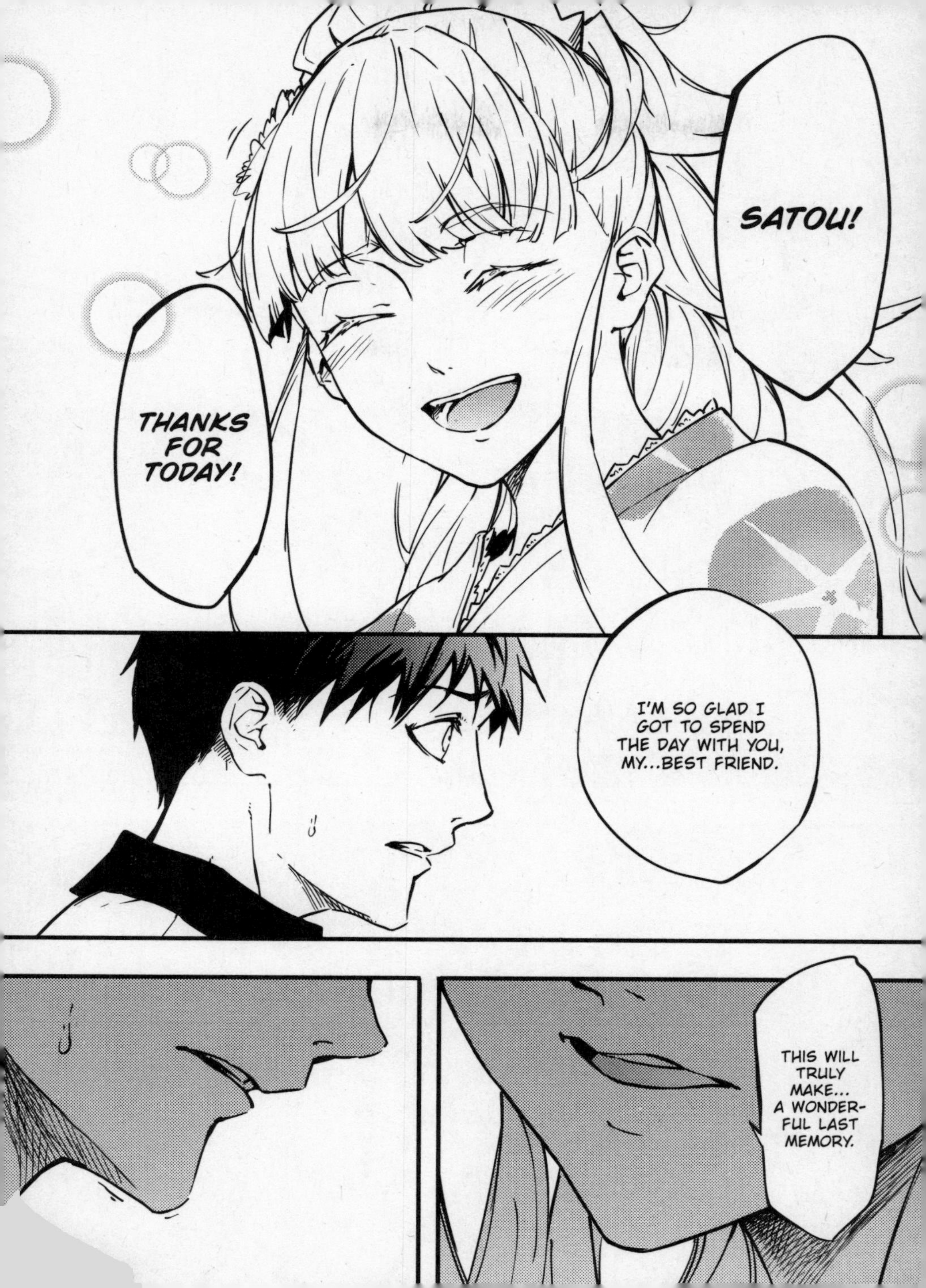
SATOU!
THANKS FOR TODAY!
I'M SO GLAD I GOT TO SPEND THE DAY WITH YOU, MY...BEST FRIEND.
THIS WILL TRULY MAKE... A WONDER-FUL LAST MEMORY.

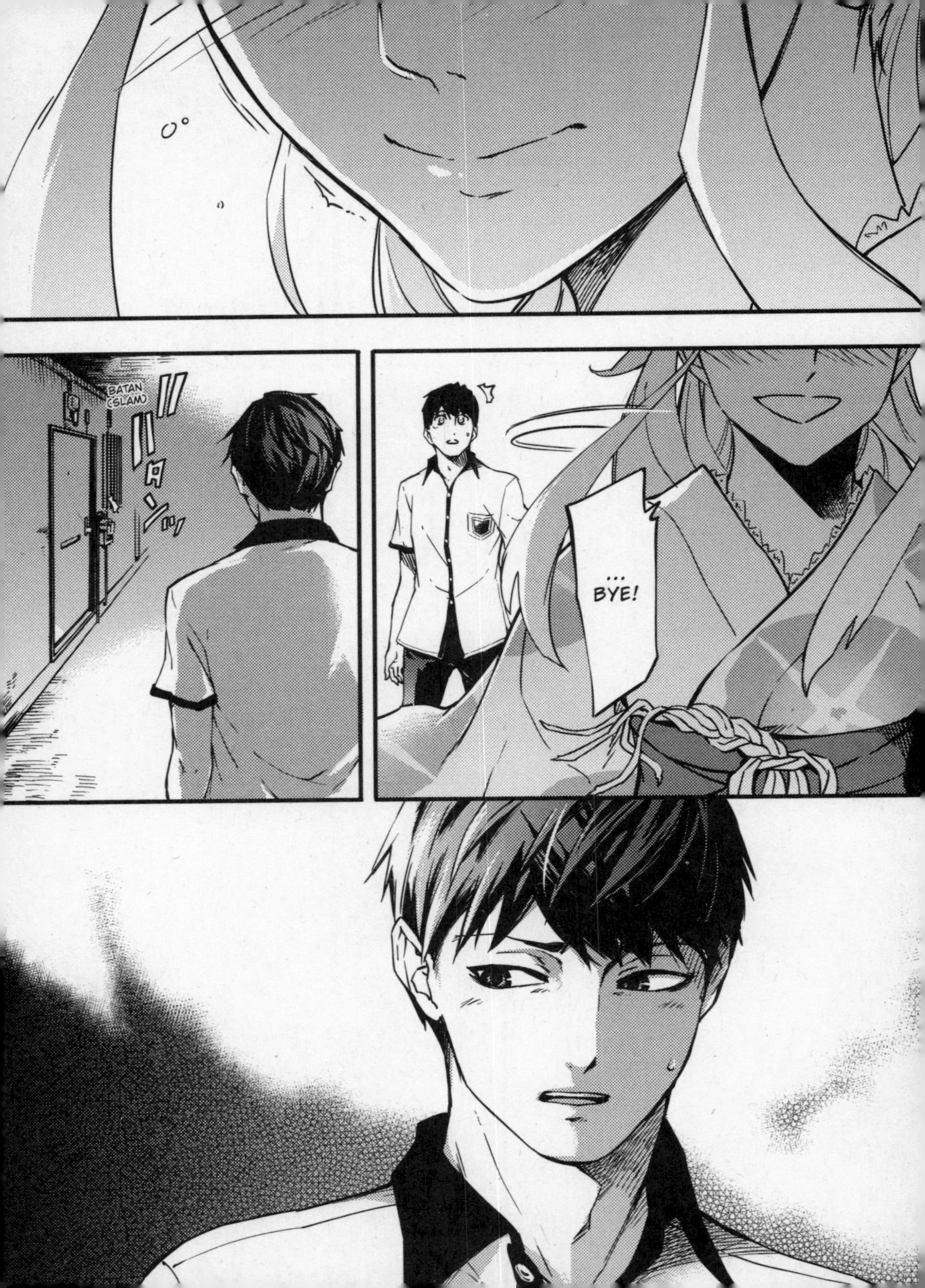
...BYE!
BATAN (SLAM)

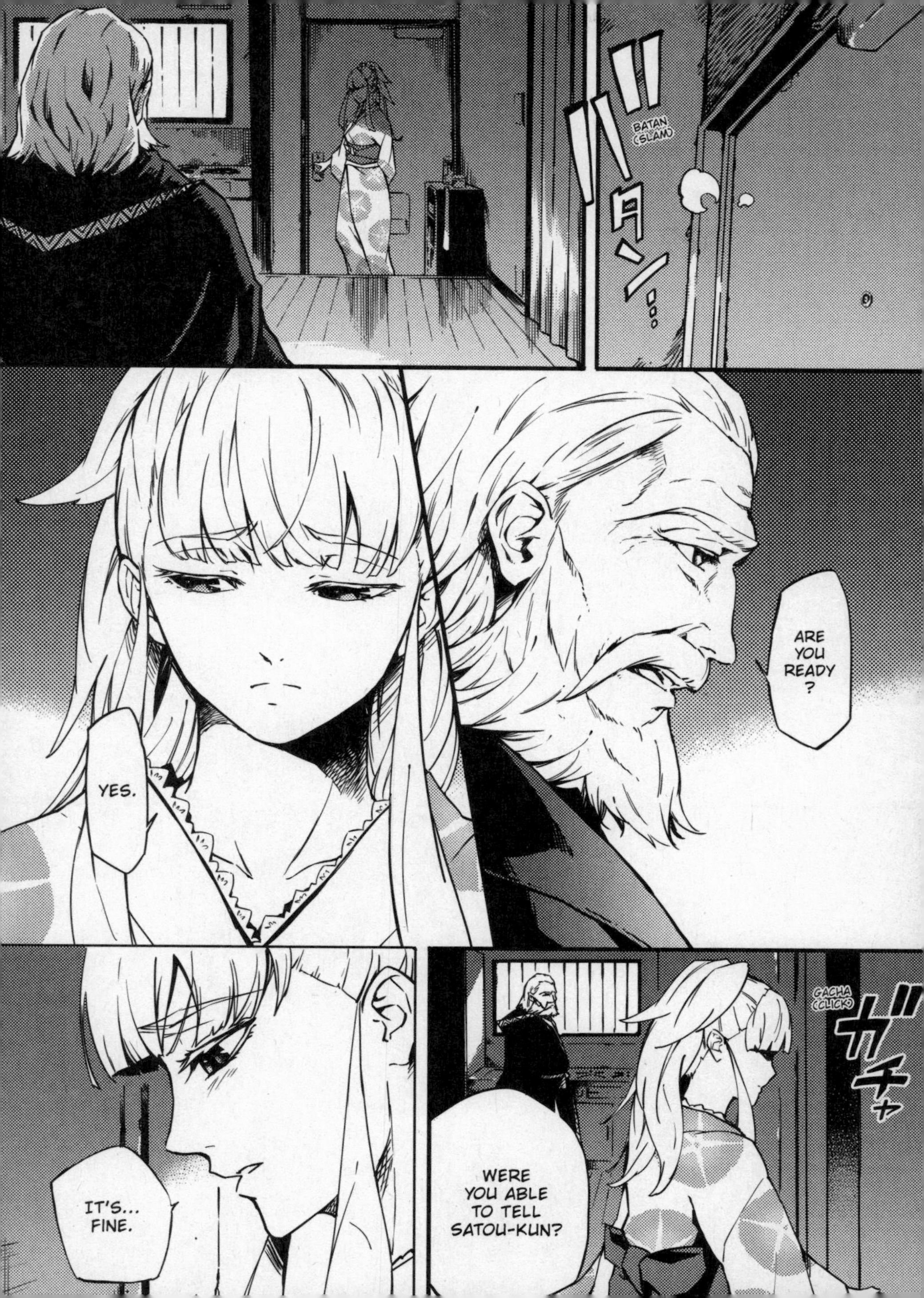
BATAN (SLAM)
ARE YOU READY?
YES.
GACHA (CLICK)
WERE YOU ABLE TO TELL SATOU-KUN?
IT'S... FINE.

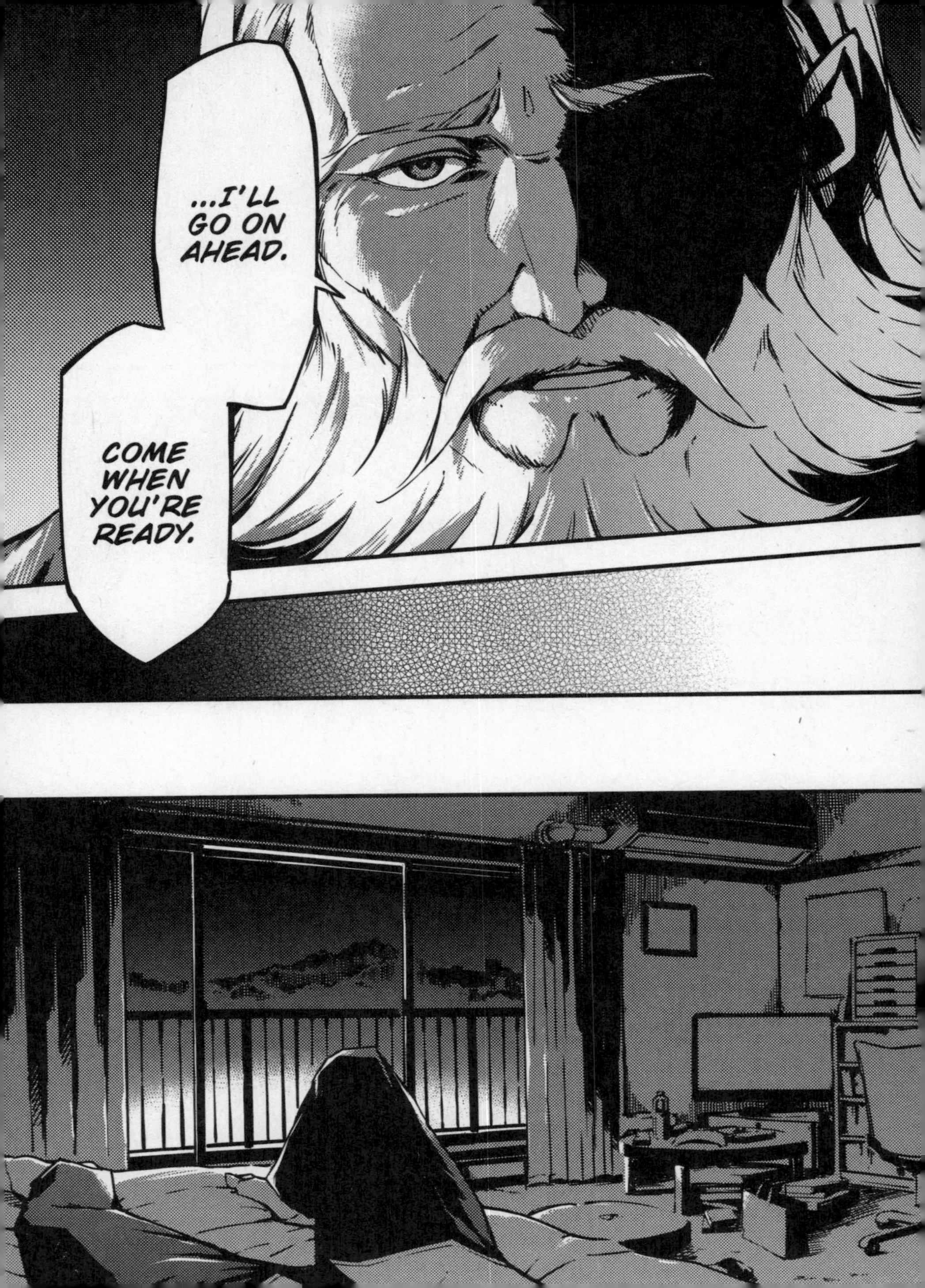
...I'LL GO ON AHEAD.
COME WHEN YOU'RE READY.

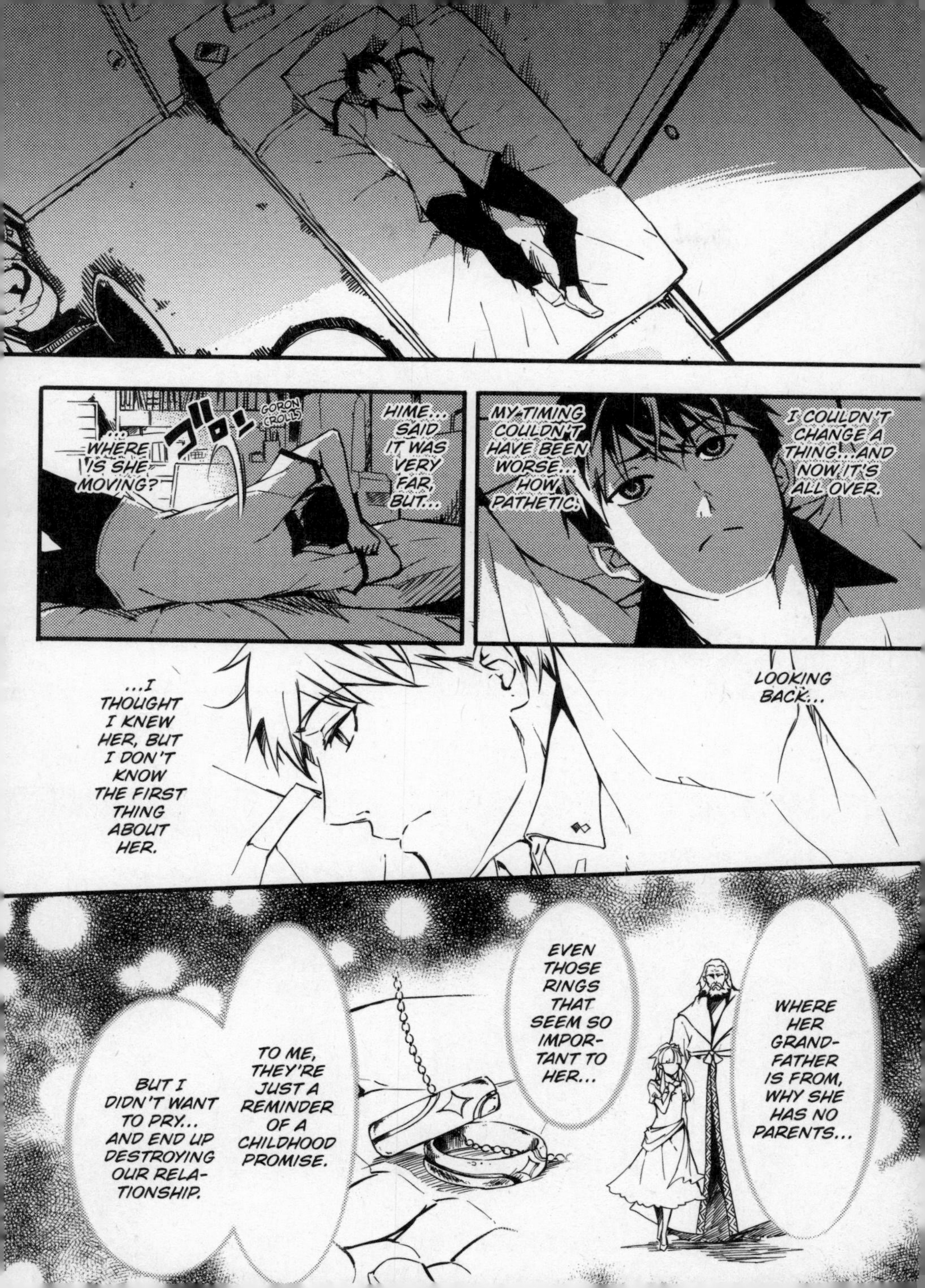

I COULDN'T CHANGE A THING... AND NOW IT'S ALL OVER.
MY TIMING COULDN'T HAVE BEEN WORSE... HOW PATHETIC.
HIME... SAID IT WAS VERY FAR, BUT...
GORON (ROLL)
...WHERE IS SHE MOVING?
LOOKING BACK...
...I THOUGHT I KNEW HER, BUT I DON'T KNOW THE FIRST THING ABOUT HER.
WHERE HER GRAND-FATHER IS FROM, WHY SHE HAS NO PARENTS...
EVEN THOSE RINGS THAT SEEM SO IMPOR-TANT TO HER...
TO ME, THEY'RE JUST A REMINDER OF A CHILDHOOD PROMISE.
BUT I DIDN'T WANT TO PRY... AND END UP DESTROYING OUR RELA-TIONSHIP.

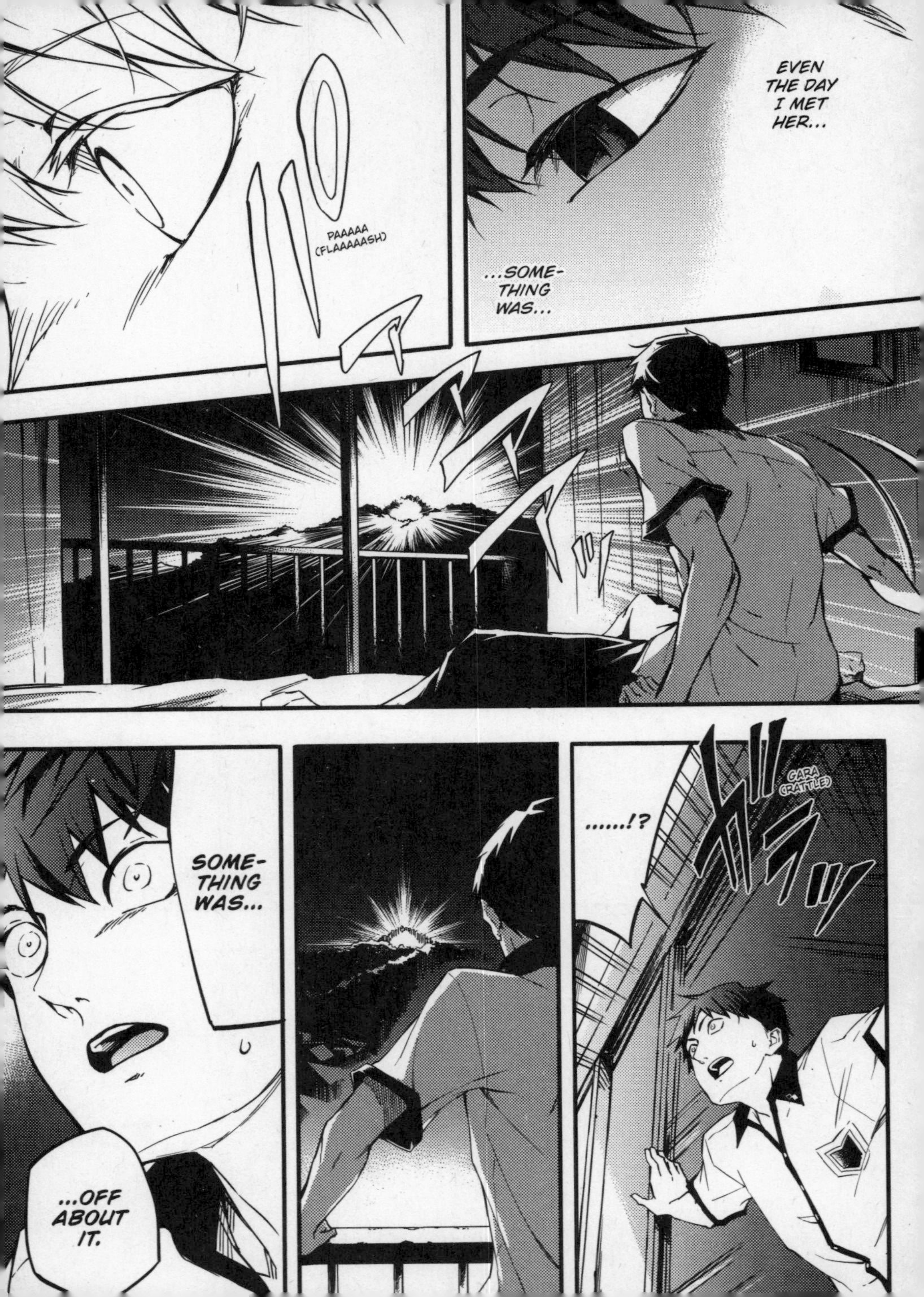
EVEN THE DAY I MET HER...
...SOME-THING WAS...
PAAAAA (FLAAAAASH)
GARA (RATTLE)
......!?
SOME-THING WAS...
...OFF ABOUT IT.

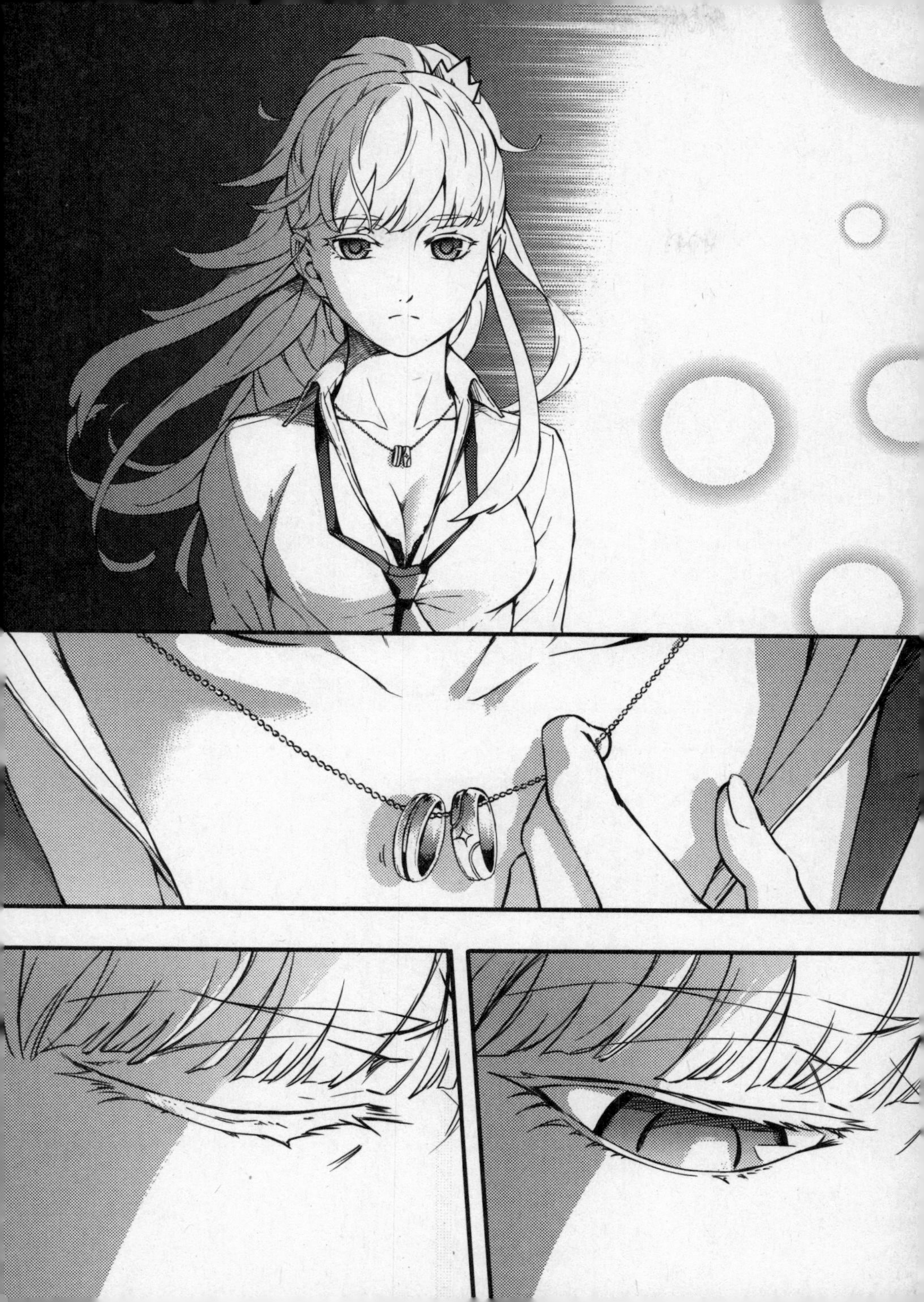

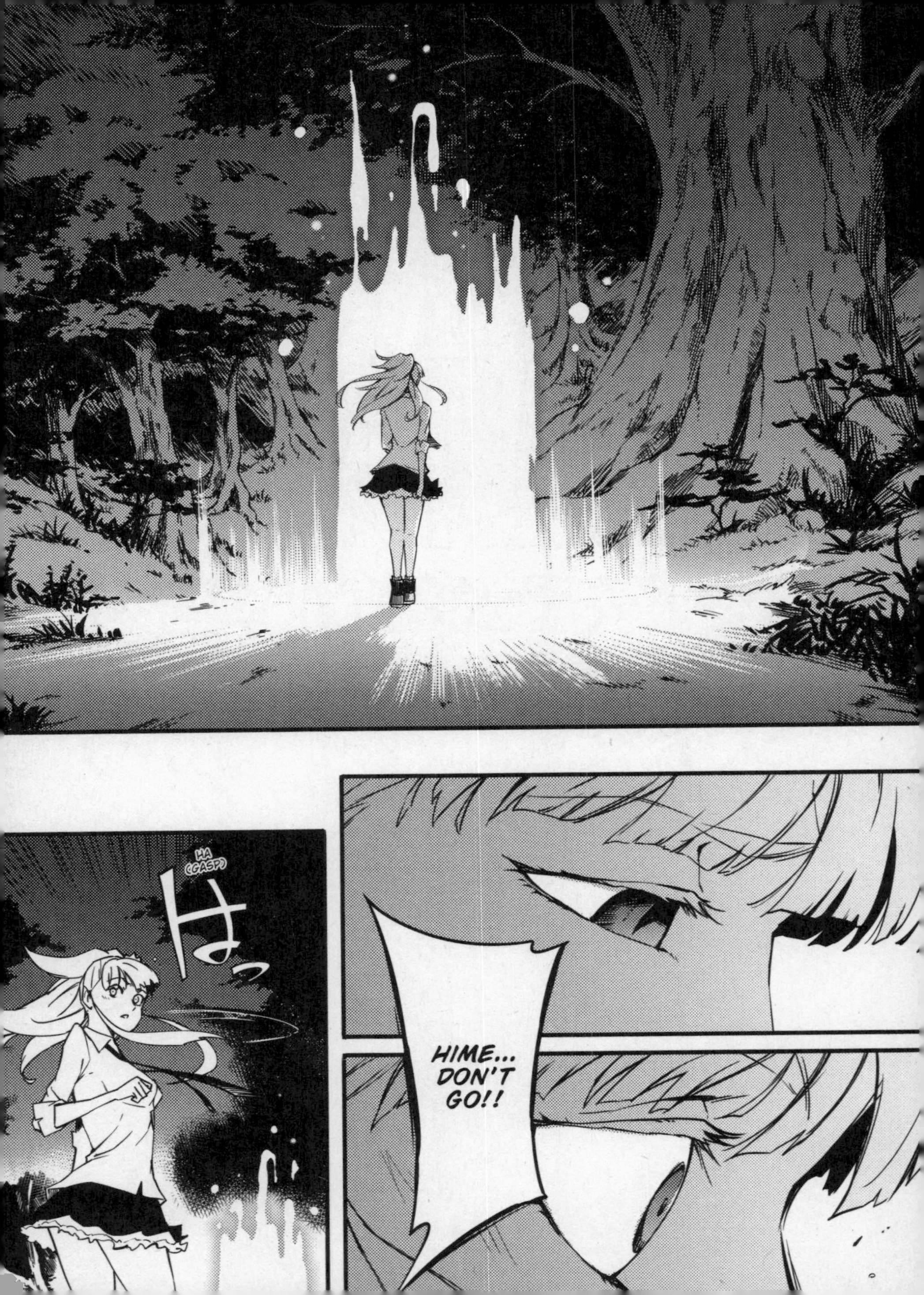
HIME... DON'T GO!!
HA (GASP)
はっ

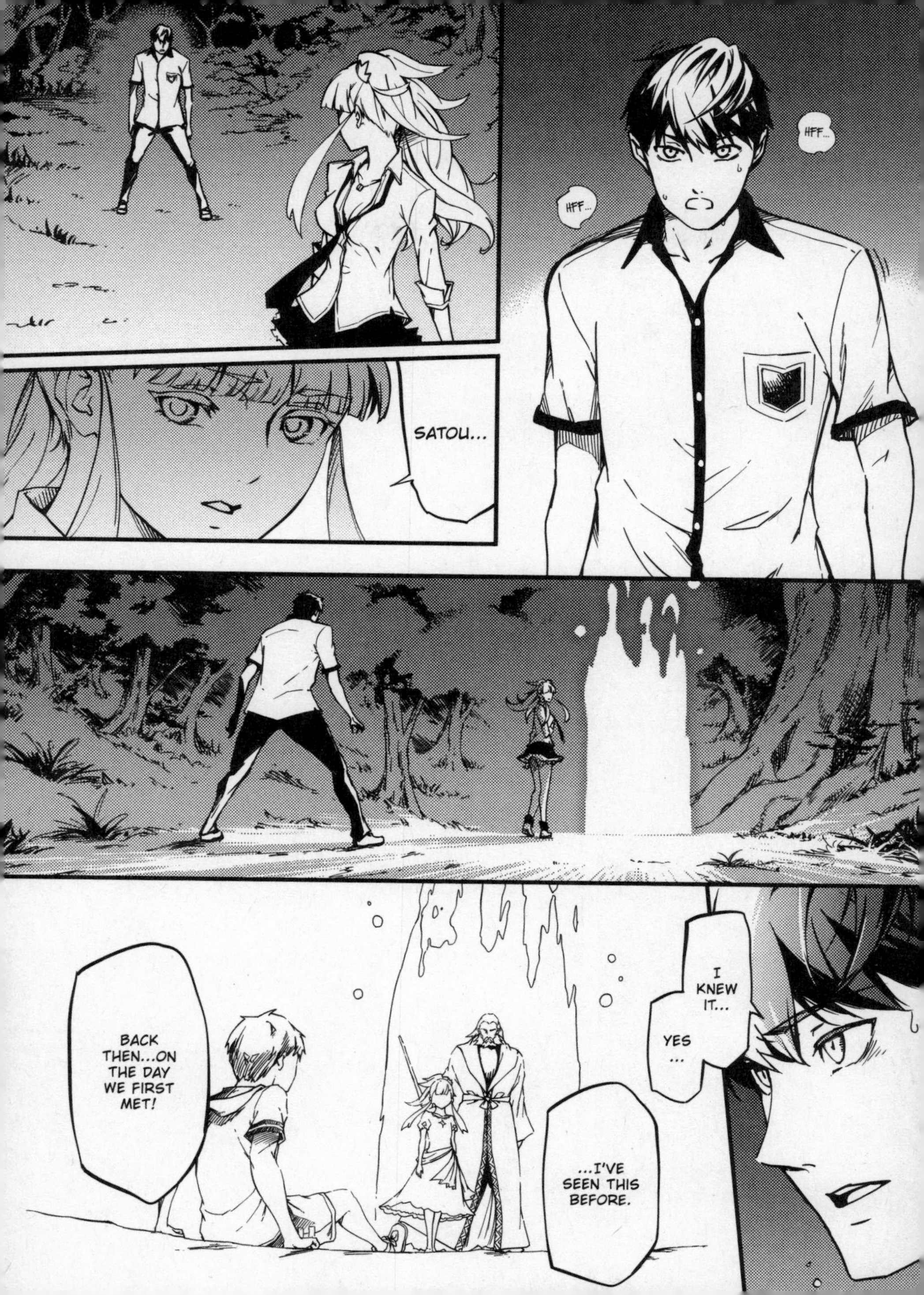
HFF...
HFF...
SATOU...
I KNEW IT...
YES...
...I'VE SEEN THIS BEFORE.
BACK THEN...ON THE DAY WE FIRST MET!

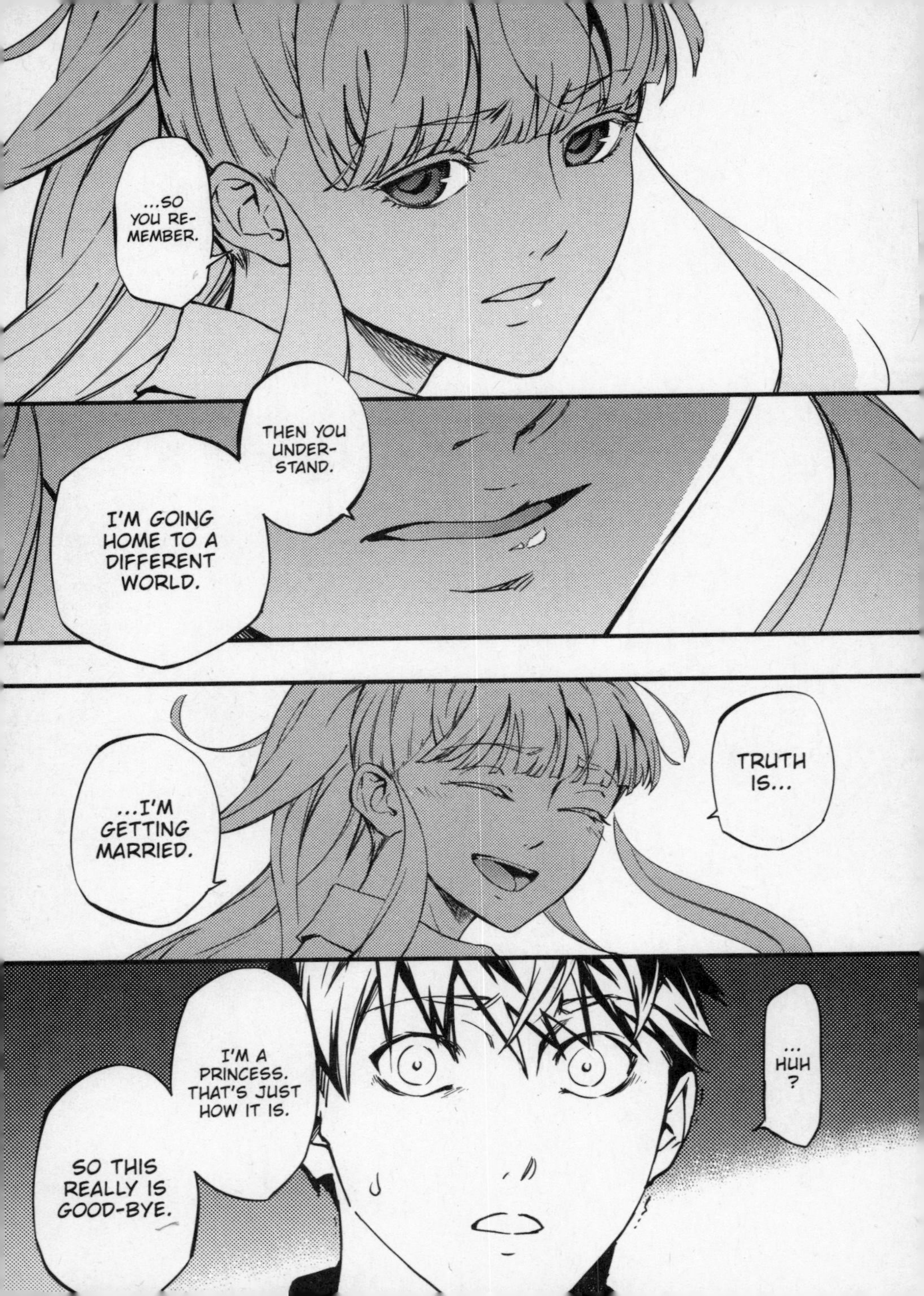
...SO YOU RE-MEMBER.
THEN YOU UNDER-STAND.
I'M GOING HOME TO A DIFFERENT WORLD.
TRUTH IS...
...I'M GETTING MARRIED.
...HUH?
I'M A PRINCESS. THAT'S JUST HOW IT IS.
SO THIS REALLY IS GOOD-BYE.

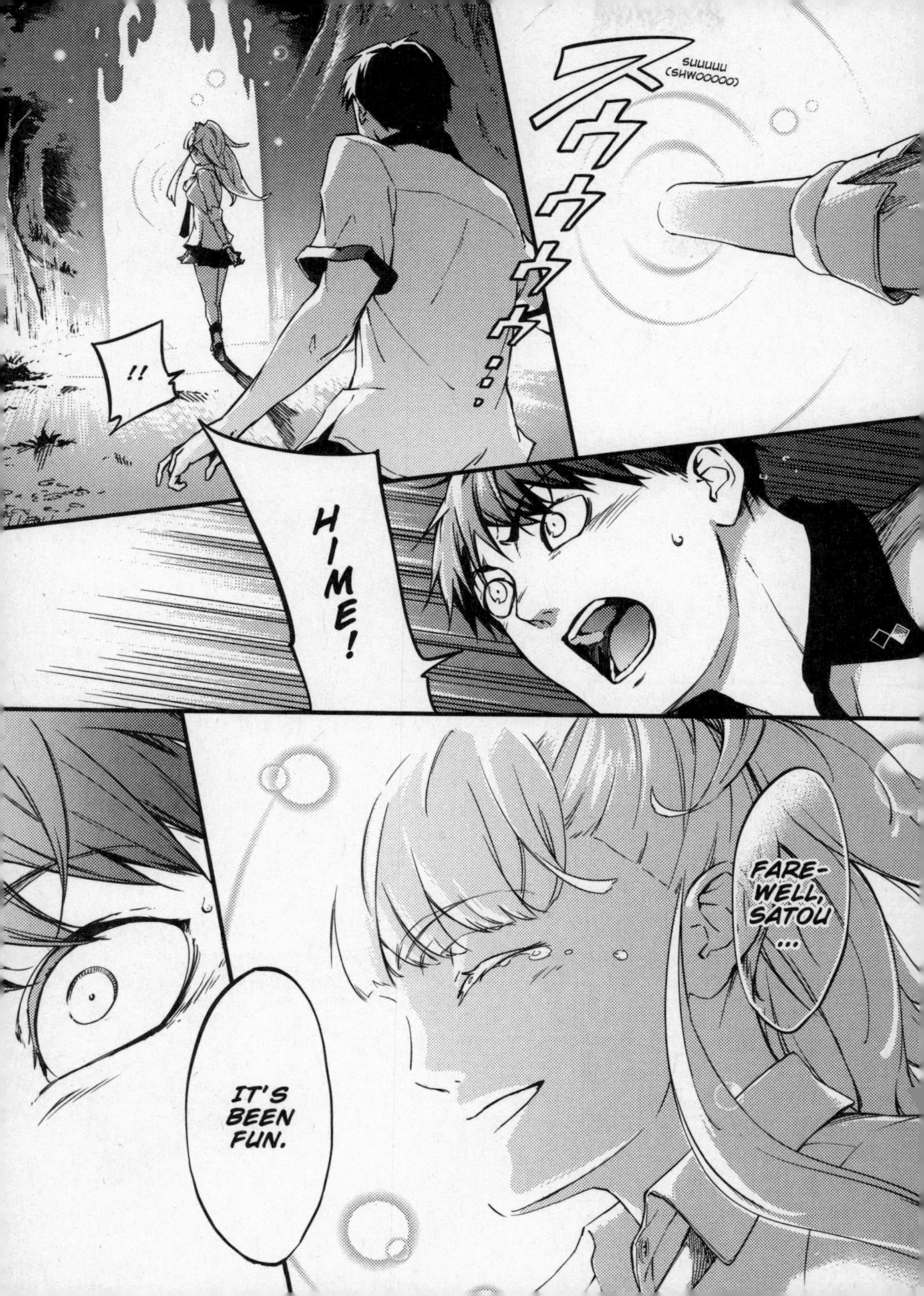
スウウウウ…
SUUUUU (SHWOOOOO)
!!
HIME!
FARE-WELL, SATOU...
IT'S BEEN FUN.

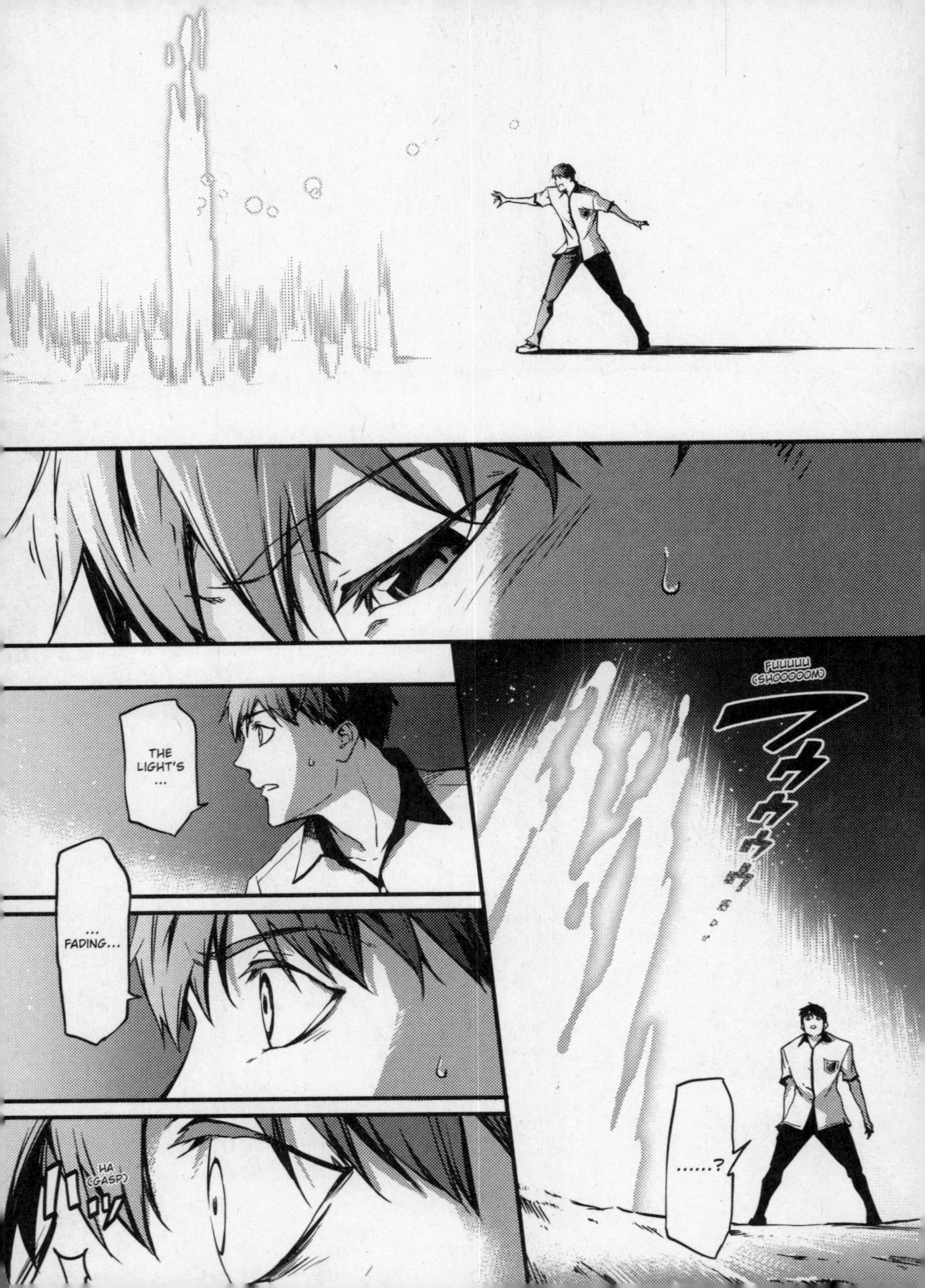
FUUUUU (SHOOOOOM)
......?
THE LIGHT'S ...
... FADING...
HA (GASP)

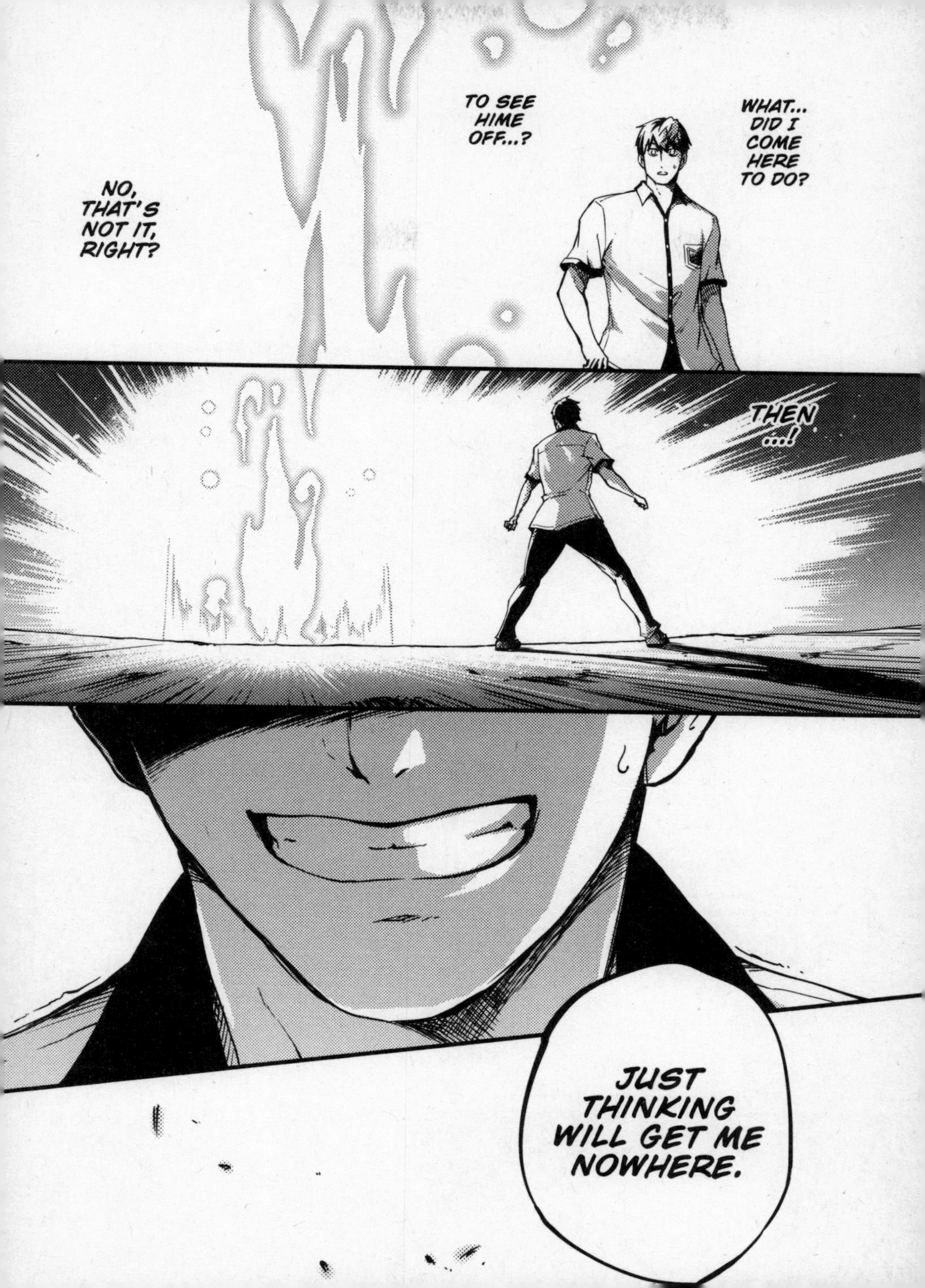
WHAT... DID I COME HERE TO DO?
TO SEE HIME OFF...?
NO, THAT'S NOT IT, RIGHT?
THEN ...!
JUST THINKING WILL GET ME NOWHERE.

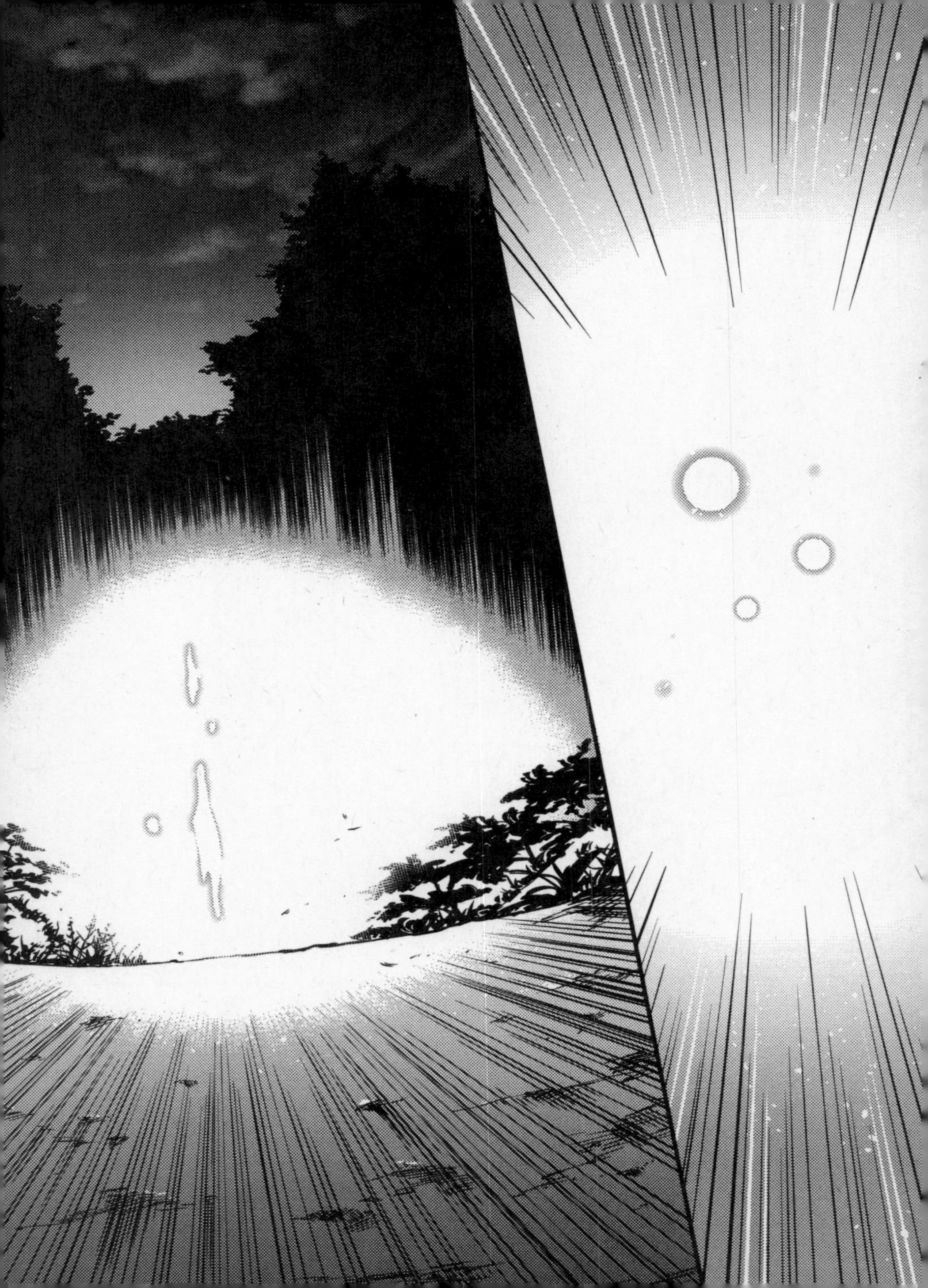

WHAT
HAPPENED
...?

IS
HIME
...?

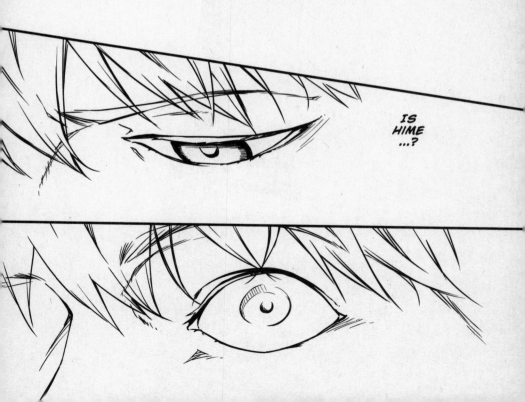

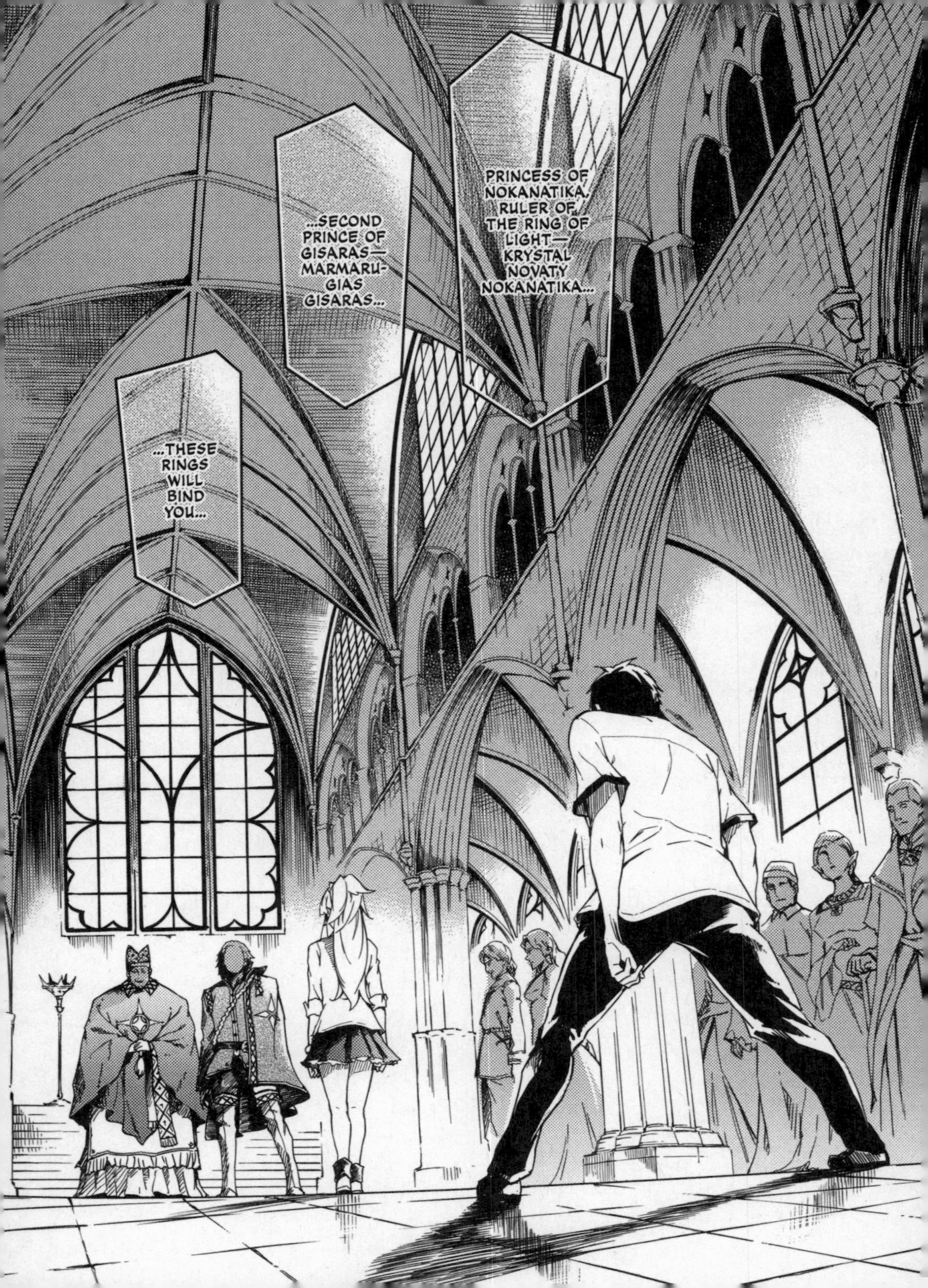
PRINCESS OF NOKANATIKA, RULER OF THE RING OF LIGHT— KRYSTAL NOVATY NOKANATIKA...
...SECOND PRINCE OF GISARAS— MARMARU-GIAS GISARAS...
...THESE RINGS WILL BIND YOU...

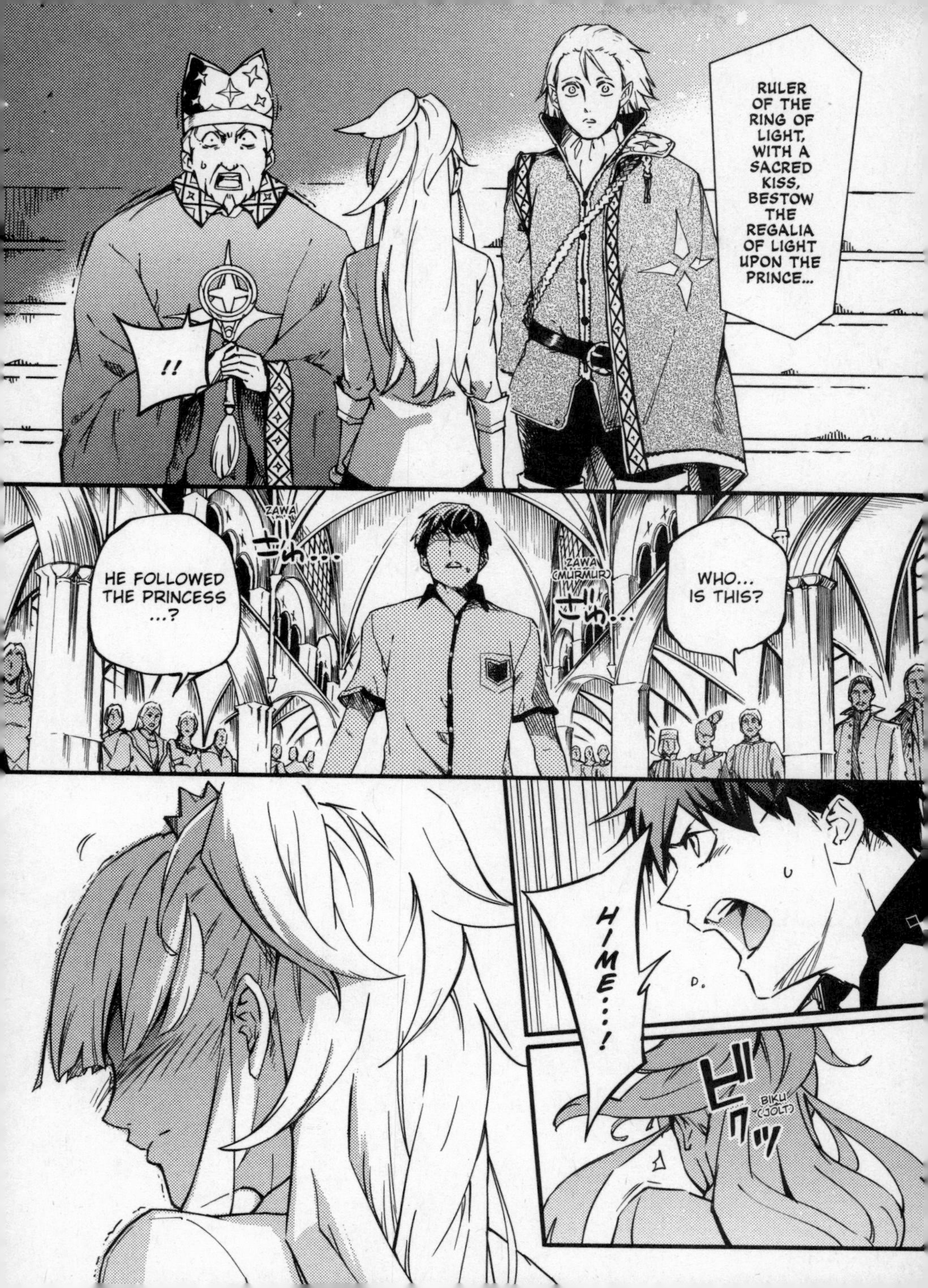
RULER OF THE RING OF LIGHT, WITH A SACRED KISS, BESTOW THE REGALIA OF LIGHT UPON THE PRINCE...
!!
WHO... IS THIS?
ZAWA (MURMUR)
ざわ...
ZAWA
ざわ...
HE FOLLOWED THE PRINCESS ...?
HIME...!
BIKU (JOLT)
ビクッ

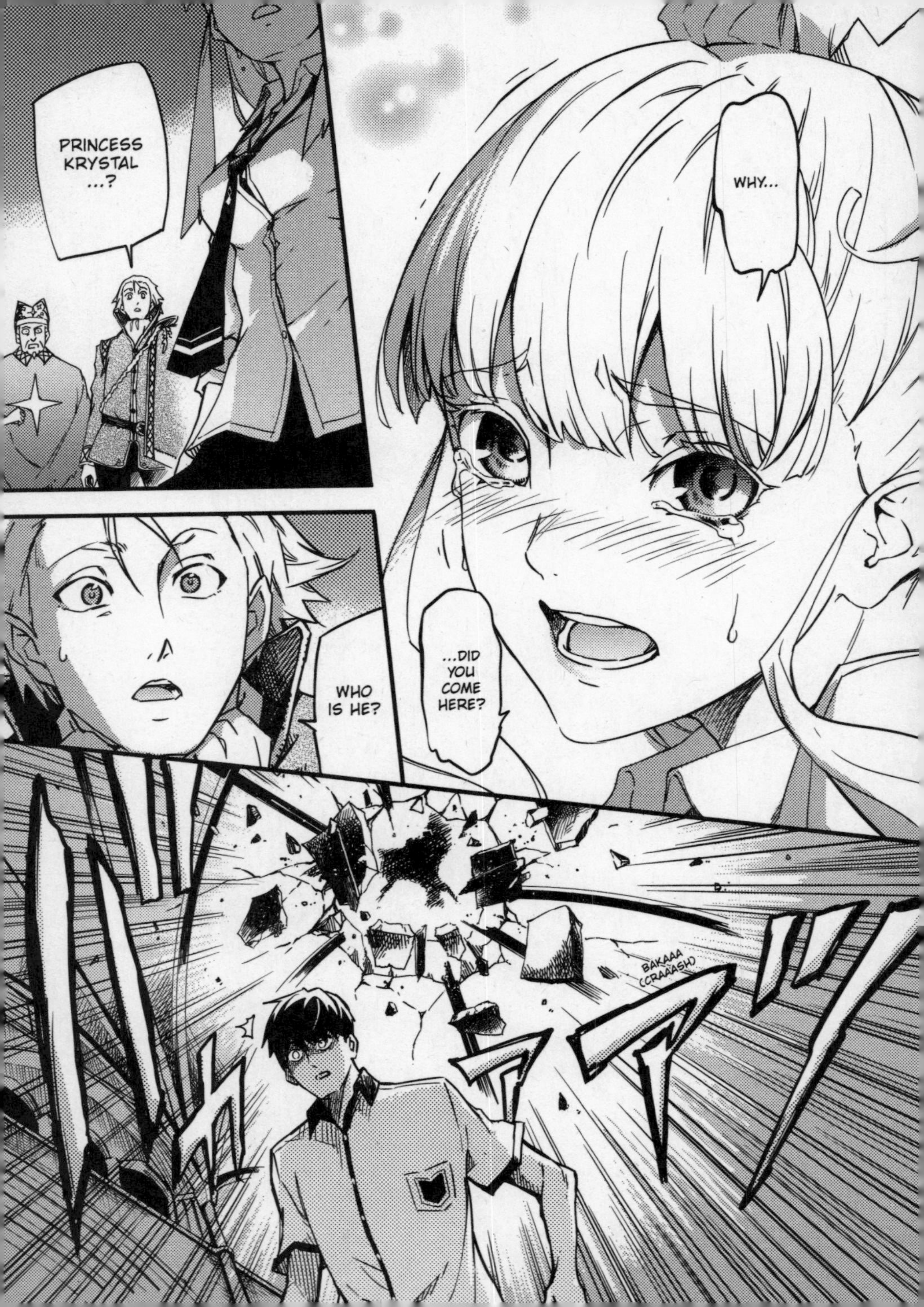
WHY...
...DID YOU COME HERE?
PRINCESS KRYSTAL ...?
WHO IS HE?
BAKAAA (CRAAASH)

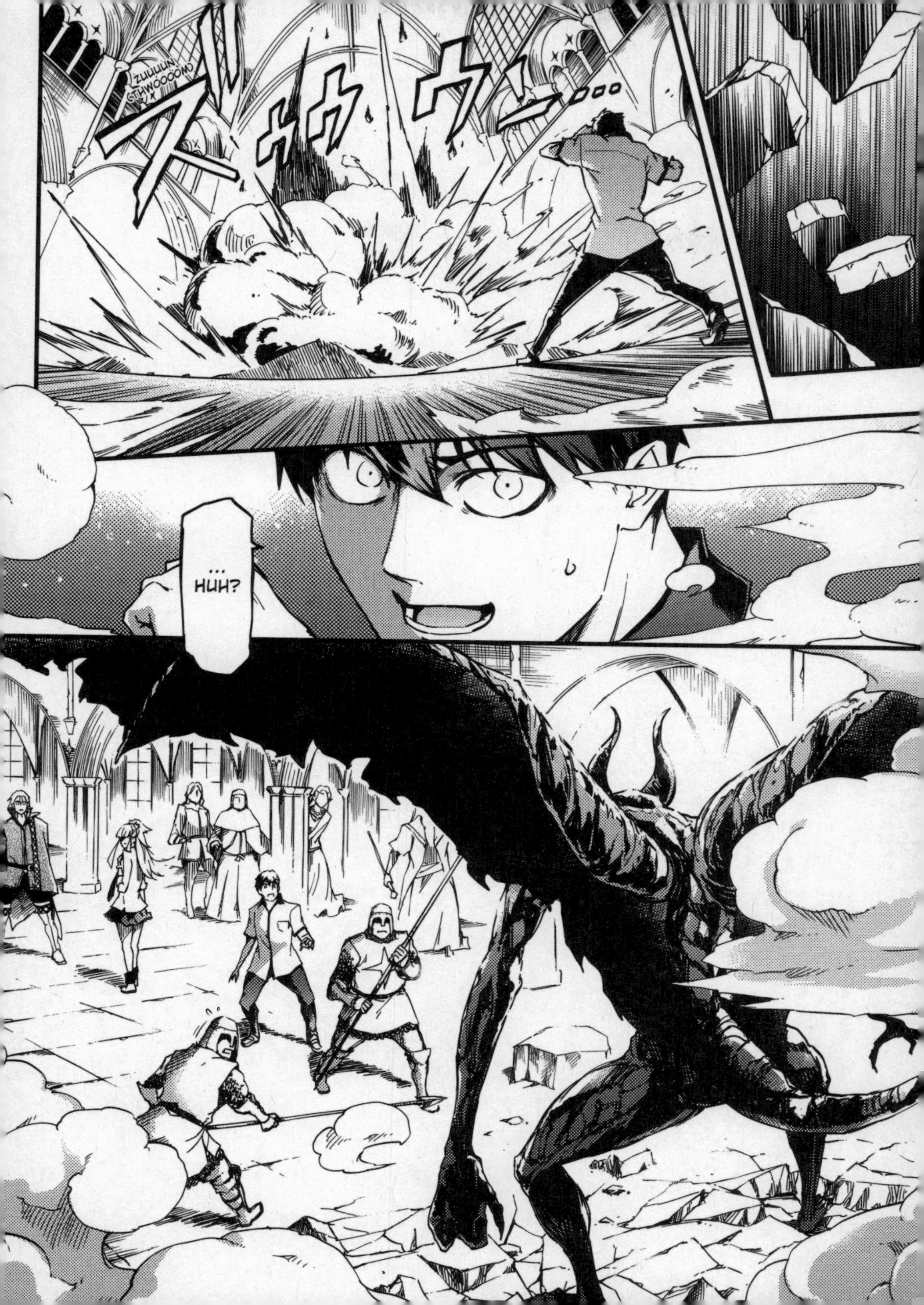
ズゥゥウン…
ZUUUUN (THWOOOOOM)
... HUH?

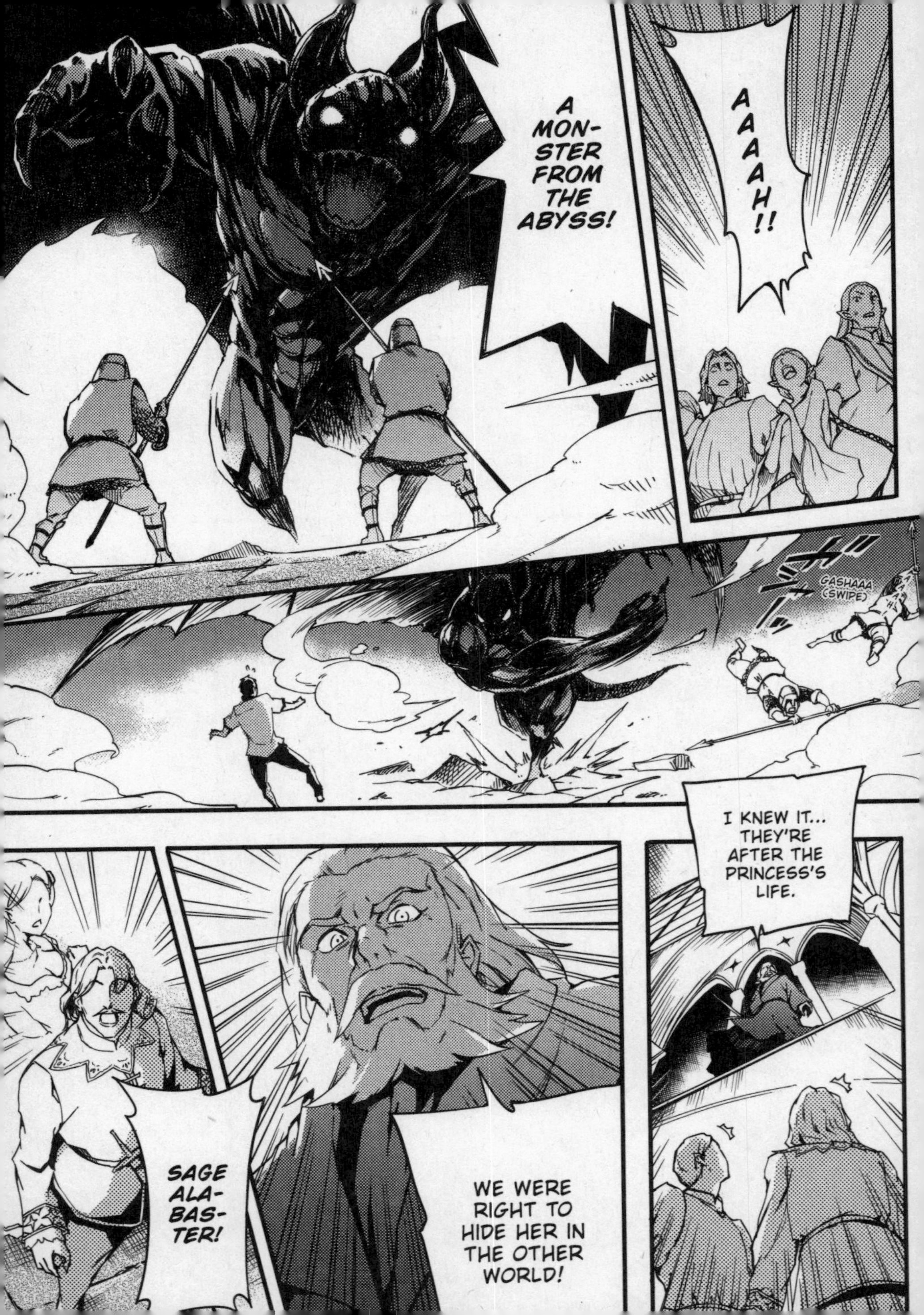
AAAAAH!!
A MON-STER FROM THE ABYSS!
GASHAAA (SWIPE)
I KNEW IT... THEY'RE AFTER THE PRINCESS'S LIFE.
WE WERE RIGHT TO HIDE HER IN THE OTHER WORLD!
SAGE ALA-BAS-TER!

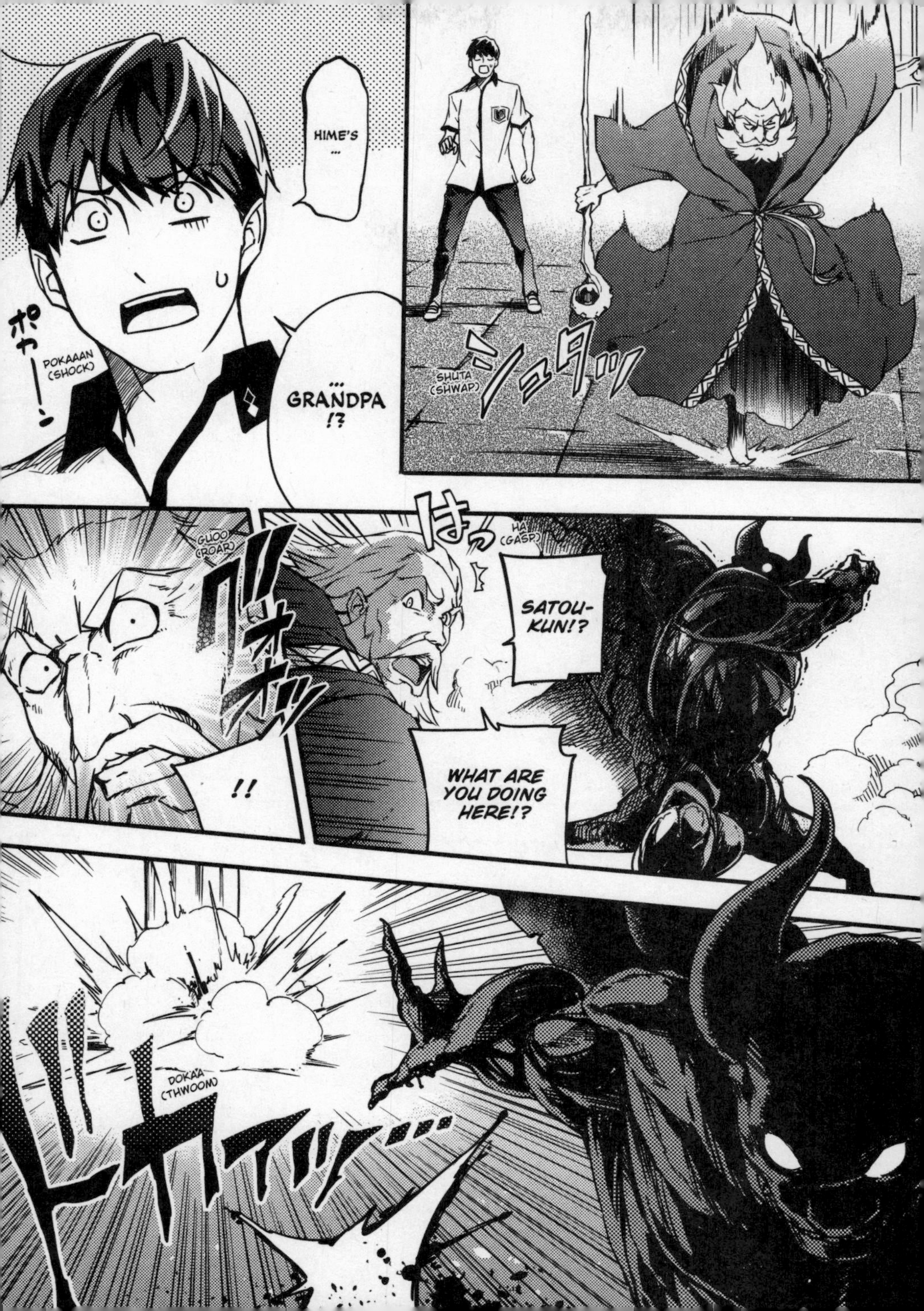
シュタッ
SHUTA (SHWAP)
HIME'S ...
ポカーン
POKAAAN (SHOCK)
... GRANDPA !?
はっ
HA (GASP)
SATOU-KUN!?
WHAT ARE YOU DOING HERE!?
グオオッ
GUOO (ROAR)
!!
ドカァッ...
DOKAA (THWOOM)

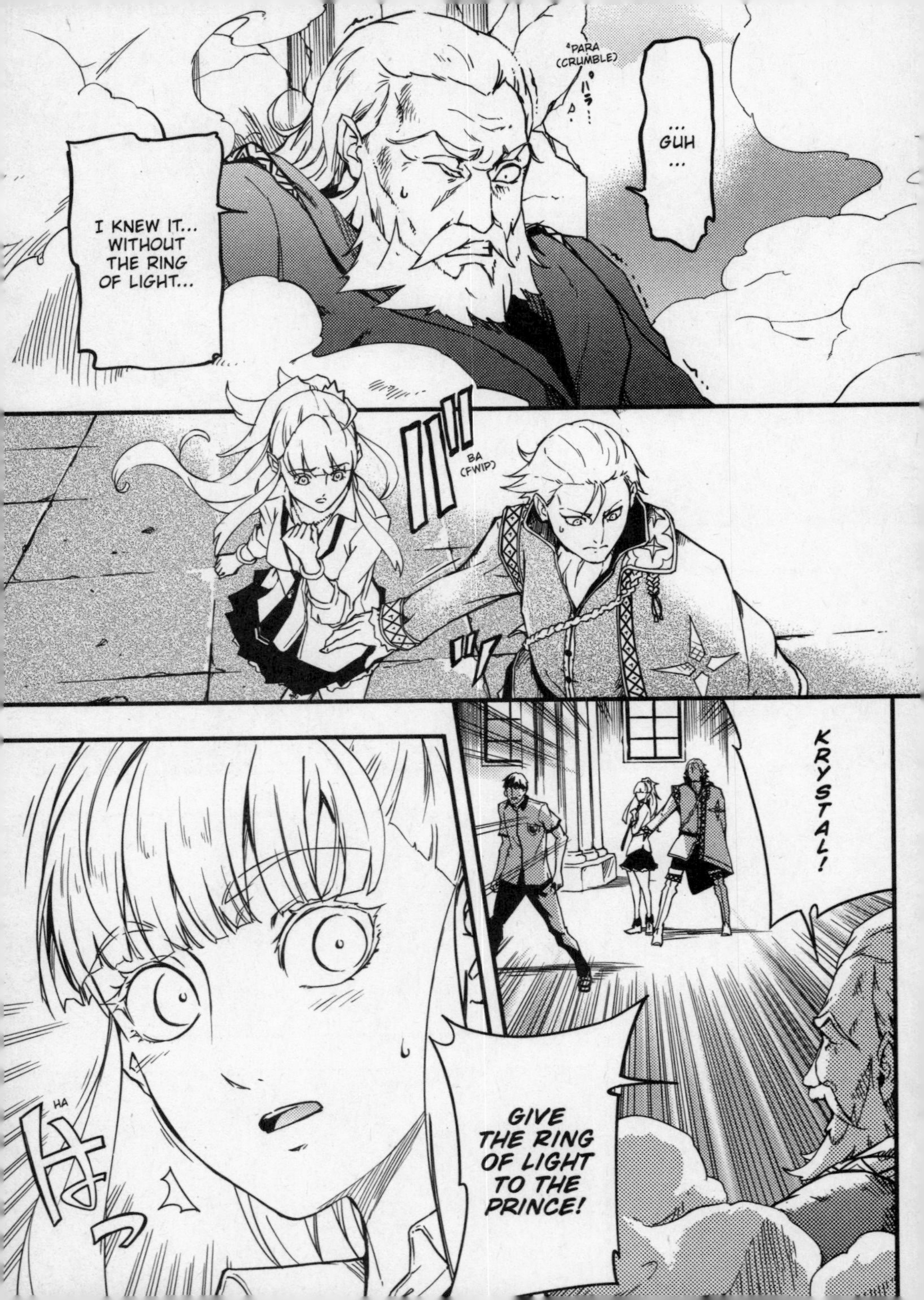
...GUH...
PARA (CRUMBLE)
パラ…
I KNEW IT... WITHOUT THE RING OF LIGHT...
BA (FWIP)
KRYSTAL!
GIVE THE RING OF LIGHT TO THE PRINCE!
HA
はっ

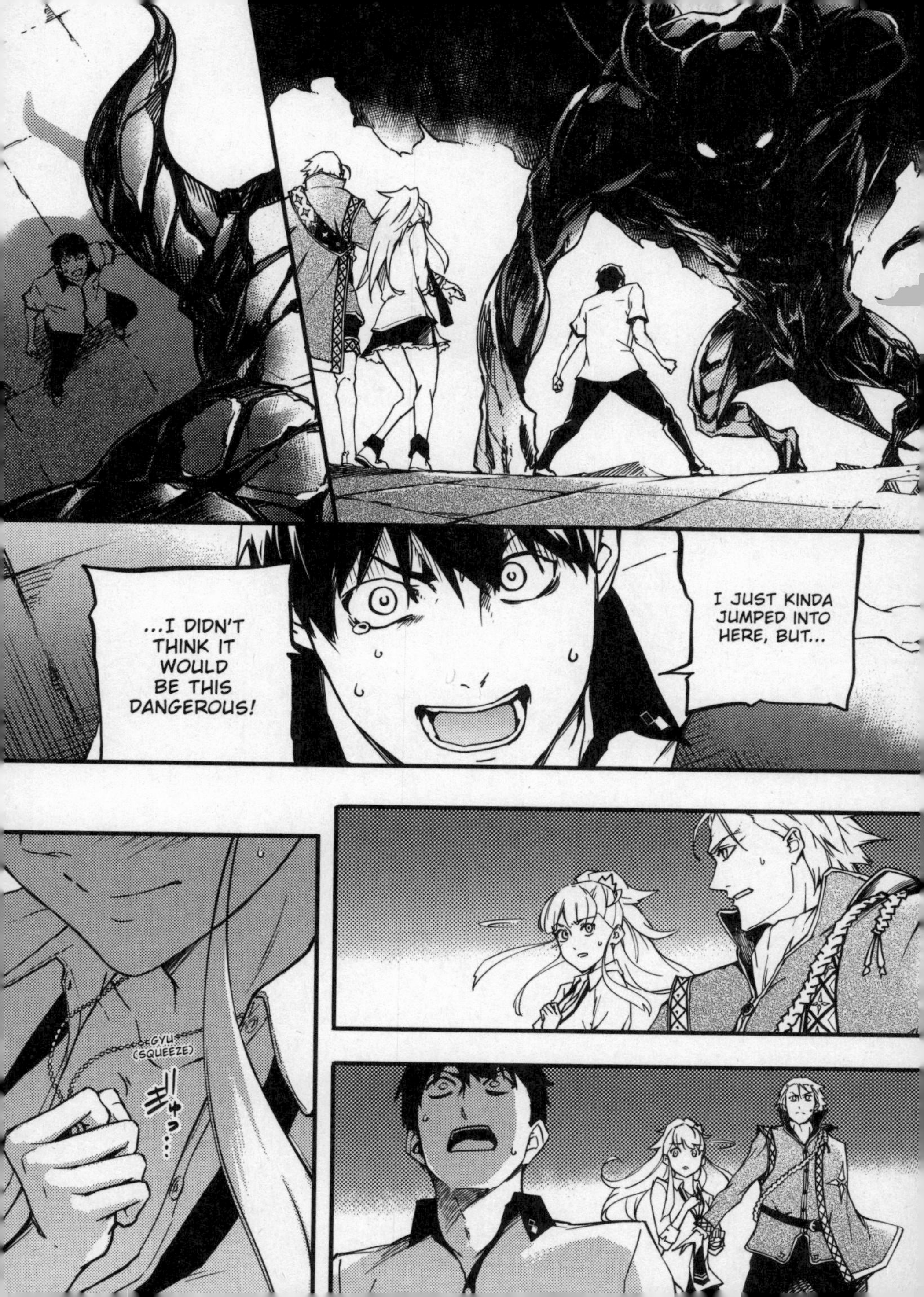
I JUST KINDA JUMPED INTO HERE, BUT...
...I DIDN'T THINK IT WOULD BE THIS DANGEROUS!
GYU (SQUEEZE)
ぎゅっ…

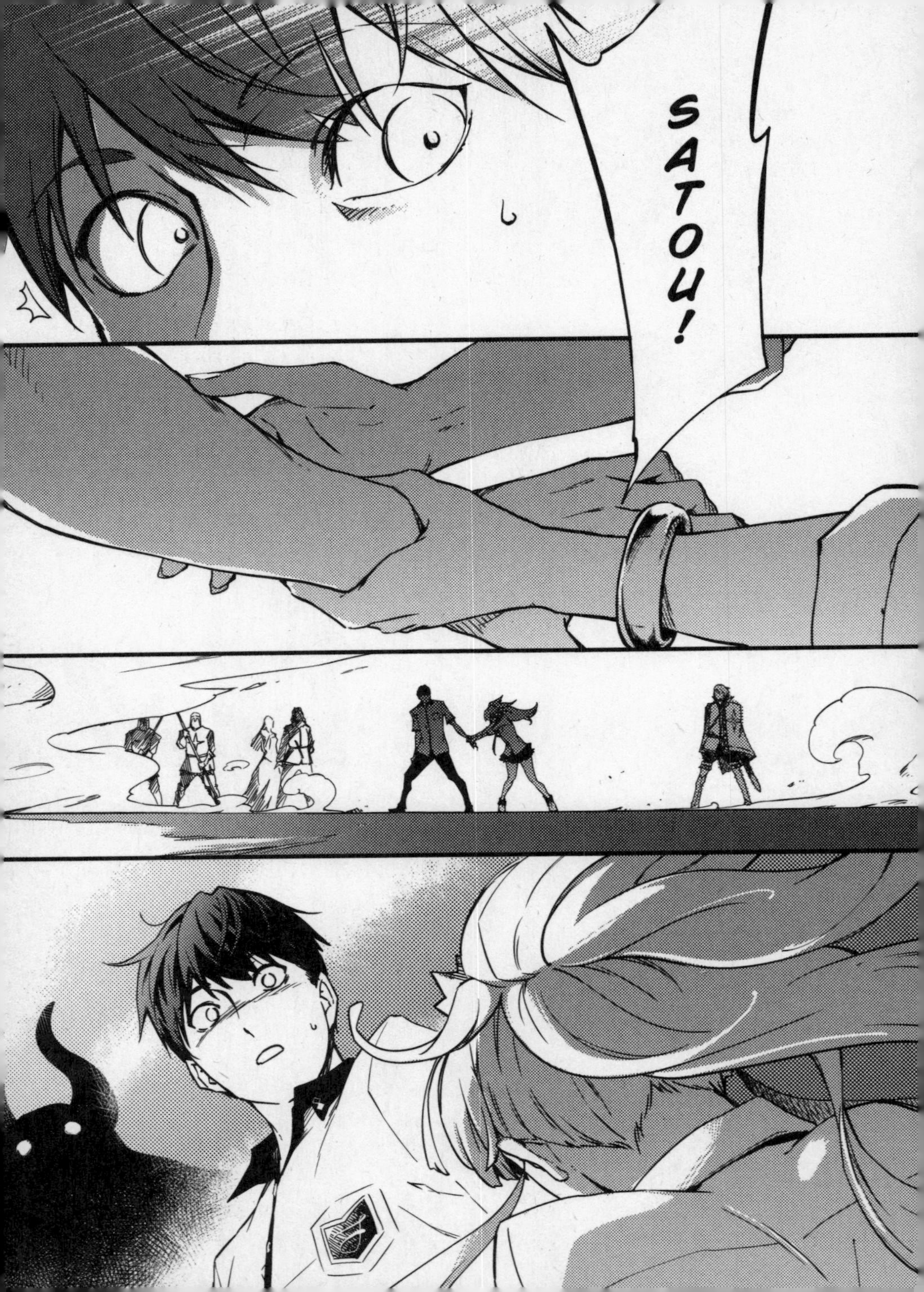
SATOU!

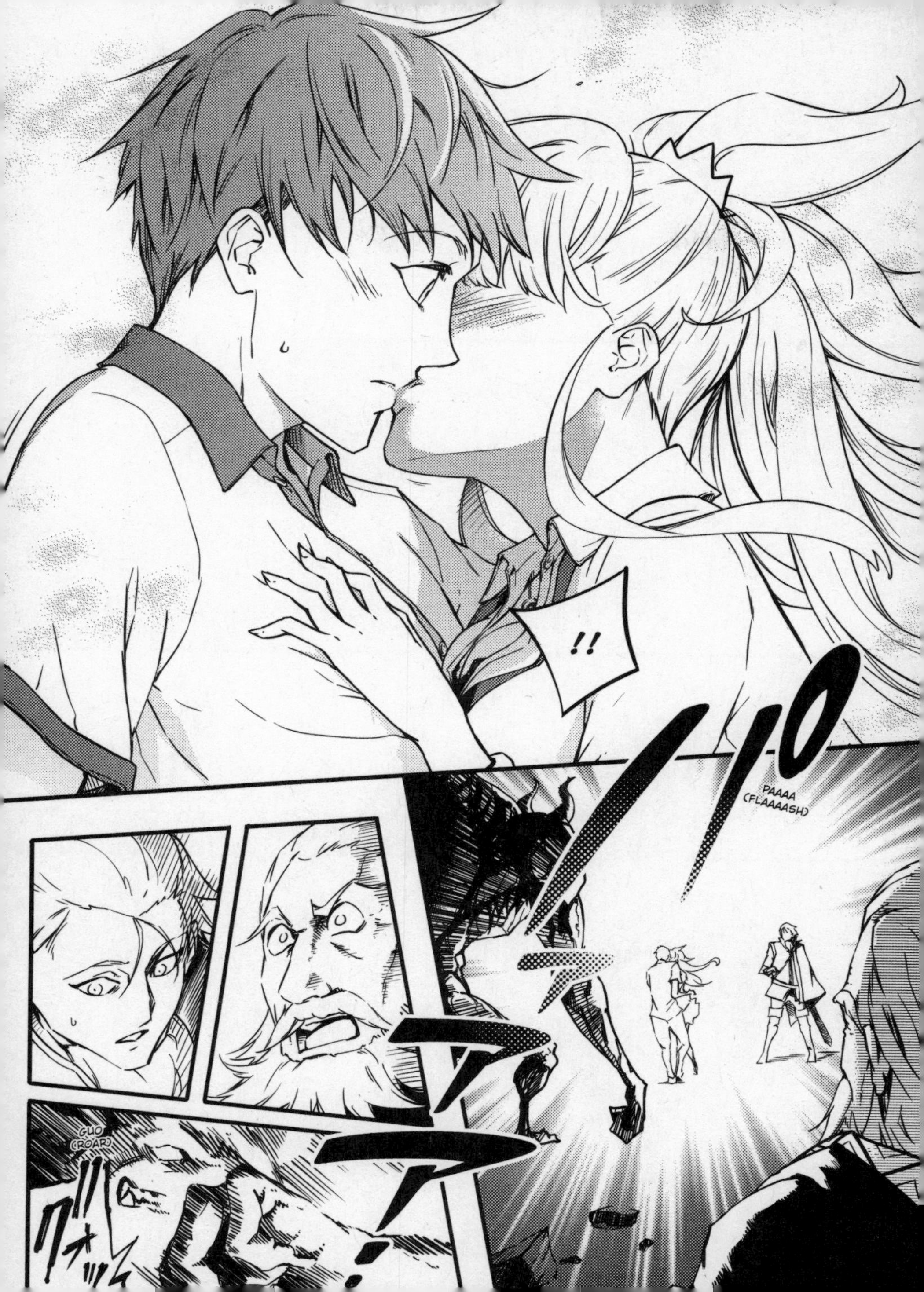

...
!!
PAAAA (FLAAAASH)
GUO (ROAR)

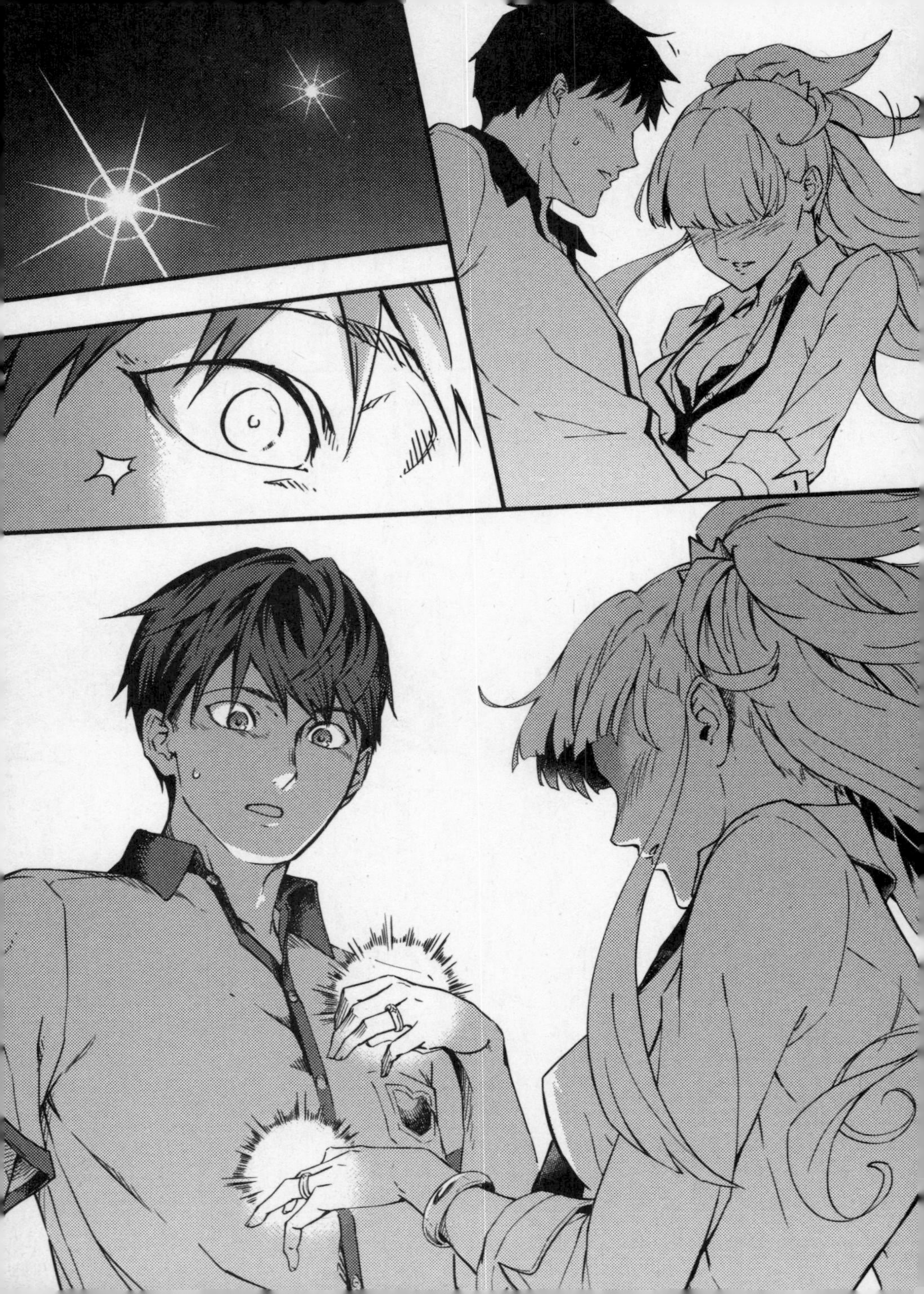

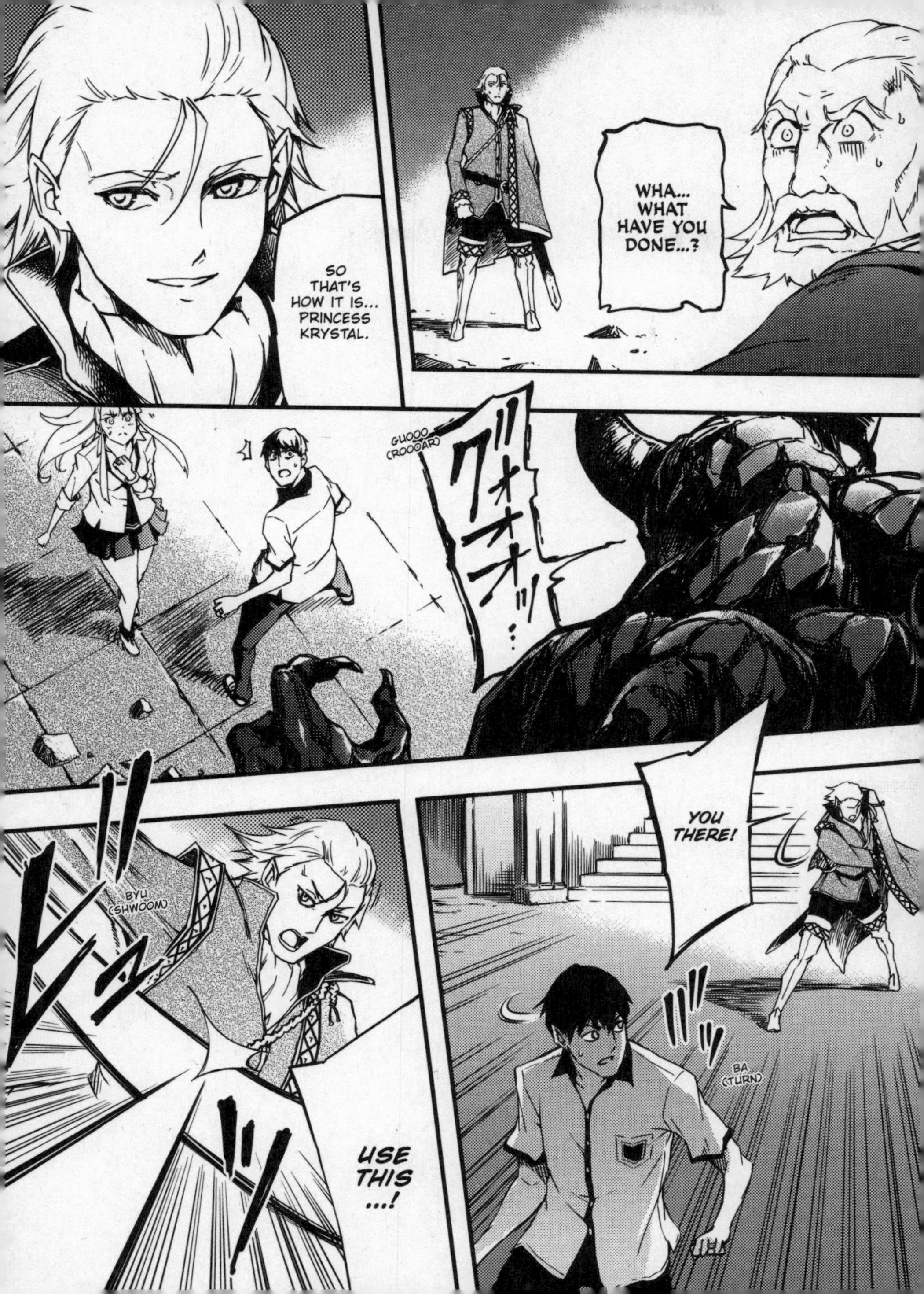
WHA... WHAT HAVE YOU DONE...?
SO THAT'S HOW IT IS... PRINCESS KRYSTAL.
GUOOO (ROOOAR)
YOU THERE!
BA (TURN)
BYU (SHWOOM)
USE THIS ...!

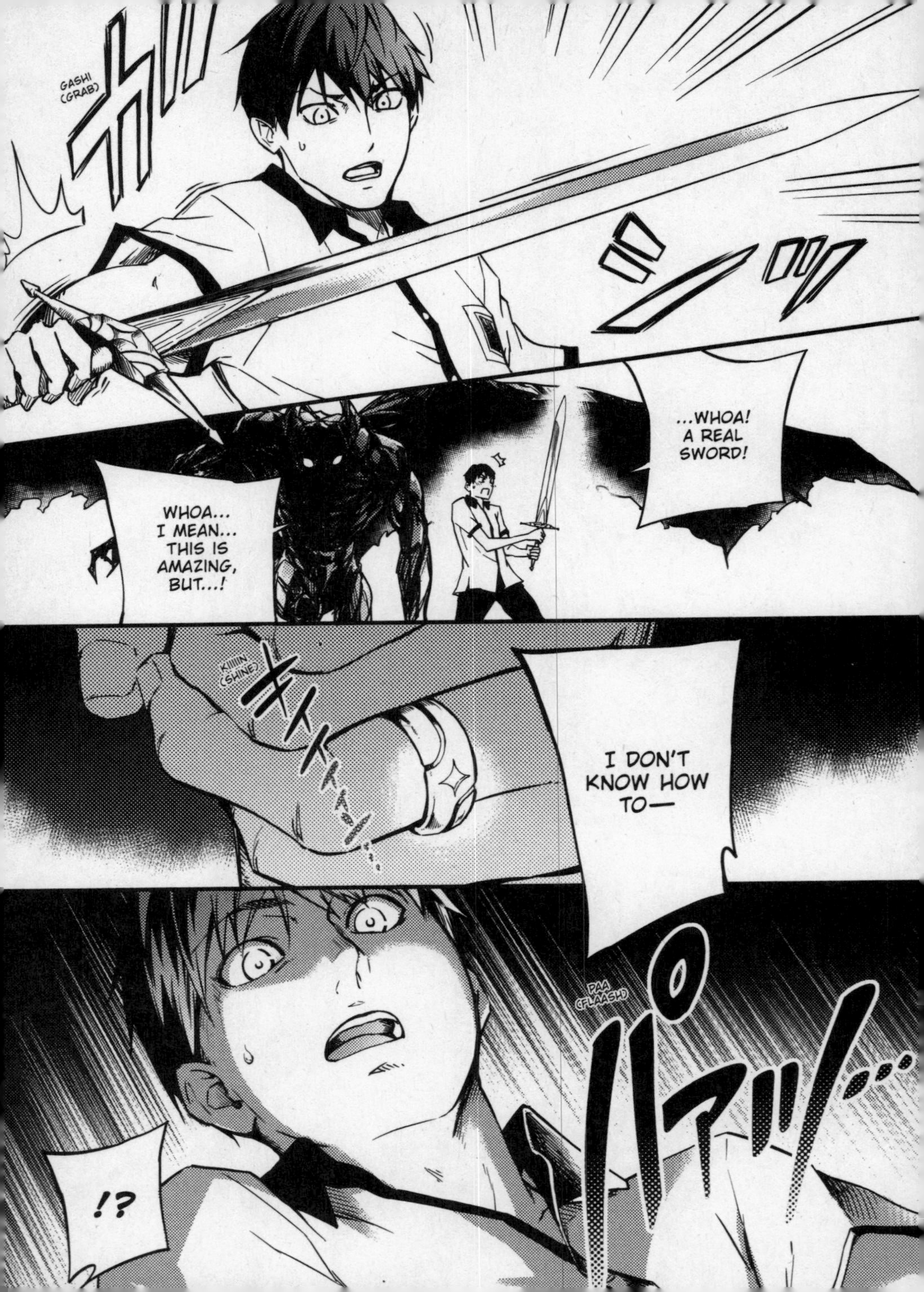
GASHI (GRAB)
...WHOA! A REAL SWORD!
WHOA... I MEAN... THIS IS AMAZING, BUT...!
KIIIIN (SHINE)
I DON'T KNOW HOW TO—
PAA (FLAASH)
!?

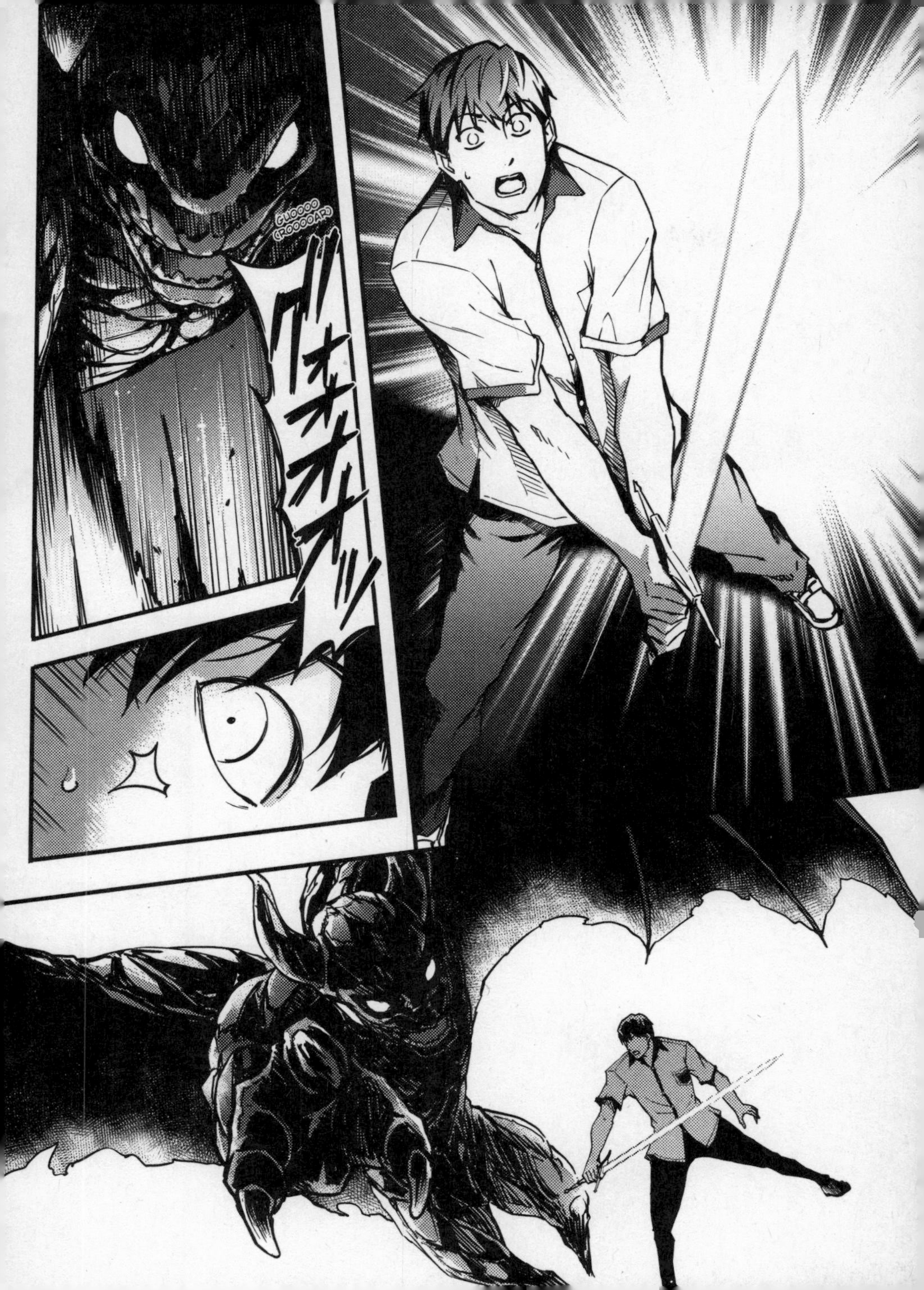
GUOOOO
(ROOOOAR)

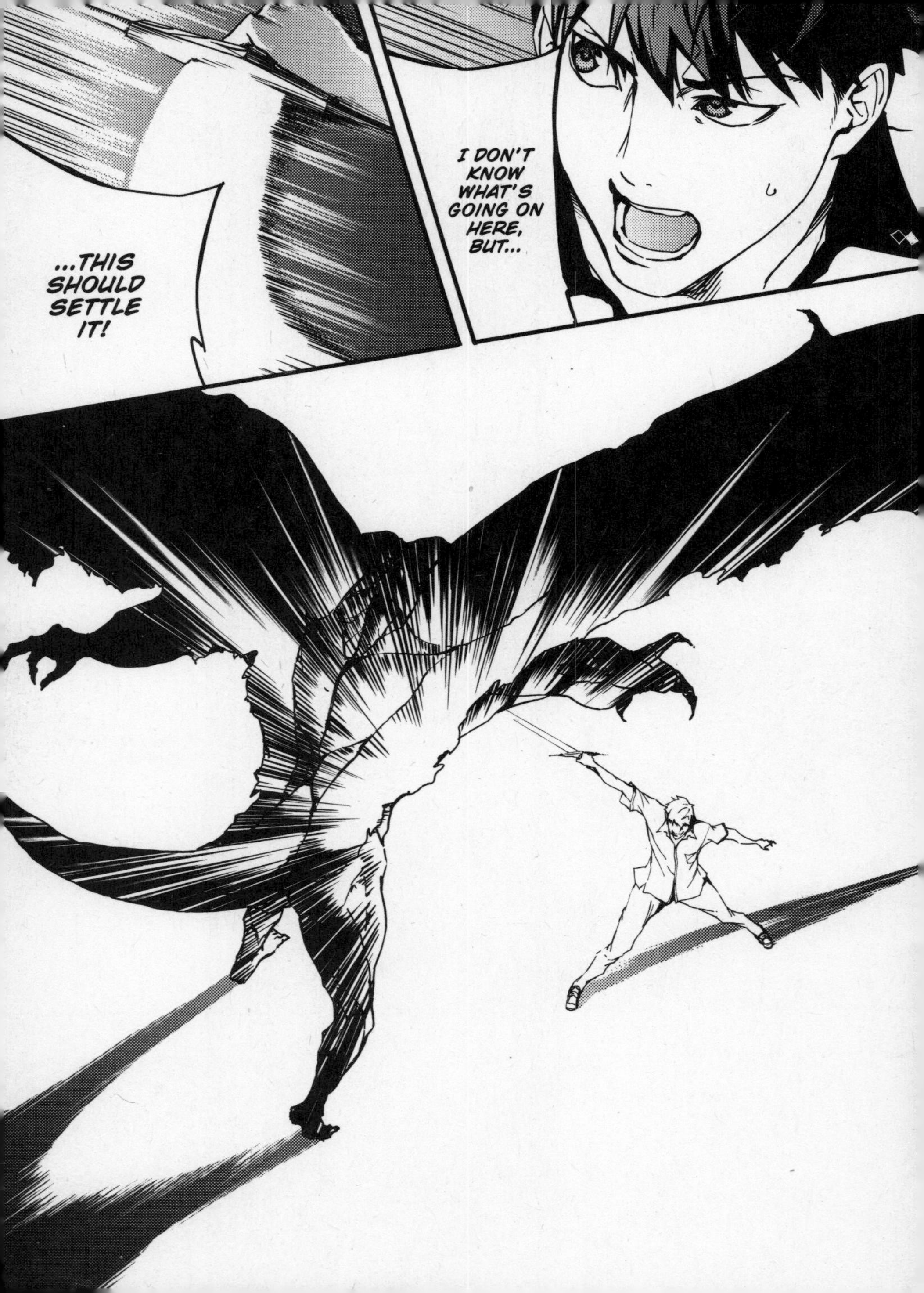
I DON'T KNOW WHAT'S GOING ON HERE, BUT...
...THIS SHOULD SETTLE IT!

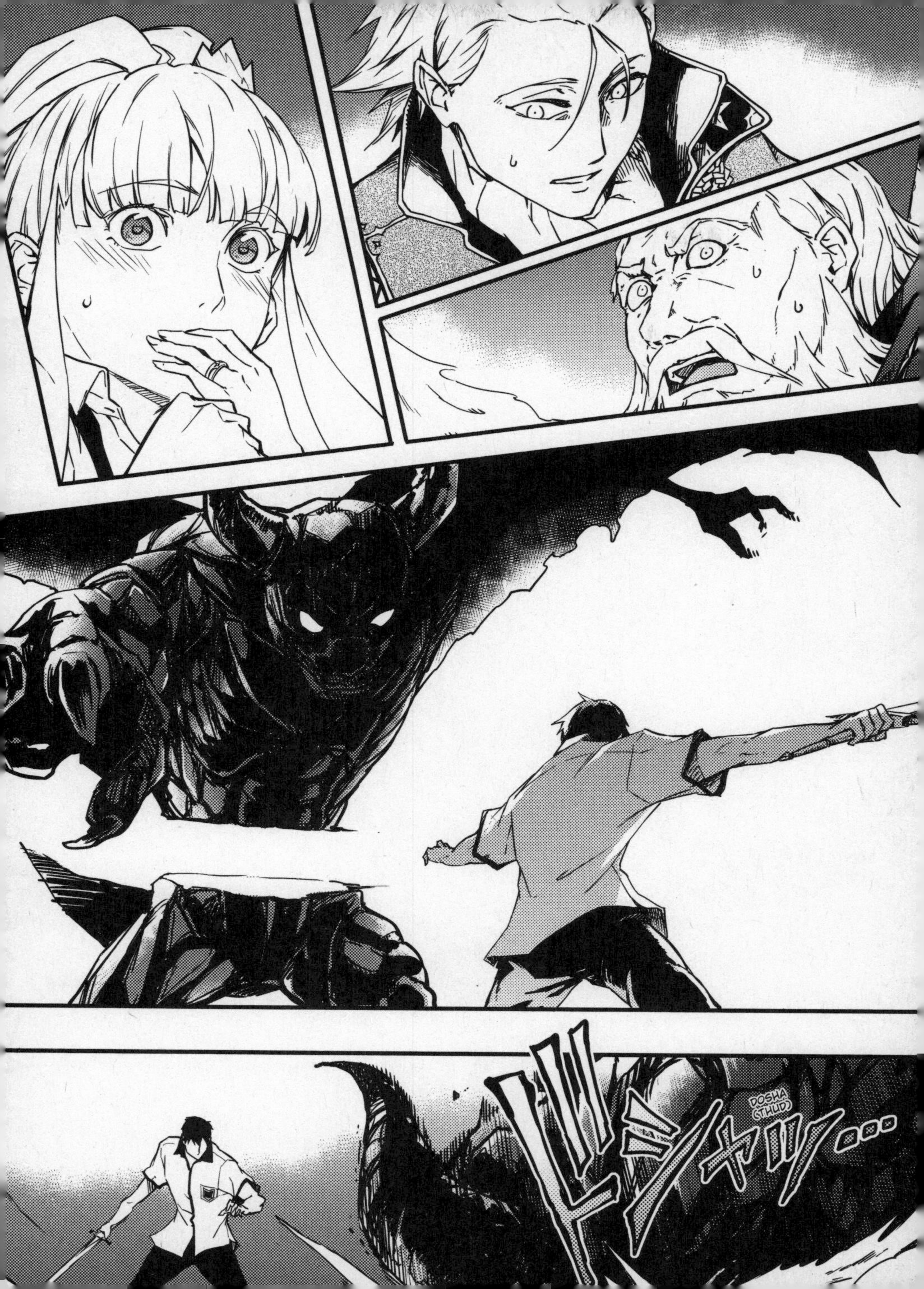
ドシャッ…
DOSHA (THUD)

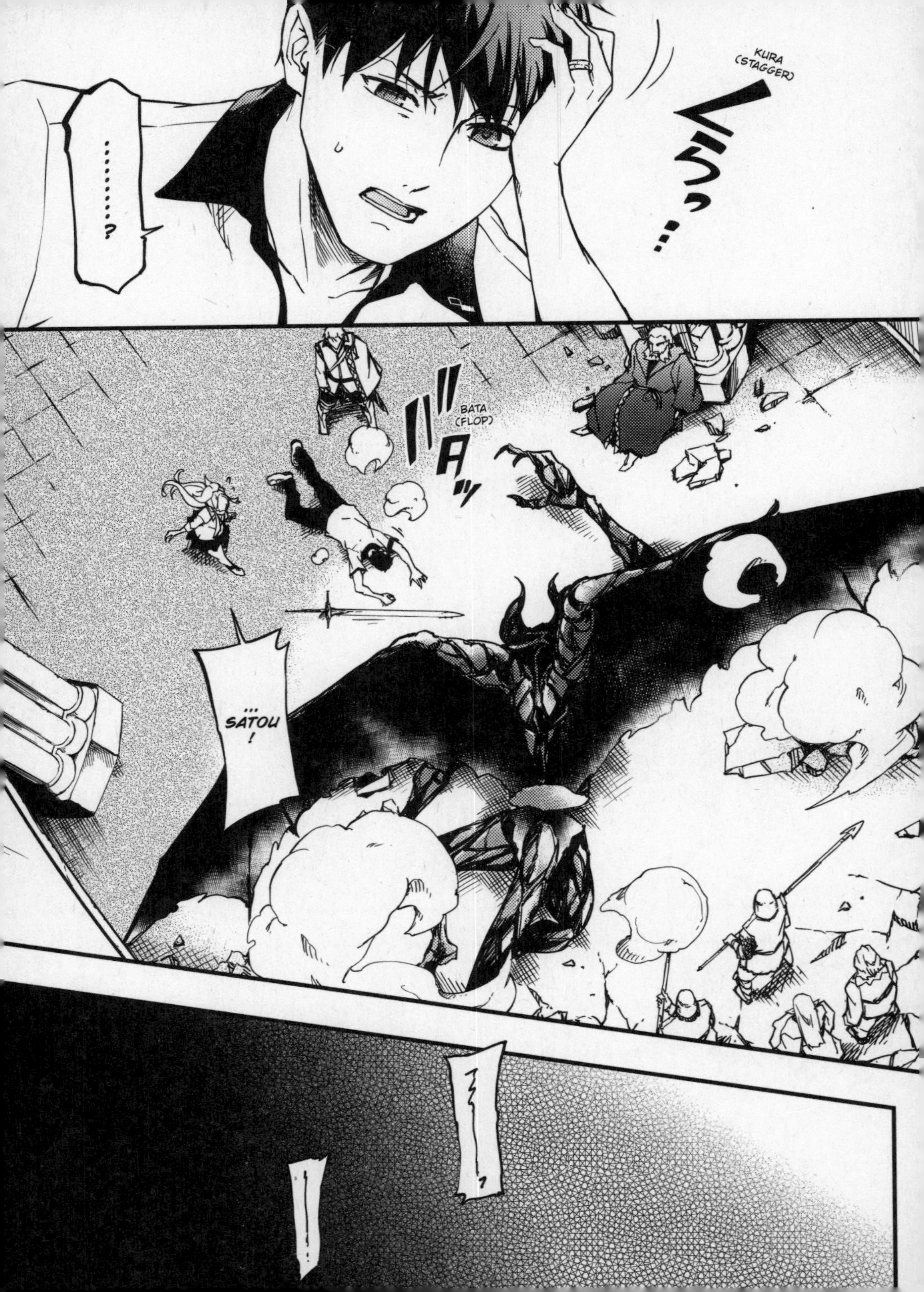
KURA (STAGGER)
......?
BATA (FLOP)
...SATOU!

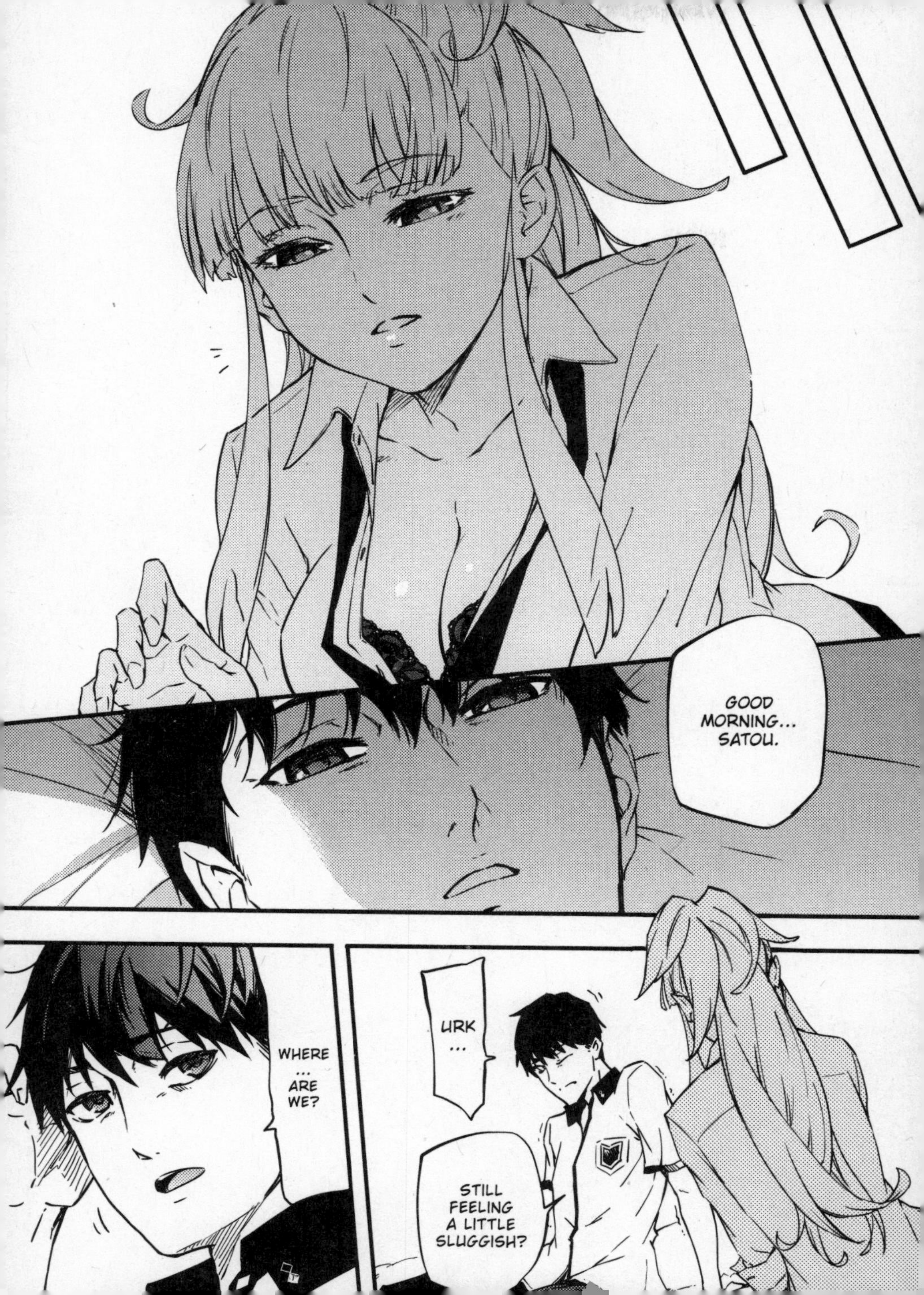
GOOD MORNING... SATOU.
URK...
STILL FEELING A LITTLE SLUGGISH?
WHERE... ARE WE?

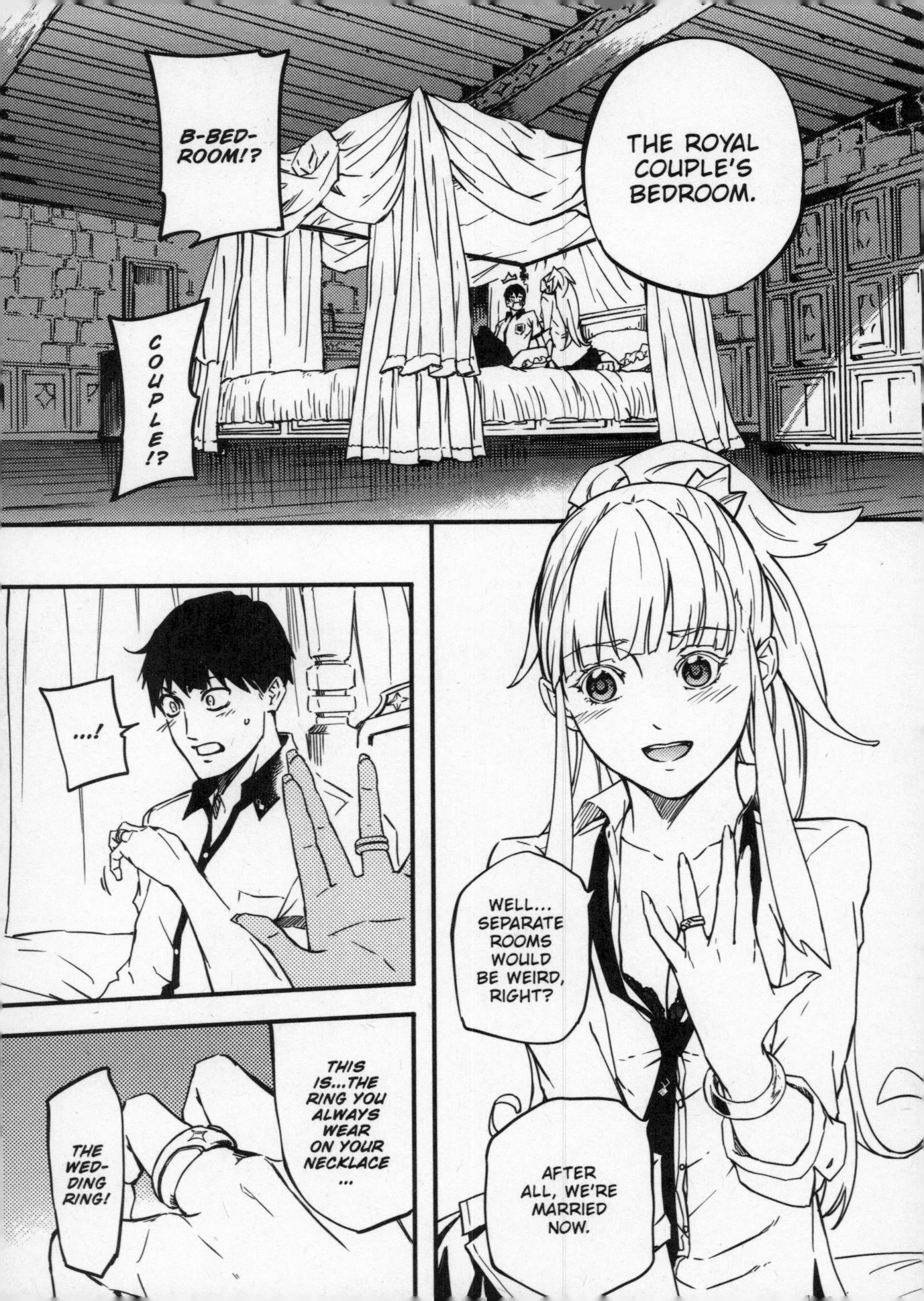
THE ROYAL COUPLE'S BEDROOM.
B-BED-ROOM!?
COUPLE!?
WELL... SEPARATE ROOMS WOULD BE WEIRD, RIGHT?
AFTER ALL, WE'RE MARRIED NOW.
...!
THIS IS...THE RING YOU ALWAYS WEAR ON YOUR NECKLACE ...
THE WED-DING RING!

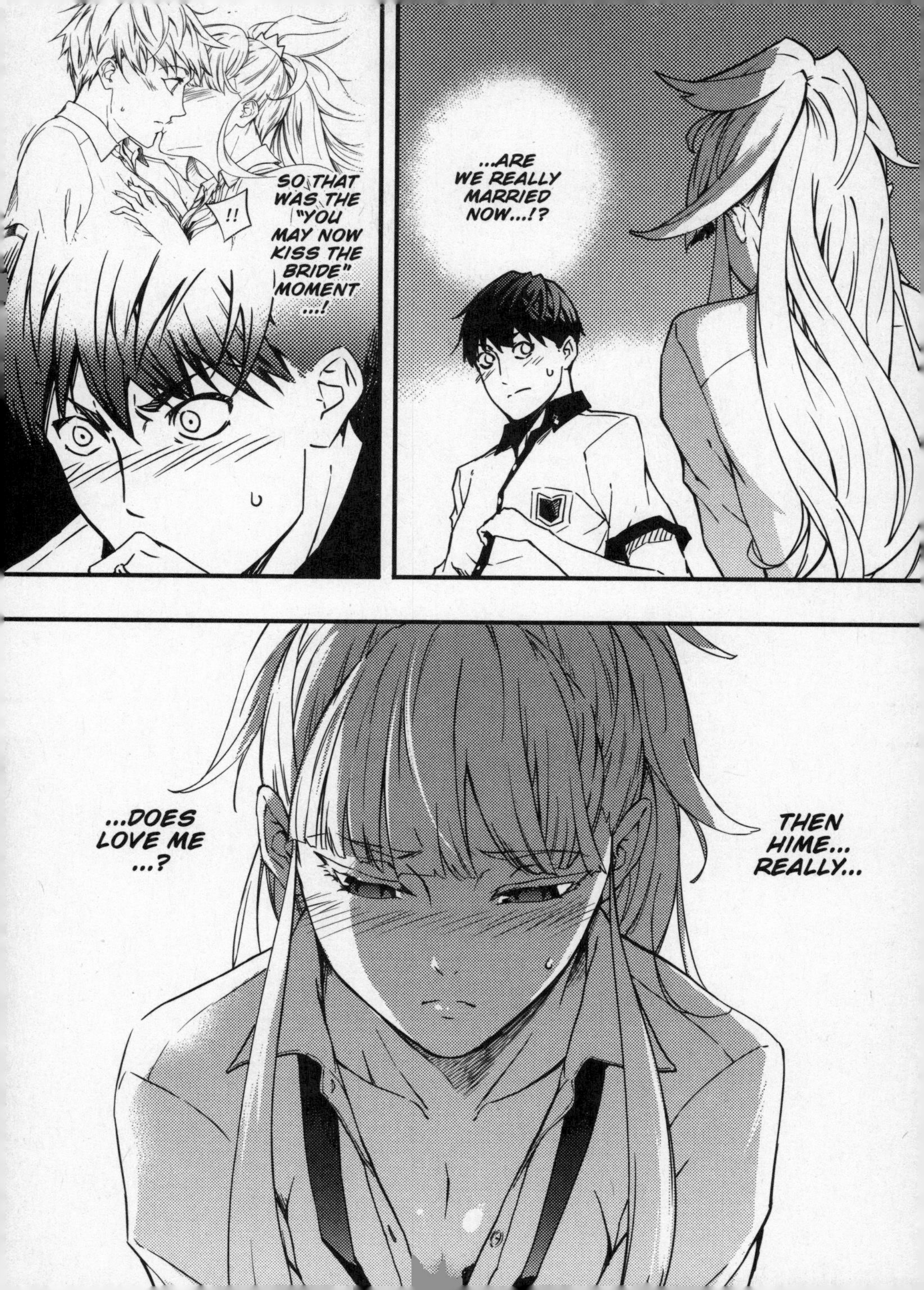
...ARE WE REALLY MARRIED NOW...!?
SO THAT WAS THE "YOU MAY NOW KISS THE BRIDE" MOMENT ...!
!!
THEN HIME... REALLY...
...DOES LOVE ME ...?

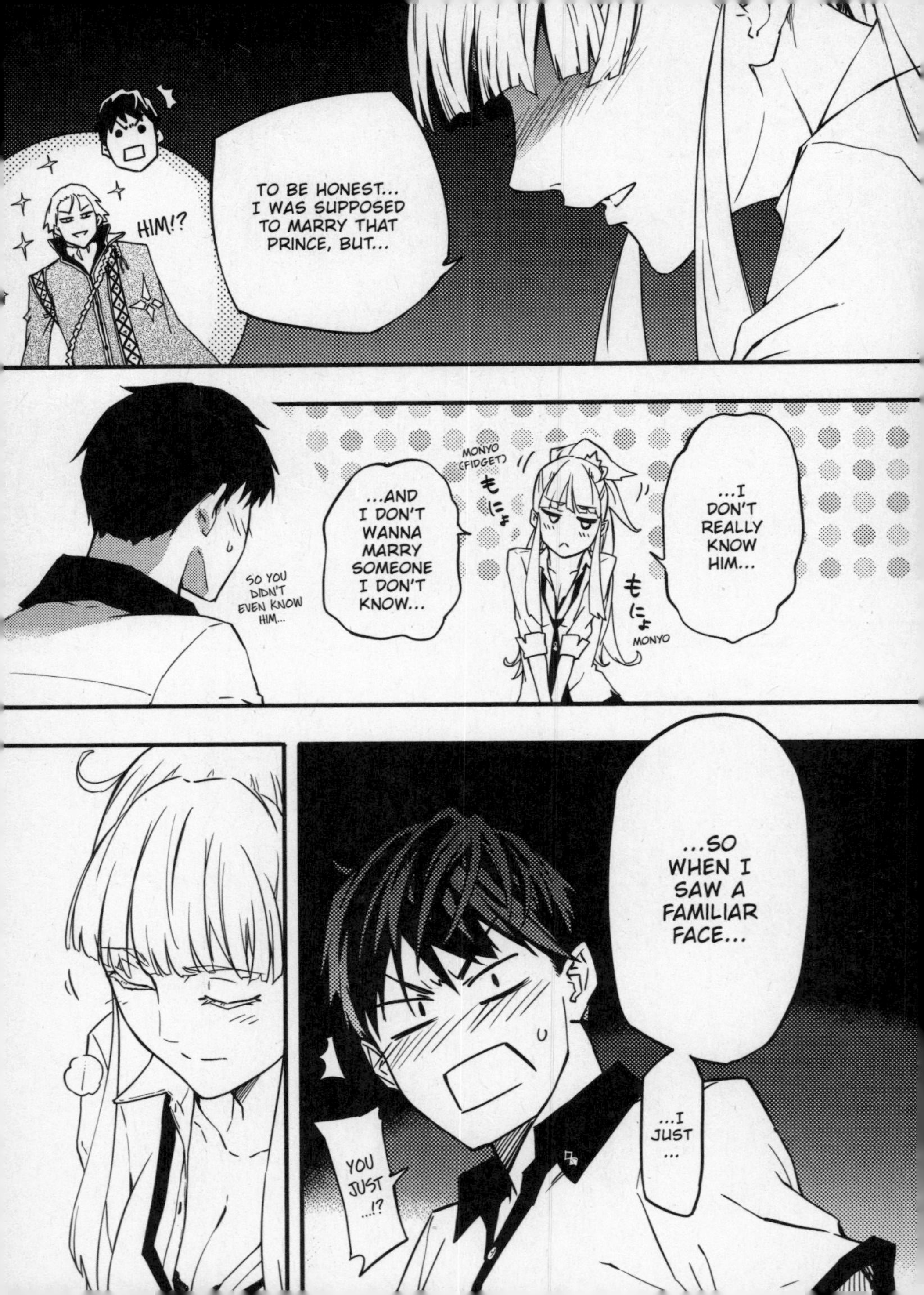
TO BE HONEST... I WAS SUPPOSED TO MARRY THAT PRINCE, BUT...
HIM!?
...I DON'T REALLY KNOW HIM...
もにょ
MONYO
MONYO (FIDGET)
もにょ
...AND I DON'T WANNA MARRY SOMEONE I DON'T KNOW...
SO YOU DIDN'T EVEN KNOW HIM...
...SO WHEN I SAW A FAMILIAR FACE...
...I JUST ...
YOU JUST ...!?

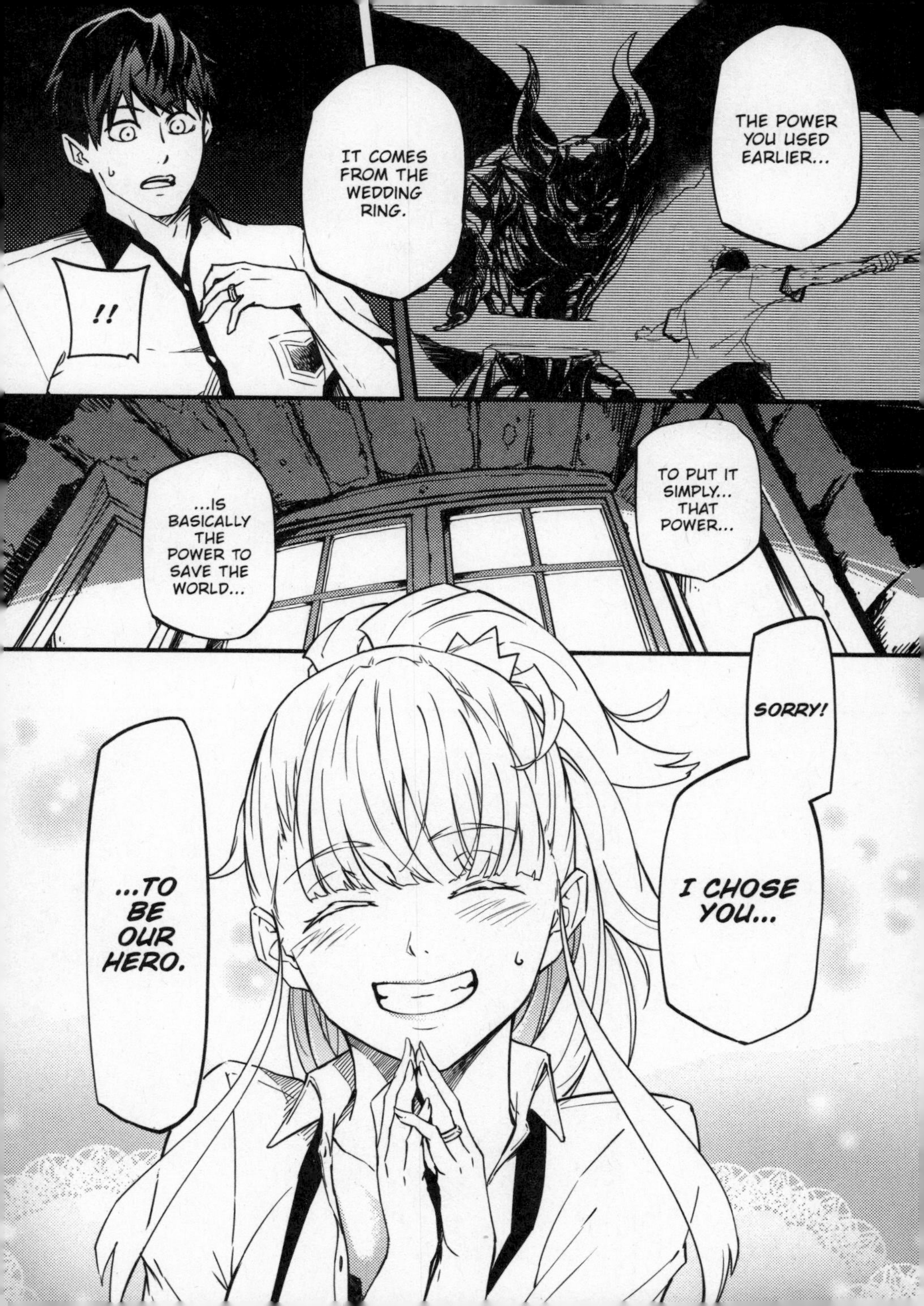
THE POWER YOU USED EARLIER...
IT COMES FROM THE WEDDING RING.
!!
TO PUT IT SIMPLY... THAT POWER...
...IS BASICALLY THE POWER TO SAVE THE WORLD...
SORRY!
I CHOSE YOU...
...TO BE OUR HERO.

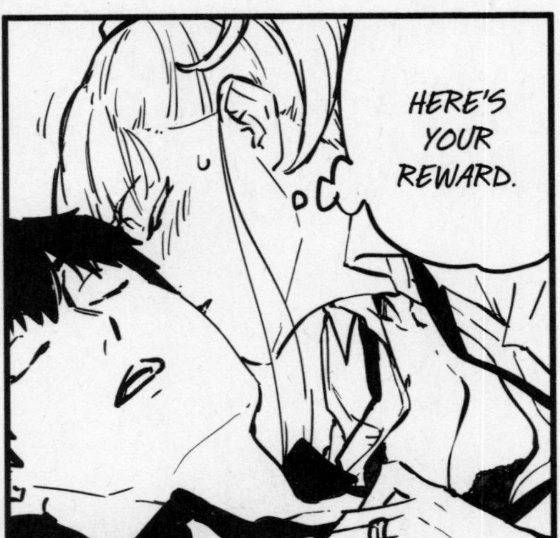
HERE'S YOUR REWARD.

Tales of
Wedding Rings

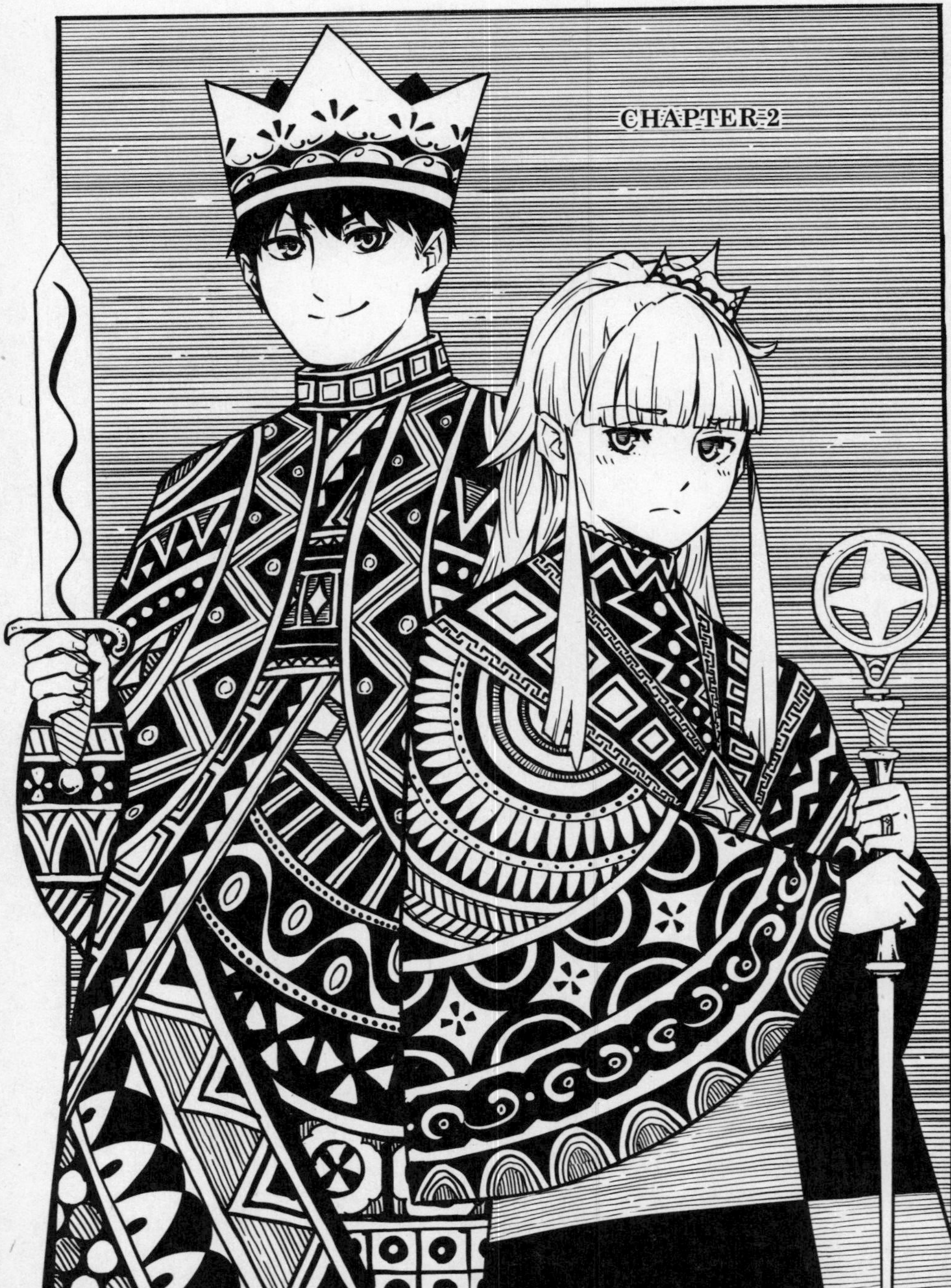
CHAPTER 2

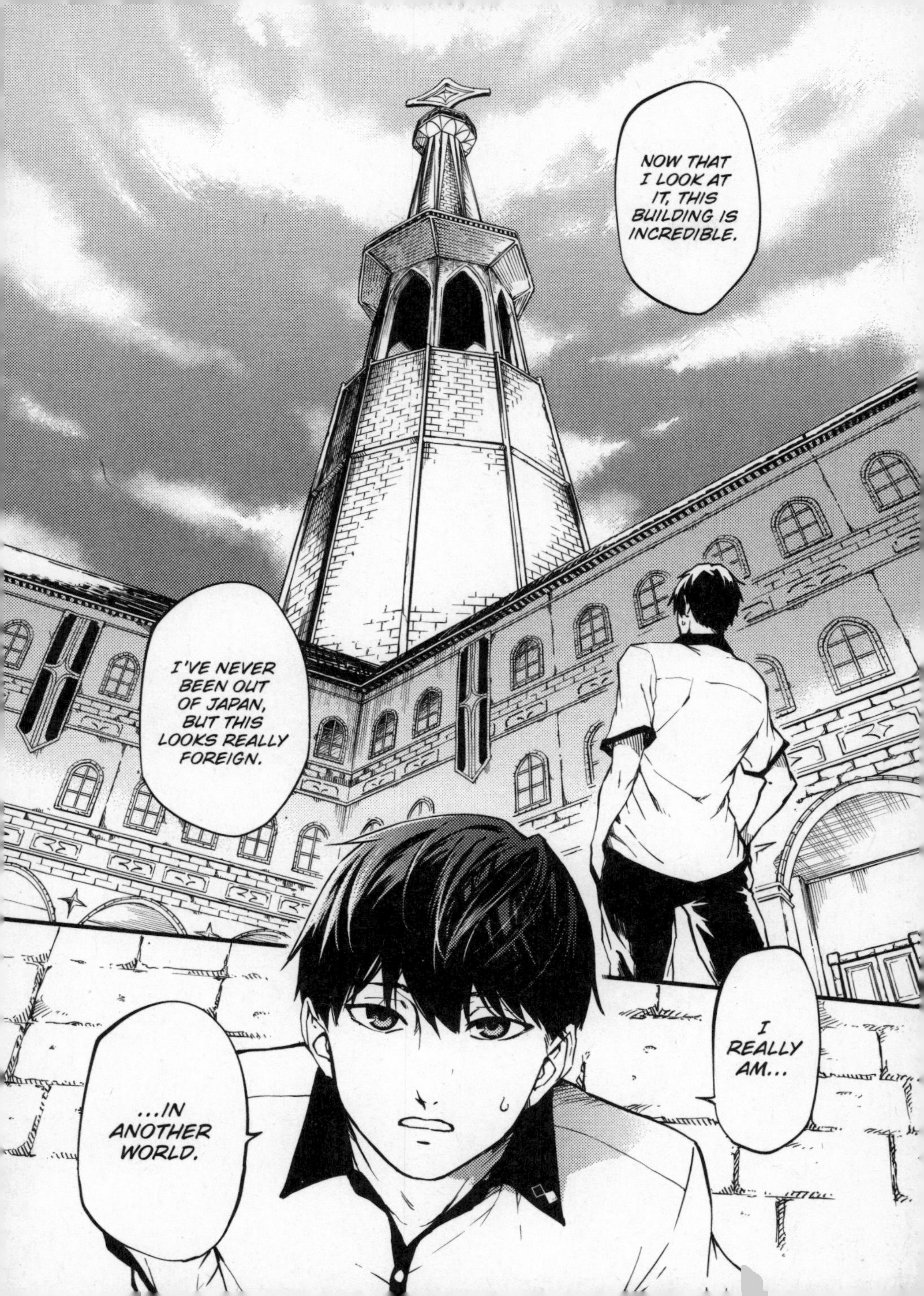
NOW THAT I LOOK AT IT, THIS BUILDING IS INCREDIBLE.
I'VE NEVER BEEN OUT OF JAPAN, BUT THIS LOOKS REALLY FOREIGN.
I REALLY AM...
...IN ANOTHER WORLD.

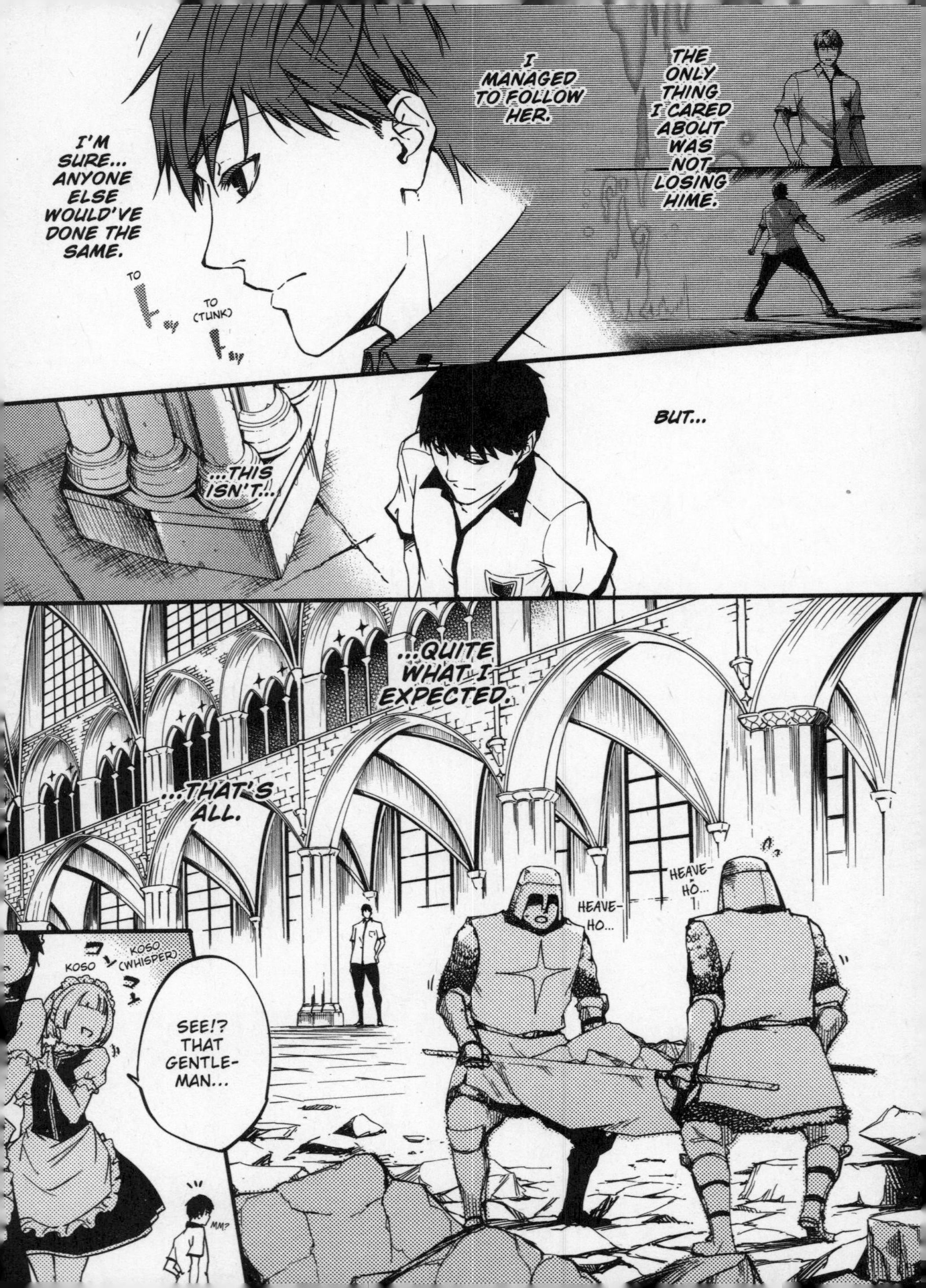
THE ONLY THING I CARED ABOUT WAS NOT LOSING HIME.
I MANAGED TO FOLLOW HER.
I'M SURE... ANYONE ELSE WOULD'VE DONE THE SAME.
TO
TO (TUNK)
BUT...
...THIS ISN'T...
...QUITE WHAT I EXPECTED.
...THAT'S ALL.
HEAVE-HO...
HEAVE-HO...
KOSO (WHISPER)
KOSO
SEE!? THAT GENTLEMAN...
MM?

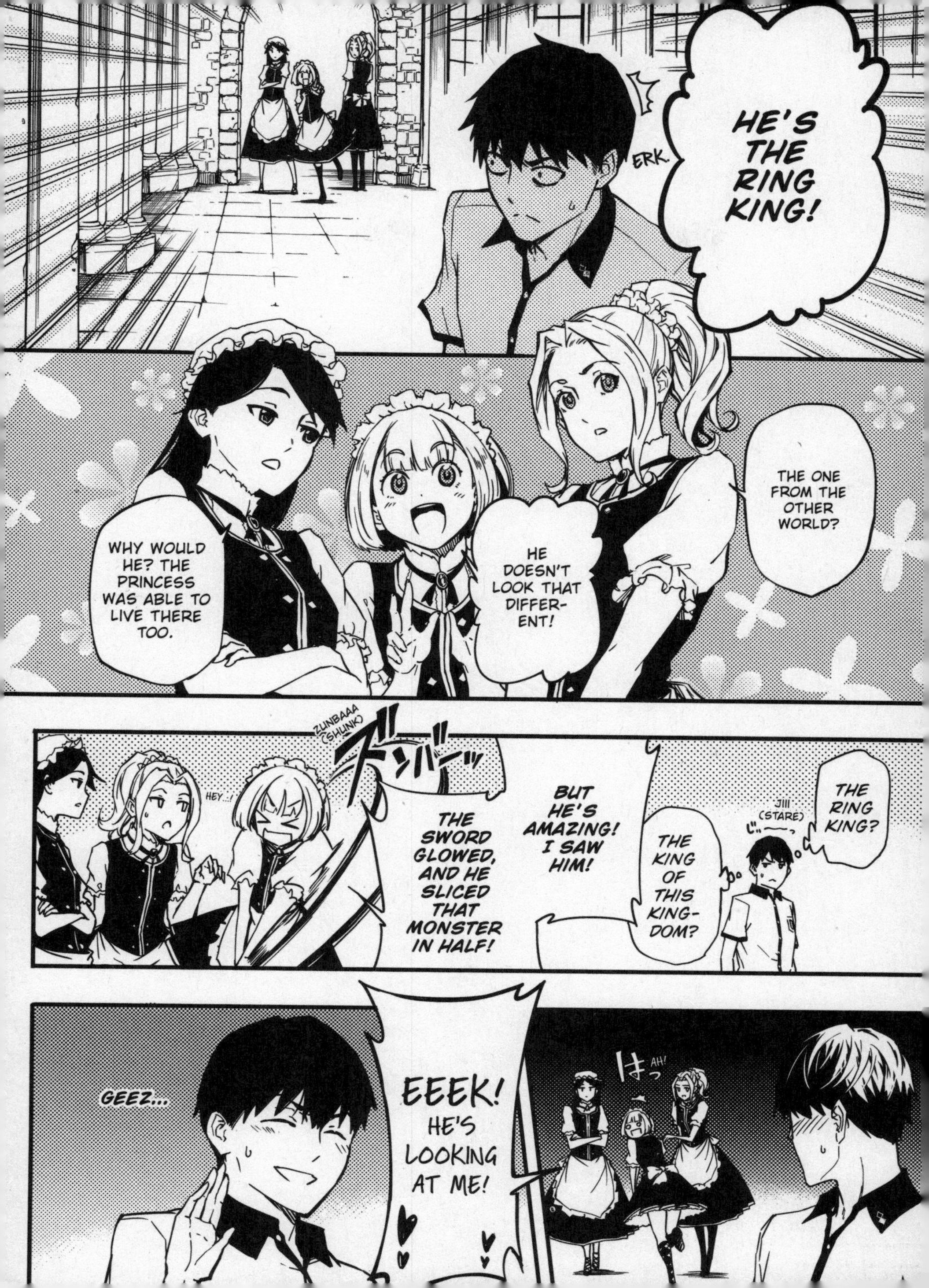

HE'S THE RING KING!
ERK.
THE ONE FROM THE OTHER WORLD?
HE DOESN'T LOOK THAT DIFFER-ENT!
WHY WOULD HE? THE PRINCESS WAS ABLE TO LIVE THERE TOO.
THE RING KING?
JIII (STARE)
THE KING OF THIS KING-DOM?
BUT HE'S AMAZING! I SAW HIM!
THE SWORD GLOWED, AND HE SLICED THAT MONSTER IN HALF!
ZUNBAAA (SHUNK)
HEY...!
AH!
EEEK! HE'S LOOKING AT ME!
GEEZ...

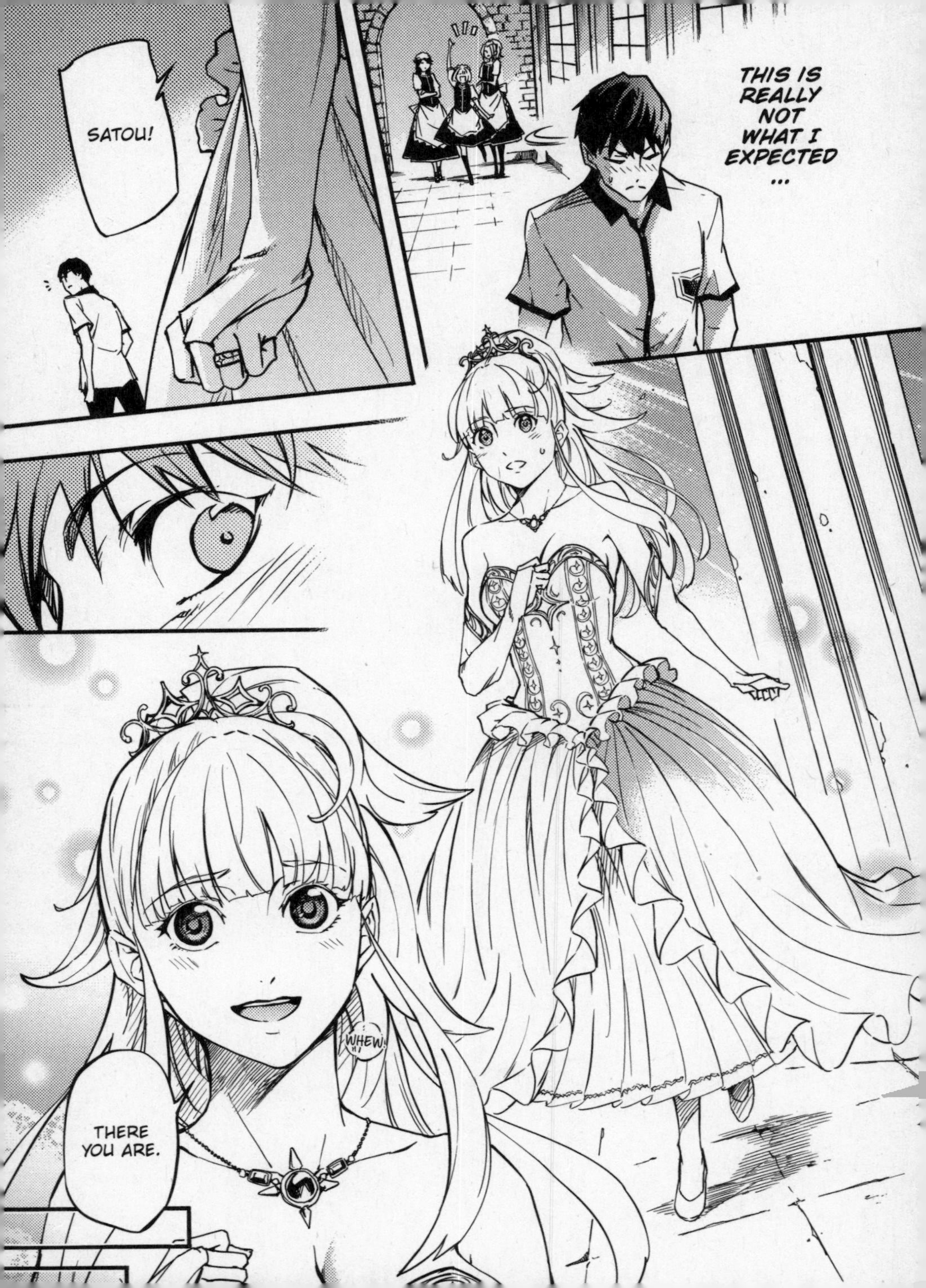
THIS IS REALLY NOT WHAT I EXPECTED...
SATOU!
WHEW!
THERE YOU ARE.

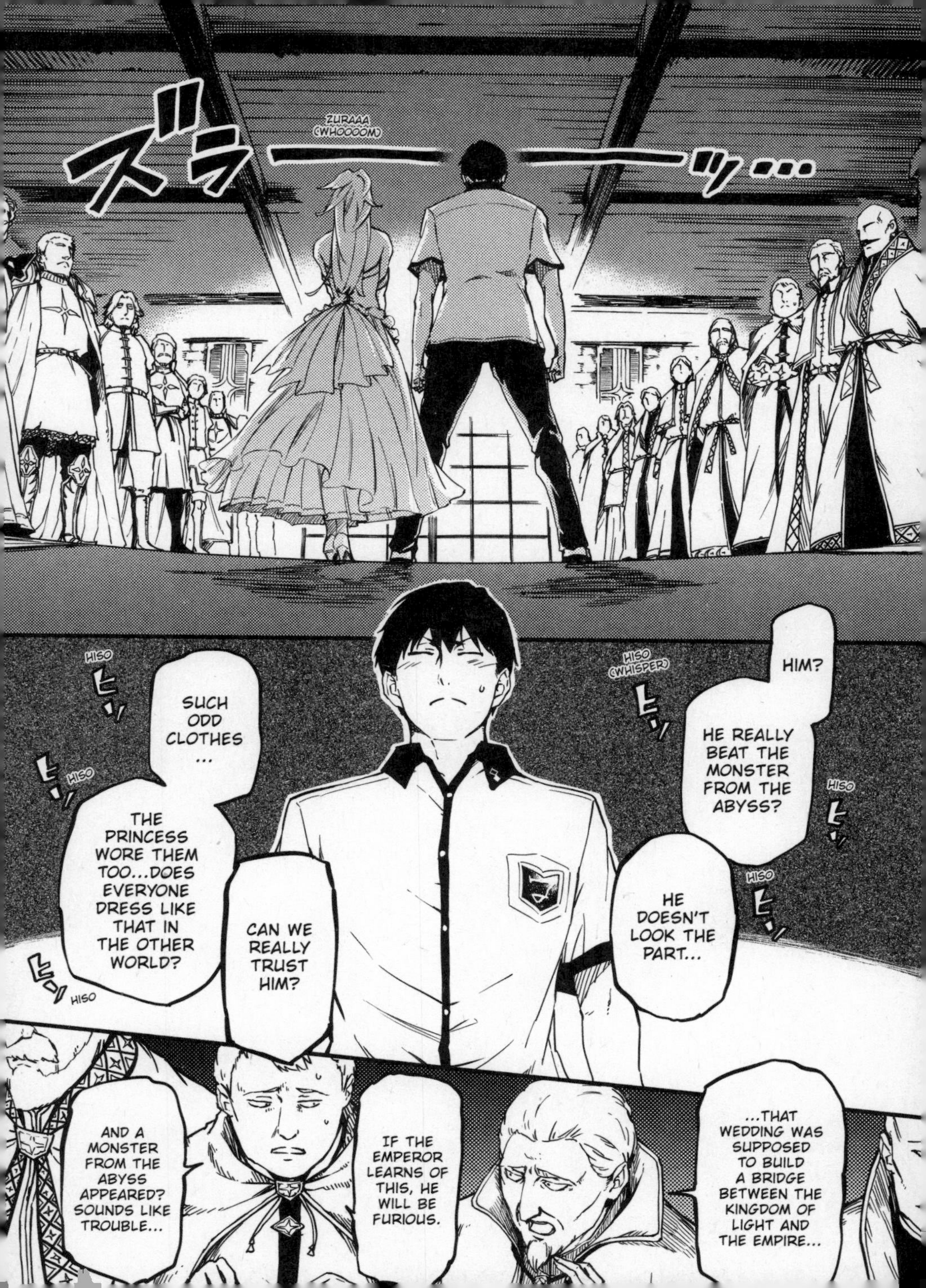
ズラーーーッ…
ZURAAA (WHOOOOM)
HIM?
HISO (WHISPER)
HE REALLY BEAT THE MONSTER FROM THE ABYSS?
HISO
HE DOESN'T LOOK THE PART...
HISO
HISO
SUCH ODD CLOTHES...
HISO
THE PRINCESS WORE THEM TOO...DOES EVERYONE DRESS LIKE THAT IN THE OTHER WORLD?
CAN WE REALLY TRUST HIM?
HISO
...THAT WEDDING WAS SUPPOSED TO BUILD A BRIDGE BETWEEN THE KINGDOM OF LIGHT AND THE EMPIRE...
IF THE EMPEROR LEARNS OF THIS, HE WILL BE FURIOUS.
AND A MONSTER FROM THE ABYSS APPEARED? SOUNDS LIKE TROUBLE...

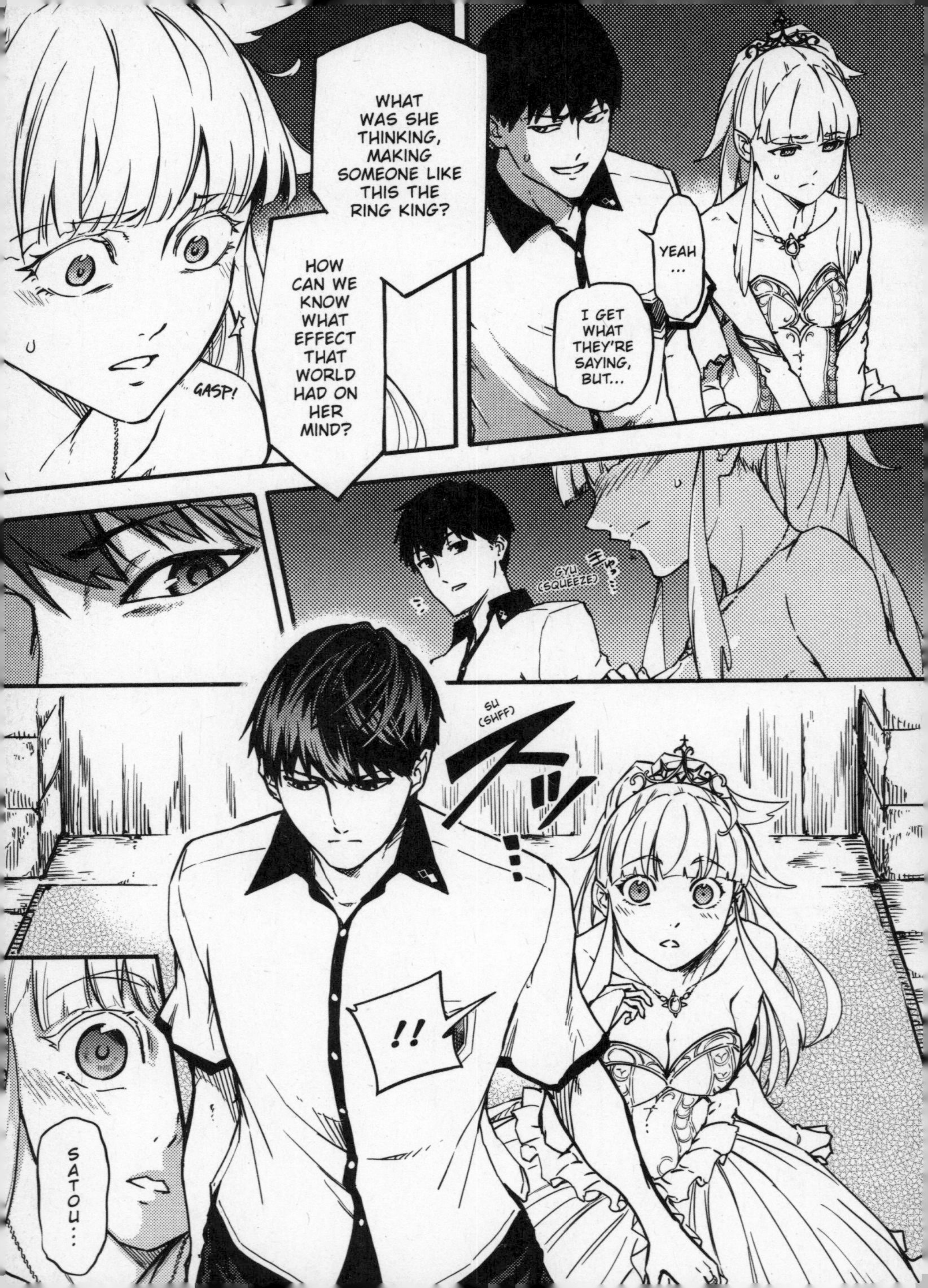

WHAT WAS SHE THINKING, MAKING SOMEONE LIKE THIS THE RING KING?
HOW CAN WE KNOW WHAT EFFECT THAT WORLD HAD ON HER MIND?
YEAH...
I GET WHAT THEY'RE SAYING, BUT...
GASP!
GYU (SQUEEZE)
SU (SHFF)
!!
SATOU...

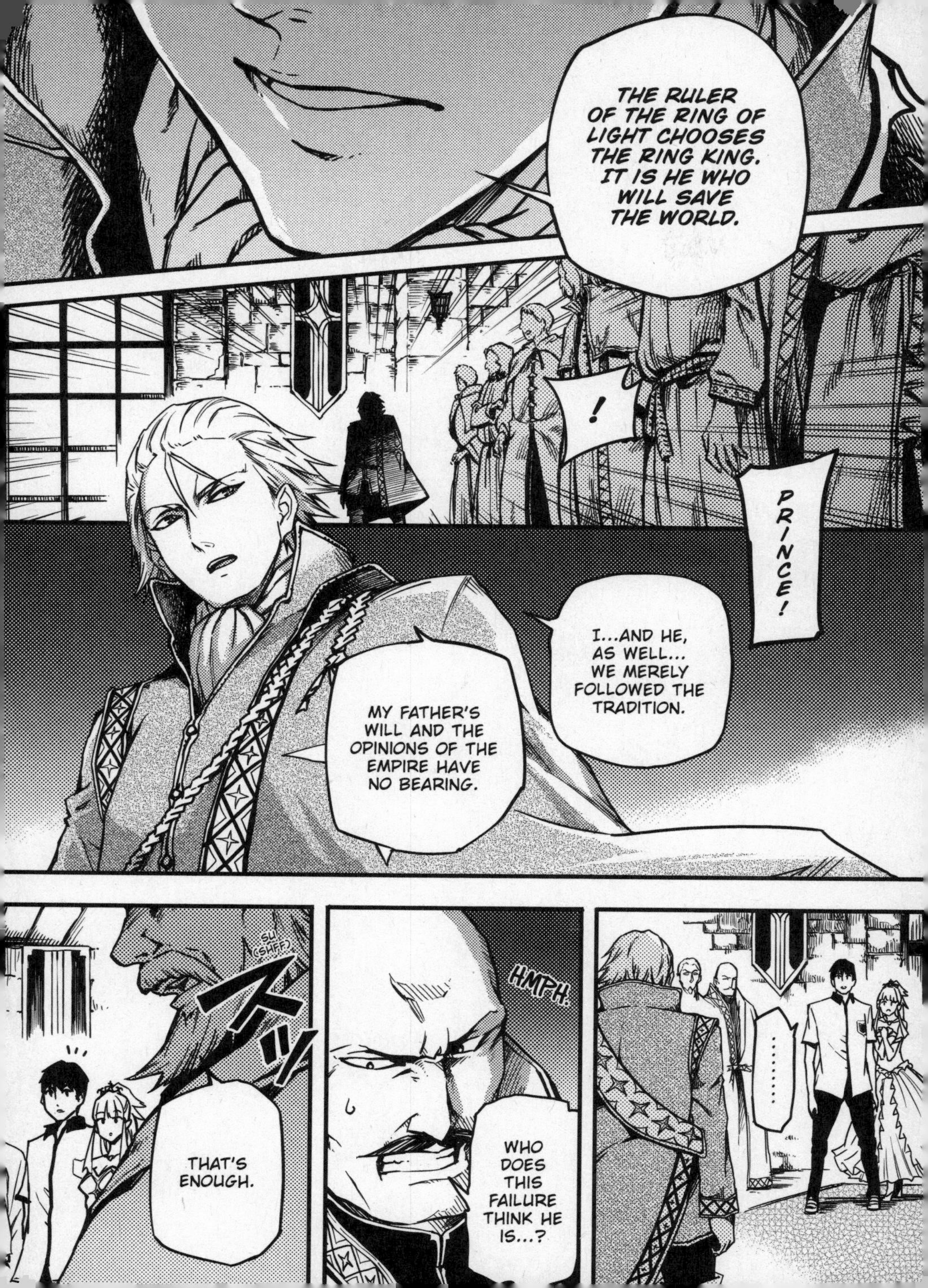
THE RULER OF THE RING OF LIGHT CHOOSES THE RING KING. IT IS HE WHO WILL SAVE THE WORLD.
!
PRINCE!
I...AND HE, AS WELL... WE MERELY FOLLOWED THE TRADITION.
MY FATHER'S WILL AND THE OPINIONS OF THE EMPIRE HAVE NO BEARING.
......
HMPH.
WHO DOES THIS FAILURE THINK HE IS...?
SU (SHFF)
THAT'S ENOUGH.

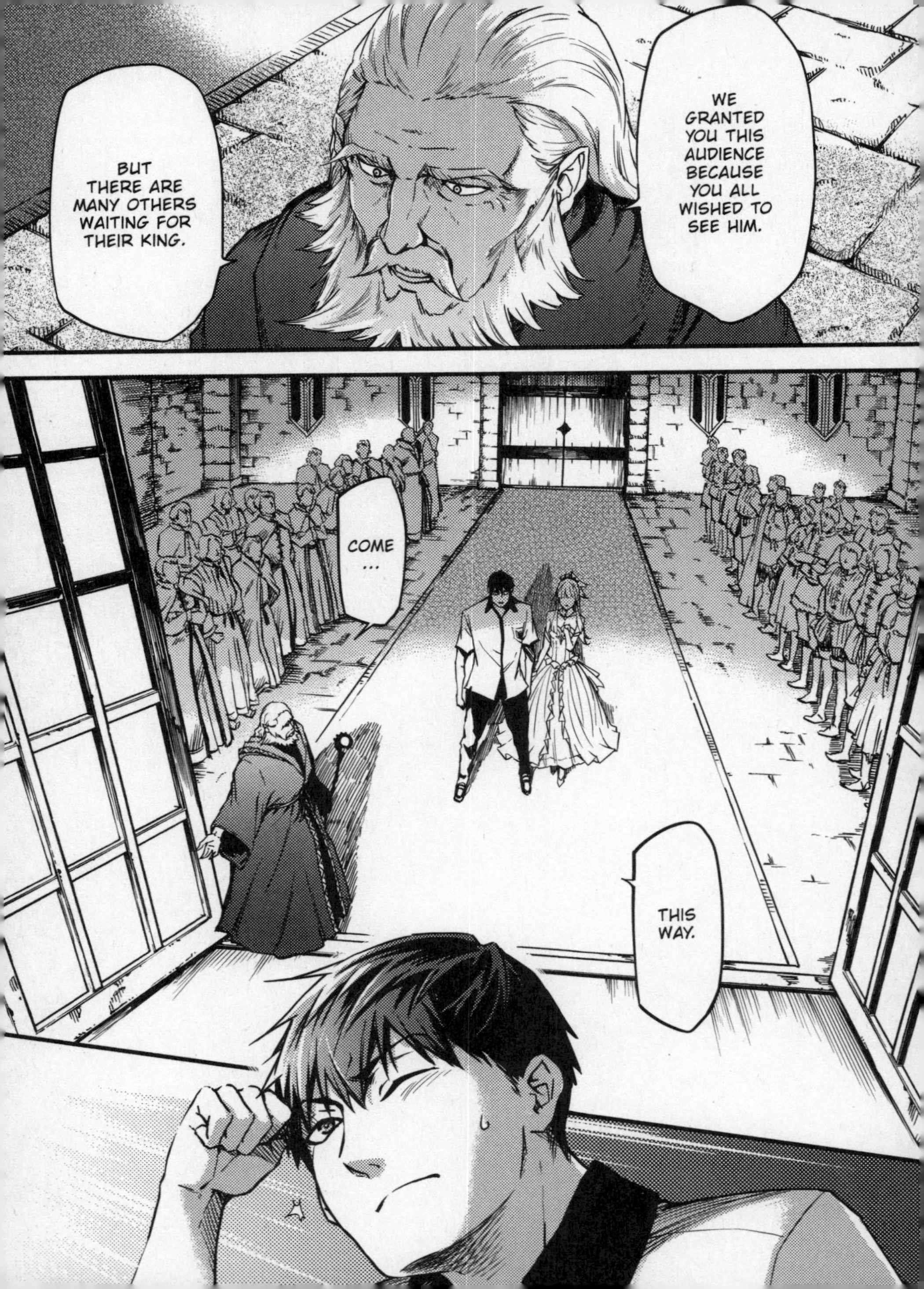
WE GRANTED YOU THIS AUDIENCE BECAUSE YOU ALL WISHED TO SEE HIM.
BUT THERE ARE MANY OTHERS WAITING FOR THEIR KING.
COME ...
THIS WAY.

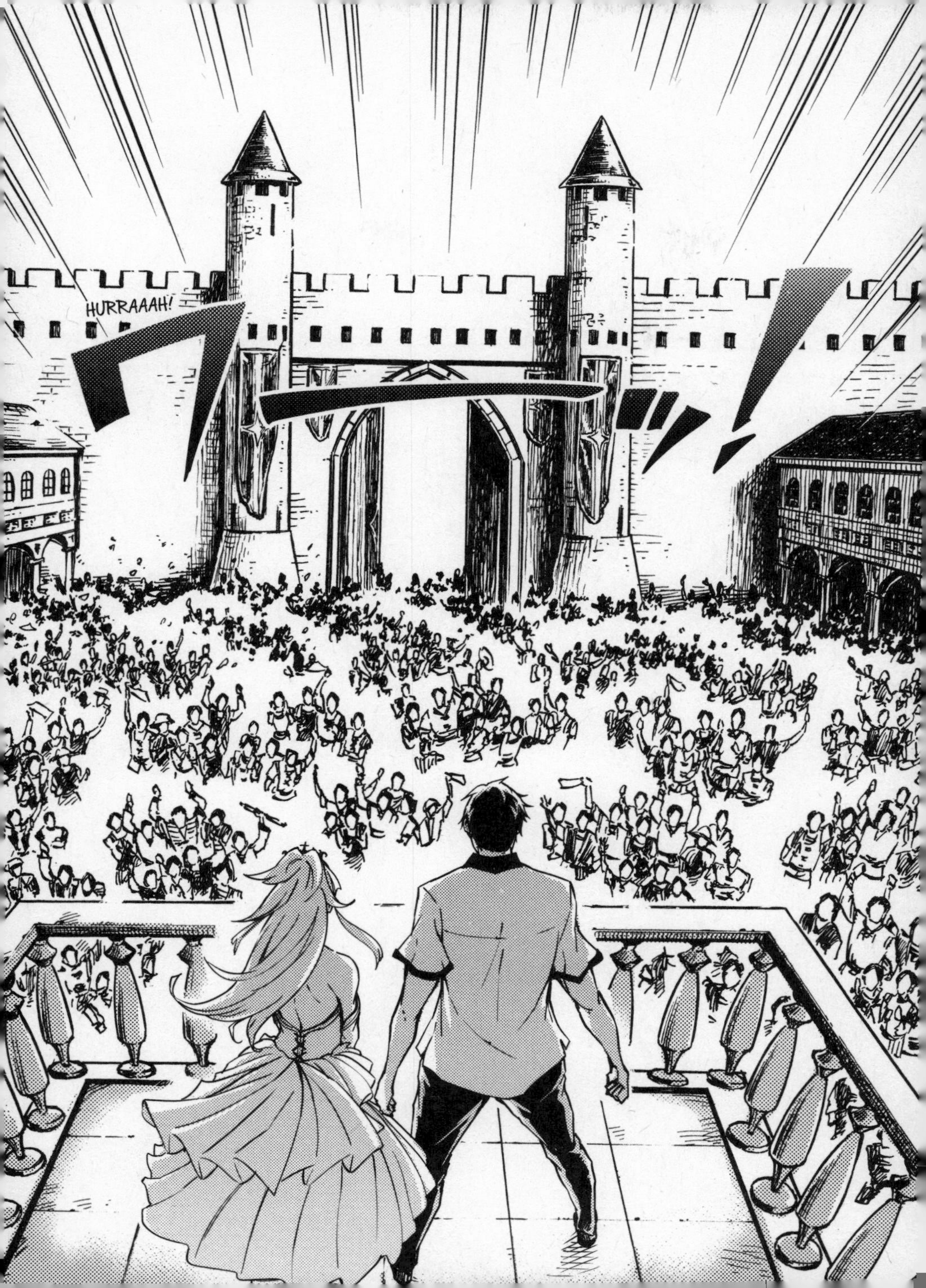
HURRAAAH!

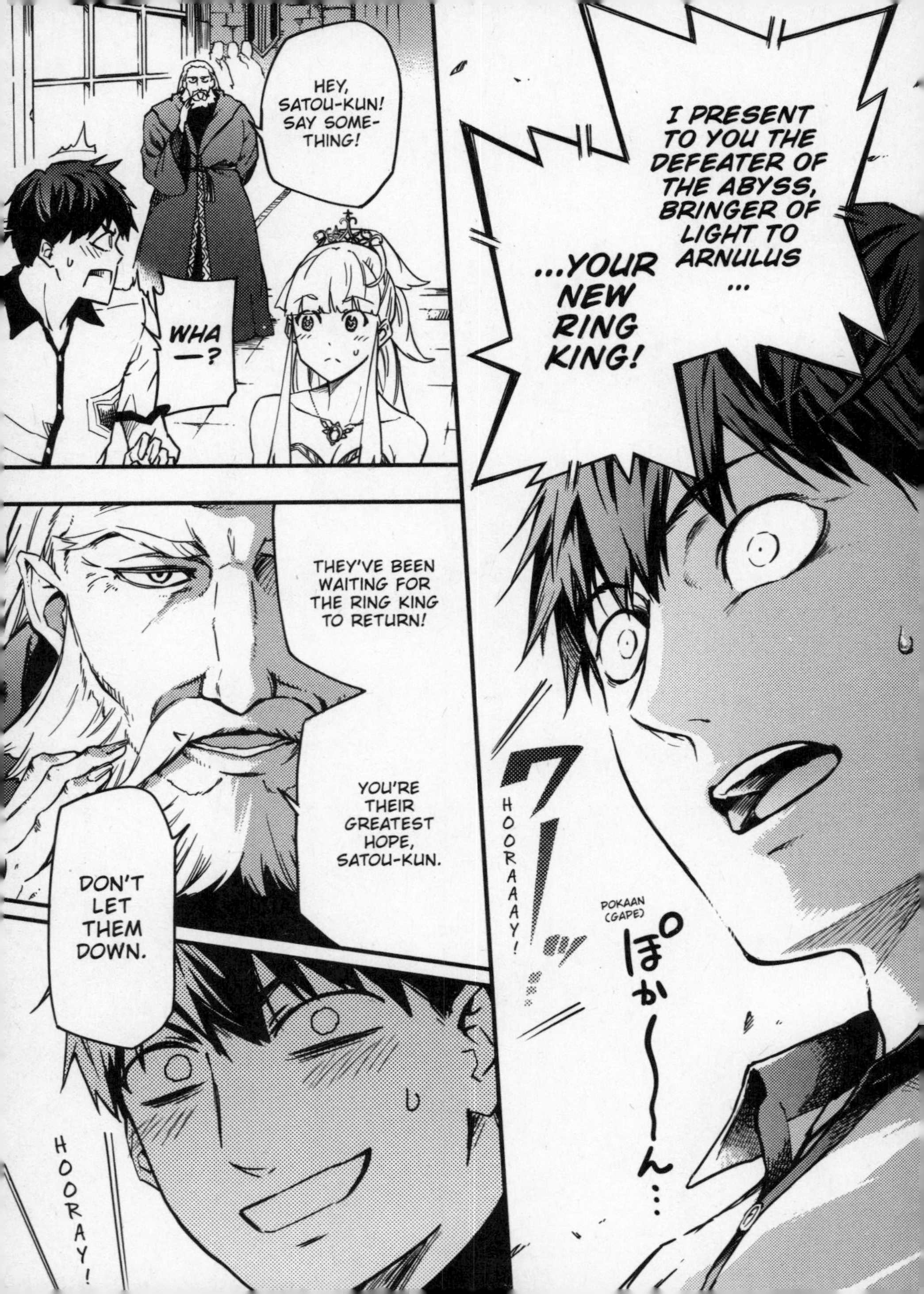
I PRESENT TO YOU THE DEFEATER OF THE ABYSS, BRINGER OF LIGHT TO ARNULUS ...
...YOUR NEW RING KING!
HOORAAAAY!
POKAAN (GAPE)
ぽか～ん…
HEY, SATOU-KUN! SAY SOME-THING!
WHA—?
THEY'VE BEEN WAITING FOR THE RING KING TO RETURN!
YOU'RE THEIR GREATEST HOPE, SATOU-KUN.
DON'T LET THEM DOWN.
HOORAY!

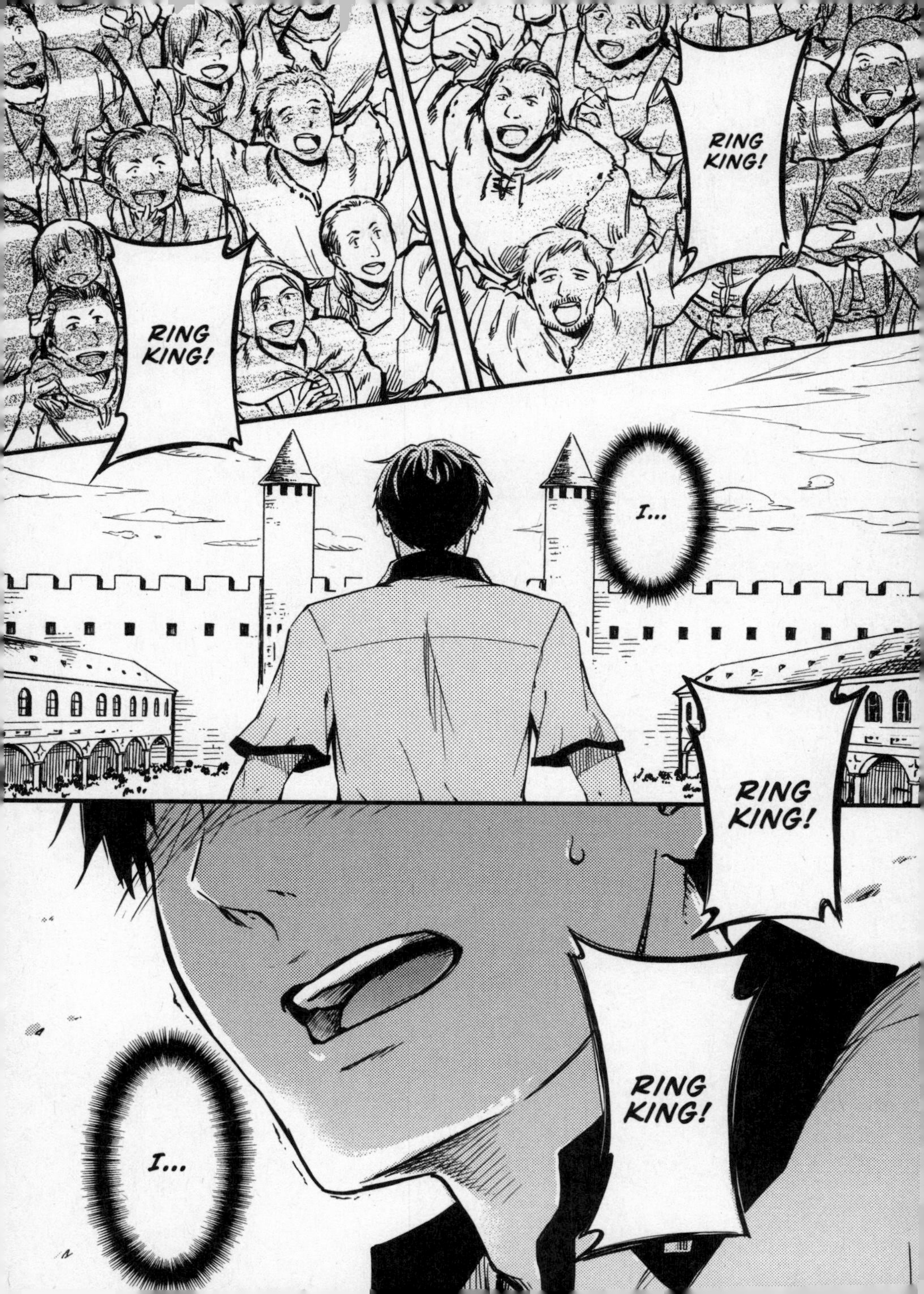
RING KING!
RING KING!
I...
RING KING!
RING KING!
I...

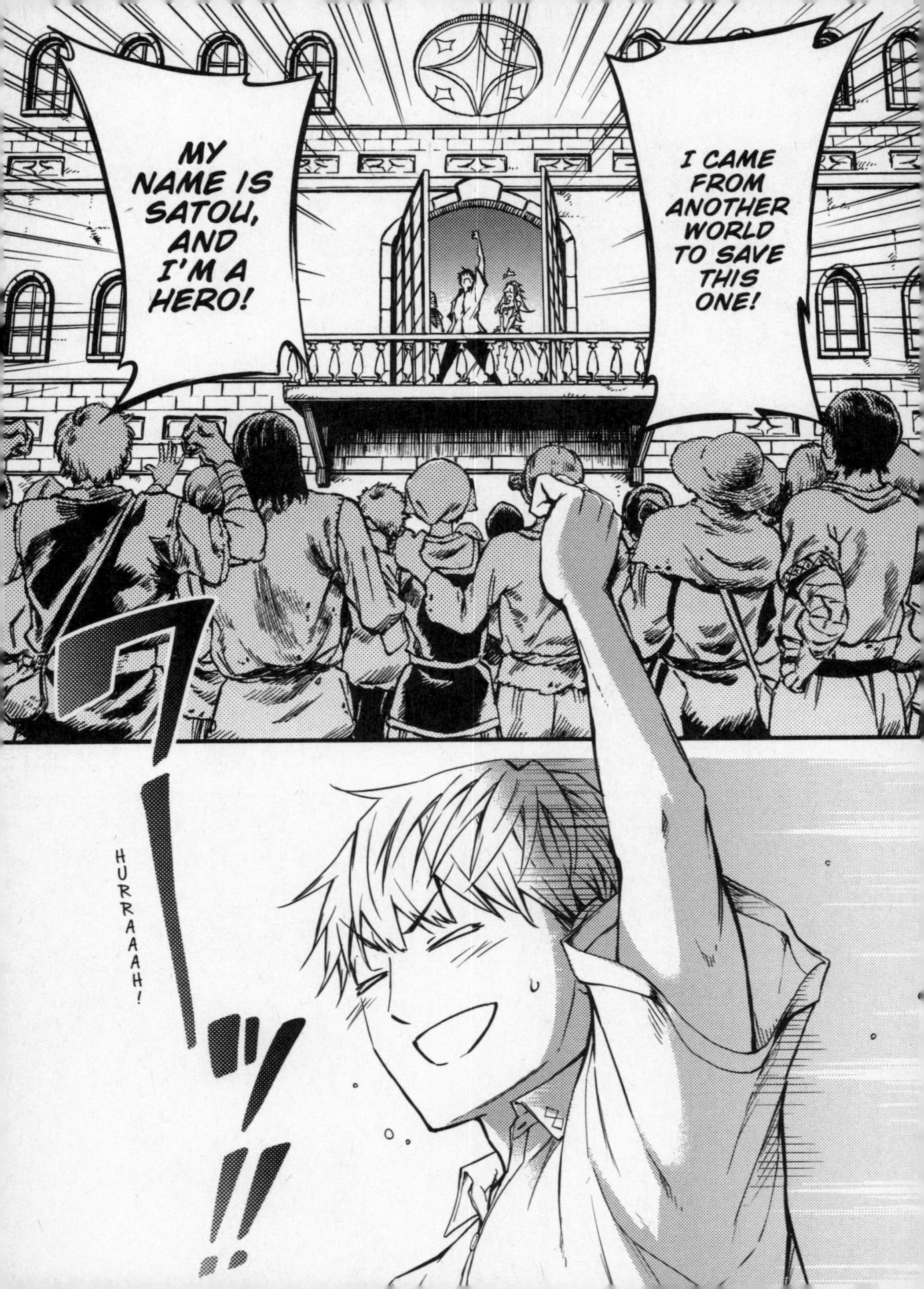
I CAME FROM ANOTHER WORLD TO SAVE THIS ONE!
MY NAME IS SATOU, AND I'M A HERO!
HURRAAAH!

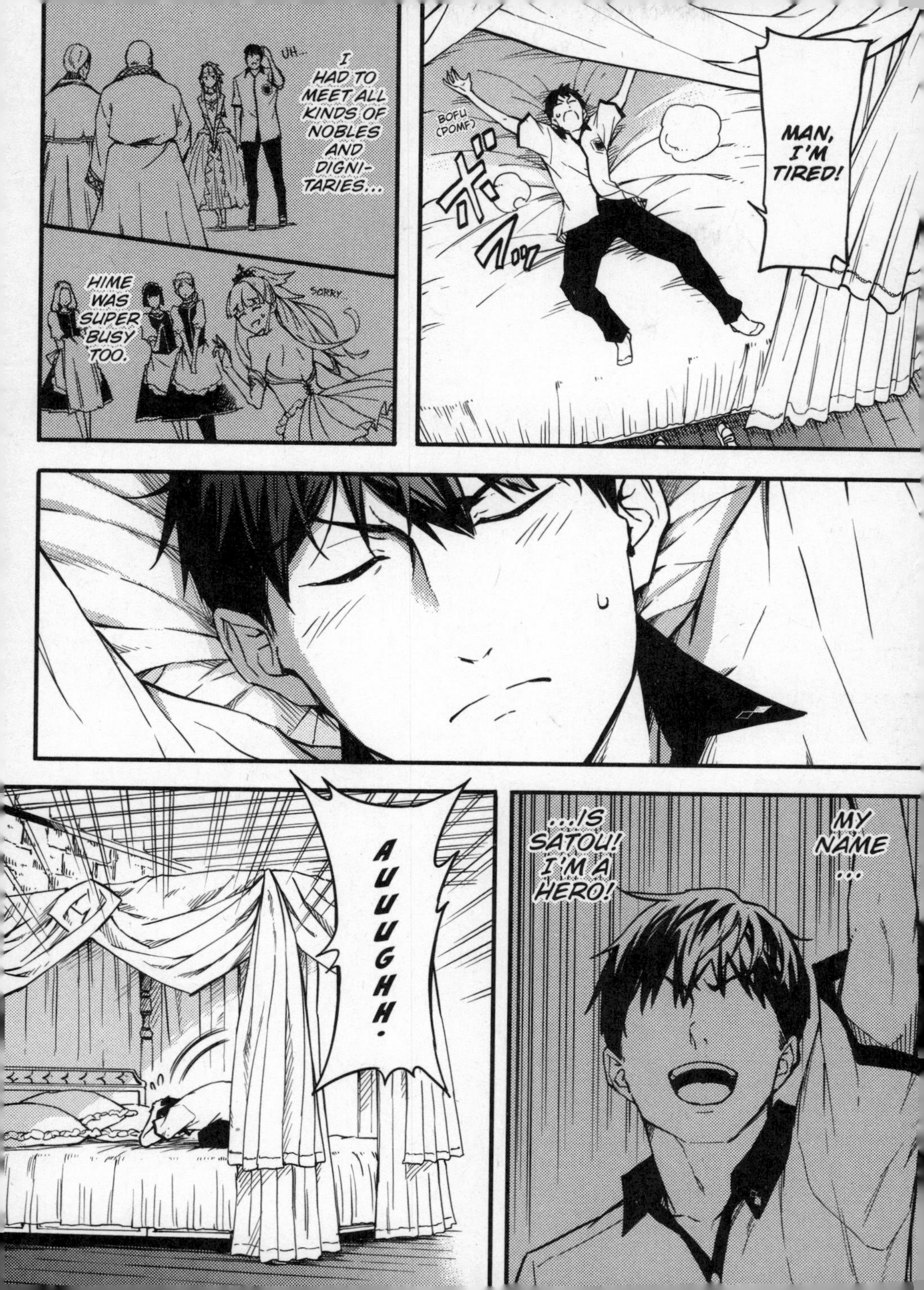
MAN, I'M TIRED!
BOFU (POMF)
I HAD TO MEET ALL KINDS OF NOBLES AND DIGNITARIES...
UH...
SORRY...
HIME WAS SUPER BUSY TOO.
MY NAME...
...IS SATOU! I'M A HERO!
AUUUGHH!

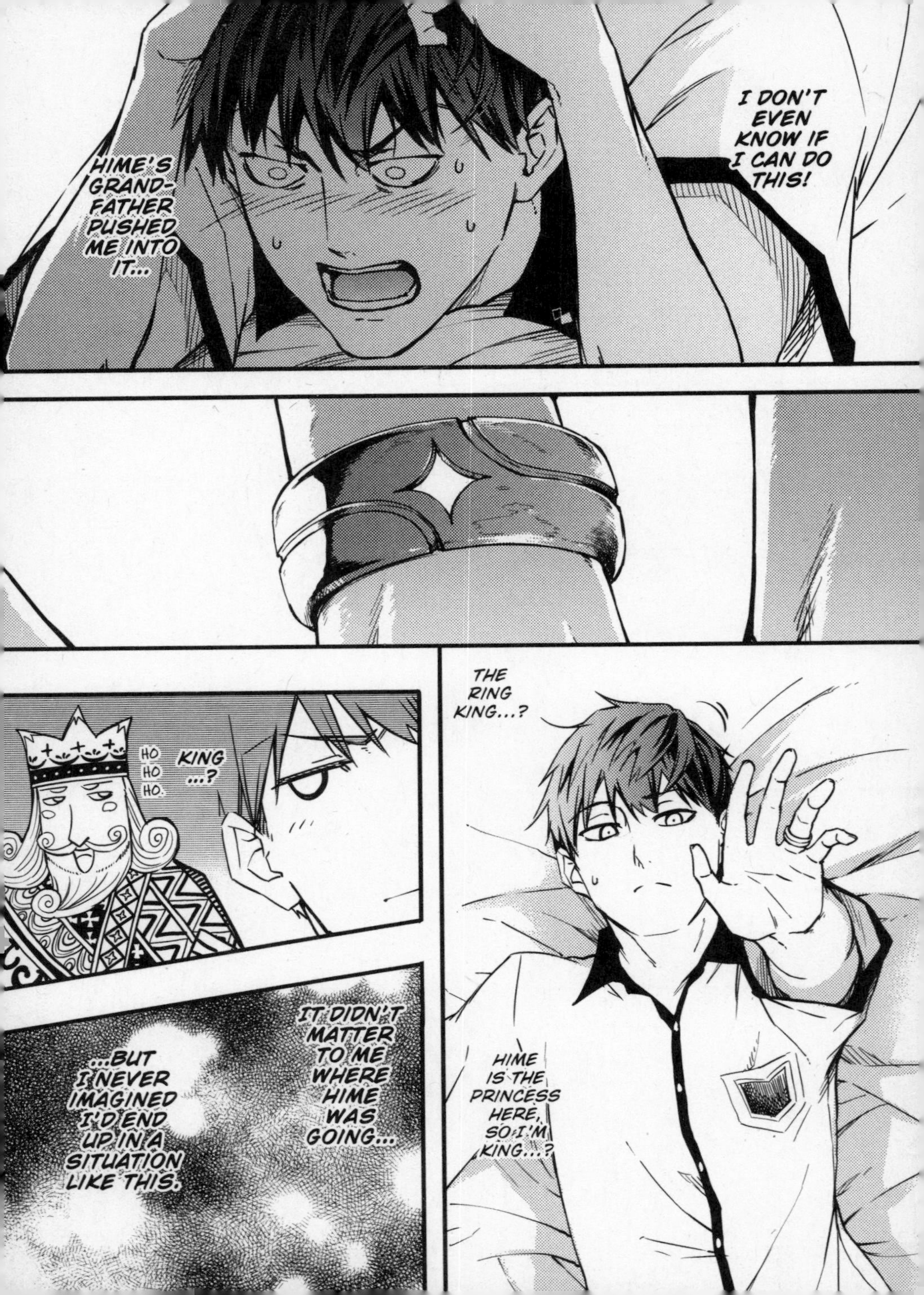
I DON'T EVEN KNOW IF I CAN DO THIS!
HIME'S GRAND-FATHER PUSHED ME INTO IT...
THE RING KING...?
HIME IS THE PRINCESS HERE, SO I'M KING...?
KING ...?
HO HO HO.
IT DIDN'T MATTER TO ME WHERE HIME WAS GOING...
...BUT I NEVER IMAGINED I'D END UP IN A SITUATION LIKE THIS.

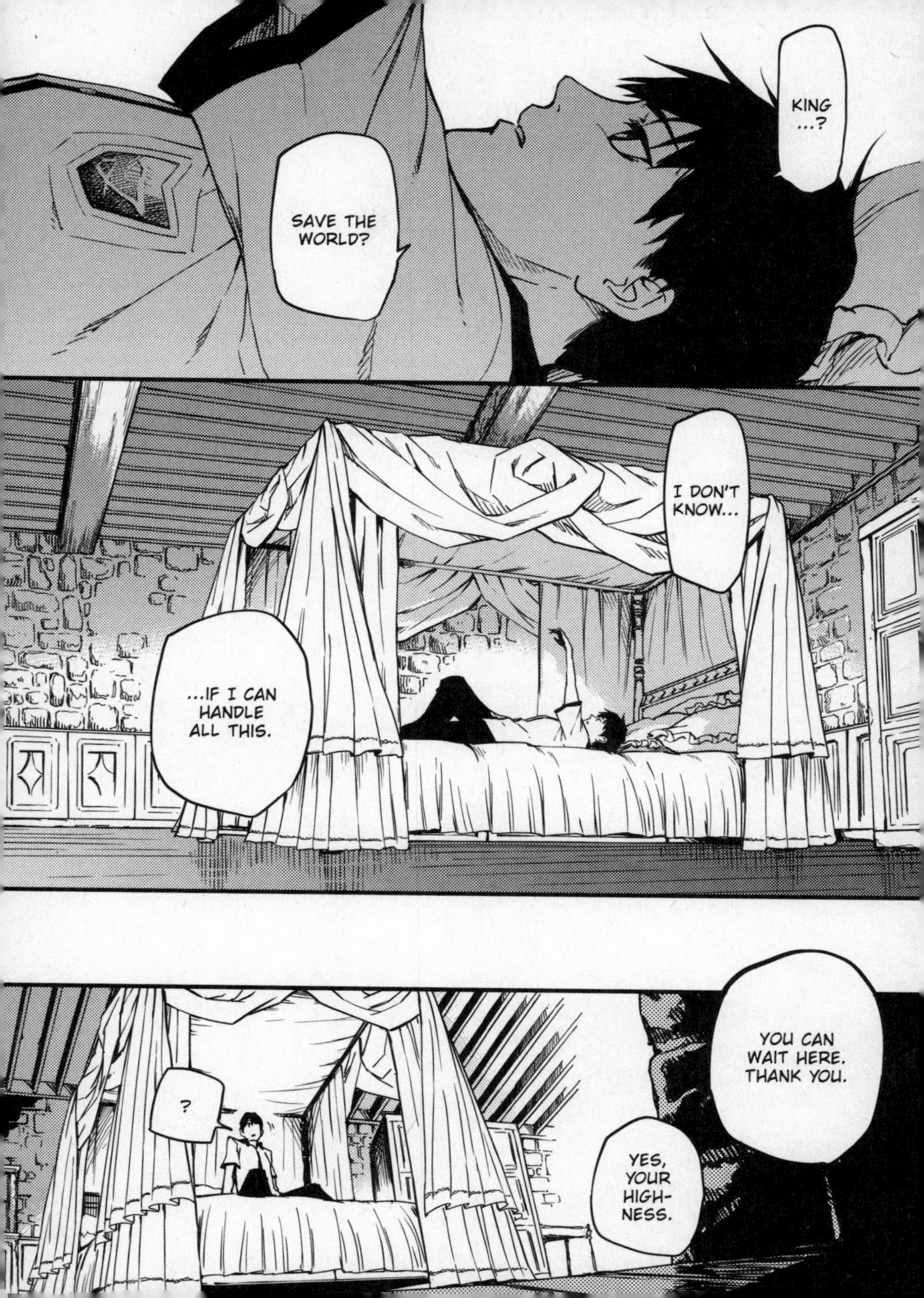
KING ...?
SAVE THE WORLD?
I DON'T KNOW...
...IF I CAN HANDLE ALL THIS.
YOU CAN WAIT HERE. THANK YOU.
YES, YOUR HIGH-NESS.
?

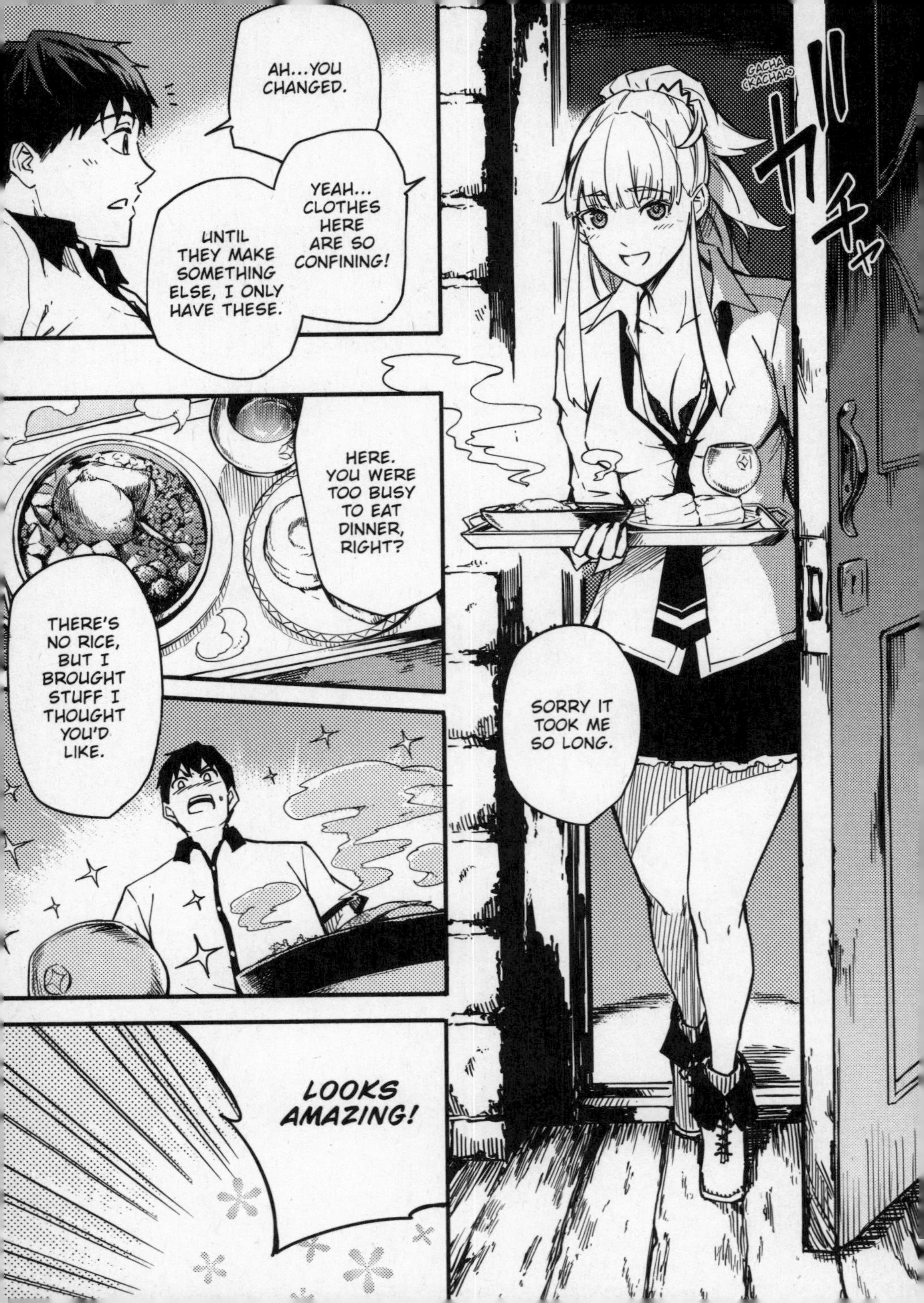
GACHA (KACHAK)
SORRY IT TOOK ME SO LONG.
AH...YOU CHANGED.
YEAH... CLOTHES HERE ARE SO CONFINING!
UNTIL THEY MAKE SOMETHING ELSE, I ONLY HAVE THESE.
HERE. YOU WERE TOO BUSY TO EAT DINNER, RIGHT?
THERE'S NO RICE, BUT I BROUGHT STUFF I THOUGHT YOU'D LIKE.
LOOKS AMAZING!

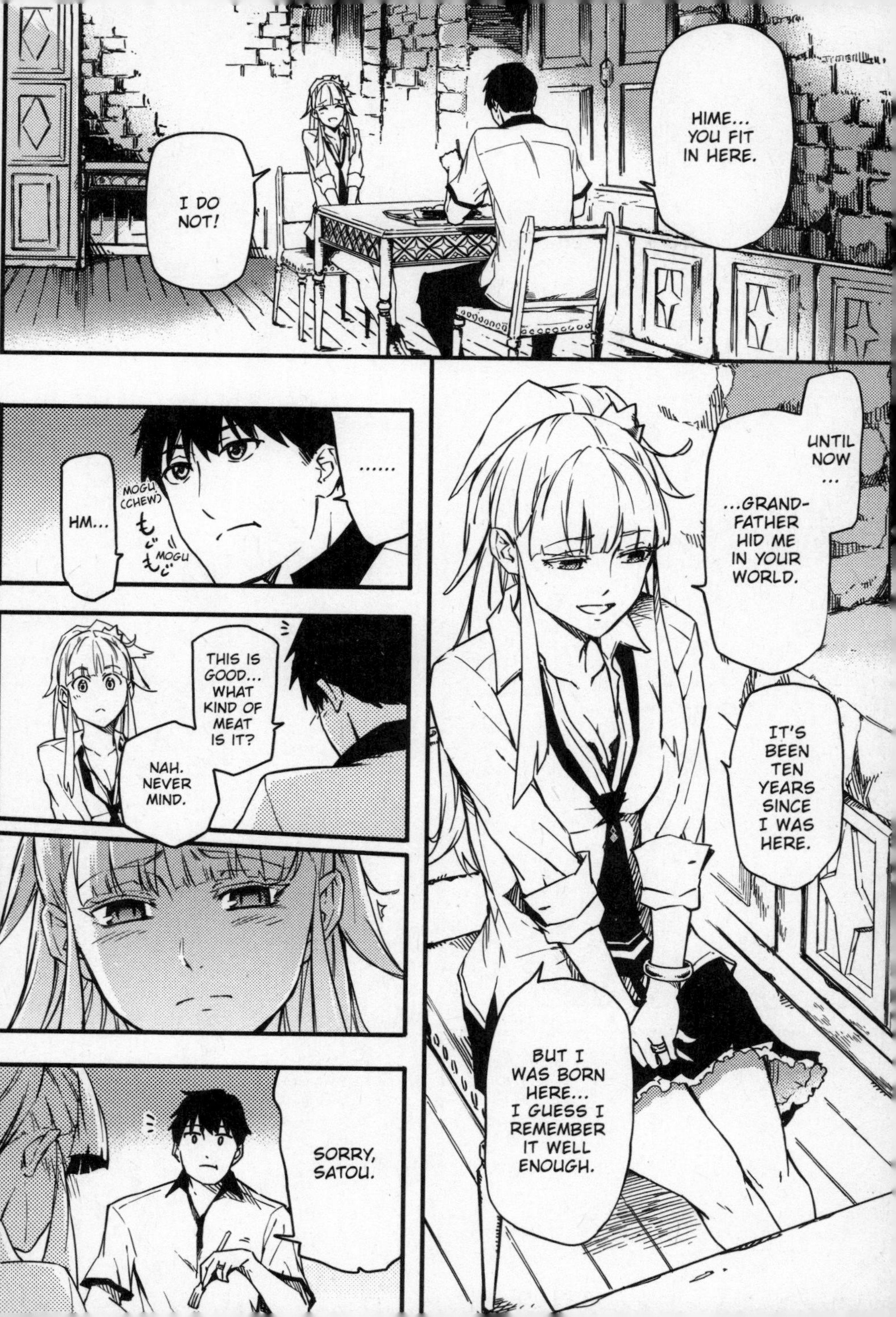
HIME... YOU FIT IN HERE.
I DO NOT!
UNTIL NOW...
...GRAND-FATHER HID ME IN YOUR WORLD.
IT'S BEEN TEN YEARS SINCE I WAS HERE.
BUT I WAS BORN HERE... I GUESS I REMEMBER IT WELL ENOUGH.
......
MOGU (CHEW)
もぐもぐ
MOGU
HM...
THIS IS GOOD... WHAT KIND OF MEAT IS IT?
NAH. NEVER MIND.
SORRY, SATOU.

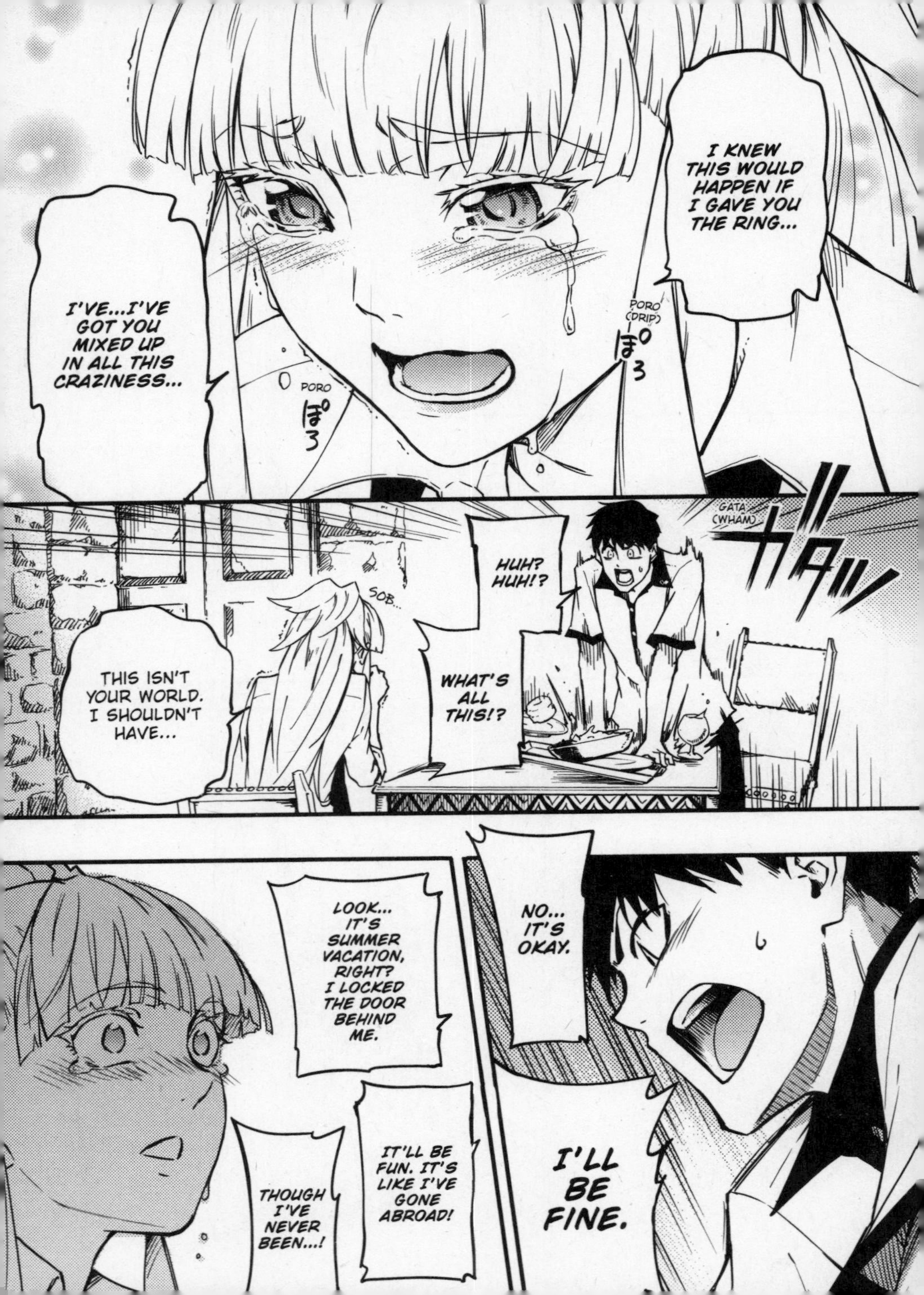

I KNEW THIS WOULD HAPPEN IF I GAVE YOU THE RING...
PORO (DRIP)
ぽろ
I'VE...I'VE GOT YOU MIXED UP IN ALL THIS CRAZINESS...
PORO
ぽろ
GATA (WHAM)
ガタッ
HUH? HUH!?
WHAT'S ALL THIS!?
SOB...
THIS ISN'T YOUR WORLD. I SHOULDN'T HAVE...
NO... IT'S OKAY.
I'LL BE FINE.
LOOK... IT'S SUMMER VACATION, RIGHT? I LOCKED THE DOOR BEHIND ME.
IT'LL BE FUN. IT'S LIKE I'VE GONE ABROAD!
THOUGH I'VE NEVER BEEN...!

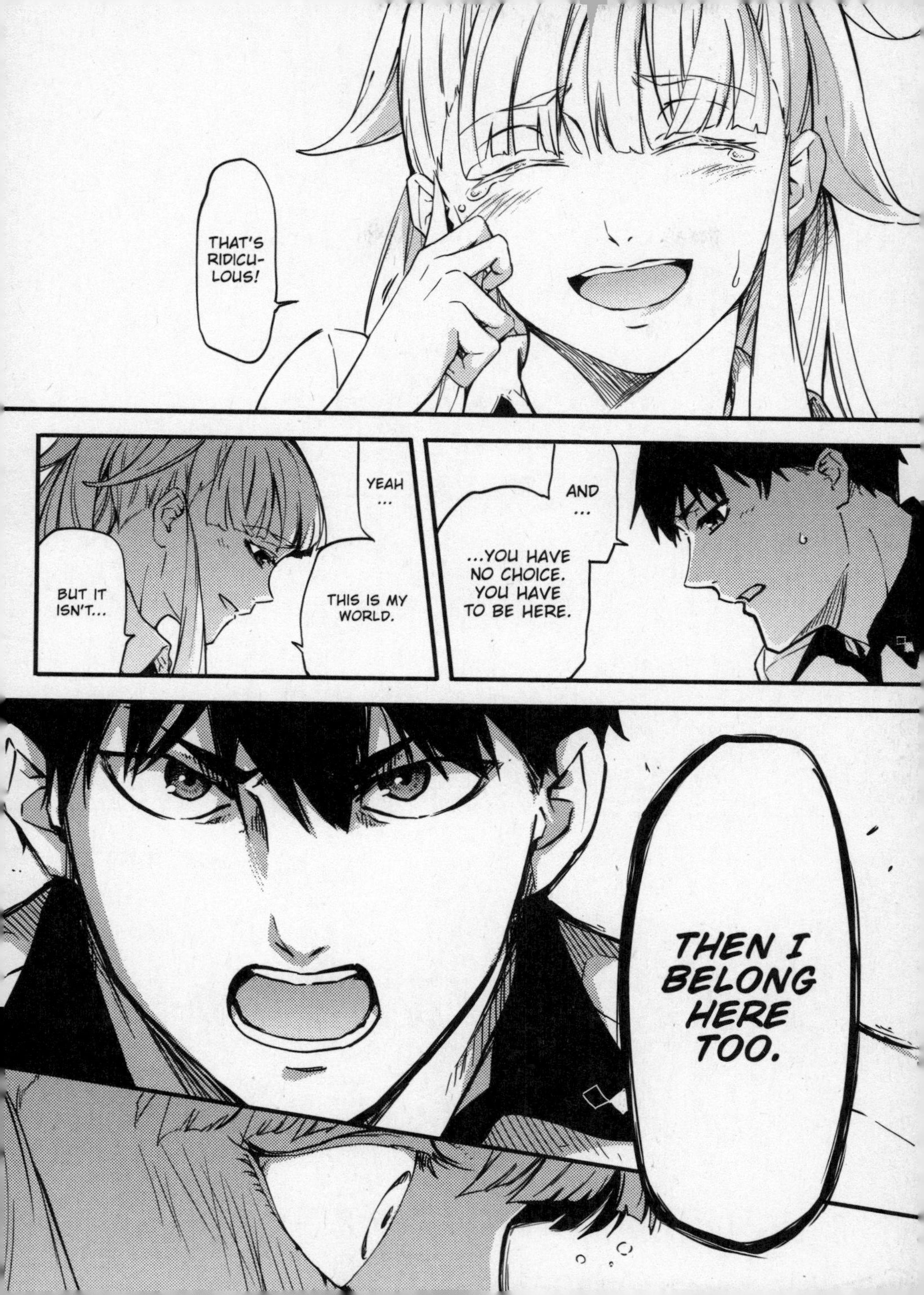
THAT'S RIDICULOUS!
AND ...
...YOU HAVE NO CHOICE. YOU HAVE TO BE HERE.
YEAH ...
THIS IS MY WORLD.
BUT IT ISN'T...
THEN I BELONG HERE TOO.

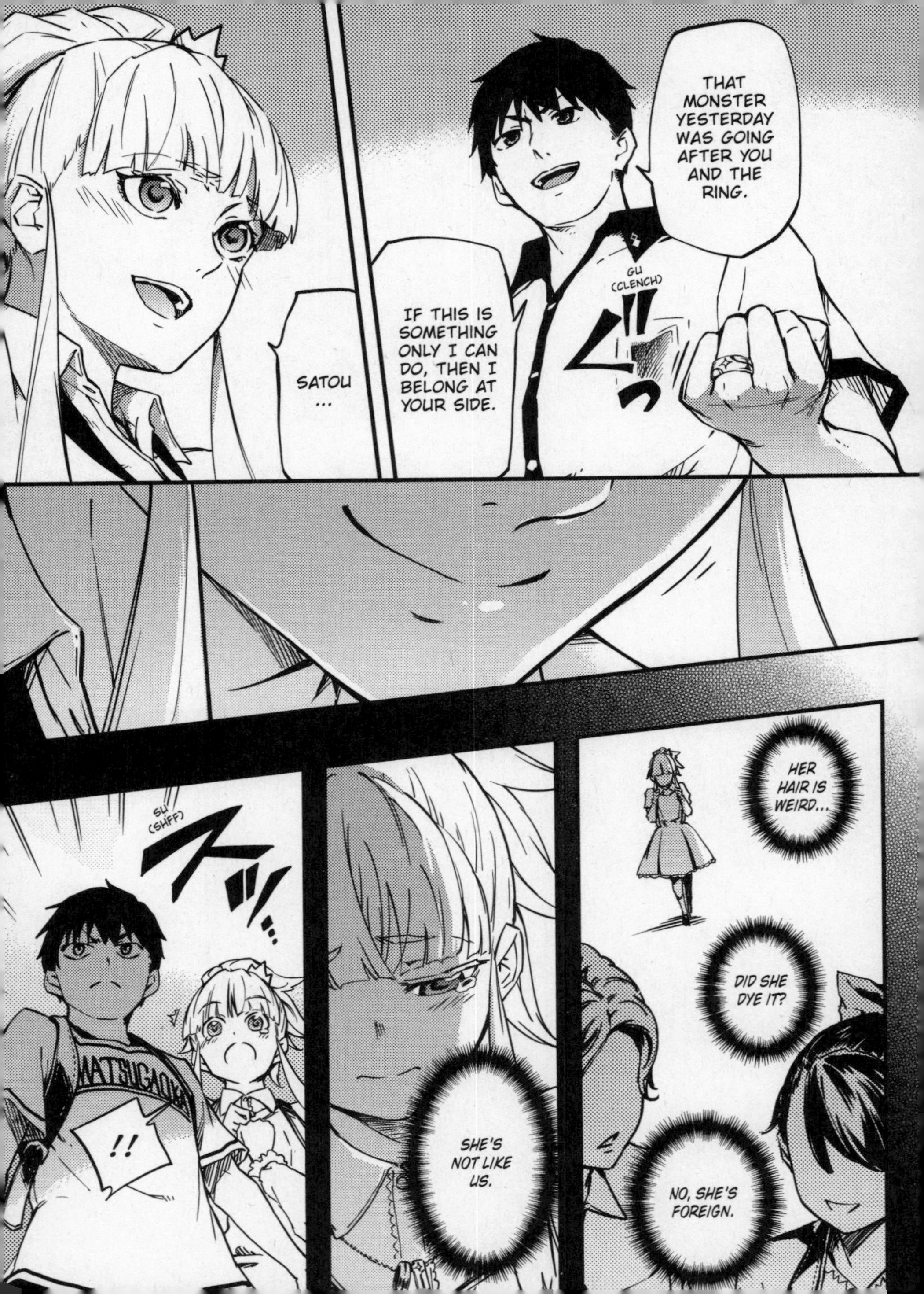
THAT MONSTER YESTERDAY WAS GOING AFTER YOU AND THE RING.
GU (CLENCH)
IF THIS IS SOMETHING ONLY I CAN DO, THEN I BELONG AT YOUR SIDE.
SATOU ...
HER HAIR IS WEIRD...
DID SHE DYE IT?
NO, SHE'S FOREIGN.
SHE'S NOT LIKE US.
SU (SHFF)
MATSUGAOKA
!!

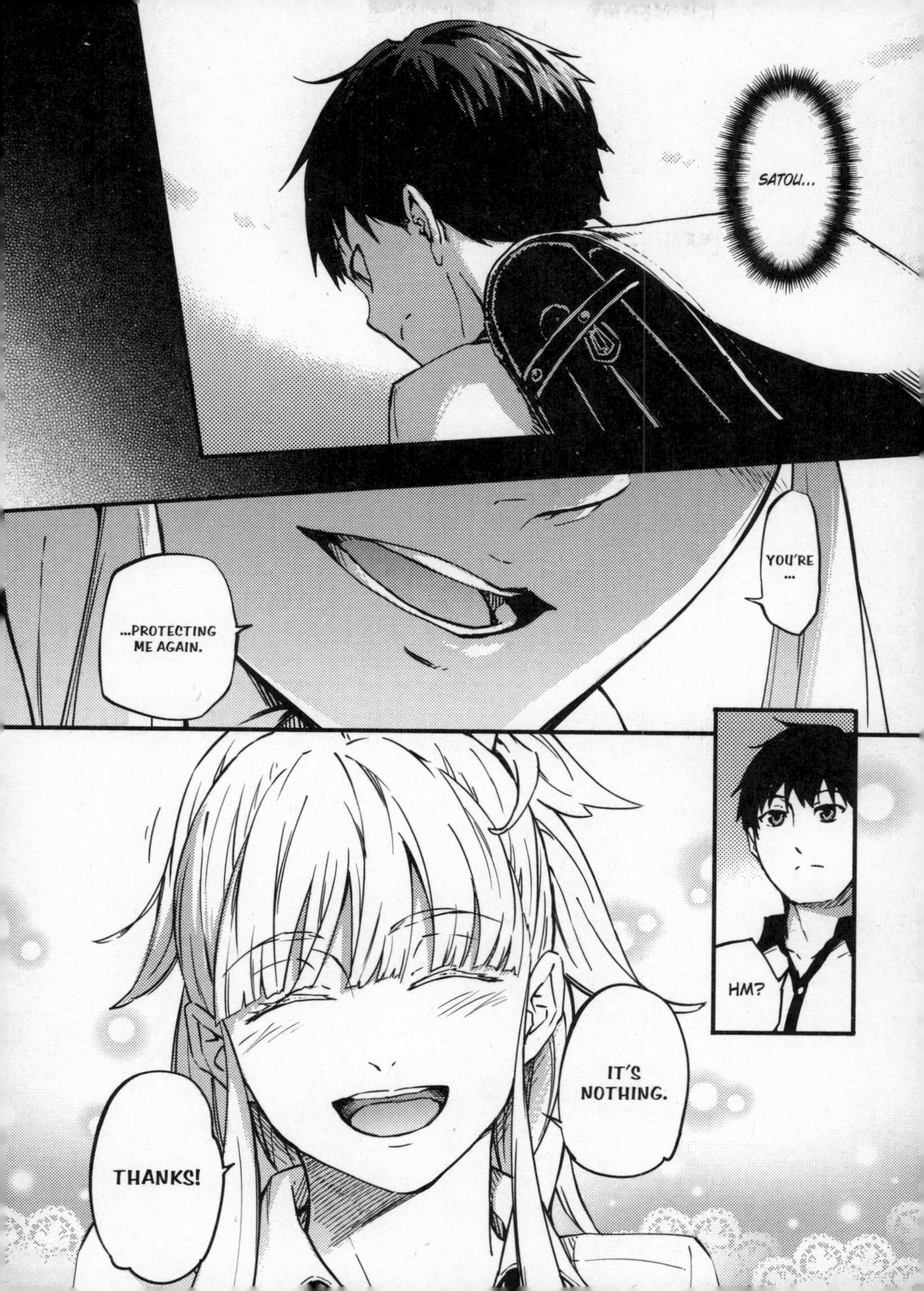
SATOU...
YOU'RE ...
...PROTECTING ME AGAIN.
HM?
IT'S NOTHING.
THANKS!

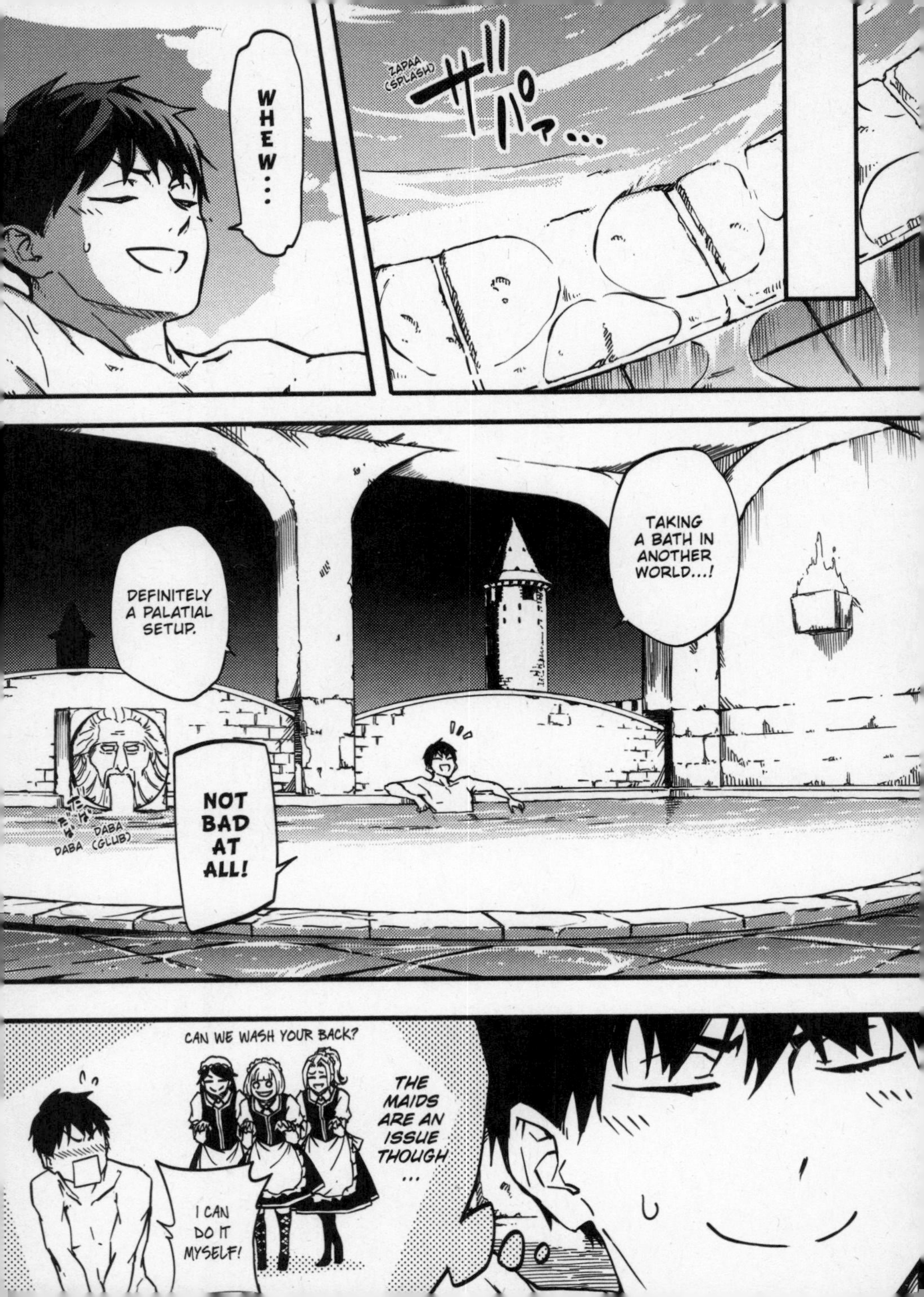
ZAPAA (SPLASH)
ザパァ...
WHEW...
TAKING A BATH IN ANOTHER WORLD...!
DEFINITELY A PALATIAL SETUP.
NOT BAD AT ALL!
DABA DABA (GLUB)
THE MAIDS ARE AN ISSUE THOUGH...
CAN WE WASH YOUR BACK?
I CAN DO IT MYSELF!

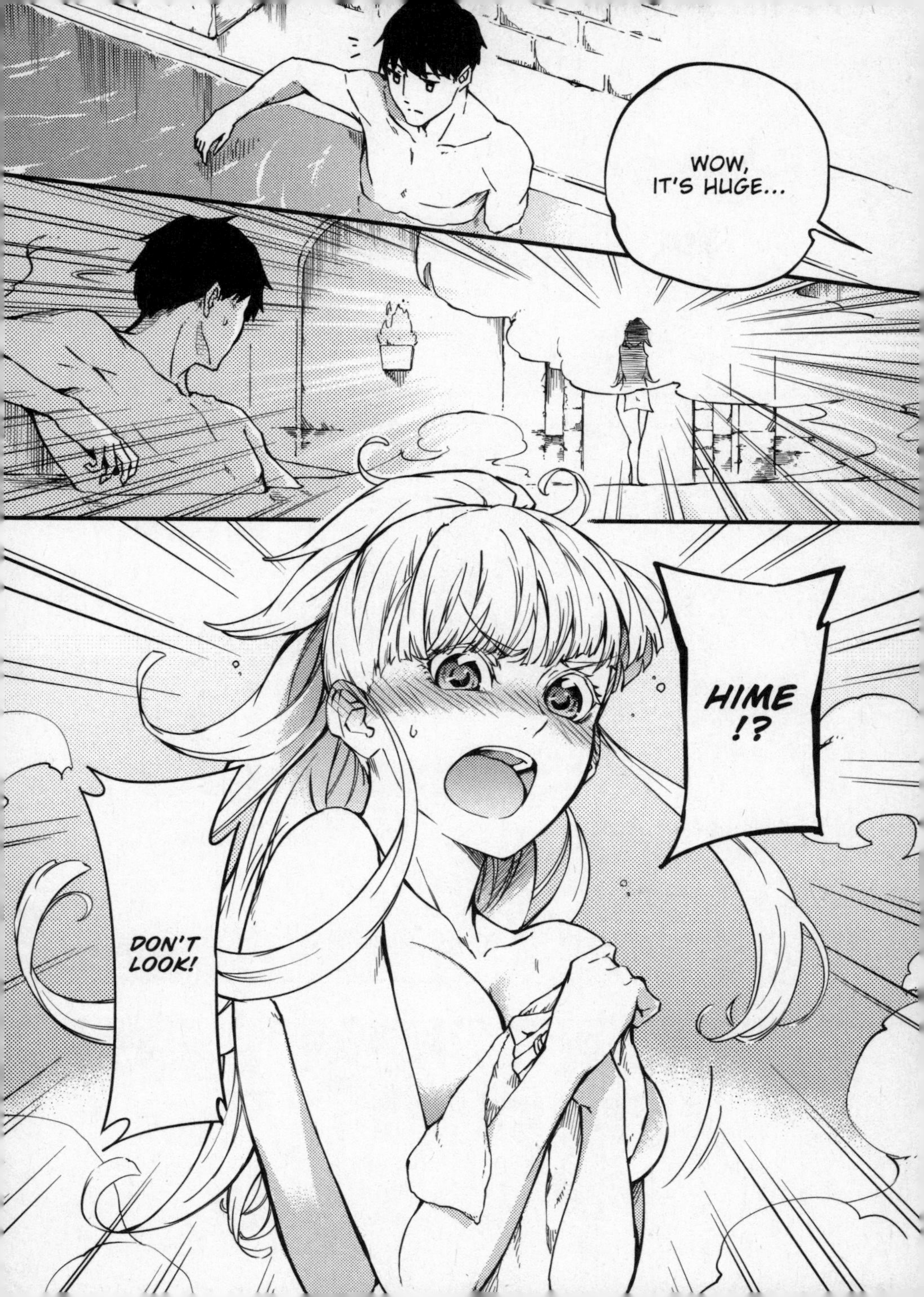
WOW, IT'S HUGE...
HIME !?
DON'T LOOK!

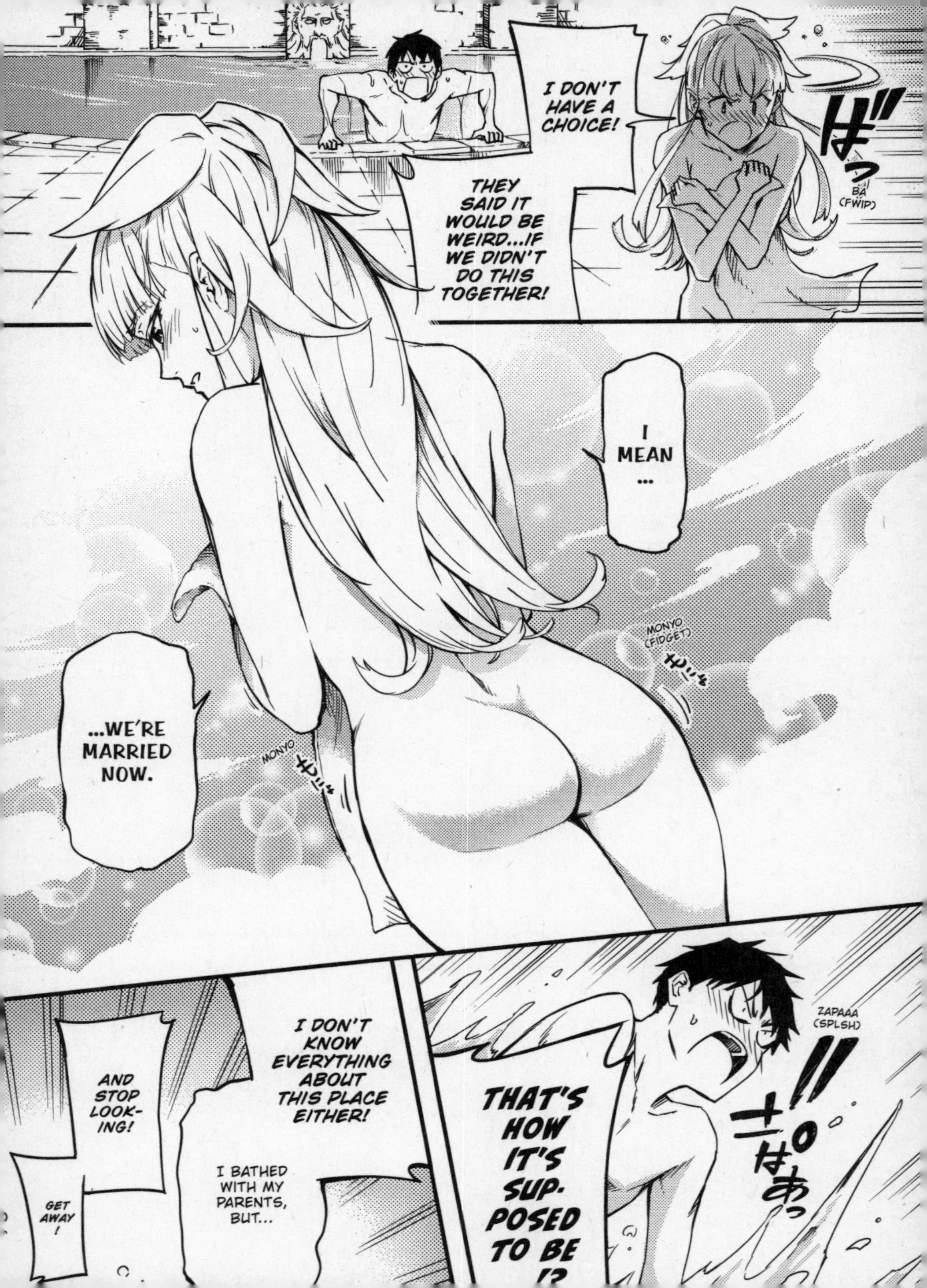
I DON'T HAVE A CHOICE!
ばっ
BA (FWIP)
THEY SAID IT WOULD BE WEIRD...IF WE DIDN'T DO THIS TOGETHER!
I MEAN...
MONYO (FIDGET)
MONYO
...WE'RE MARRIED NOW.
ZAPAAA (SPLSH)
ざぱあっ!!
THAT'S HOW IT'S SUP-POSED TO BE!?
I DON'T KNOW EVERYTHING ABOUT THIS PLACE EITHER!
I BATHED WITH MY PARENTS, BUT...
AND STOP LOOKING!
GET AWAY!

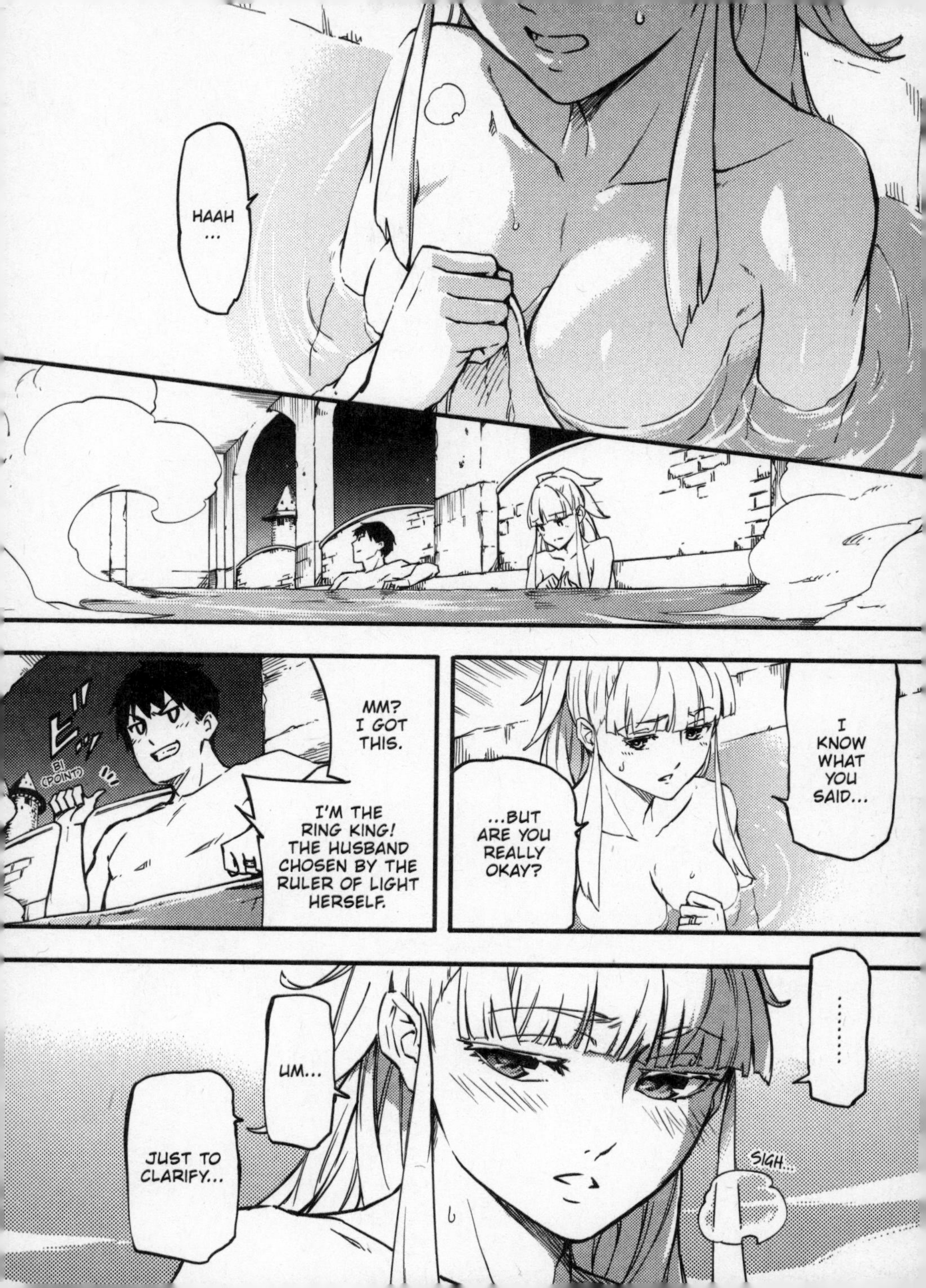
HAAH ...
I KNOW WHAT YOU SAID...
...BUT ARE YOU REALLY OKAY?
MM? I GOT THIS.
I'M THE RING KING! THE HUSBAND CHOSEN BY THE RULER OF LIGHT HERSELF.
BI (POINT)
......
SIGH...
UM...
JUST TO CLARIFY...

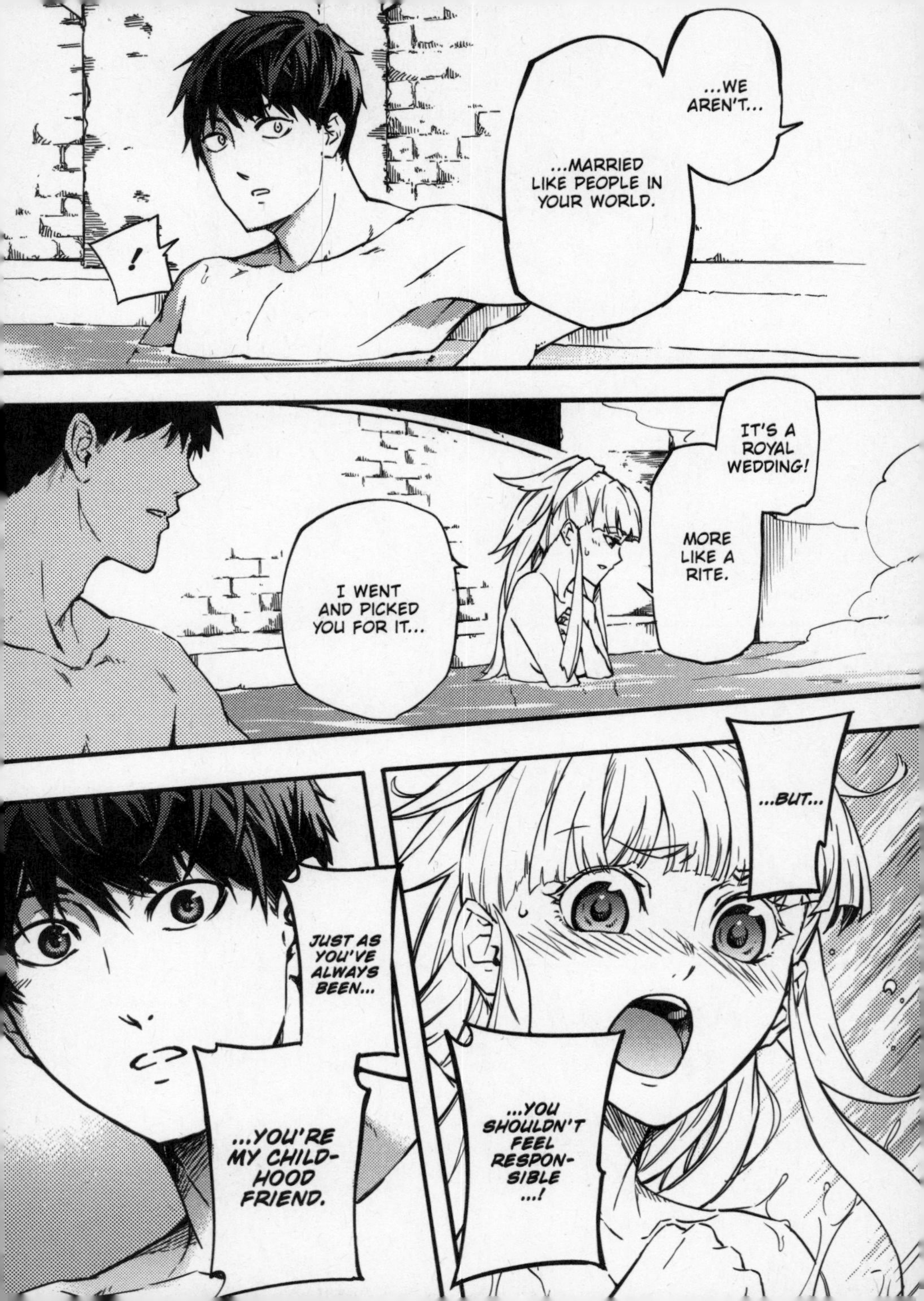
...WE AREN'T...
...MARRIED LIKE PEOPLE IN YOUR WORLD.
!
IT'S A ROYAL WEDDING!
MORE LIKE A RITE.
I WENT AND PICKED YOU FOR IT...
...BUT...
...YOU SHOULDN'T FEEL RESPONSIBLE...!
JUST AS YOU'VE ALWAYS BEEN...
...YOU'RE MY CHILDHOOD FRIEND.

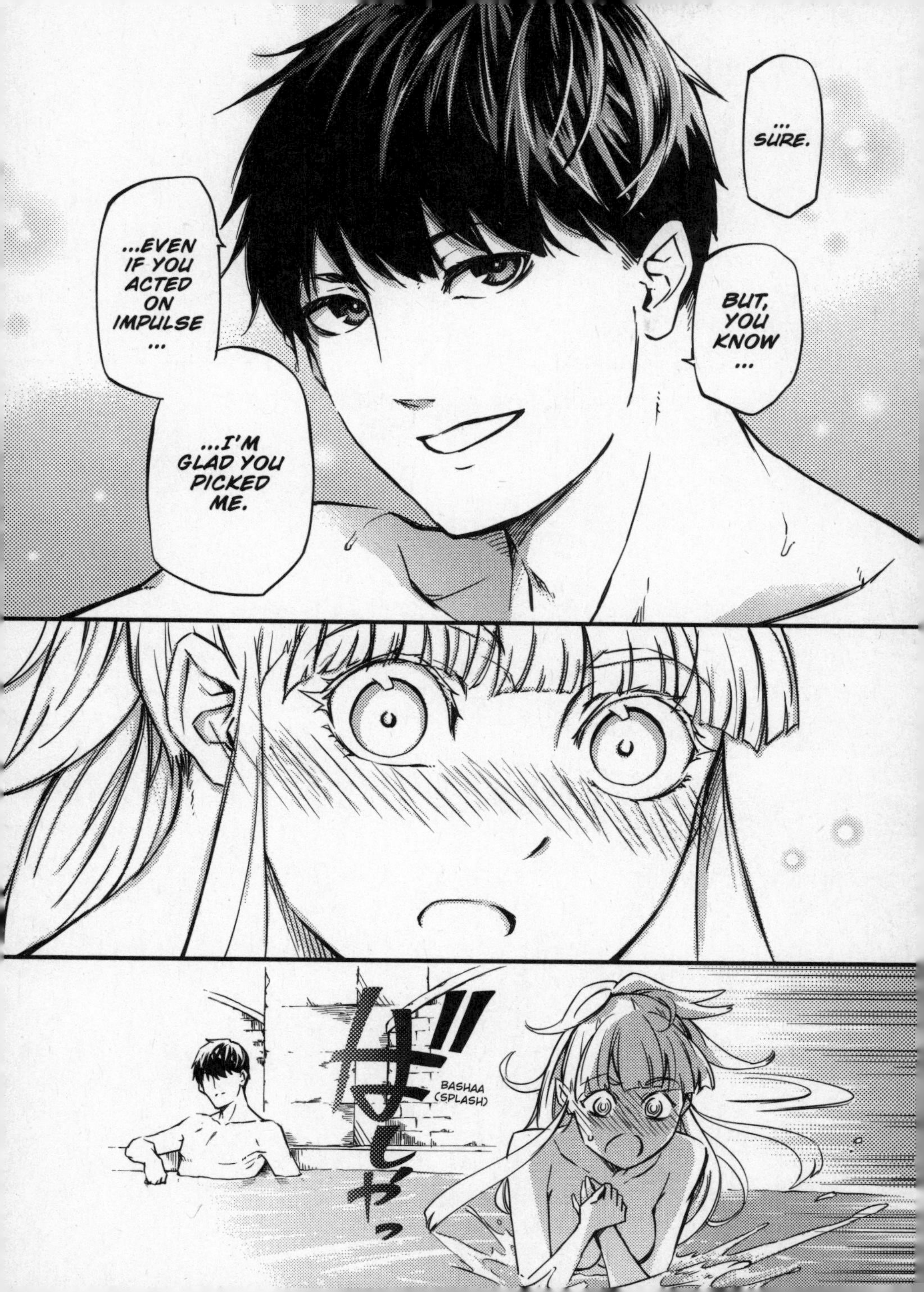

... SURE.
BUT, YOU KNOW ...
...EVEN IF YOU ACTED ON IMPULSE ...
...I'M GLAD YOU PICKED ME.
ばしゃっ
BASHAA (SPLASH)

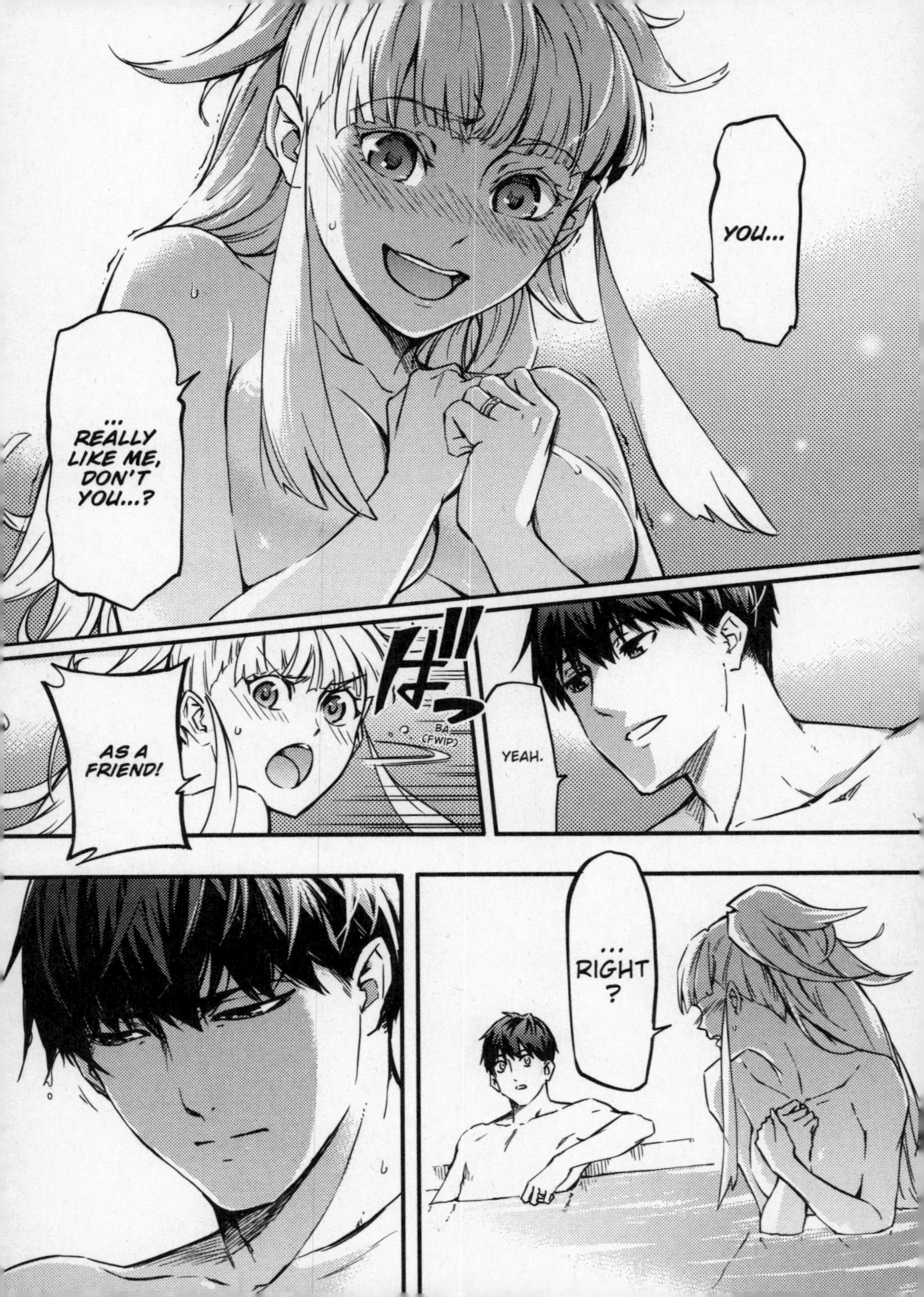
YOU...
...REALLY LIKE ME, DON'T YOU...?
YEAH.
ばっ
BA (FWIP)
AS A FRIEND!
...RIGHT?

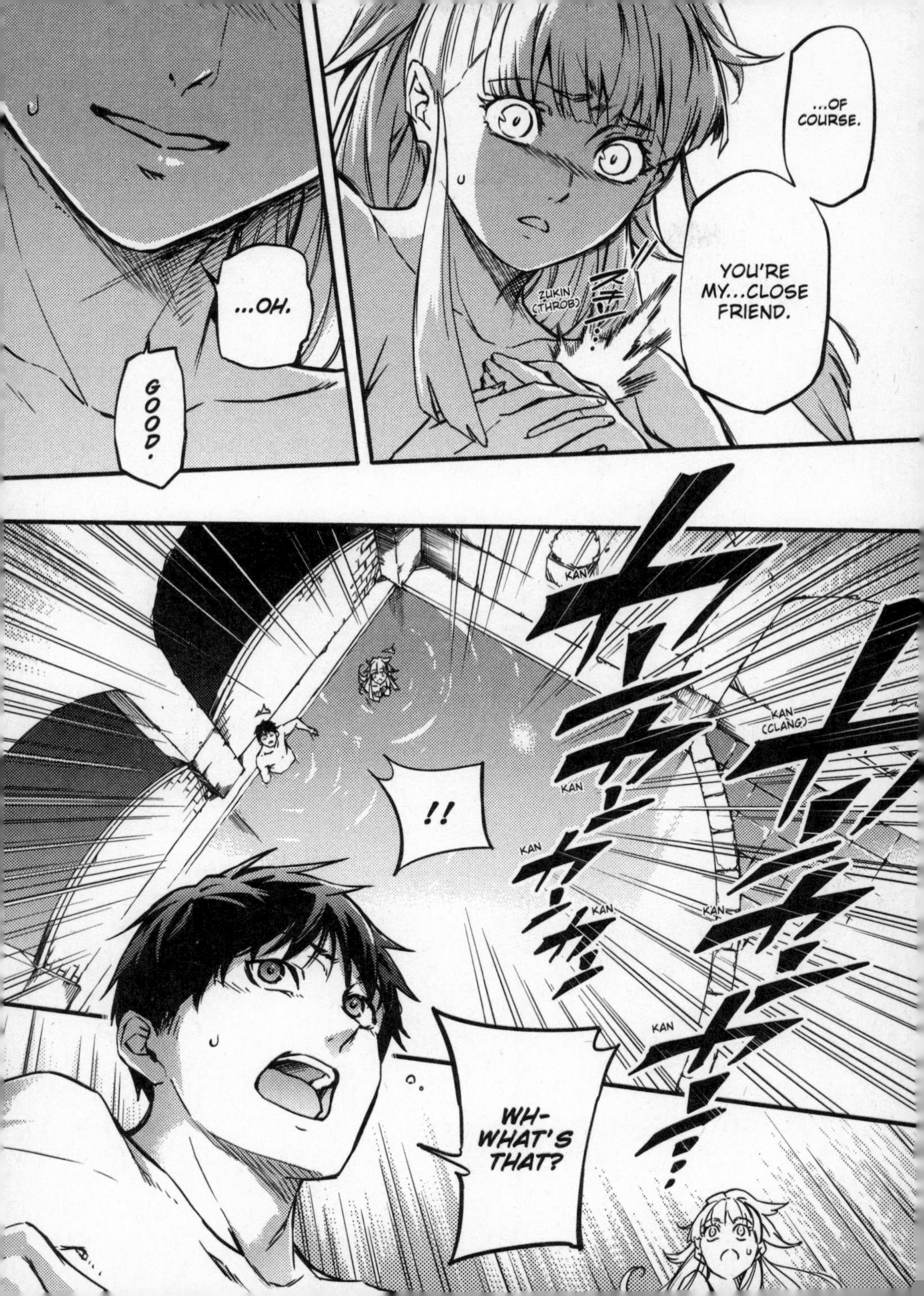
...OF COURSE.
YOU'RE MY...CLOSE FRIEND.
ZUKIN (THROB)
...OH.
GOOD.
KAN
KAN (CLANG)
KAN
KAN
KAN
KAN
KAN
!!
WH-WHAT'S THAT?

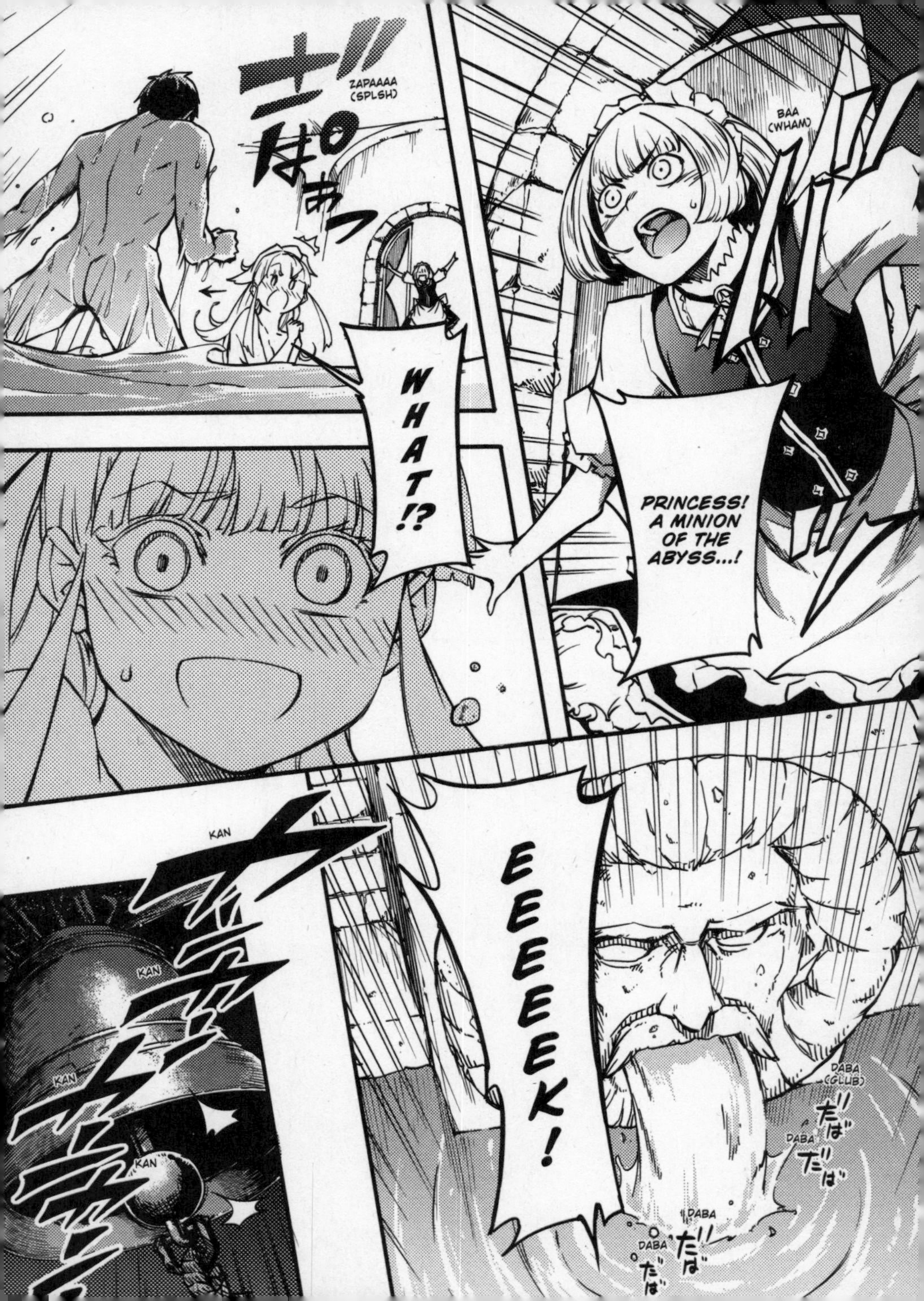
BAA (WHAM)
ZAPAAAA (SPLSH)
PRINCESS! A MINION OF THE ABYSS...!
WHAT!?
EEEEEEK!
DABA (GLUB)
DABA
DABA
DABA
KAN
KAN
KAN
KAN

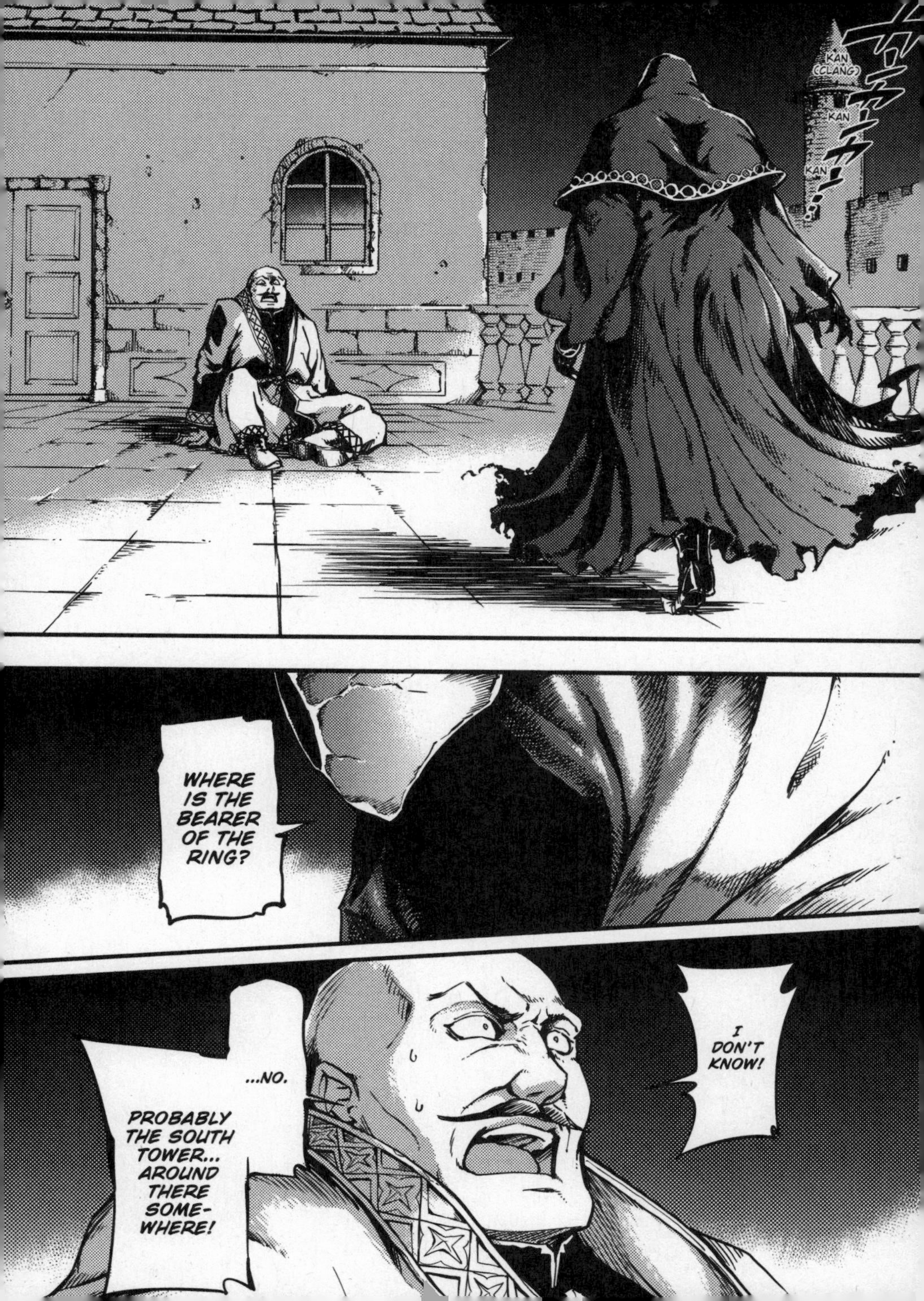
KAN (CLANG)
KAN
KAN
WHERE IS THE BEARER OF THE RING?
I DON'T KNOW!
...NO.
PROBABLY THE SOUTH TOWER... AROUND THERE SOME-WHERE!

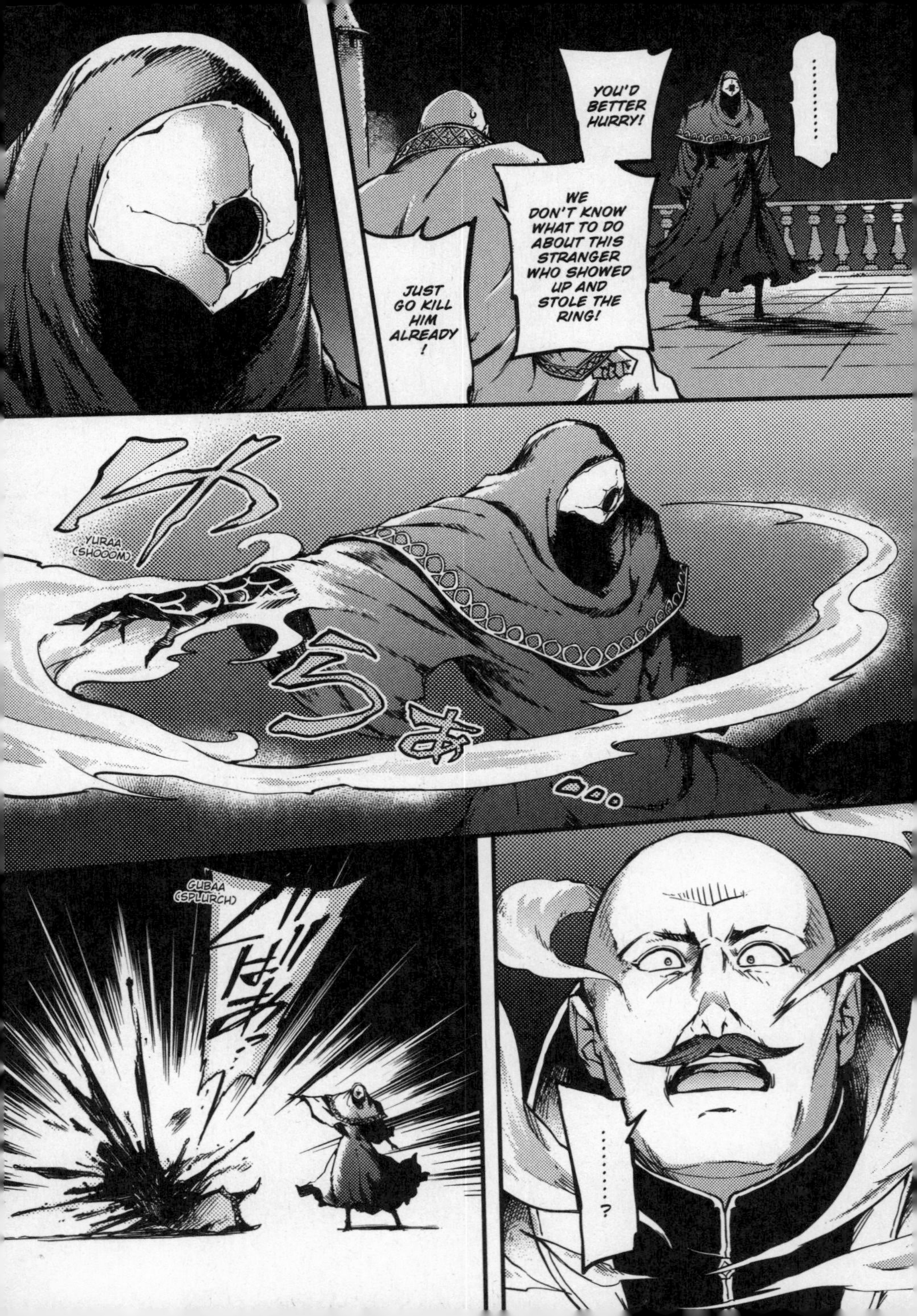

......
YOU'D BETTER HURRY!
WE DON'T KNOW WHAT TO DO ABOUT THIS STRANGER WHO SHOWED UP AND STOLE THE RING!
JUST GO KILL HIM ALREADY!
YURAA (SHOOOM)
ゆらぁ...
GUBAA (SPLURCH)
ゴバぁっ
......?

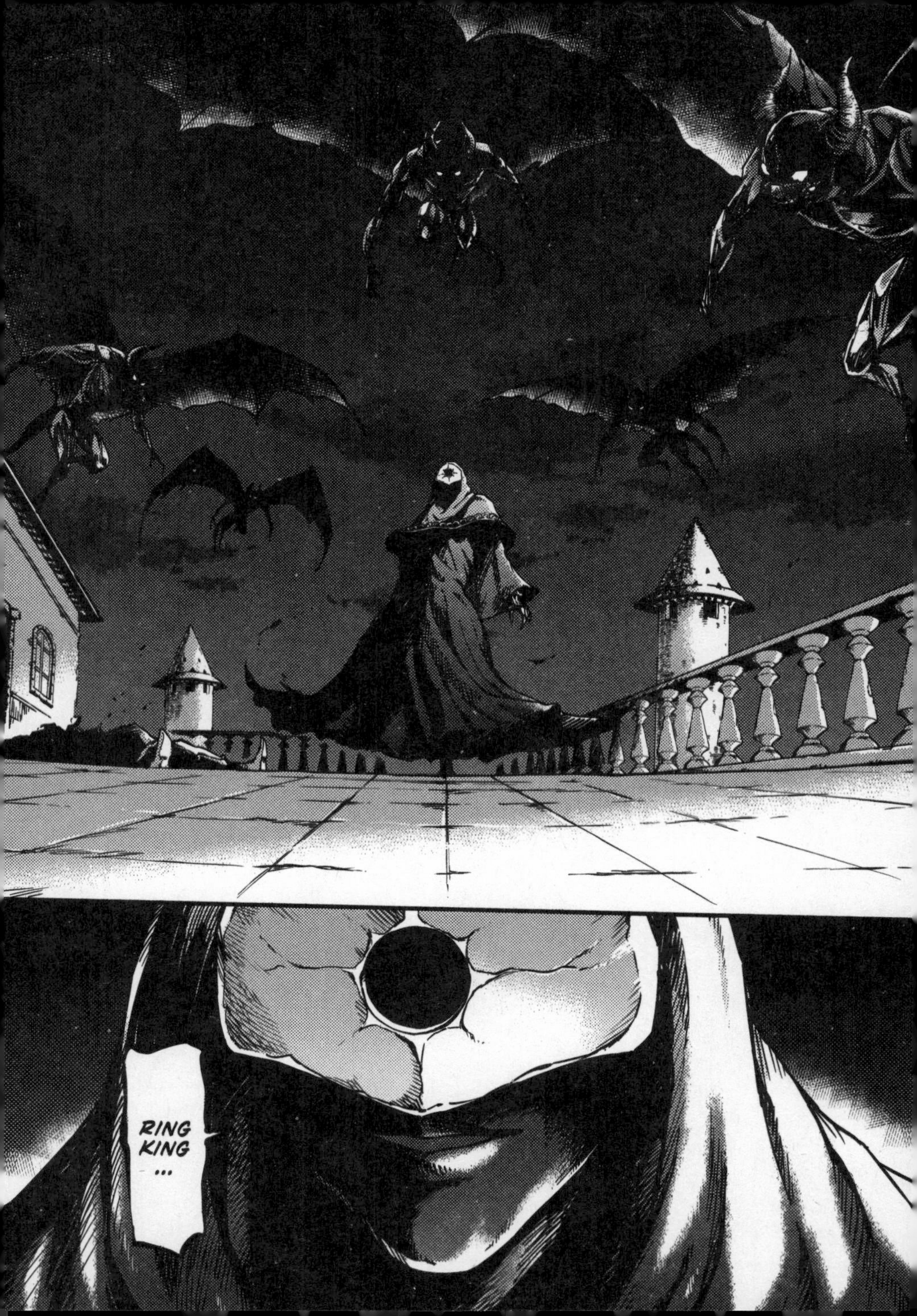
RING KING
—...

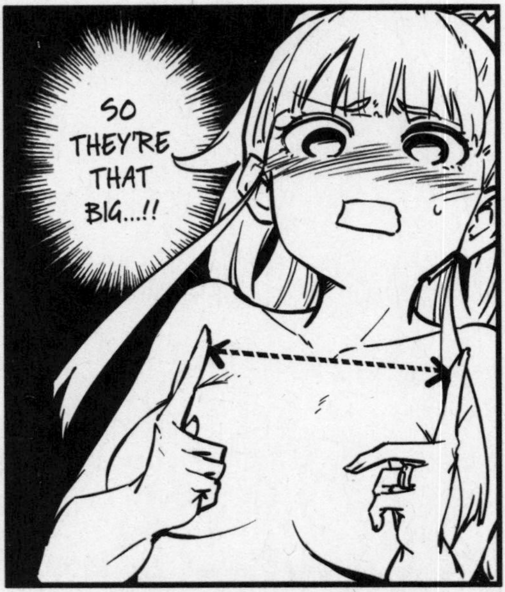
SO THEY'RE THAT BIG...!!

Tales of Wedding Rings

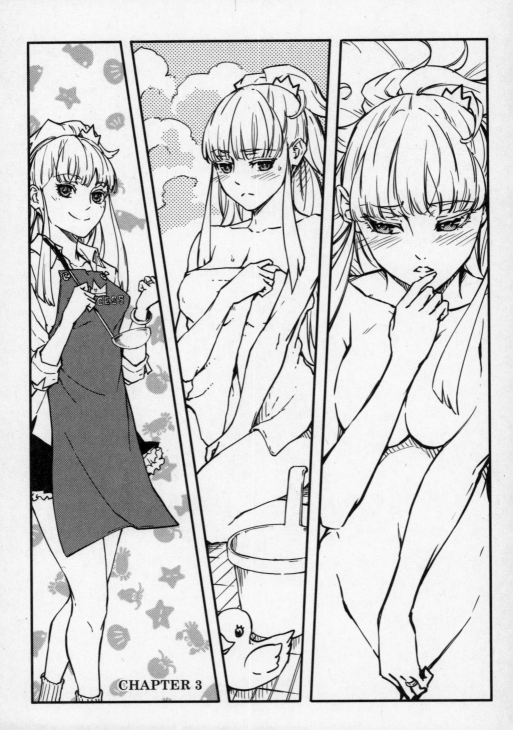

CHAPTER 3

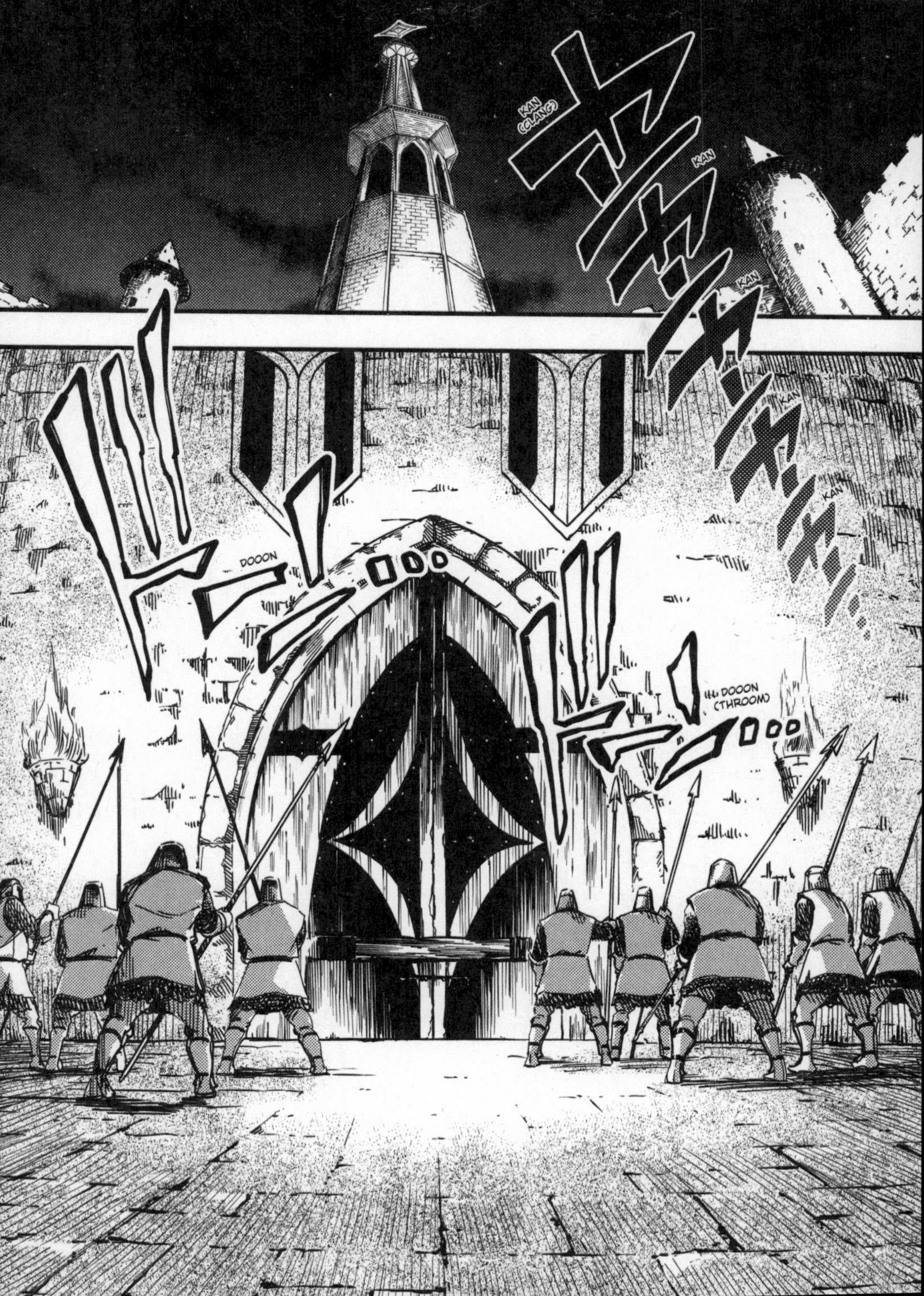
KAN (CLANG)
KAN
KAN
KAN
KAN
DOOON (THROOM)
DOOON

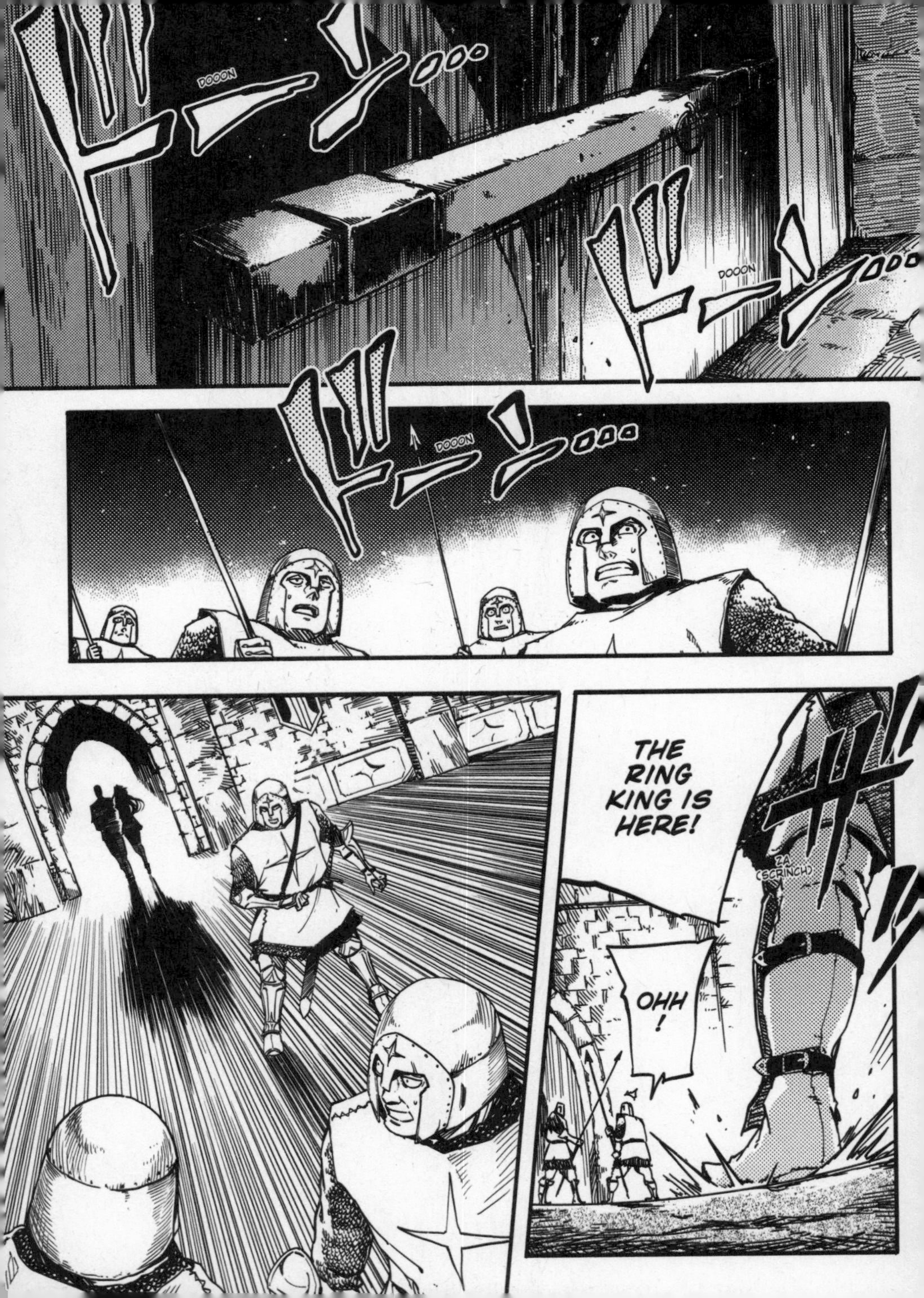
DOOON
DOOON
DOOON
THE RING KING IS HERE!
ZA (SCRINCH)
OHH!

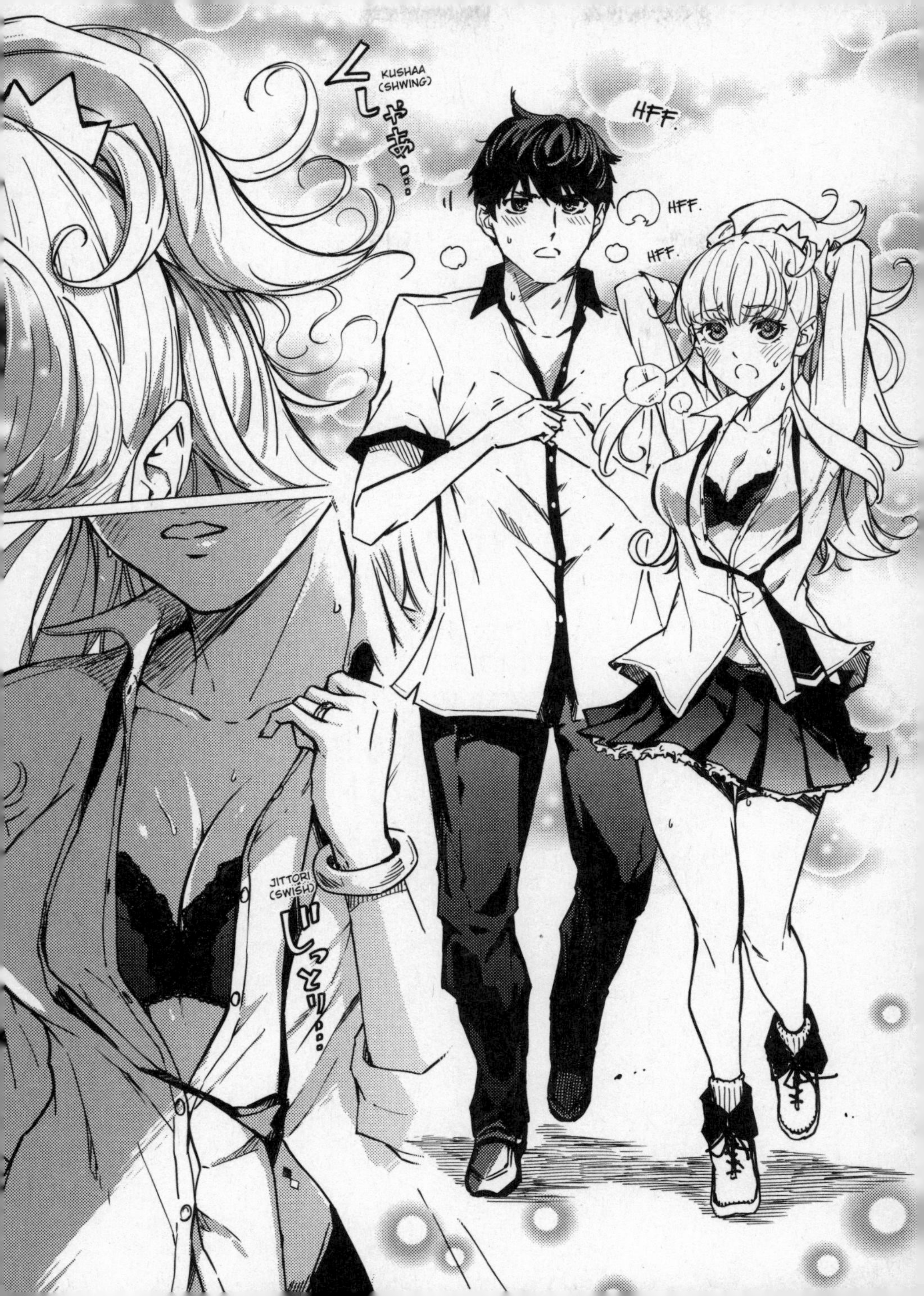
HFF.
HFF.
HFF.
KUSHAA (SHWING)
くしゃあ...
JITTORI (SWISH)
じっとり...

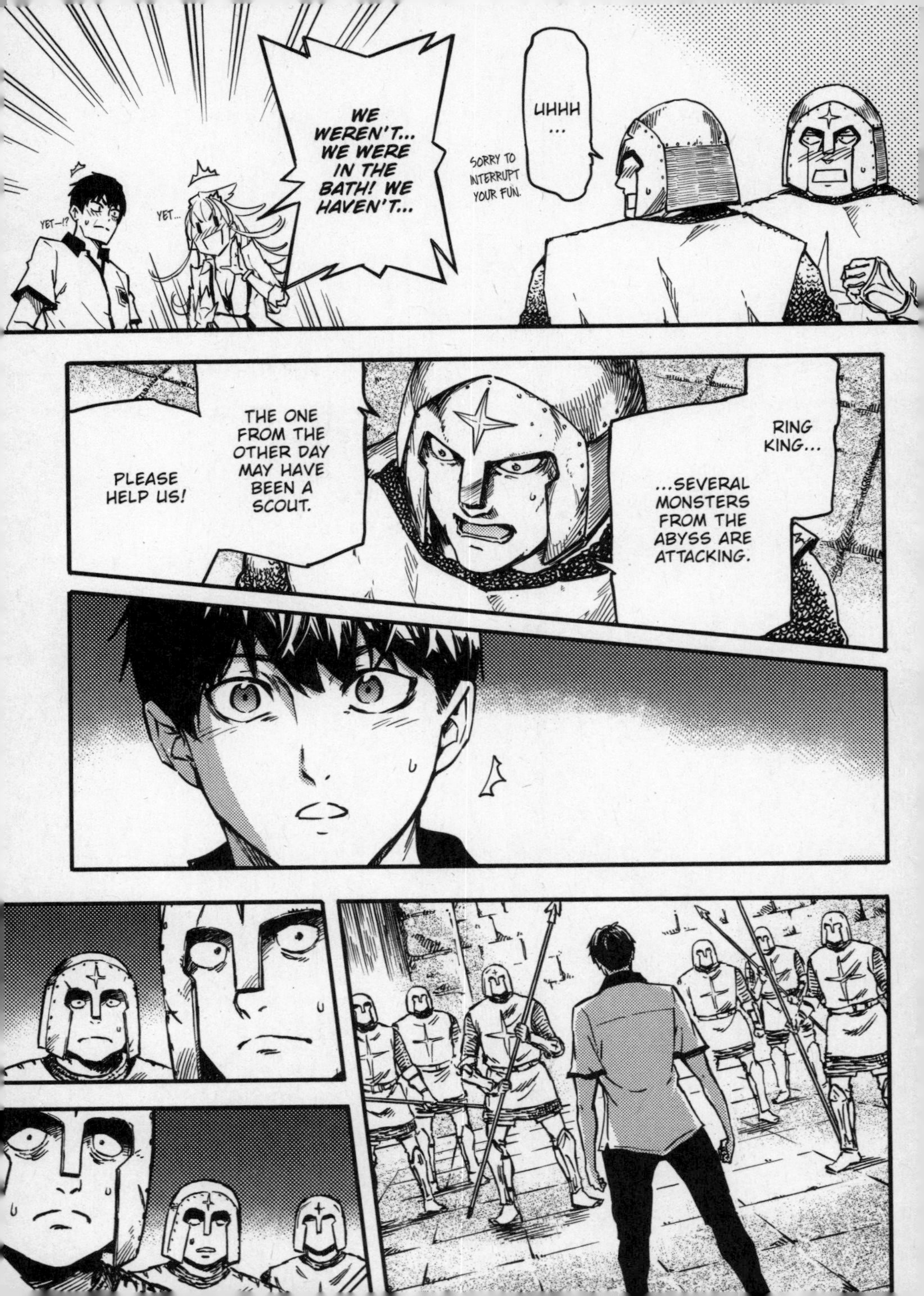
UHHH ...
SORRY TO INTERRUPT YOUR FUN.
WE WEREN'T... WE WERE IN THE BATH! WE HAVEN'T...
YET...
YET—!?
RING KING...
...SEVERAL MONSTERS FROM THE ABYSS ARE ATTACKING.
THE ONE FROM THE OTHER DAY MAY HAVE BEEN A SCOUT.
PLEASE HELP US!

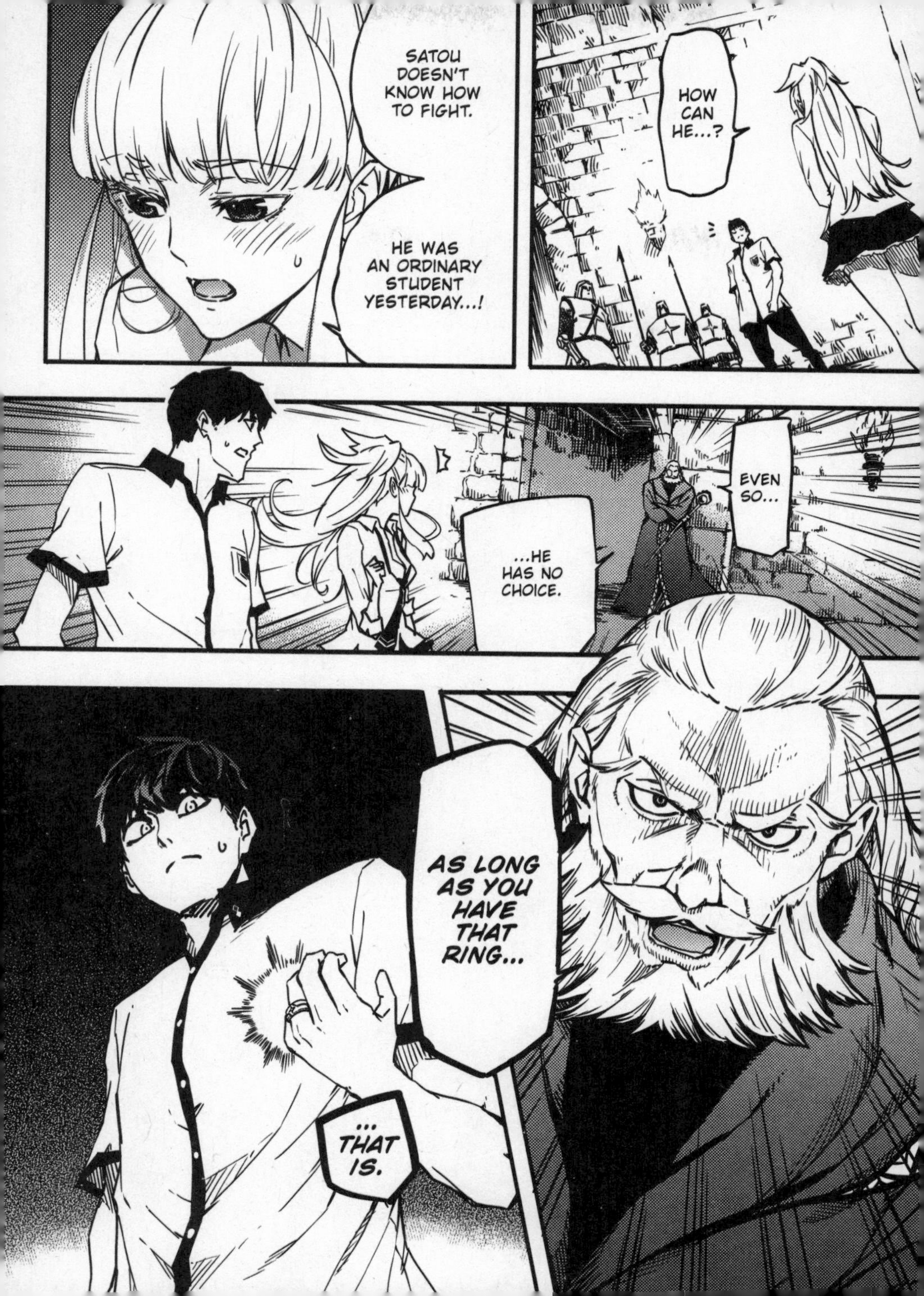
HOW CAN HE...?
SATOU DOESN'T KNOW HOW TO FIGHT.
HE WAS AN ORDINARY STUDENT YESTERDAY...!
EVEN SO...
...HE HAS NO CHOICE.
AS LONG AS YOU HAVE THAT RING...
... THAT IS.

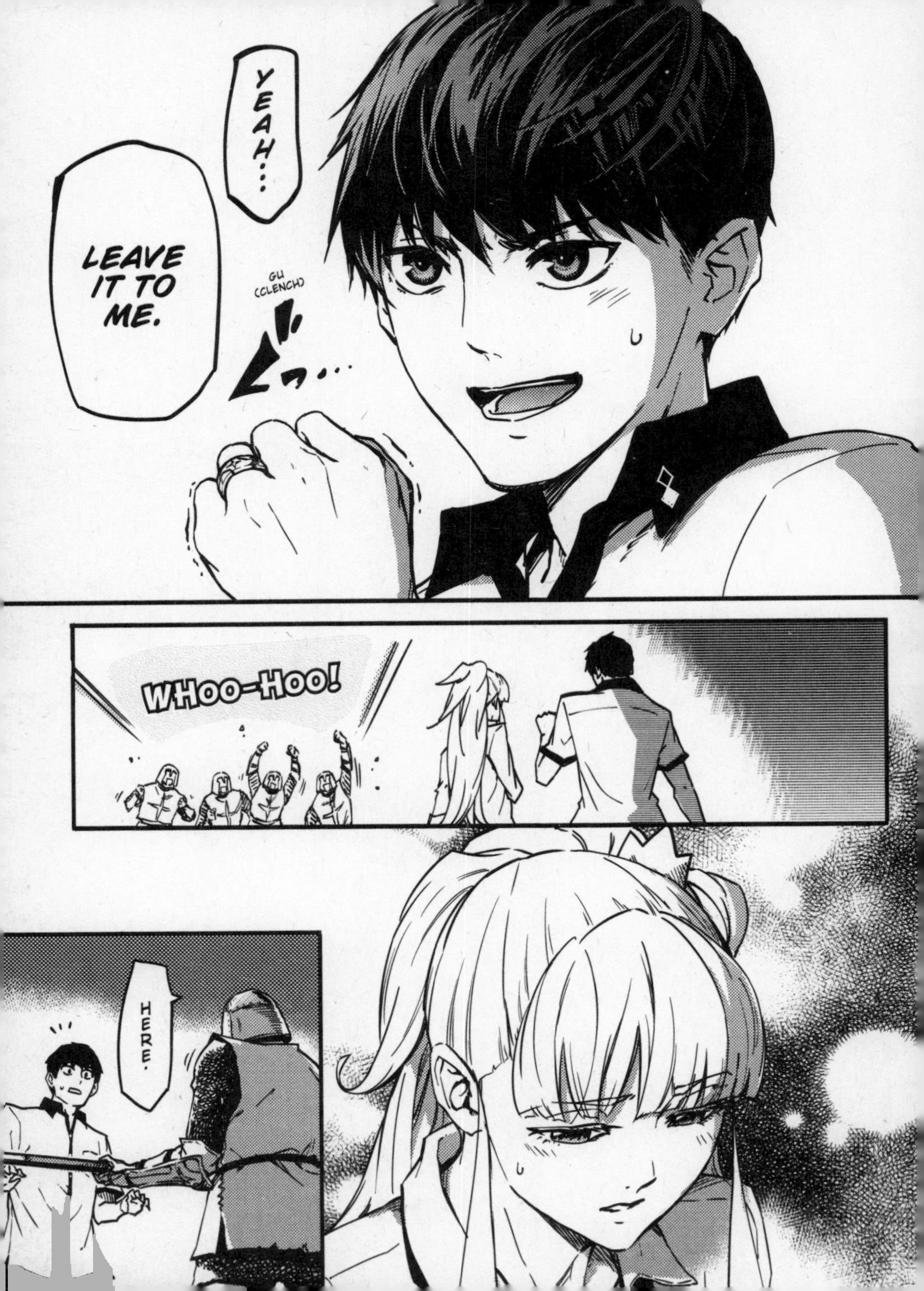
YEAH...
LEAVE IT TO ME.
GU (CLENCH)
WHOO-HOO!
HERE.

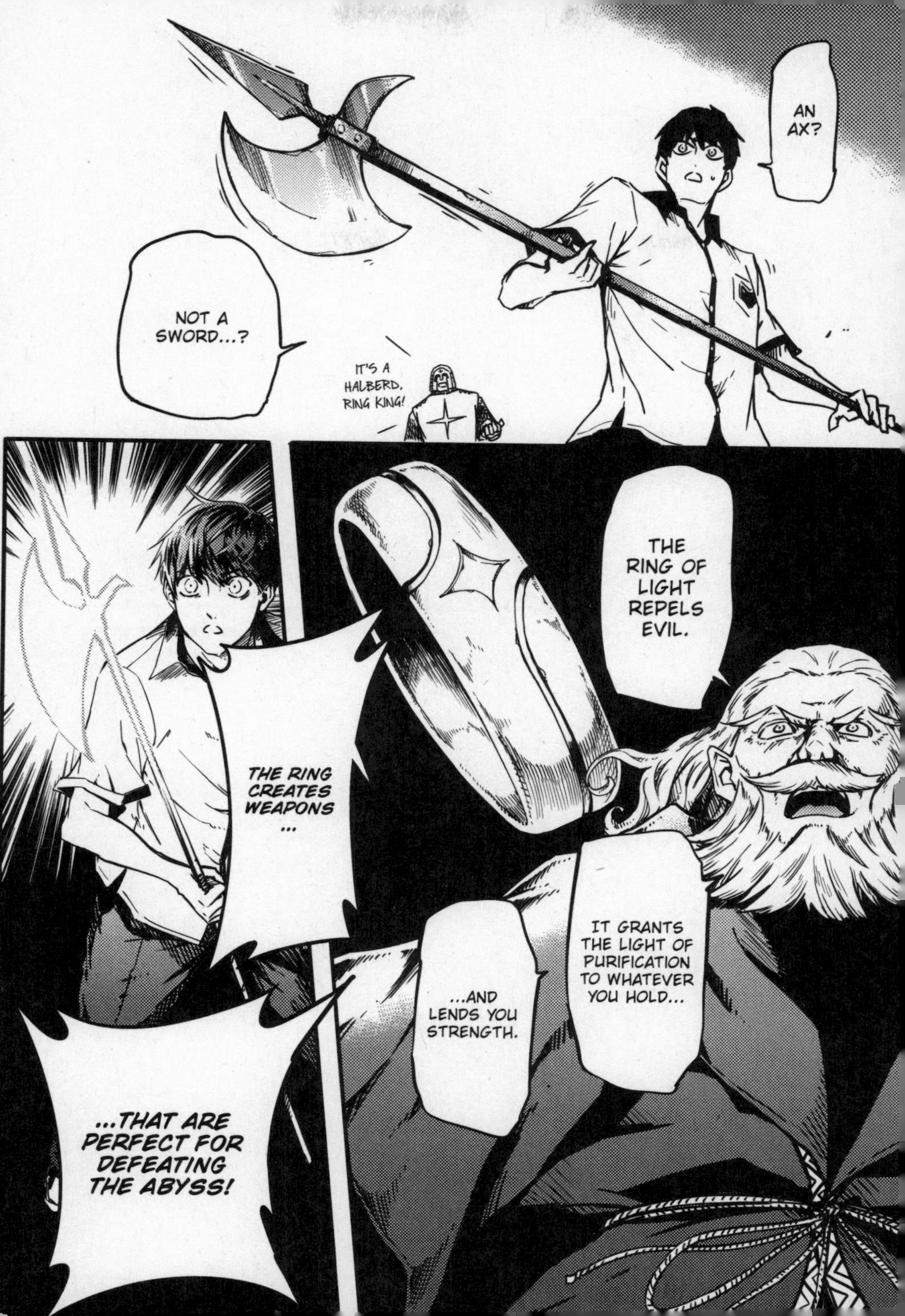
AN AX?
NOT A SWORD...?
IT'S A HALBERD, RING KING!
THE RING OF LIGHT REPELS EVIL.
IT GRANTS THE LIGHT OF PURIFICATION TO WHATEVER YOU HOLD...
...AND LENDS YOU STRENGTH.
THE RING CREATES WEAPONS ...
...THAT ARE PERFECT FOR DEFEATING THE ABYSS!

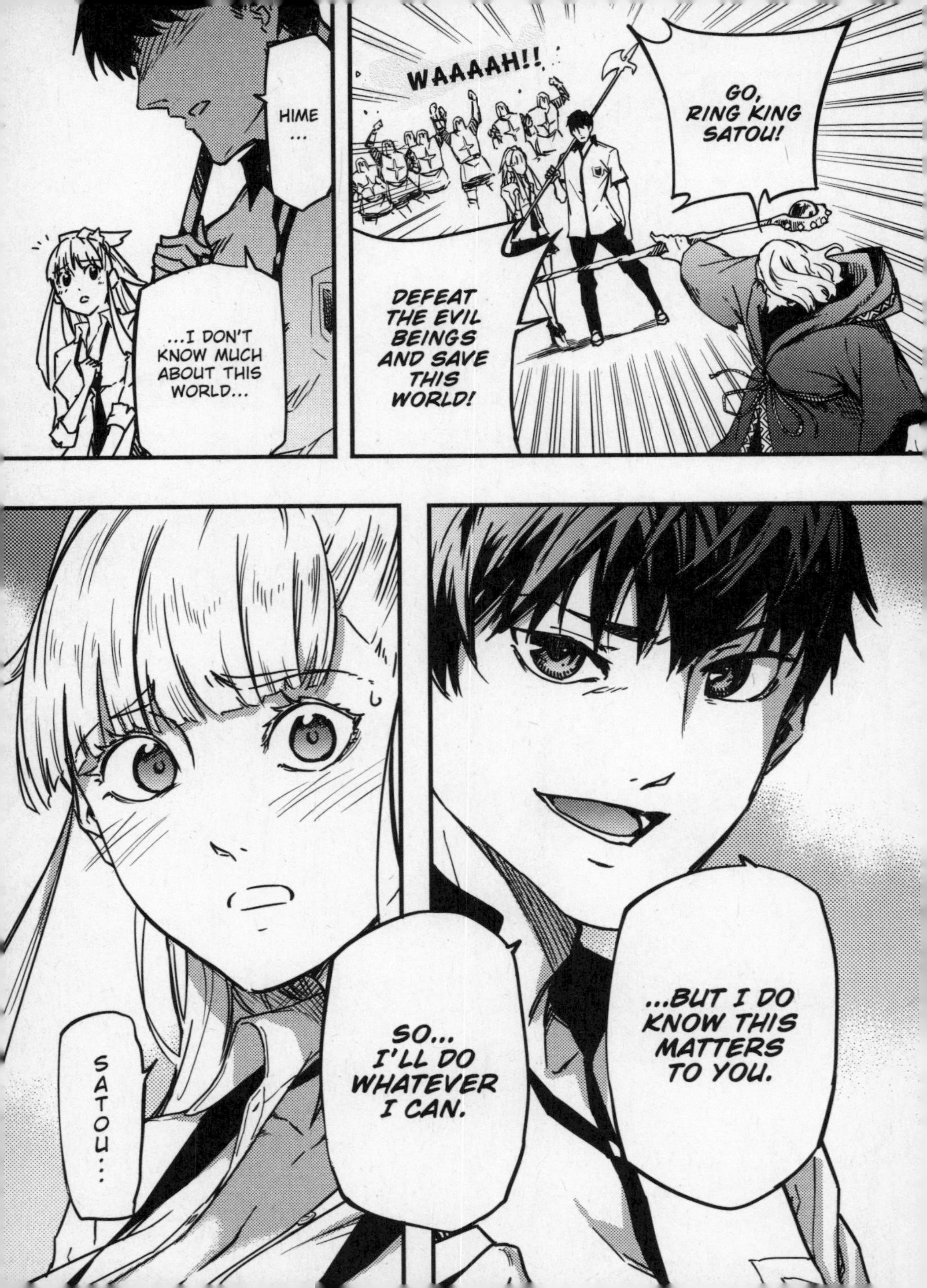
HIME ...
...I DON'T KNOW MUCH ABOUT THIS WORLD...
WAAAAH!!
GO, RING KING SATOU!
DEFEAT THE EVIL BEINGS AND SAVE THIS WORLD!
...BUT I DO KNOW THIS MATTERS TO YOU.
SO... I'LL DO WHATEVER I CAN.
SATOU...

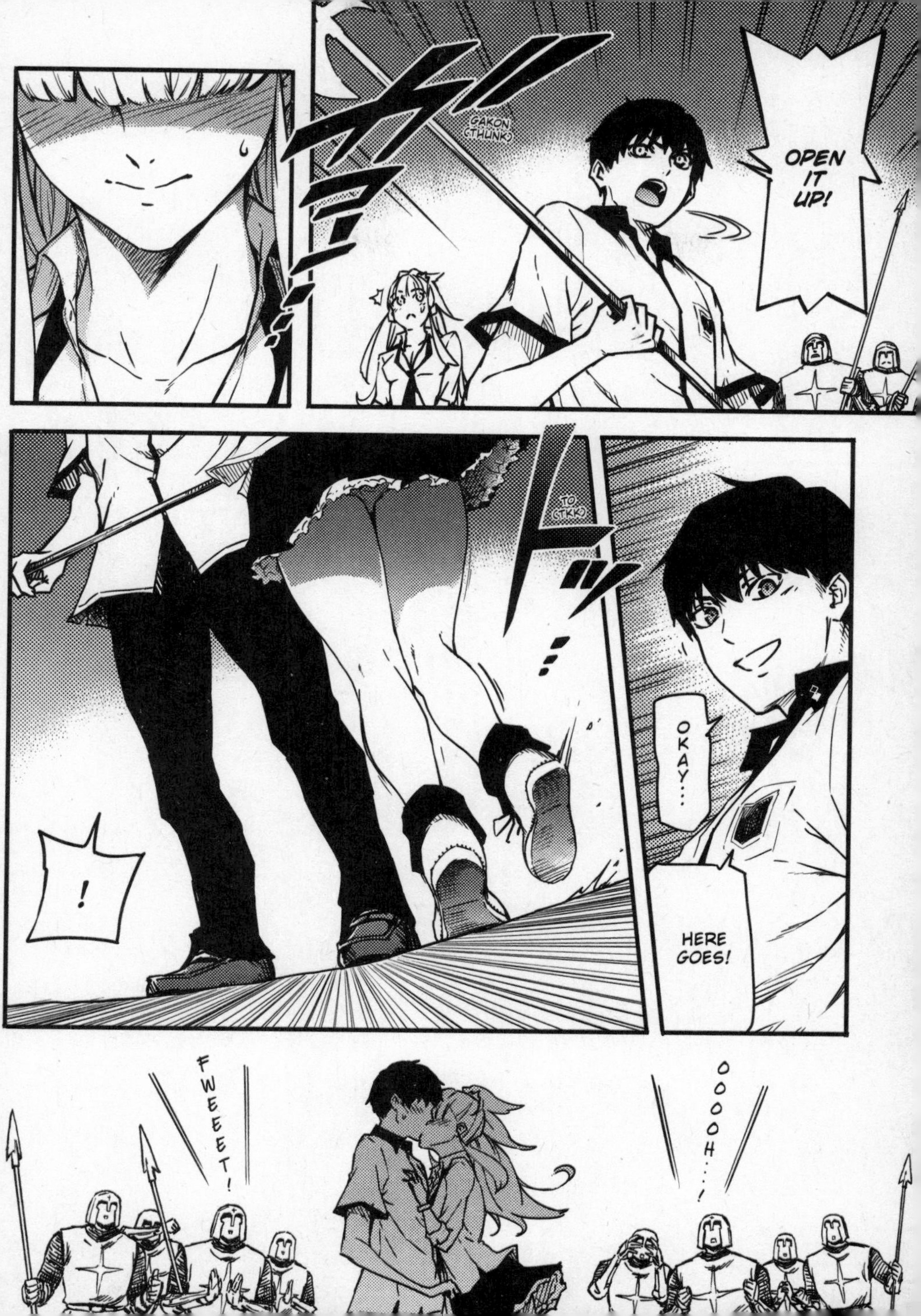
OPEN IT UP!
GAKON (THUNK)
OKAY...
HERE GOES!
TO (TKK)
!
OOOOH...!
FWEEET!

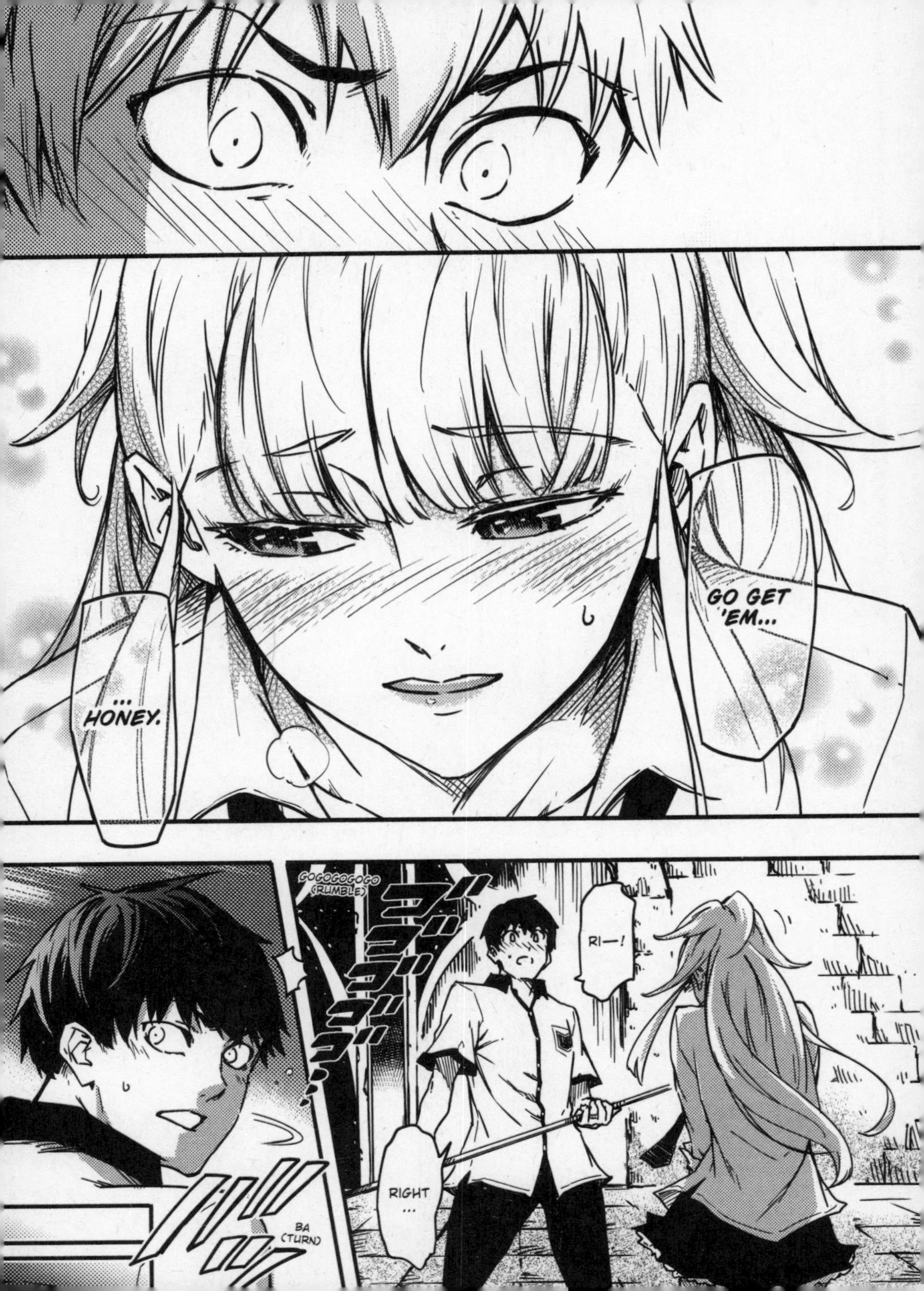
GO GET 'EM...
... HONEY.
GOGOGOGOGO (RUMBLE)
RI—!
RIGHT ...
BA (TURN)

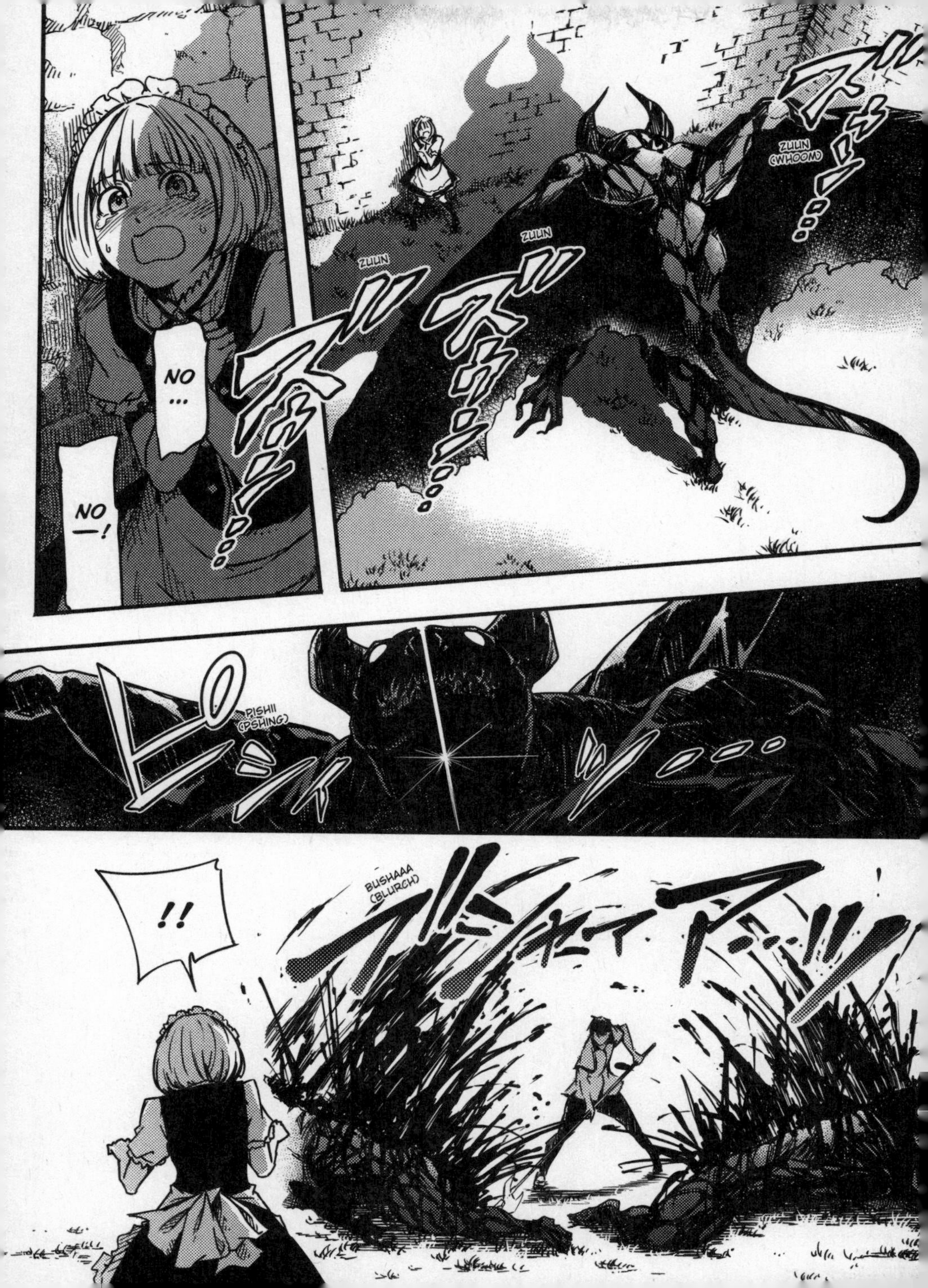
ZUUN (WHOOM)
ZUUN
ZUUN
NO ...
NO —!
PISHII (PSHING)
BUSHAAA (BLURCH)
!!

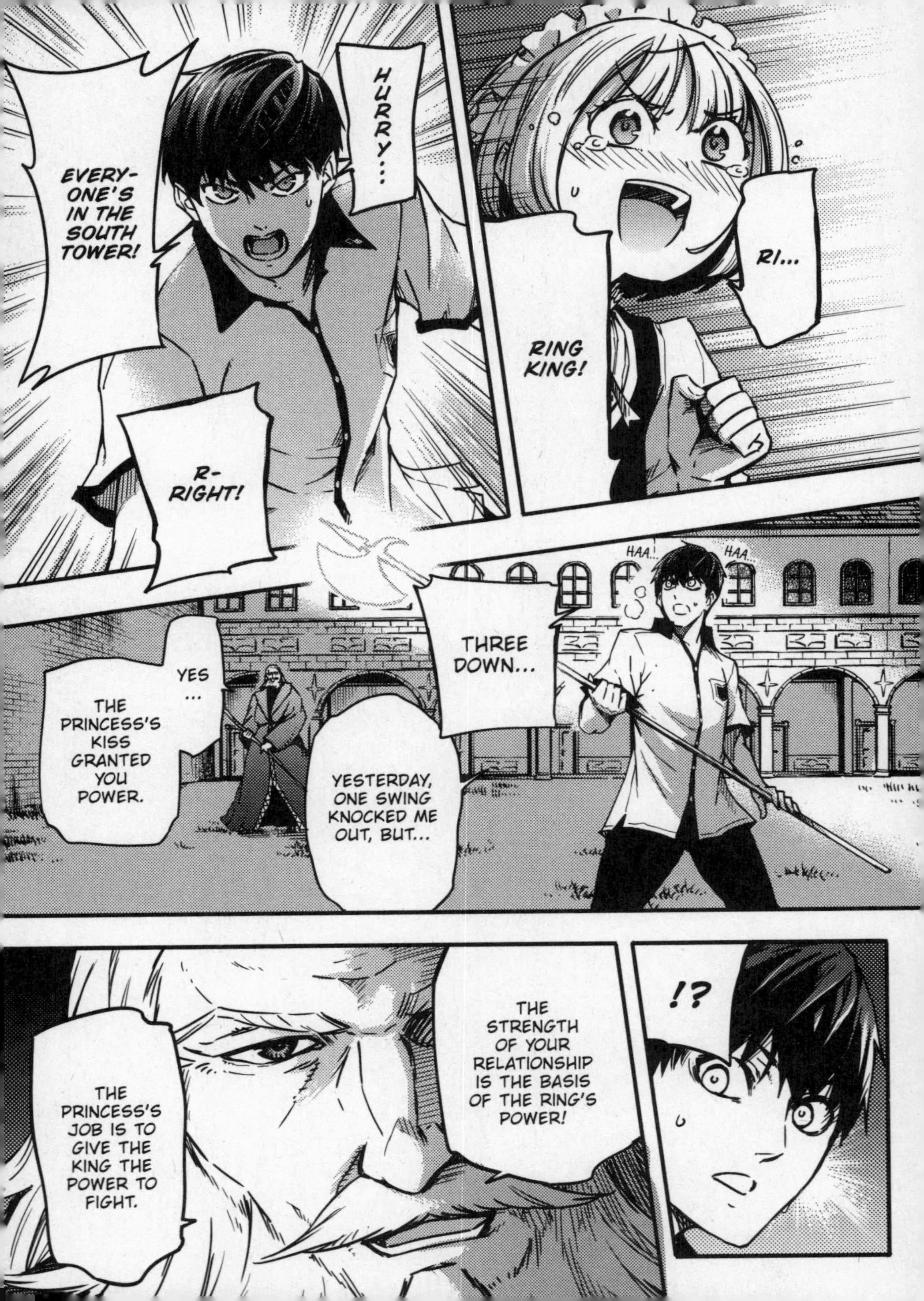
RI...
RING KING!
HURRY...
EVERYONE'S IN THE SOUTH TOWER!
R-RIGHT!
HAA..!
HAA...
THREE DOWN...
YESTERDAY, ONE SWING KNOCKED ME OUT, BUT...
YES...
THE PRINCESS'S KISS GRANTED YOU POWER.
!?
THE STRENGTH OF YOUR RELATIONSHIP IS THE BASIS OF THE RING'S POWER!
THE PRINCESS'S JOB IS TO GIVE THE KING THE POWER TO FIGHT.

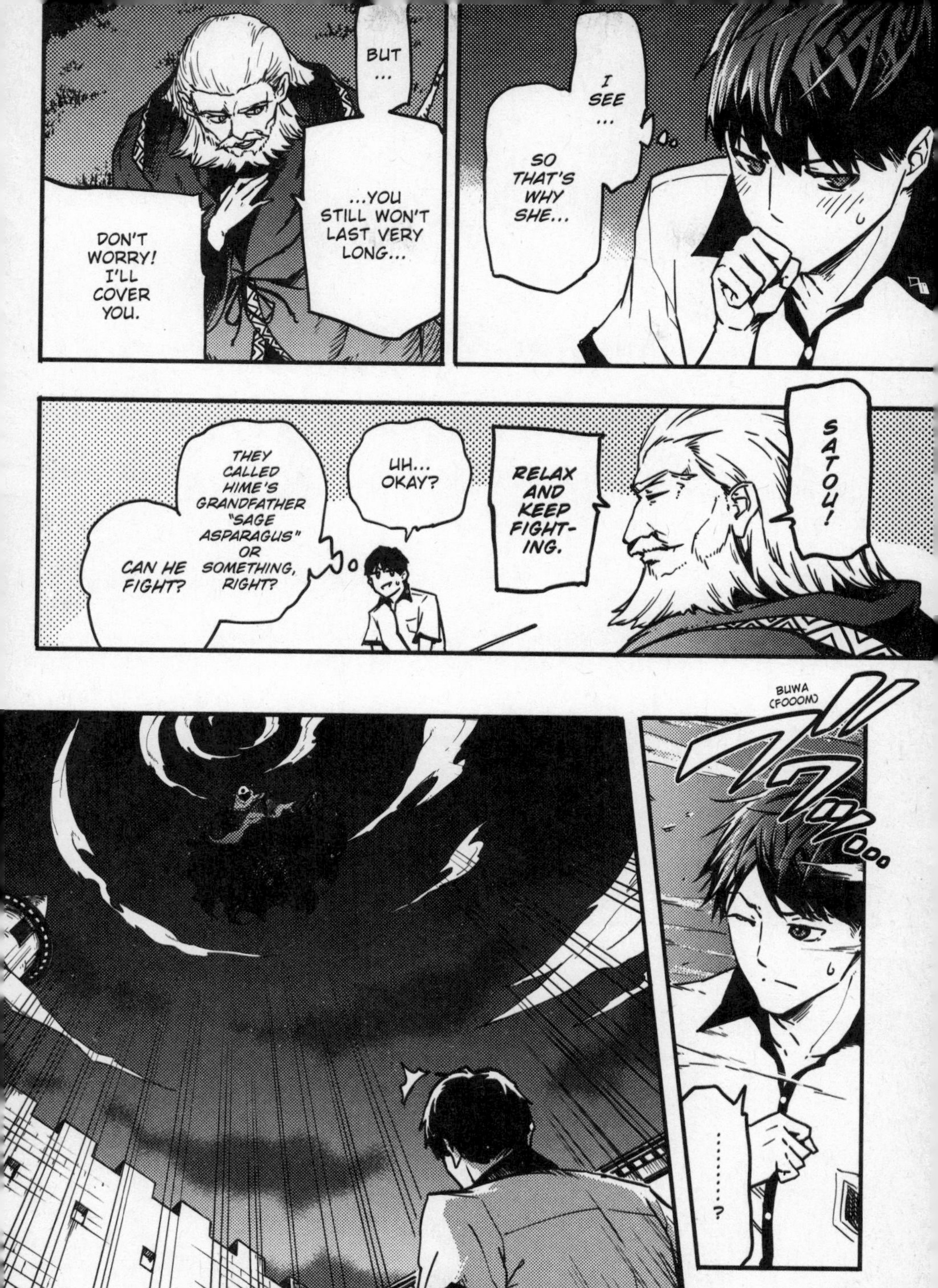
I SEE...
SO THAT'S WHY SHE...
BUT...
...YOU STILL WON'T LAST VERY LONG...
DON'T WORRY! I'LL COVER YOU.
SATOU!
RELAX AND KEEP FIGHTING.
UH... OKAY?
THEY CALLED HIME'S GRANDFATHER "SAGE ASPARAGUS" OR SOMETHING, RIGHT?
CAN HE FIGHT?
BUWA (FOOOM)
.......?

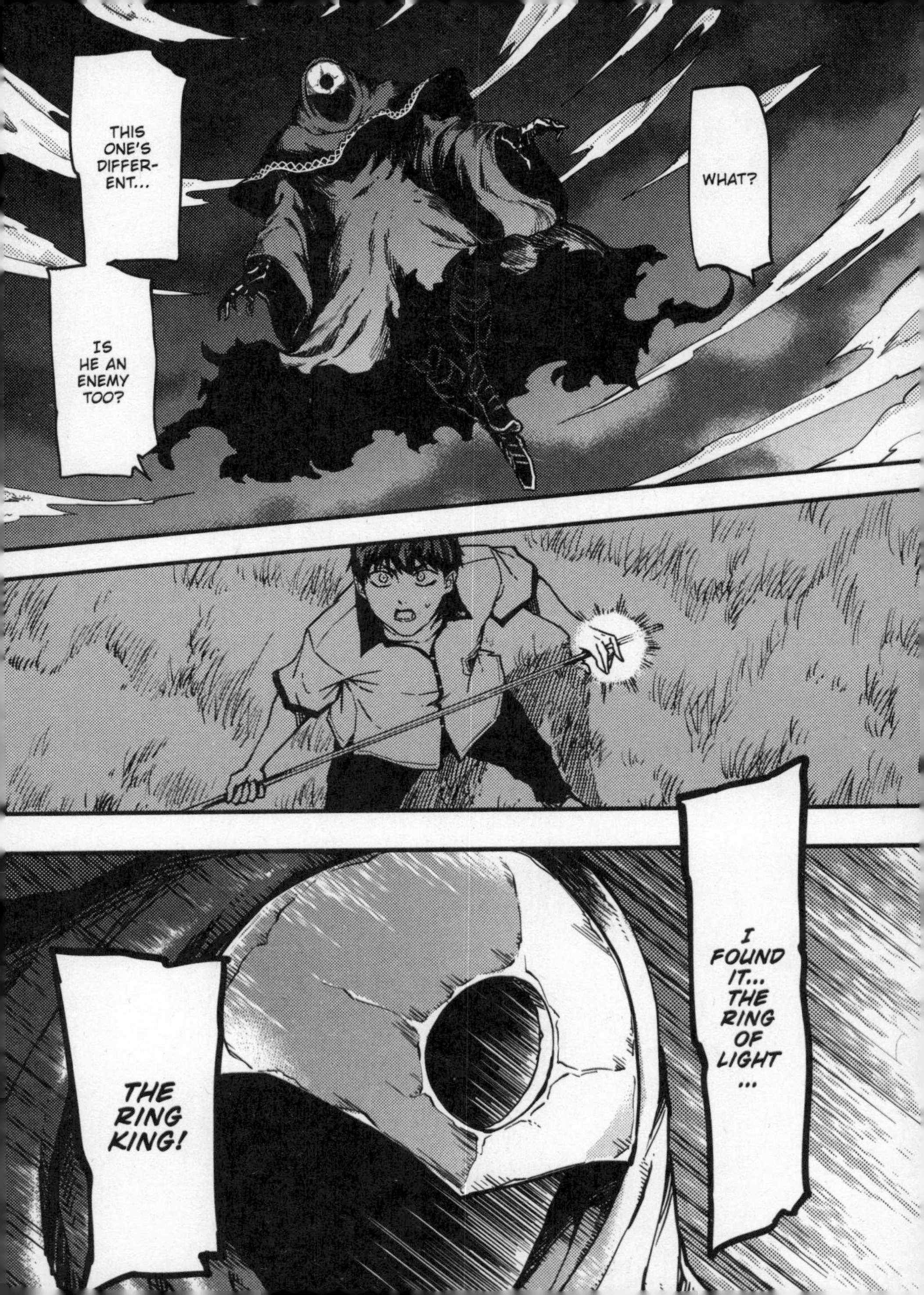
WHAT?
THIS ONE'S DIFFERENT...
IS HE AN ENEMY TOO?
I FOUND IT... THE RING OF LIGHT...
THE RING KING!

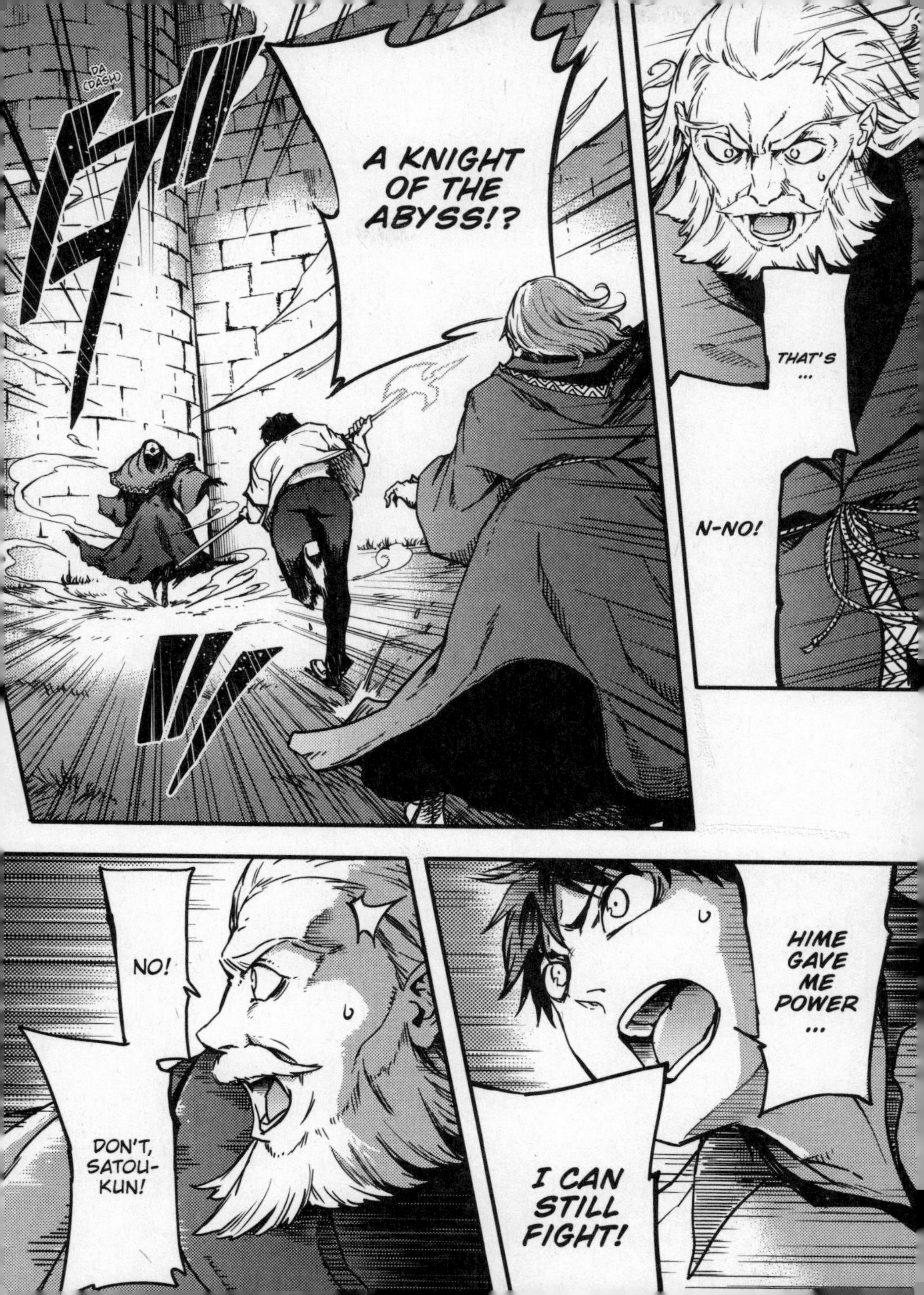
THAT'S...
N-NO!
A KNIGHT OF THE ABYSS!?
DA (DASH)
HIME GAVE ME POWER...
I CAN STILL FIGHT!
NO!
DON'T, SATOU-KUN!

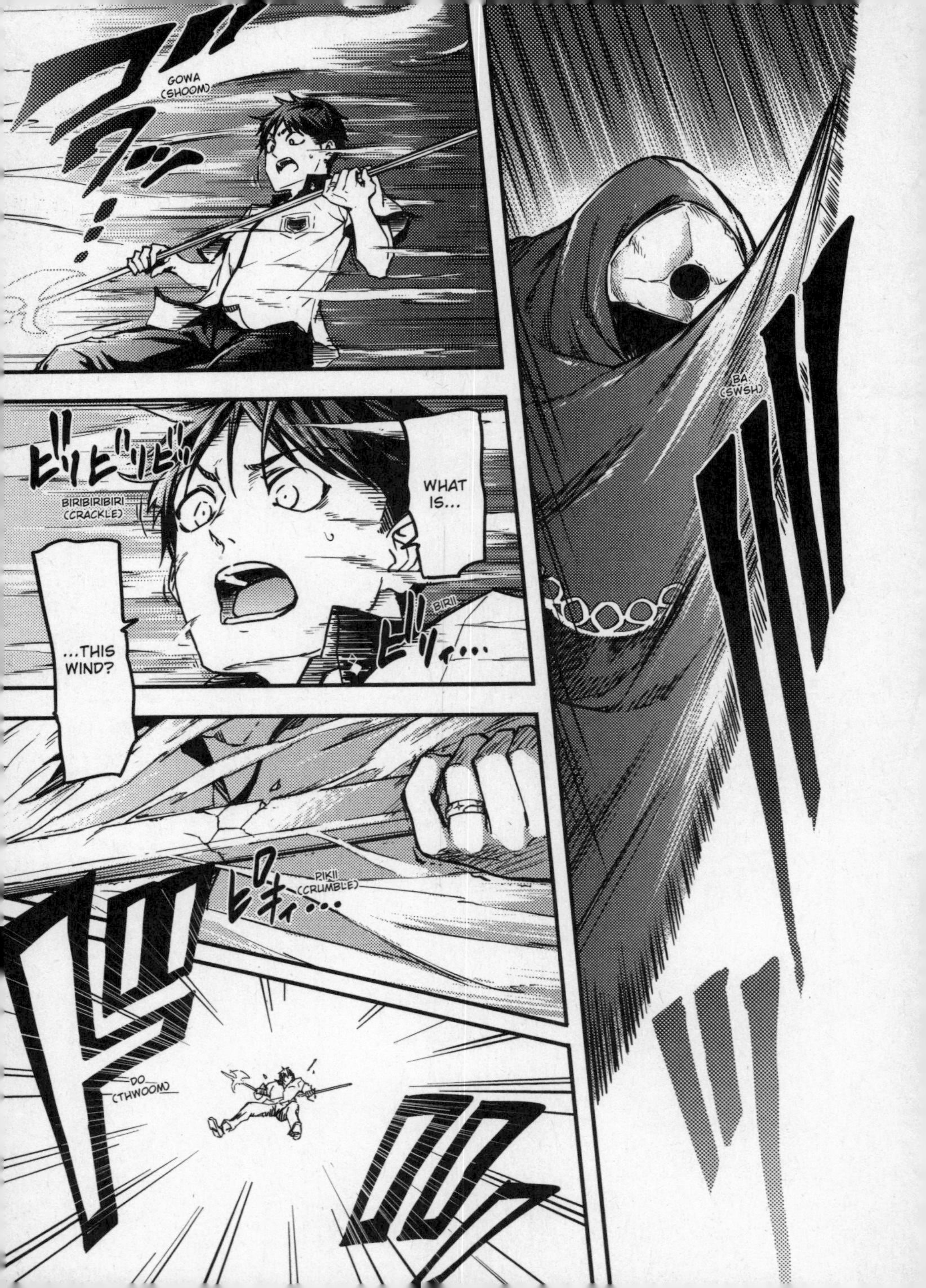
BA
(SWSH)
GOWA
(SHOOM)
WHAT IS...
BIRIBIRIBIRI
(CRACKLE)
BIRII
...THIS WIND?
PIKII
(CRUMBLE)
DO
(THWOOM)

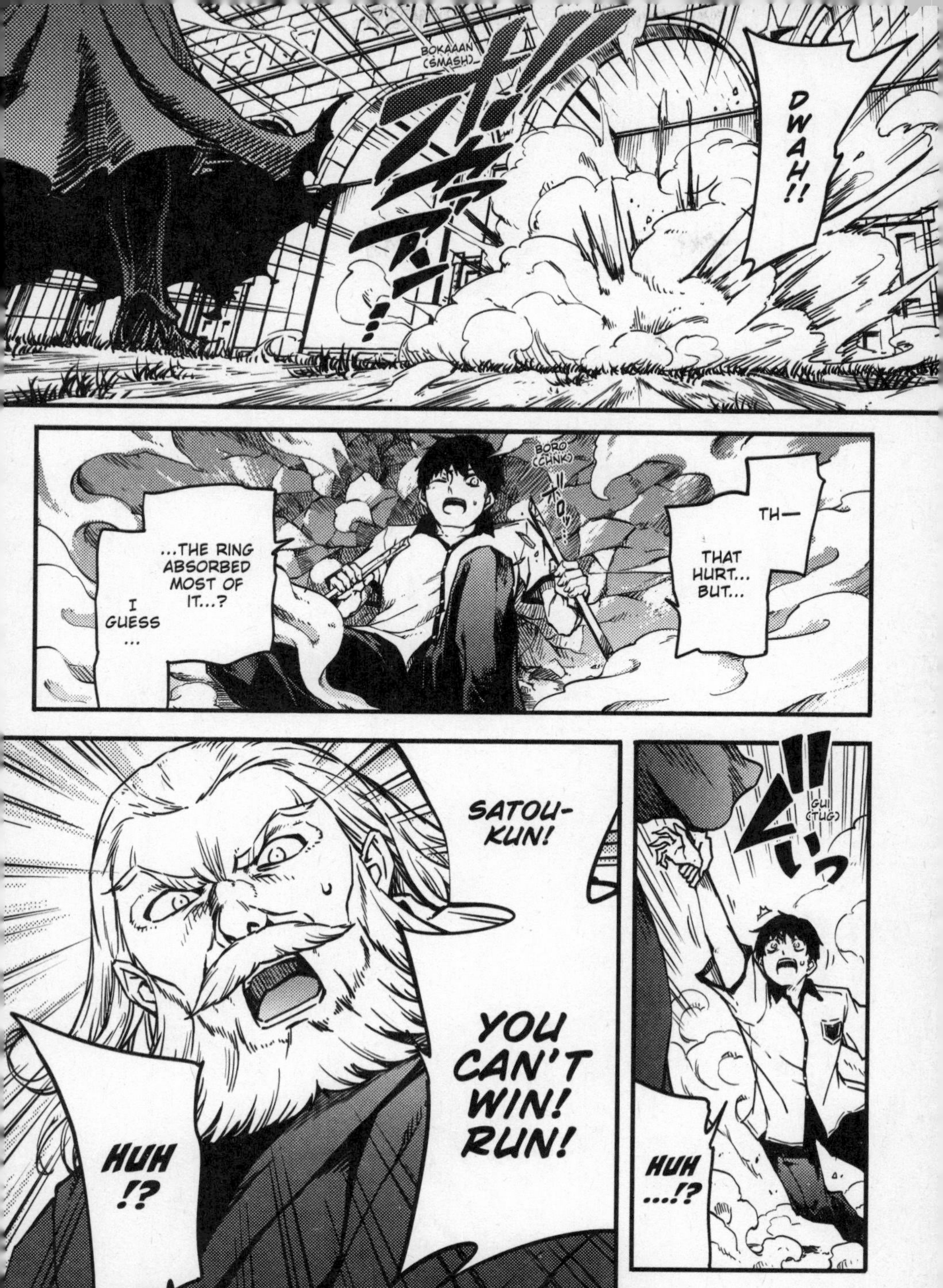
DWAH!!
BOKAAAN (SMASH)
TH—
THAT HURT... BUT...
BORO (CHNK)
...THE RING ABSORBED MOST OF IT...?
I GUESS...
GUI (TUG)
HUH...!?
SATOU-KUN!
YOU CAN'T WIN! RUN!
HUH!?

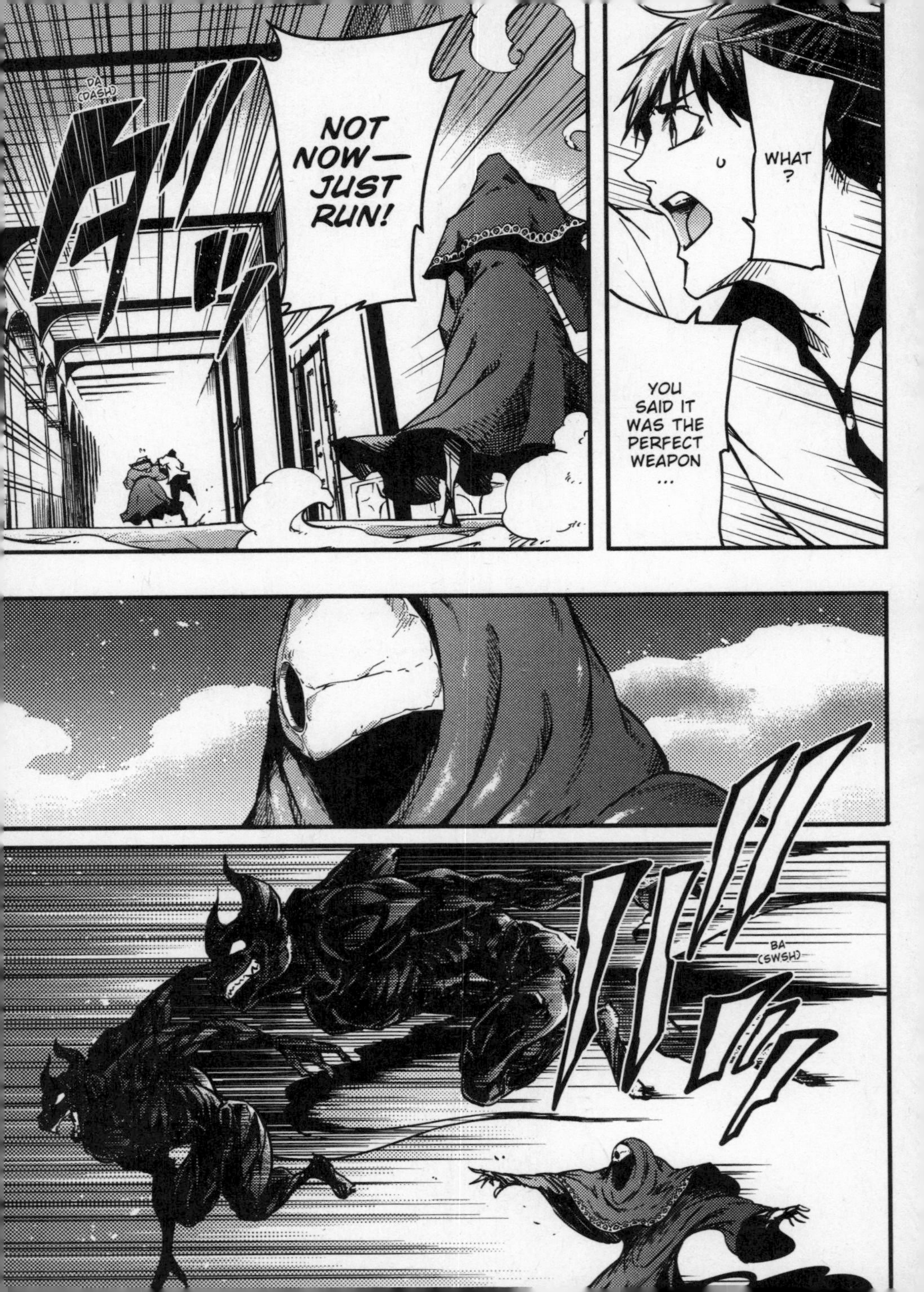
WHAT?
YOU SAID IT WAS THE PERFECT WEAPON...
NOT NOW—JUST RUN!
DA (DASH)
BA (SWSH)

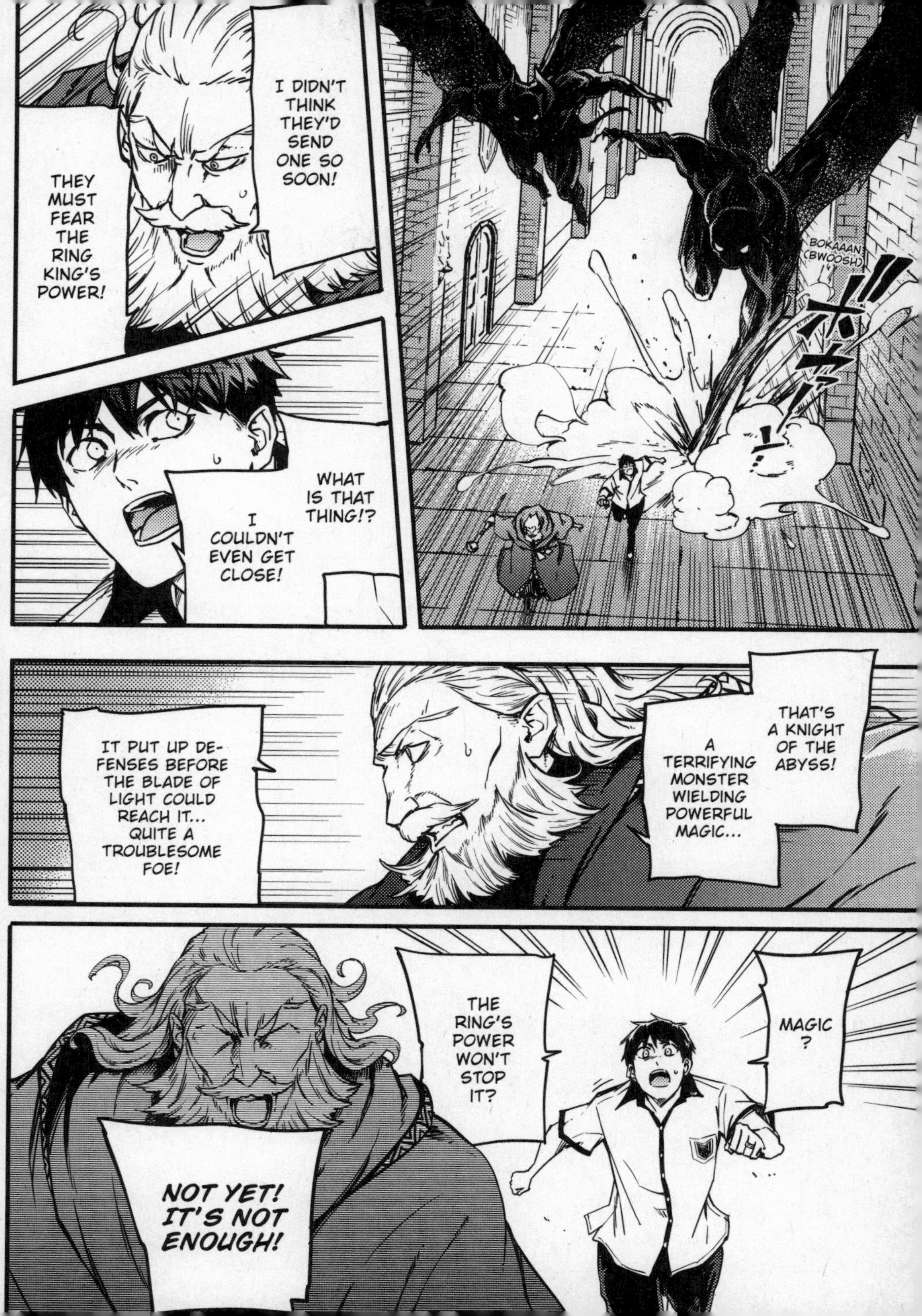
BOKAAAN (BWOOSH)
I DIDN'T THINK THEY'D SEND ONE SO SOON!
THEY MUST FEAR THE RING KING'S POWER!
WHAT IS THAT THING!?
I COULDN'T EVEN GET CLOSE!
THAT'S A KNIGHT OF THE ABYSS!
A TERRIFYING MONSTER WIELDING POWERFUL MAGIC...
IT PUT UP DE-FENSES BEFORE THE BLADE OF LIGHT COULD REACH IT... QUITE A TROUBLESOME FOE!
MAGIC?
THE RING'S POWER WON'T STOP IT?
NOT YET! IT'S NOT ENOUGH!

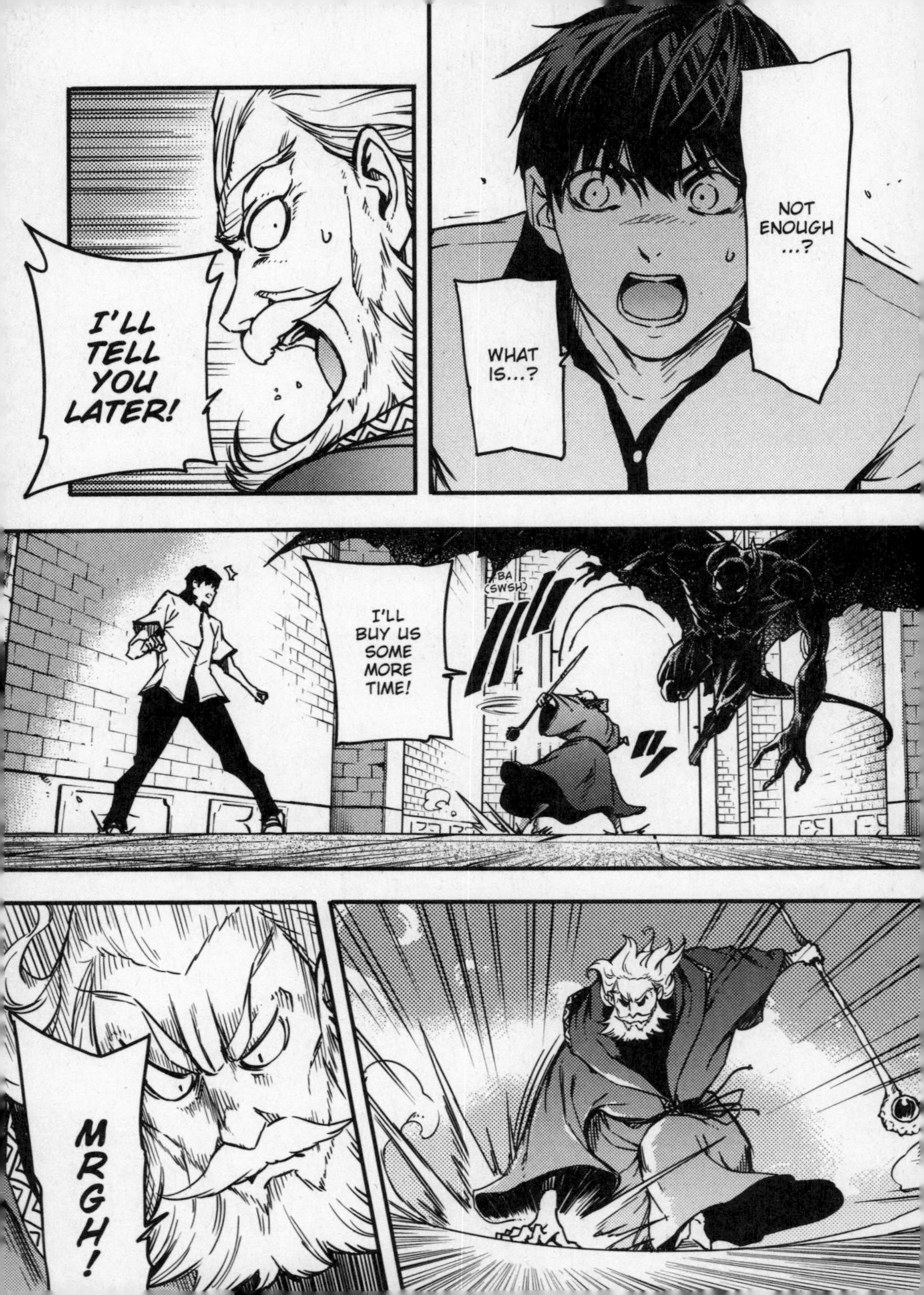
NOT ENOUGH ...?
WHAT IS...?
I'LL TELL YOU LATER!
BA (SWSH)
I'LL BUY US SOME MORE TIME!
MRGH!

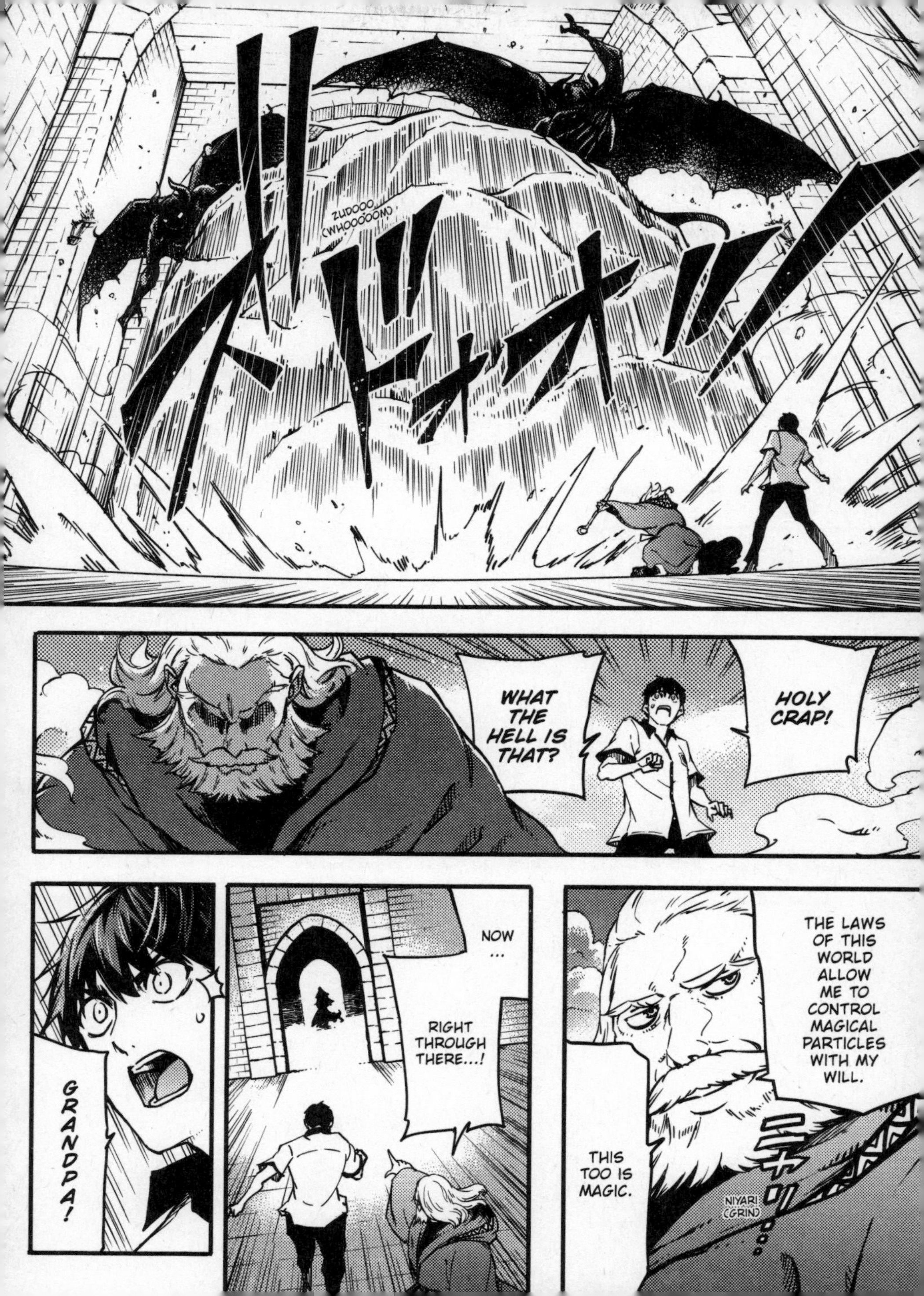
ZUDOOO (WHOOOOOM)
HOLY CRAP!
WHAT THE HELL IS THAT?
THE LAWS OF THIS WORLD ALLOW ME TO CONTROL MAGICAL PARTICLES WITH MY WILL.
THIS TOO IS MAGIC.
NIYARI (GRIN)
NOW...
RIGHT THROUGH THERE...!
GRANDPA!

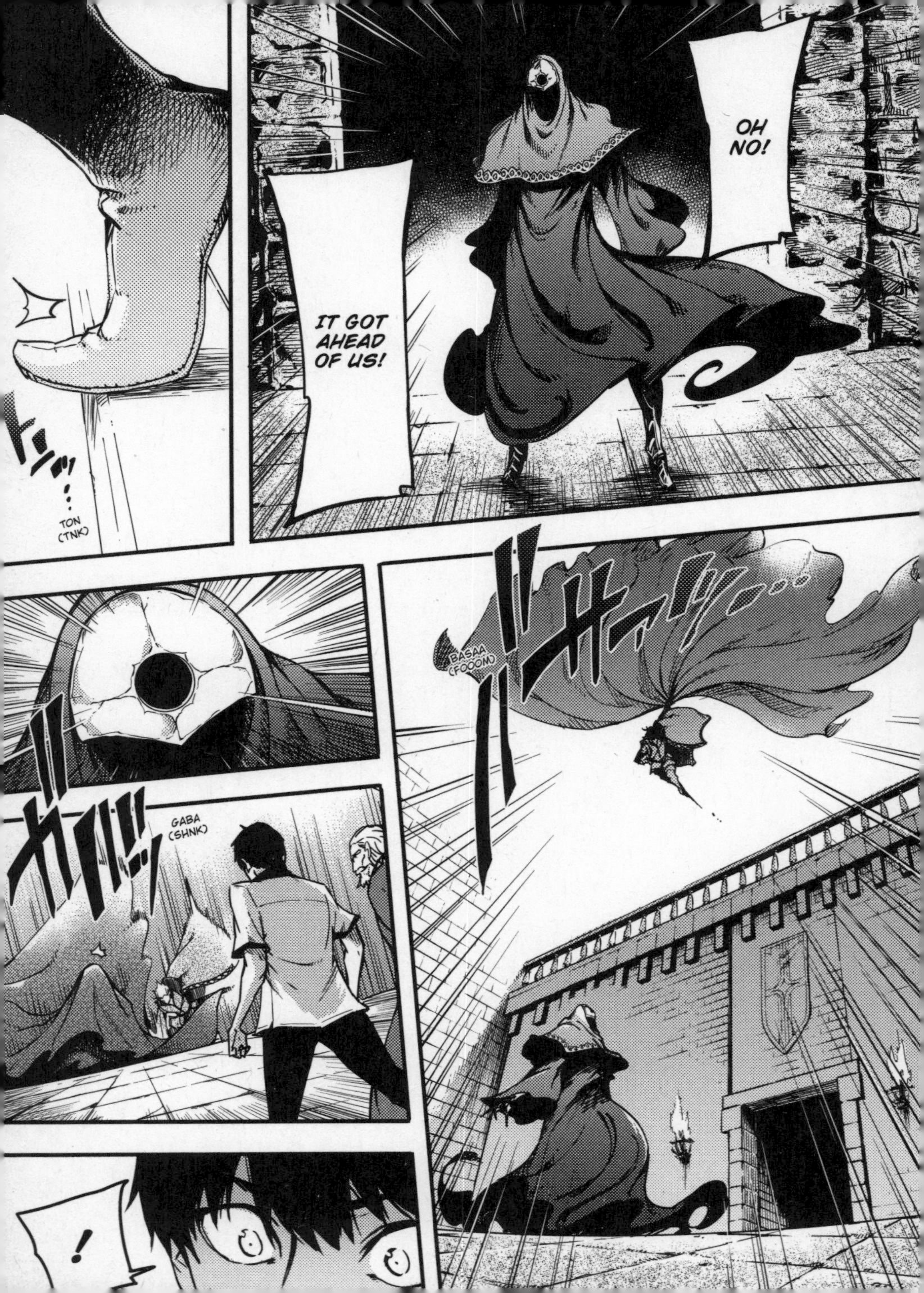
OH NO!
IT GOT AHEAD OF US!
TON (TNK)
BASAA (FOOOM)
GABA (SHNK)
!

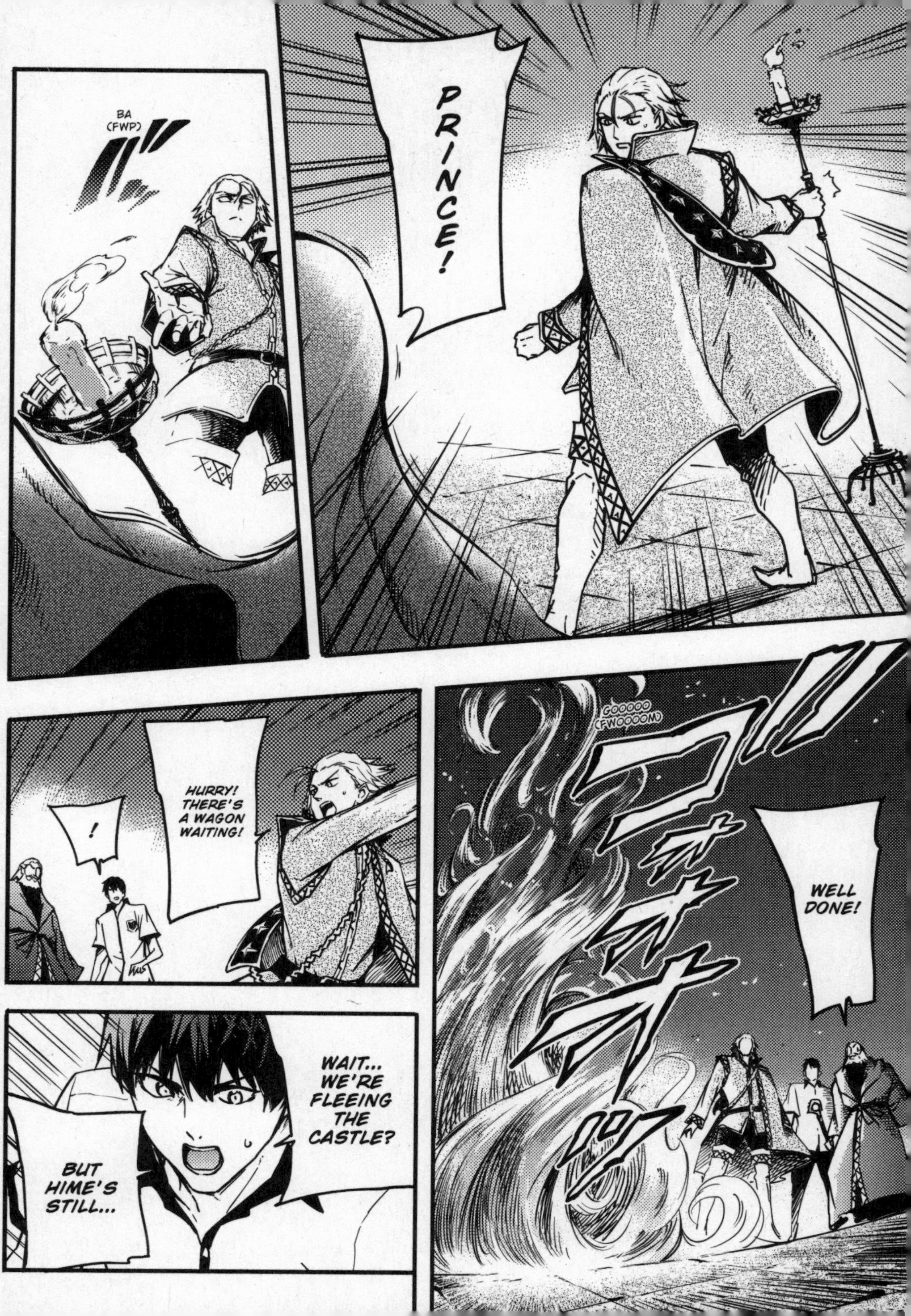
PRINCE!
BA
(FWP)
GOOOOO
(FWOOOOM)
WELL DONE!
HURRY! THERE'S A WAGON WAITING!
!
WAIT... WE'RE FLEEING THE CASTLE?
BUT HIME'S STILL...

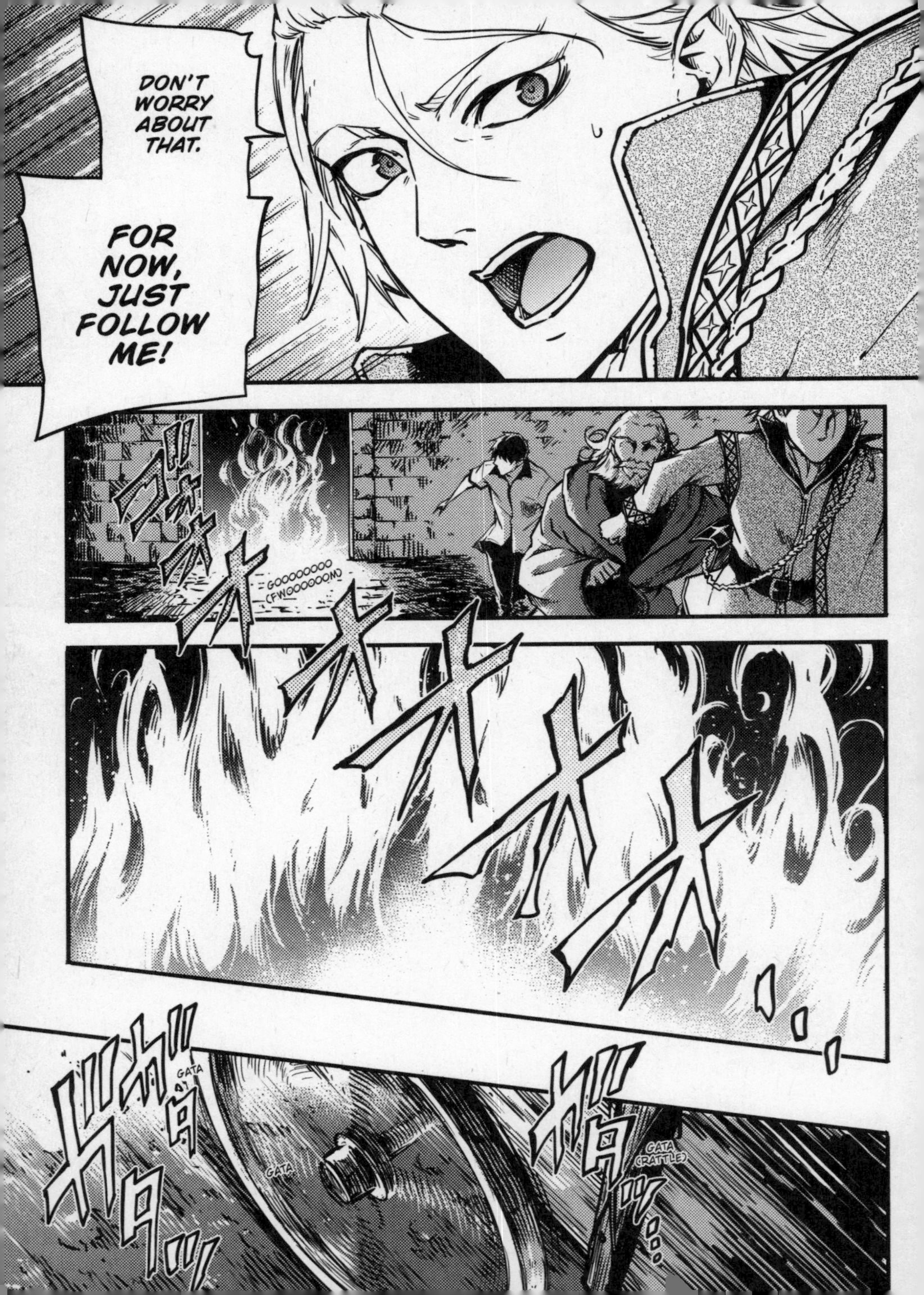

DON'T WORRY ABOUT THAT.
FOR NOW, JUST FOLLOW ME!
GOOOOOOOOO (FWOOOOOOM)
GATA (RATTLE)
GATA
GATA

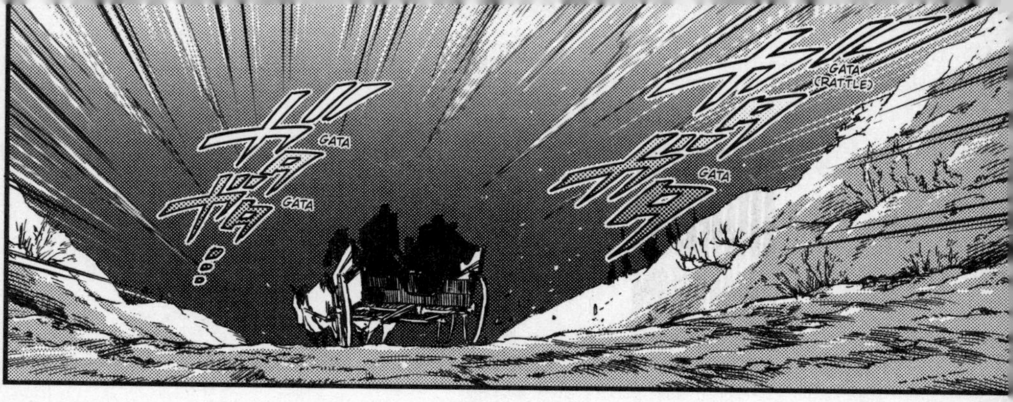
GATA (RATTLE)
GATA
GATA
GATA

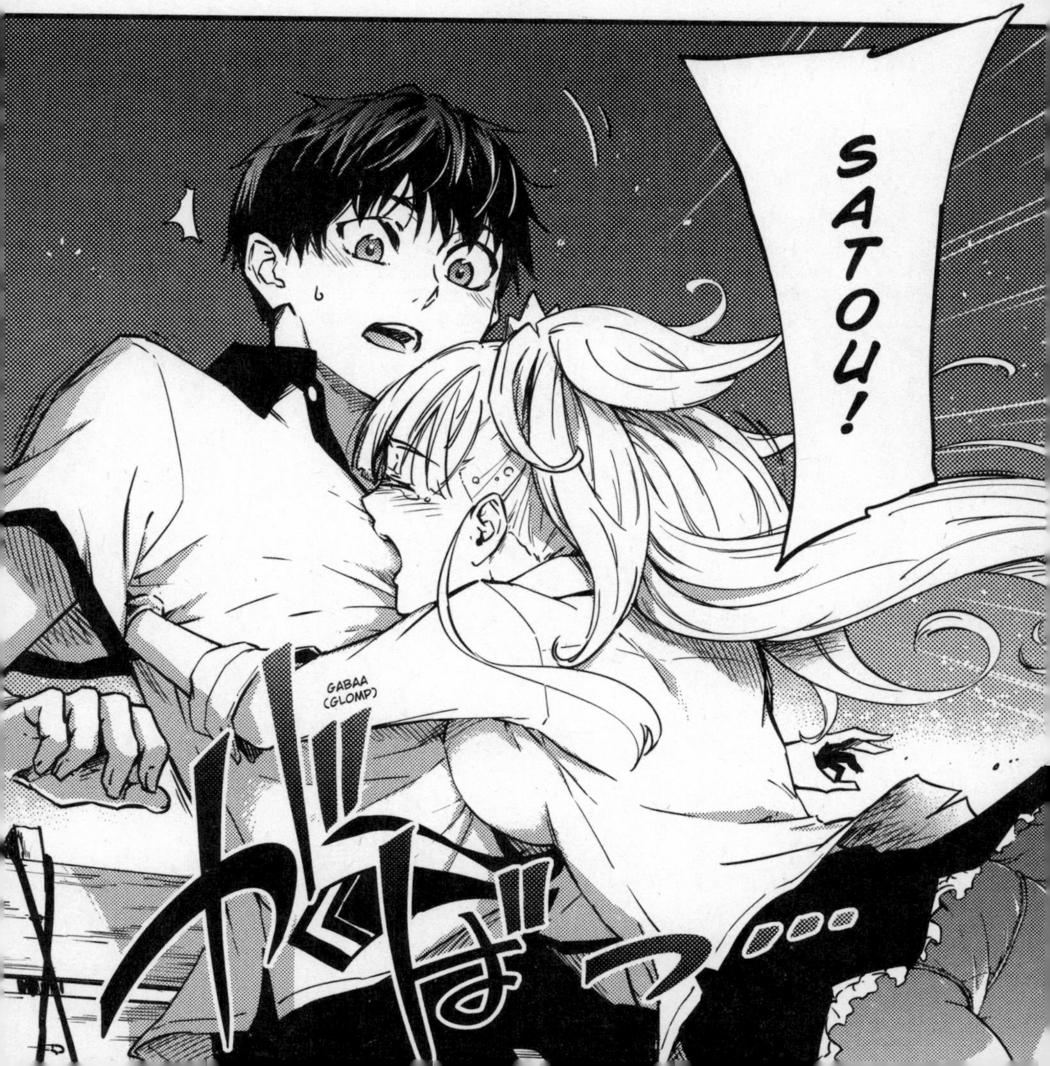
SATOU!
GABAA (GLOMP)

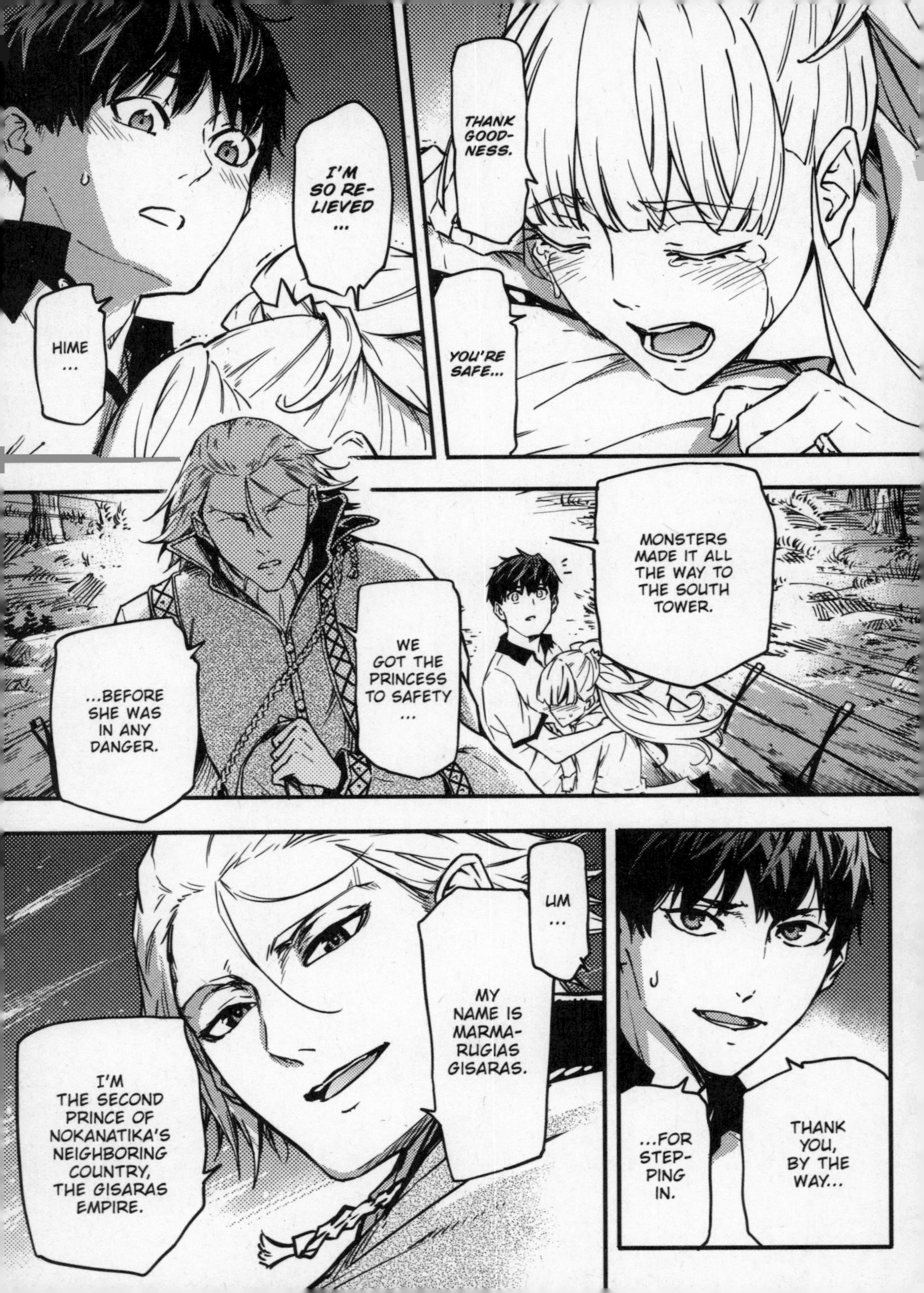
THANK GOODNESS.
YOU'RE SAFE...
I'M SO RELIEVED...
HIME...
MONSTERS MADE IT ALL THE WAY TO THE SOUTH TOWER.
WE GOT THE PRINCESS TO SAFETY...
...BEFORE SHE WAS IN ANY DANGER.
THANK YOU, BY THE WAY...
...FOR STEPPING IN.
UM...
MY NAME IS MARMARUGIAS GISARAS.
I'M THE SECOND PRINCE OF NOKANATIKA'S NEIGHBORING COUNTRY, THE GISARAS EMPIRE.

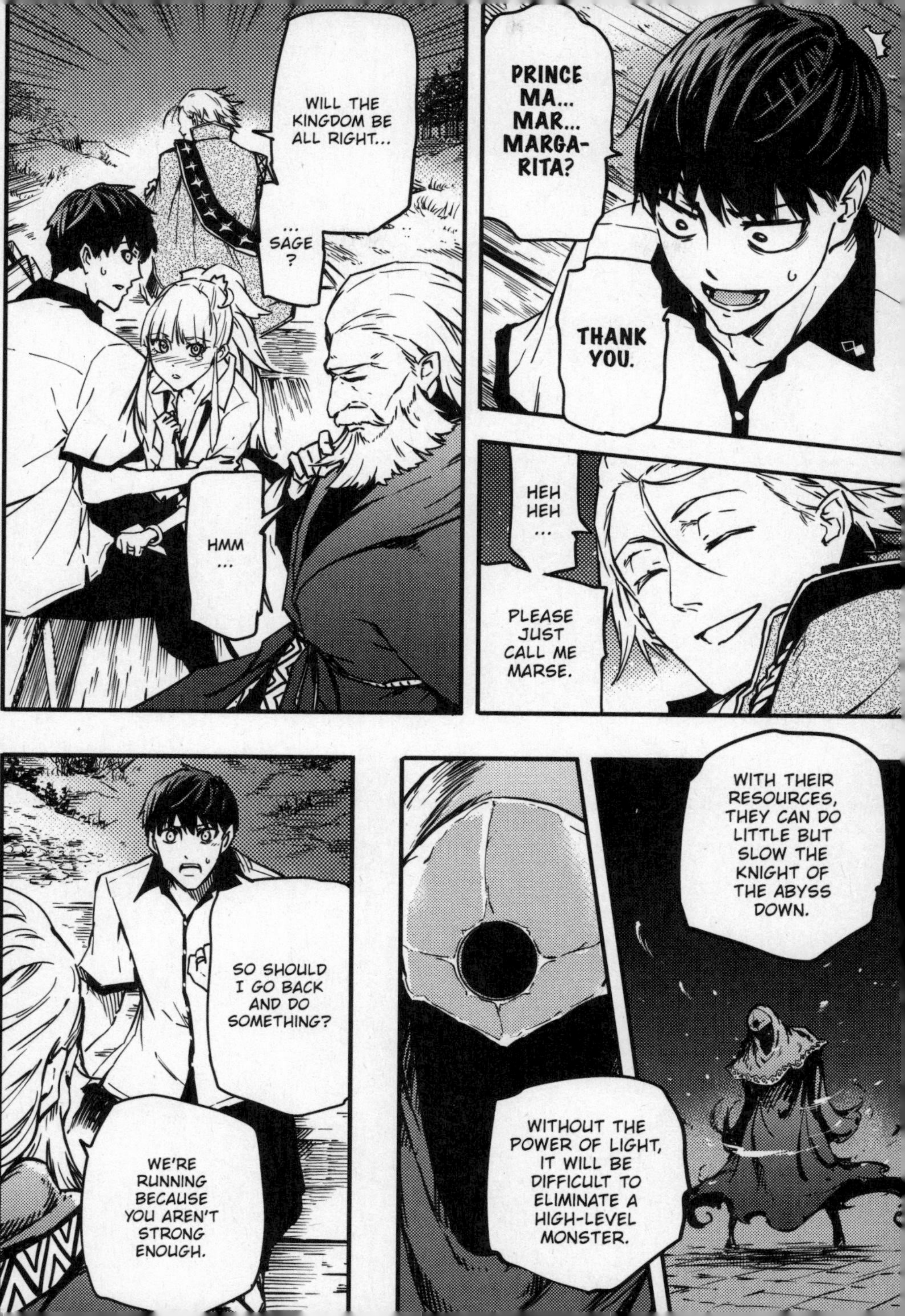
PRINCE MA... MAR... MARGARITA?
THANK YOU.
HEH HEH...
PLEASE JUST CALL ME MARSE.
WILL THE KINGDOM BE ALL RIGHT...
...SAGE?
HMM...
WITH THEIR RESOURCES, THEY CAN DO LITTLE BUT SLOW THE KNIGHT OF THE ABYSS DOWN.
WITHOUT THE POWER OF LIGHT, IT WILL BE DIFFICULT TO ELIMINATE A HIGH-LEVEL MONSTER.
SO SHOULD I GO BACK AND DO SOMETHING?
WE'RE RUNNING BECAUSE YOU AREN'T STRONG ENOUGH.

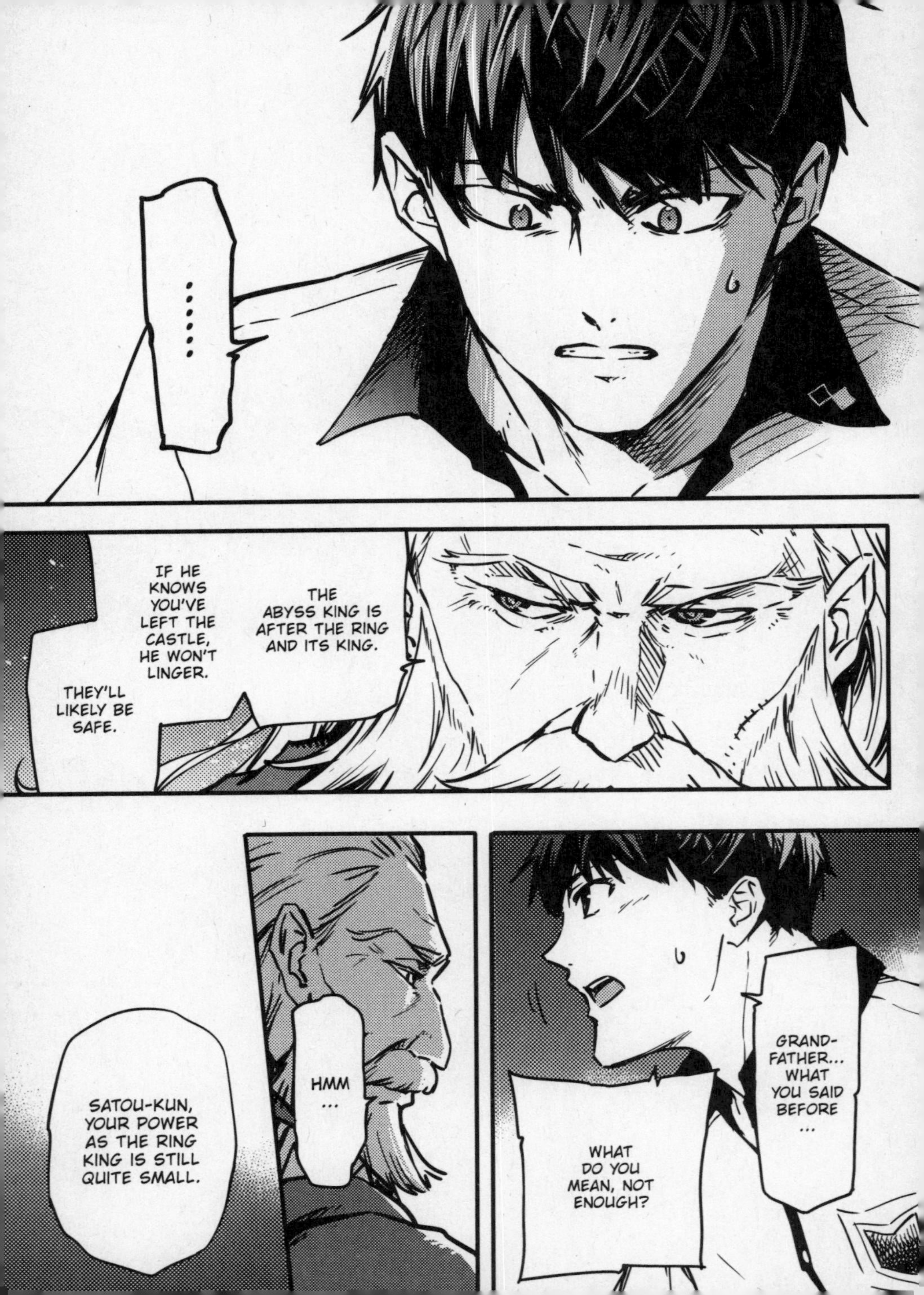
......
THE ABYSS KING IS AFTER THE RING AND ITS KING.
IF HE KNOWS YOU'VE LEFT THE CASTLE, HE WON'T LINGER.
THEY'LL LIKELY BE SAFE.
GRAND-FATHER... WHAT YOU SAID BEFORE...
WHAT DO YOU MEAN, NOT ENOUGH?
HMM...
SATOU-KUN, YOUR POWER AS THE RING KING IS STILL QUITE SMALL.

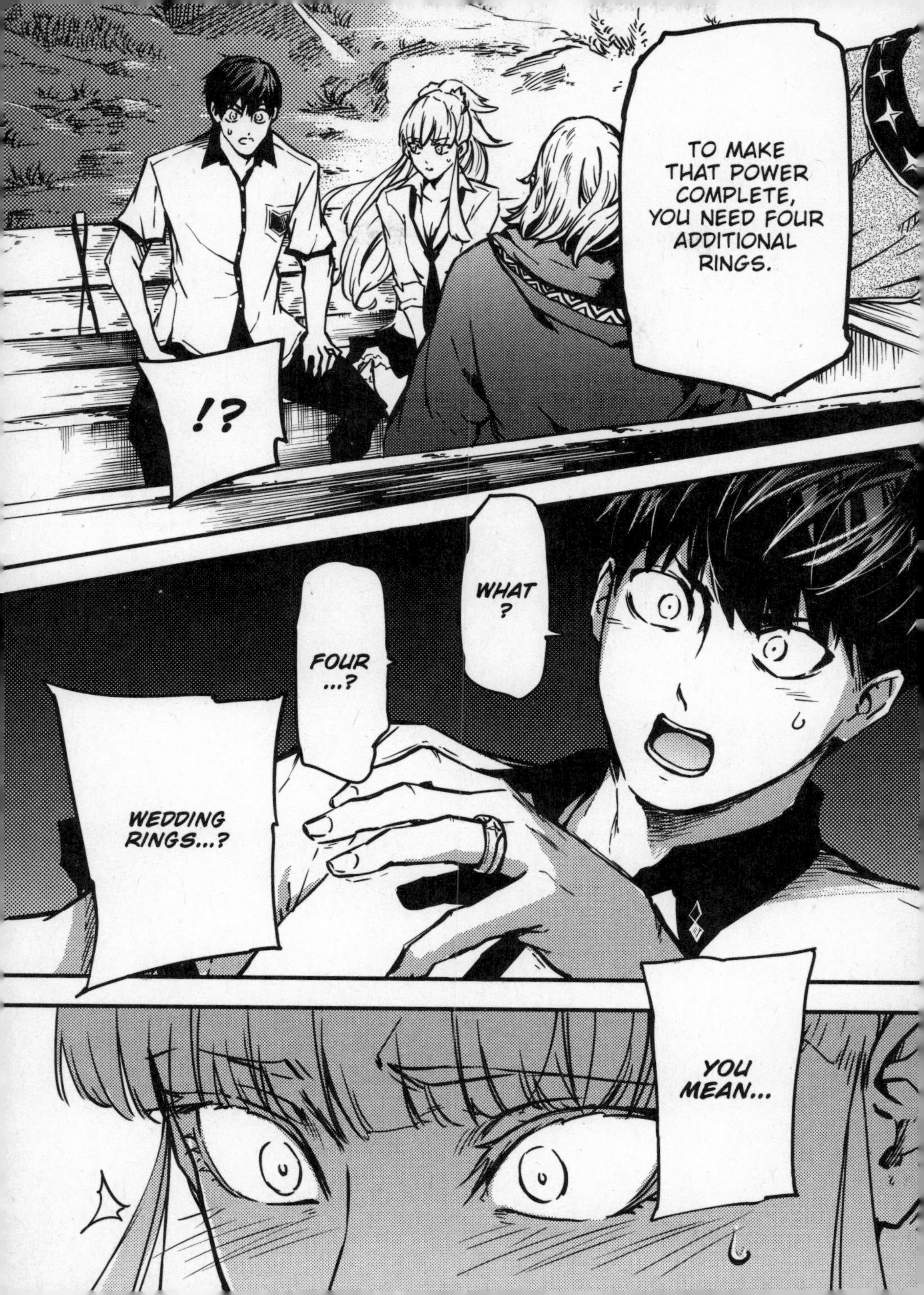
TO MAKE THAT POWER COMPLETE, YOU NEED FOUR ADDITIONAL RINGS.
!?
WHAT?
FOUR...?
WEDDING RINGS...?
YOU MEAN...

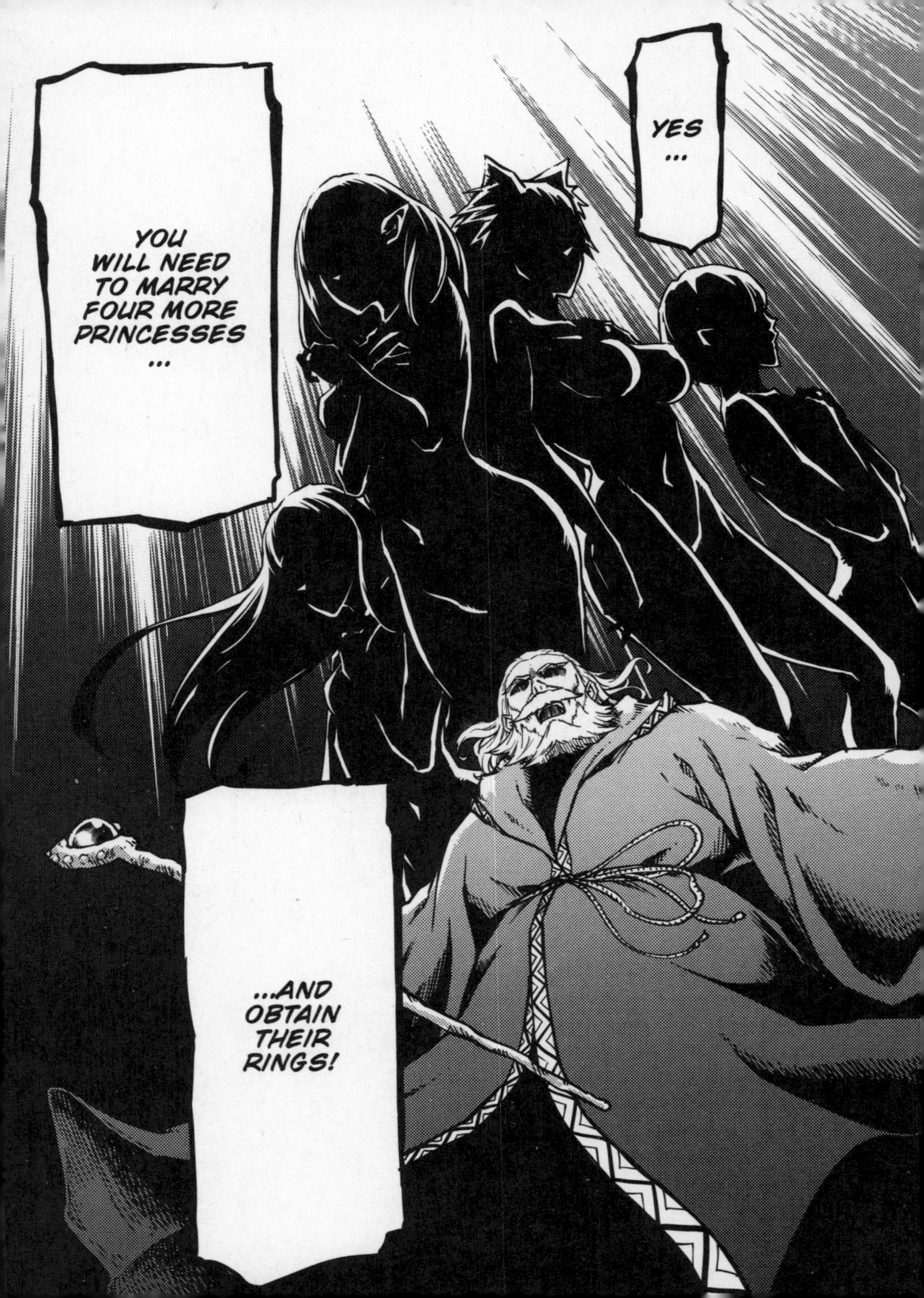
YES ...
YOU WILL NEED TO MARRY FOUR MORE PRINCESSES ...
...AND OBTAIN THEIR RINGS!

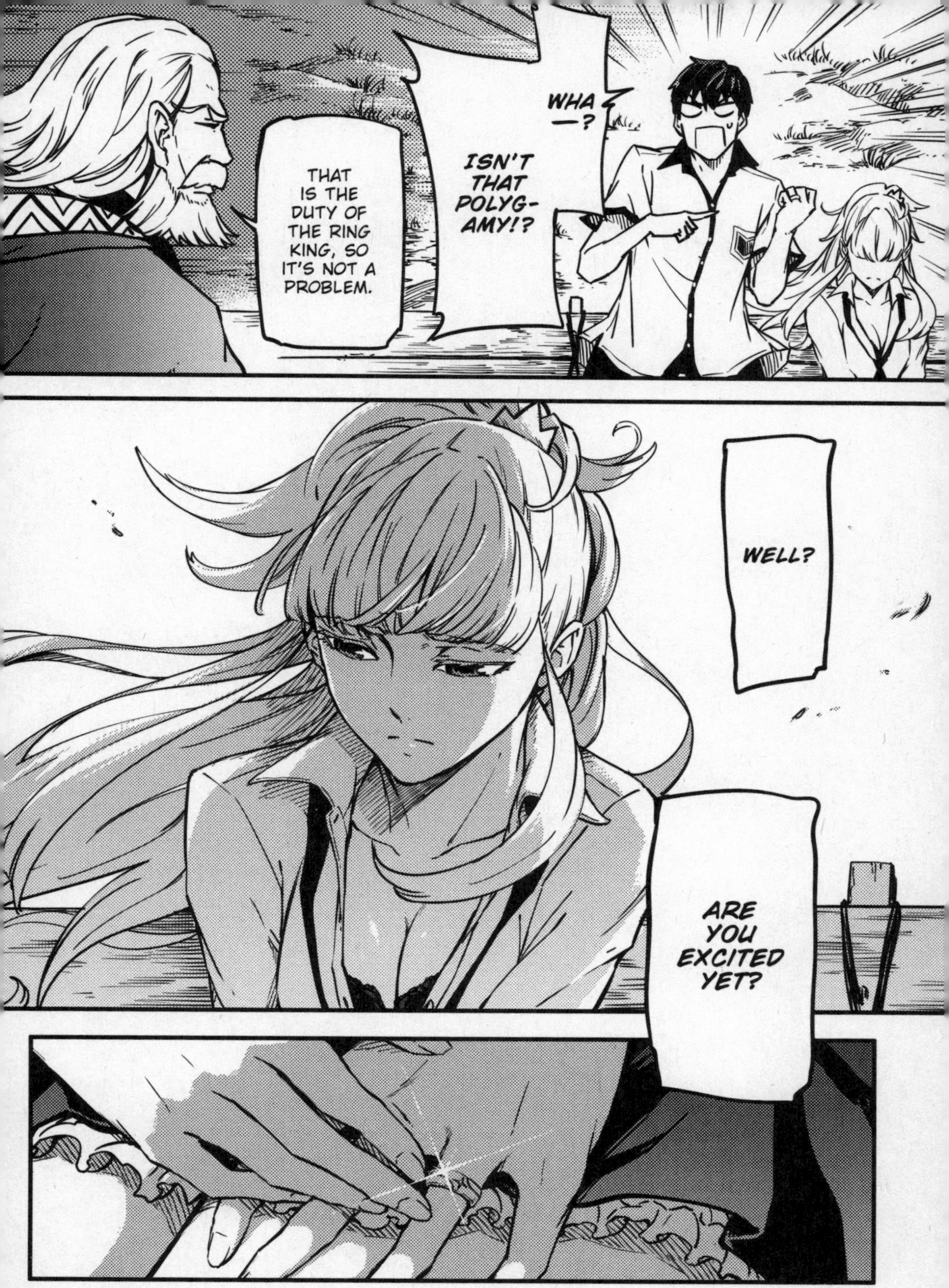
WHA—?
ISN'T THAT POLYGAMY!?
THAT IS THE DUTY OF THE RING KING, SO IT'S NOT A PROBLEM.
WELL?
ARE YOU EXCITED YET?

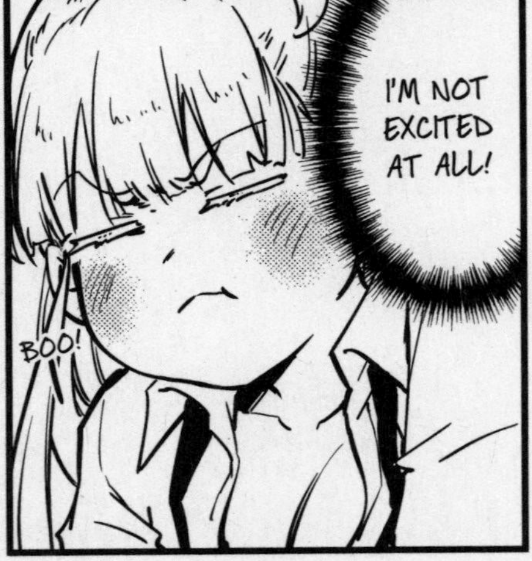
I'M NOT EXCITED AT ALL!
BOO!

Tales of Wedding Rings

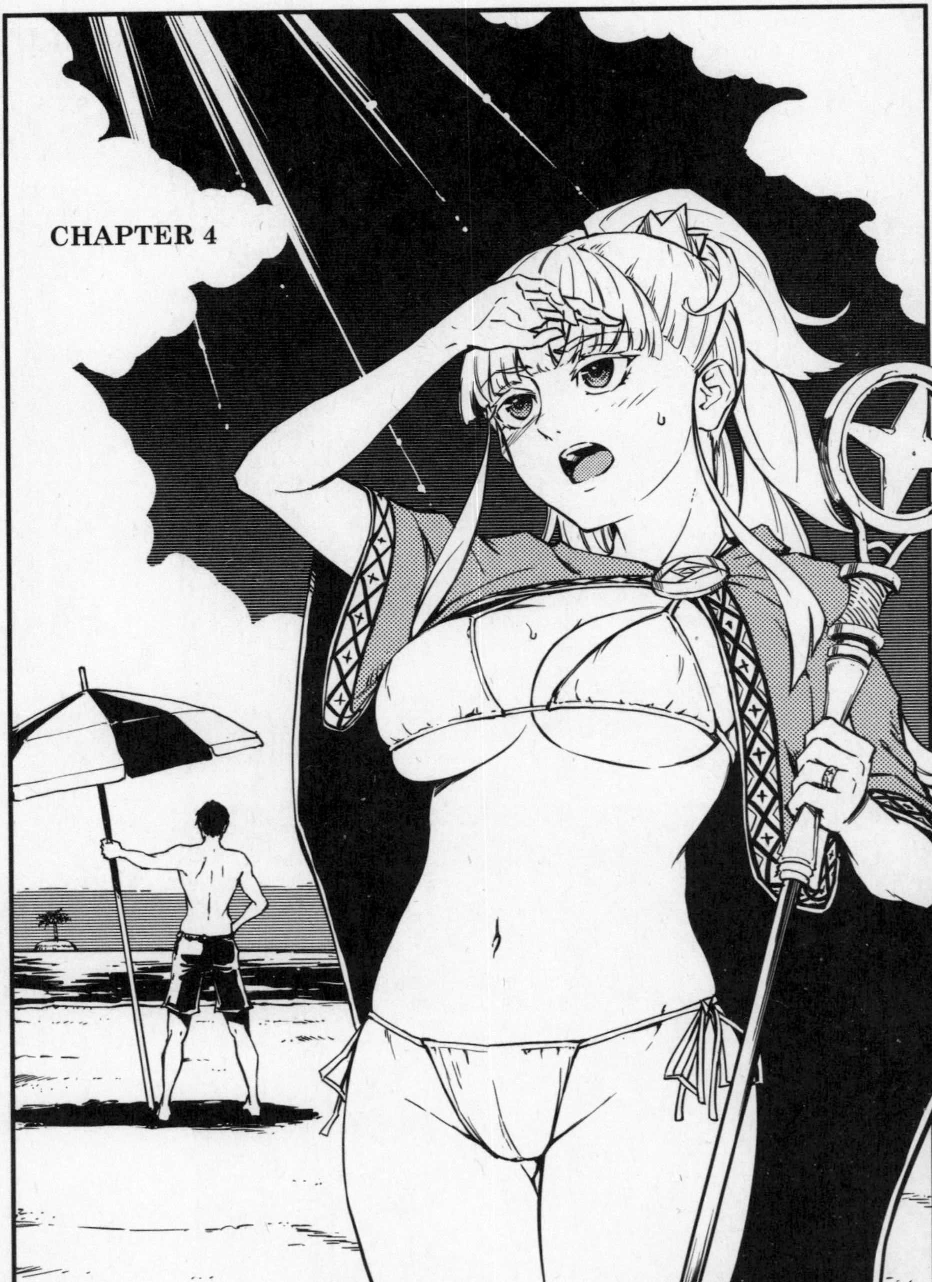
CHAPTER 4

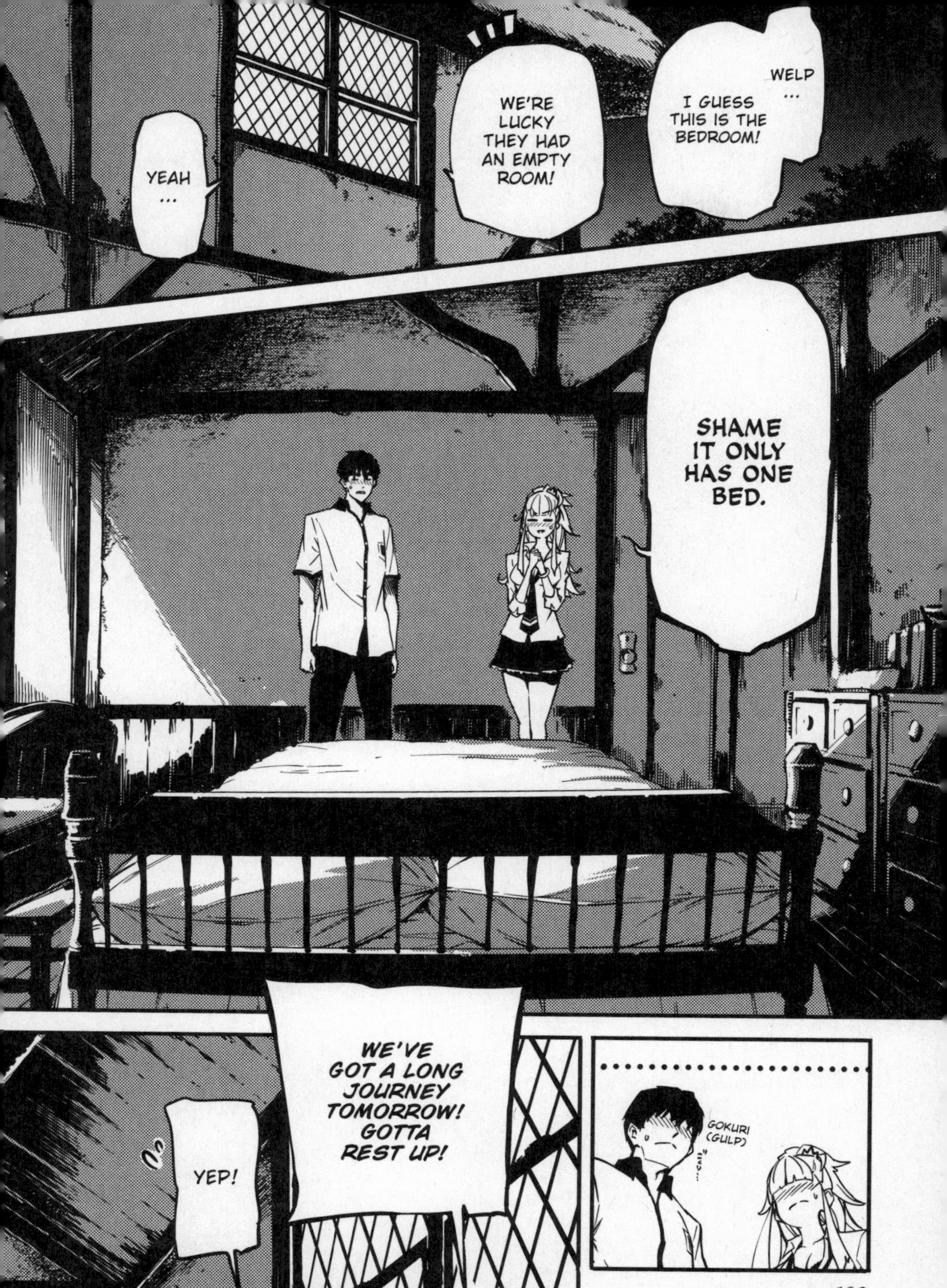
WELP ... I GUESS THIS IS THE BEDROOM!
WE'RE LUCKY THEY HAD AN EMPTY ROOM!
YEAH ...
SHAME IT ONLY HAS ONE BED.
..........
GOKURI (GULP)
WE'VE GOT A LONG JOURNEY TOMORROW! GOTTA REST UP!
YEP!

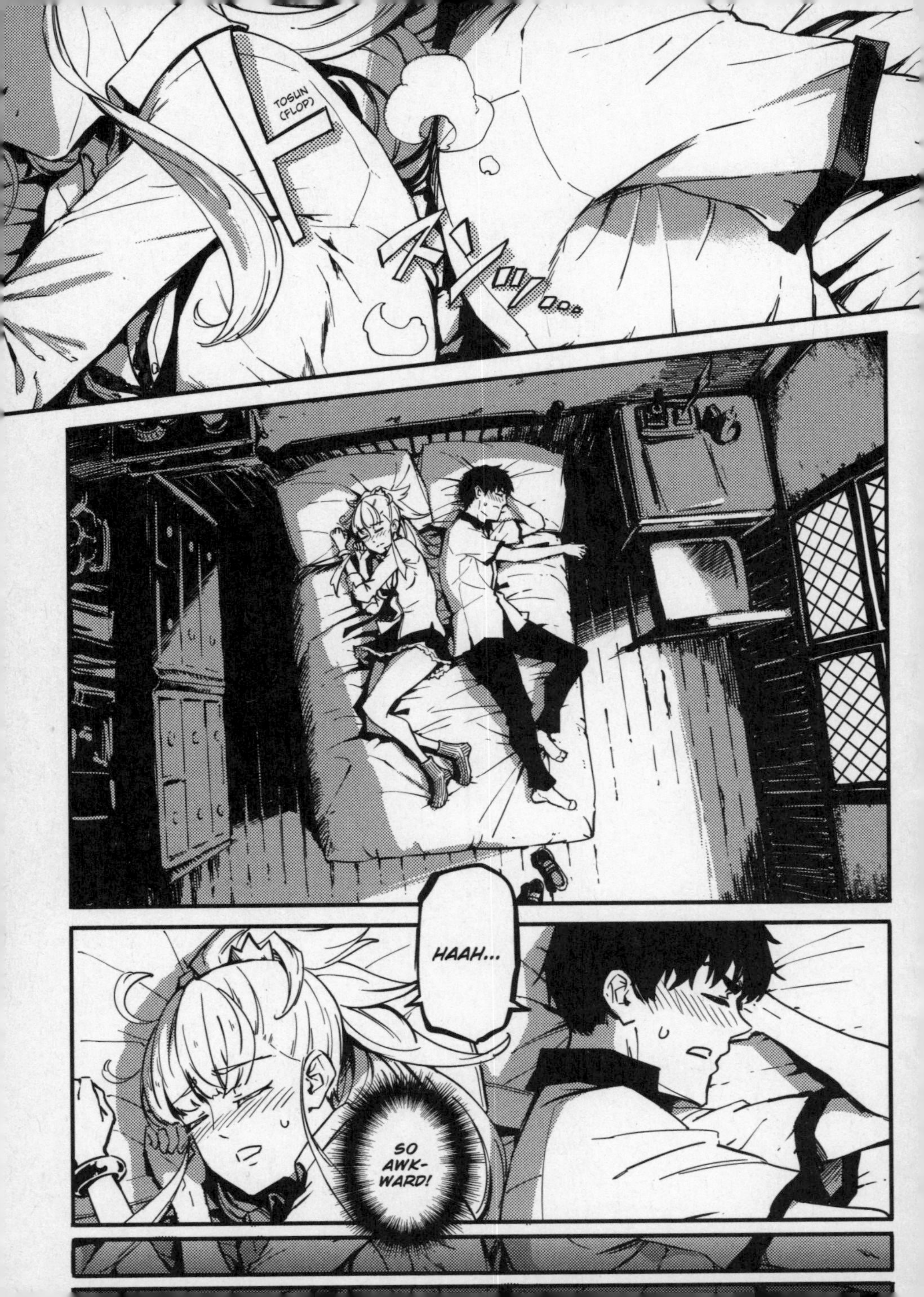
TOSUN (FLOP)
HAAH...
SO AWK-WARD!

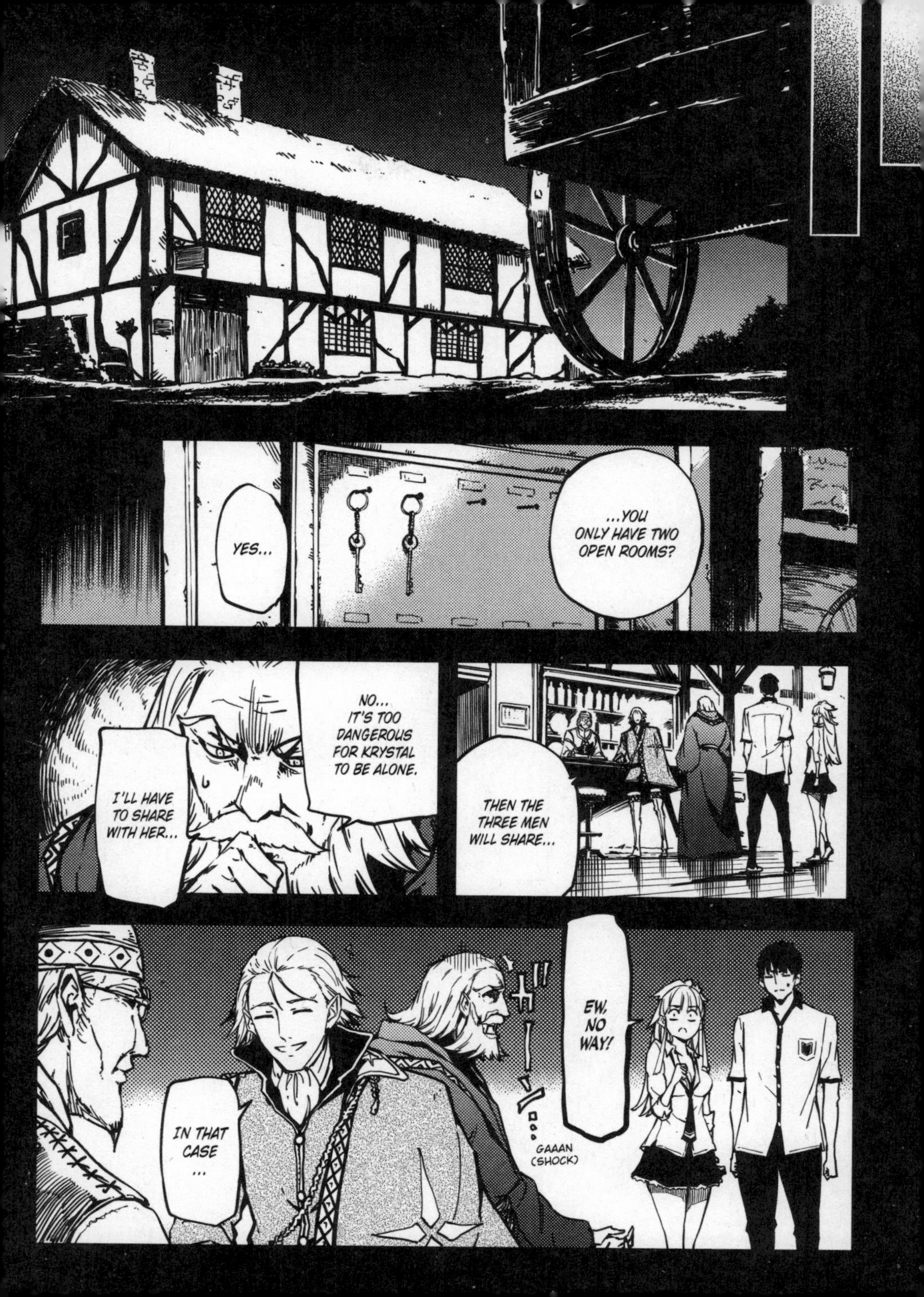
...YOU ONLY HAVE TWO OPEN ROOMS?
YES...
THEN THE THREE MEN WILL SHARE...
NO... IT'S TOO DANGEROUS FOR KRYSTAL TO BE ALONE.
I'LL HAVE TO SHARE WITH HER...
EW, NO WAY!
GAAAN (SHOCK)
IN THAT CASE ...

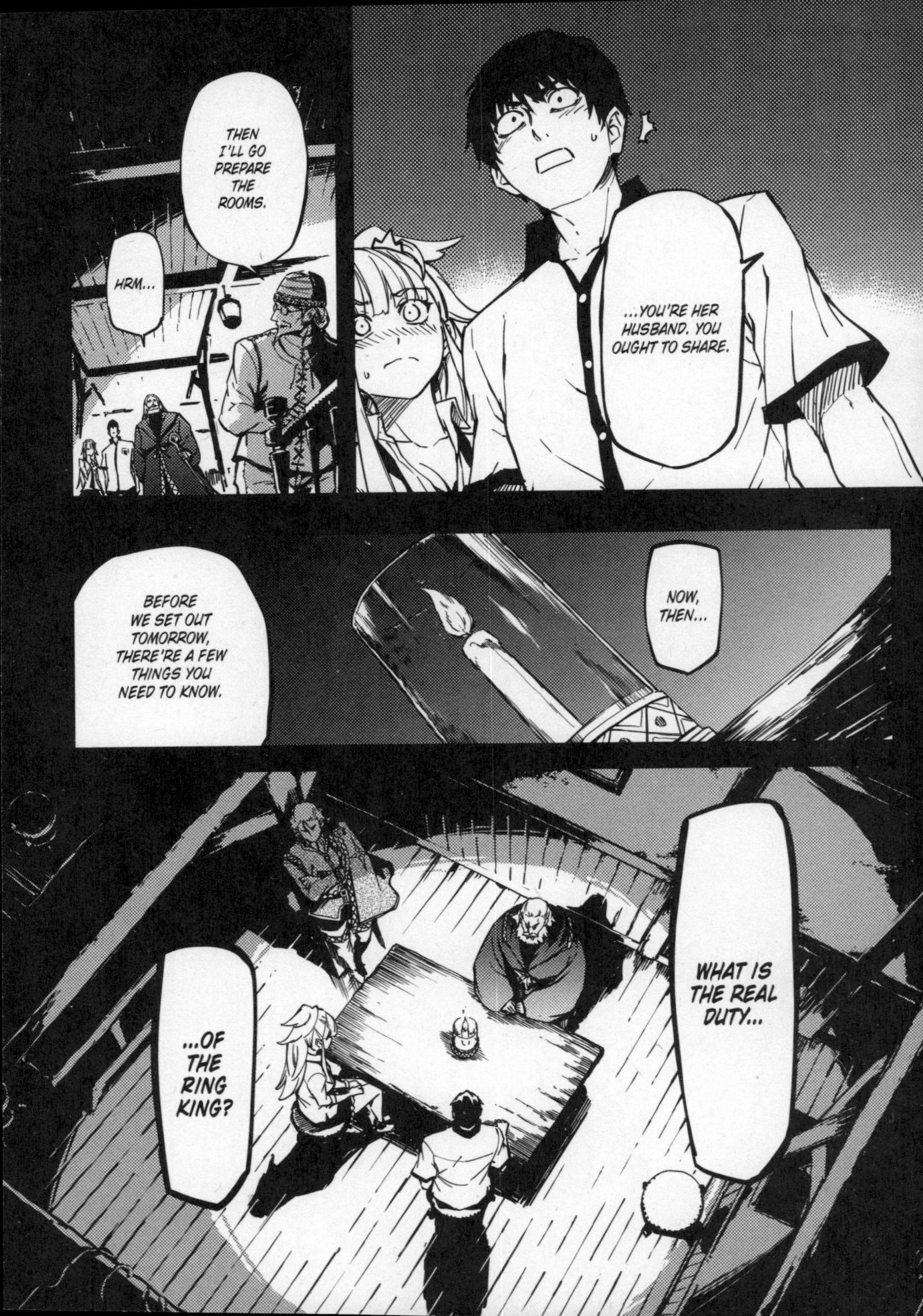
...YOU'RE HER HUSBAND. YOU OUGHT TO SHARE.
THEN I'LL GO PREPARE THE ROOMS.
HRM...
NOW, THEN...
BEFORE WE SET OUT TOMORROW, THERE'RE A FEW THINGS YOU NEED TO KNOW.
WHAT IS THE REAL DUTY...
...OF THE RING KING?

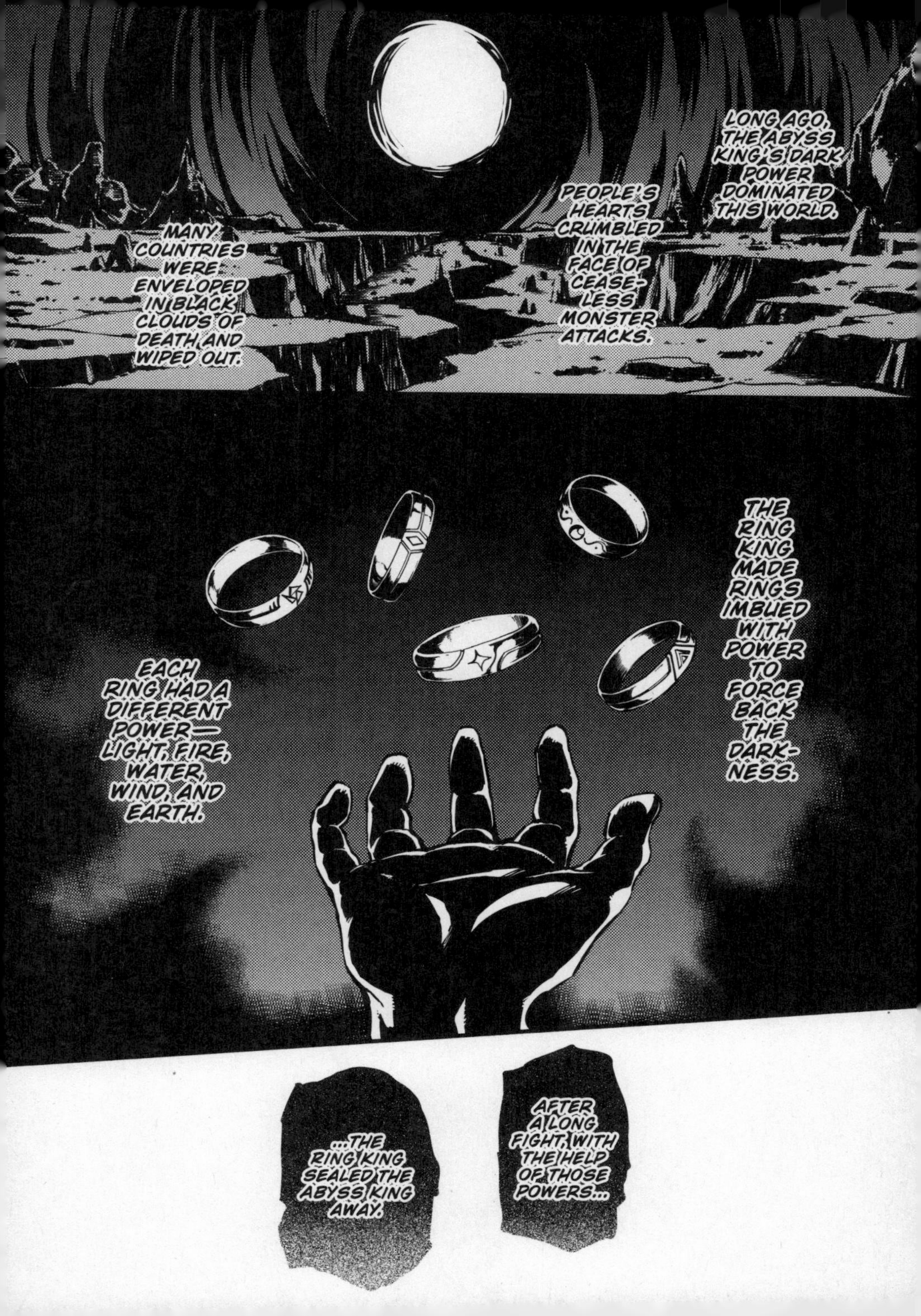
LONG AGO, THE ABYSS KING'S DARK POWER DOMINATED THIS WORLD.
PEOPLE'S HEARTS CRUMBLED IN THE FACE OF CEASE-LESS MONSTER ATTACKS.
MANY COUNTRIES WERE ENVELOPED IN BLACK CLOUDS OF DEATH AND WIPED OUT.
THE RING KING MADE RINGS IMBUED WITH POWER TO FORCE BACK THE DARK-NESS.
EACH RING HAD A DIFFERENT POWER—LIGHT, FIRE, WATER, WIND, AND EARTH.
AFTER A LONG FIGHT, WITH THE HELP OF THOSE POWERS...
...THE RING KING SEALED THE ABYSS KING AWAY.

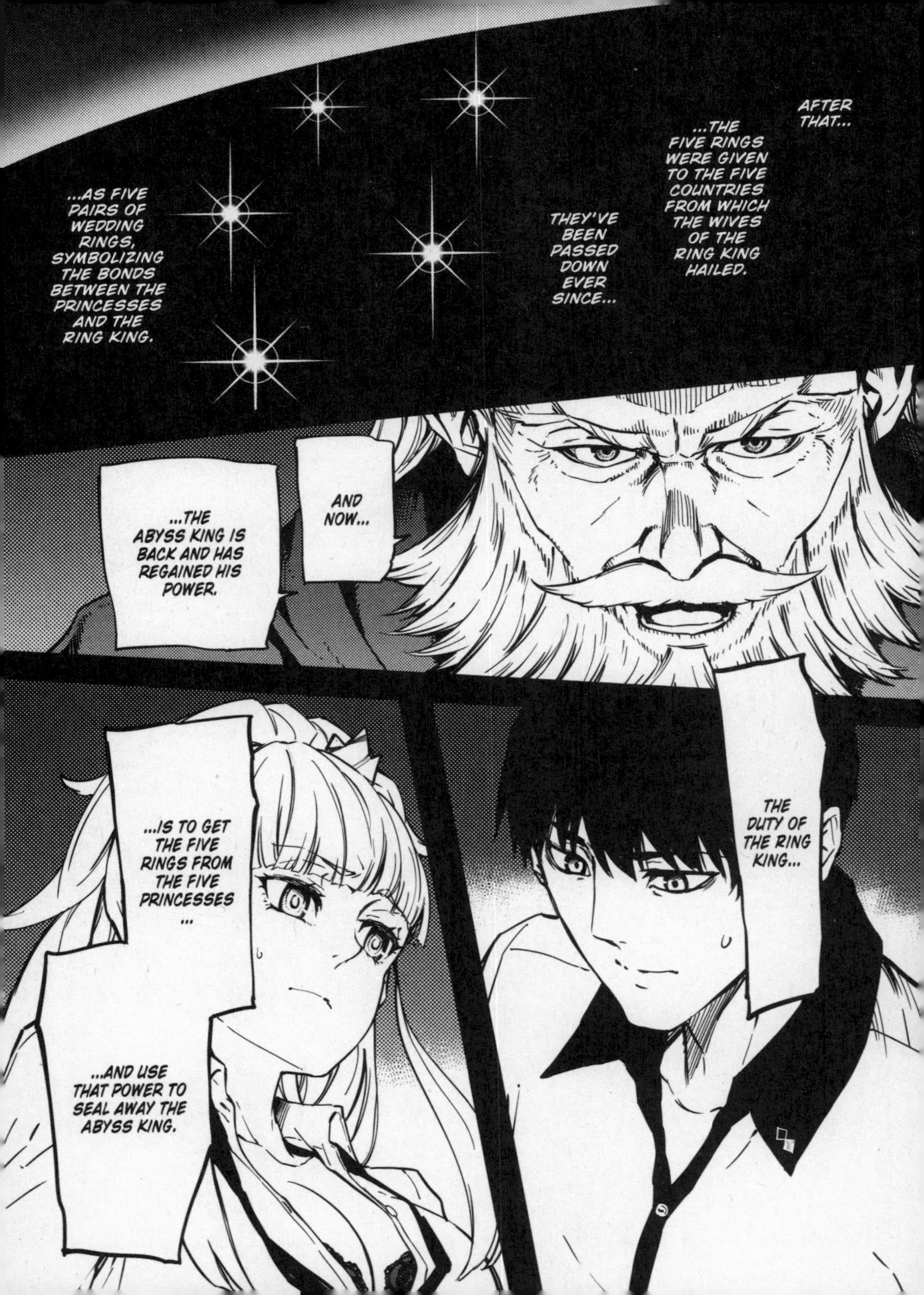
AFTER THAT...
...THE FIVE RINGS WERE GIVEN TO THE FIVE COUNTRIES FROM WHICH THE WIVES OF THE RING KING HAILED.
THEY'VE BEEN PASSED DOWN EVER SINCE...
...AS FIVE PAIRS OF WEDDING RINGS, SYMBOLIZING THE BONDS BETWEEN THE PRINCESSES AND THE RING KING.
AND NOW...
...THE ABYSS KING IS BACK AND HAS REGAINED HIS POWER.
THE DUTY OF THE RING KING...
...IS TO GET THE FIVE RINGS FROM THE FIVE PRINCESSES ...
...AND USE THAT POWER TO SEAL AWAY THE ABYSS KING.

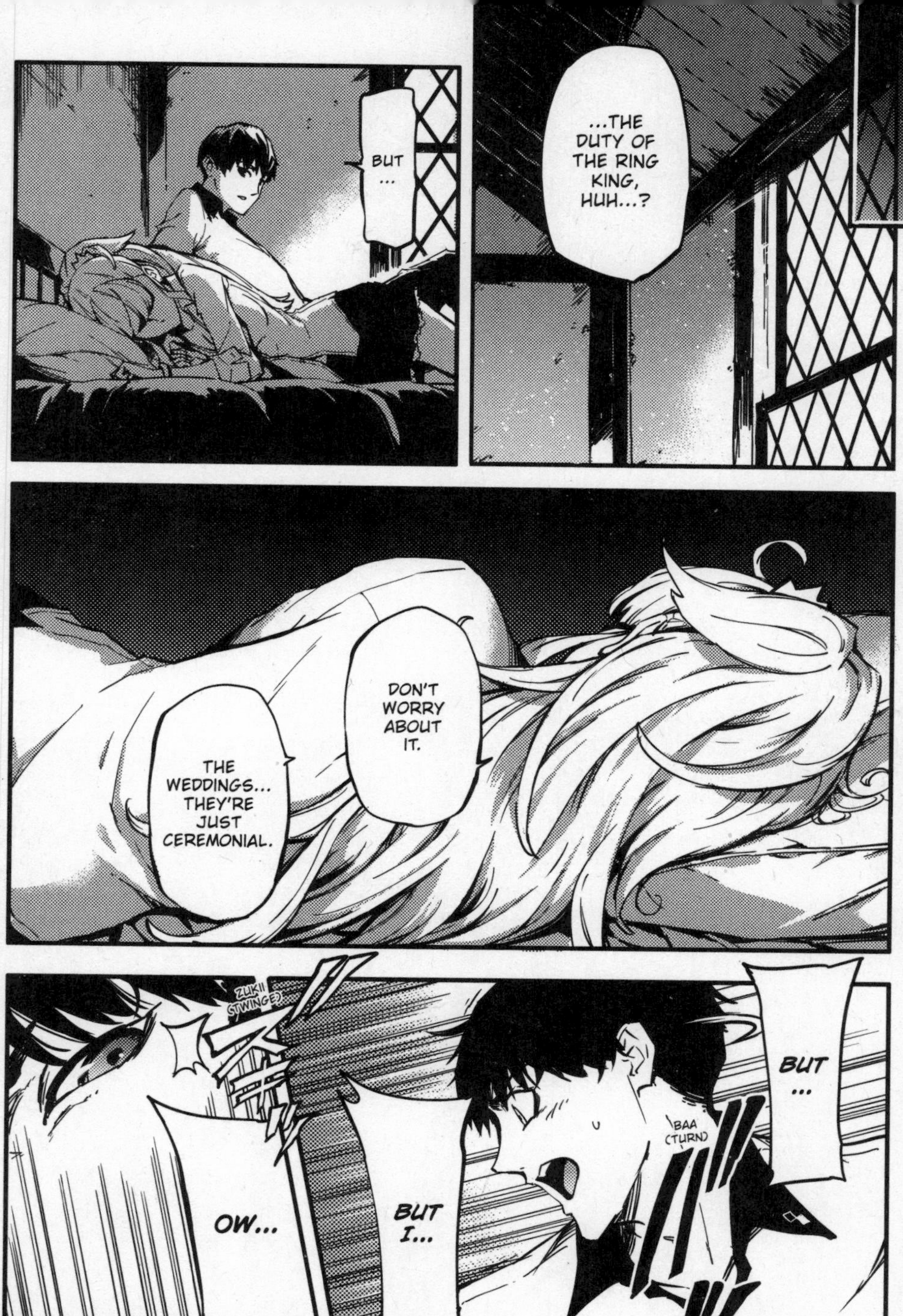
...THE DUTY OF THE RING KING, HUH...?
BUT ...
DON'T WORRY ABOUT IT.
THE WEDDINGS... THEY'RE JUST CEREMONIAL.
BUT ...
BAA (TURN)
BUT I...
ZUKII (TWINGE)
OW...

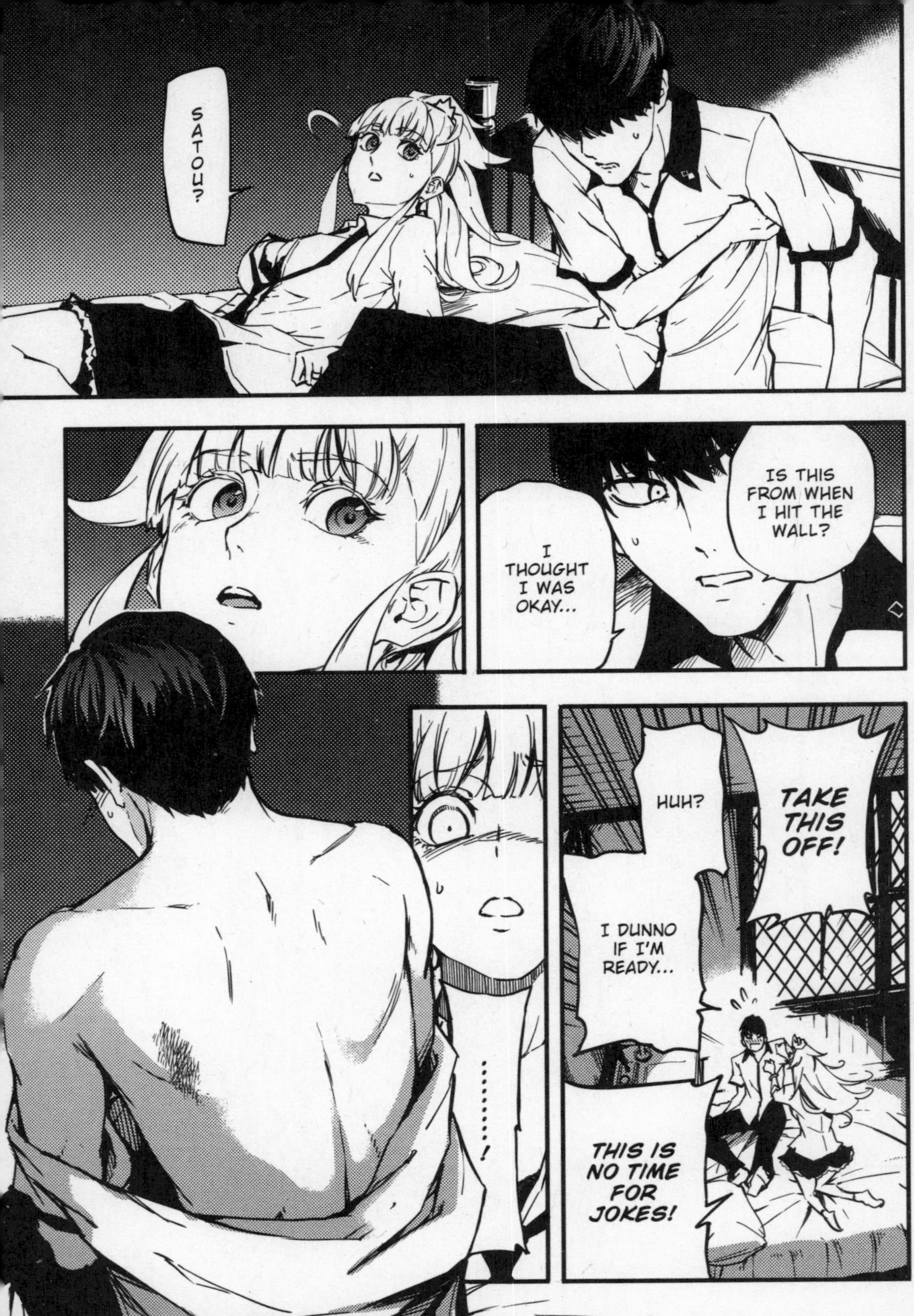
SATOU?
IS THIS FROM WHEN I HIT THE WALL?
I THOUGHT I WAS OKAY...
TAKE THIS OFF!
HUH?
I DUNNO IF I'M READY...
THIS IS NO TIME FOR JOKES!
......!

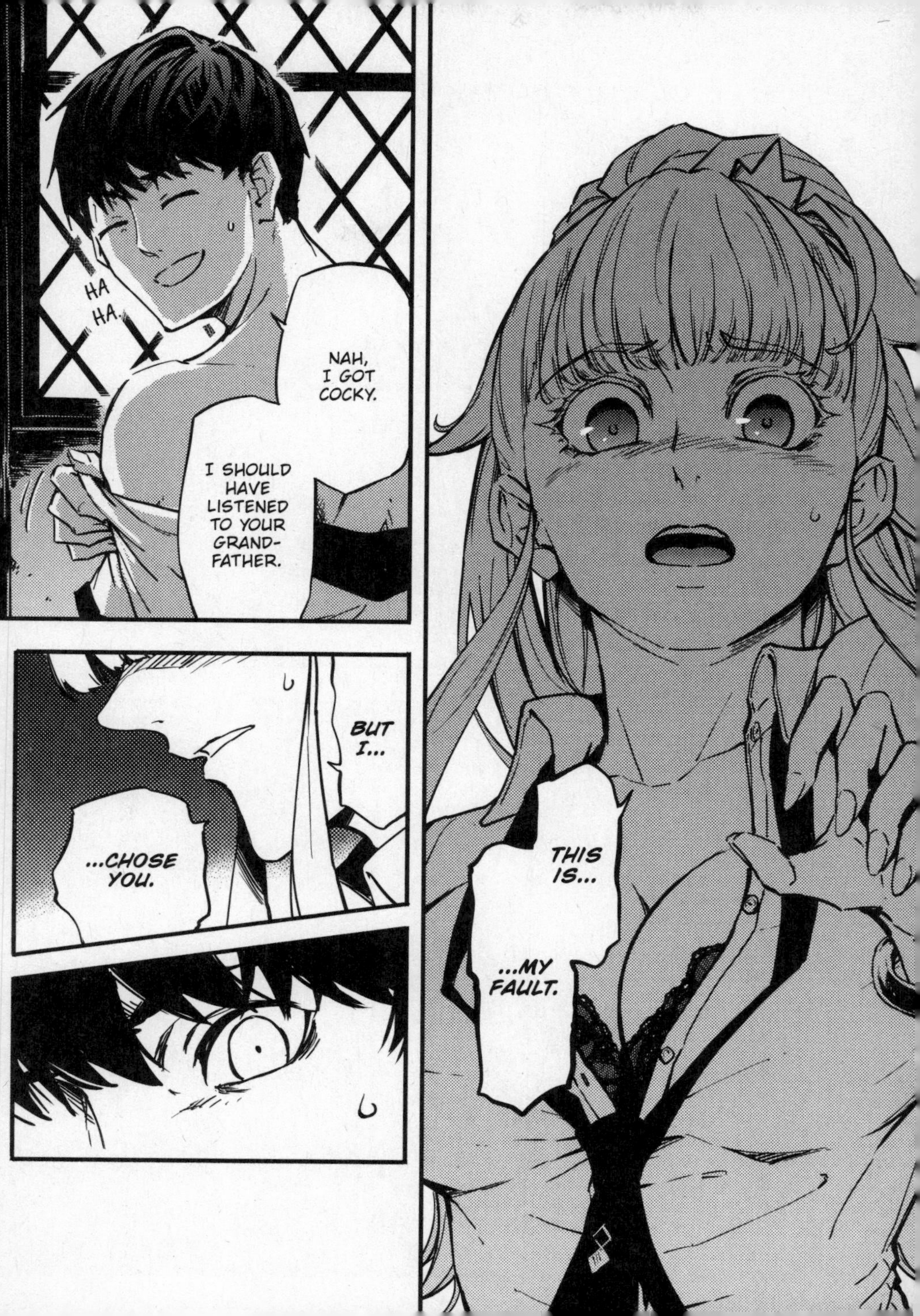
THIS IS...
...MY FAULT.
HA HA.
NAH, I GOT COCKY.
I SHOULD HAVE LISTENED TO YOUR GRAND-FATHER.
BUT I...
...CHOSE YOU.

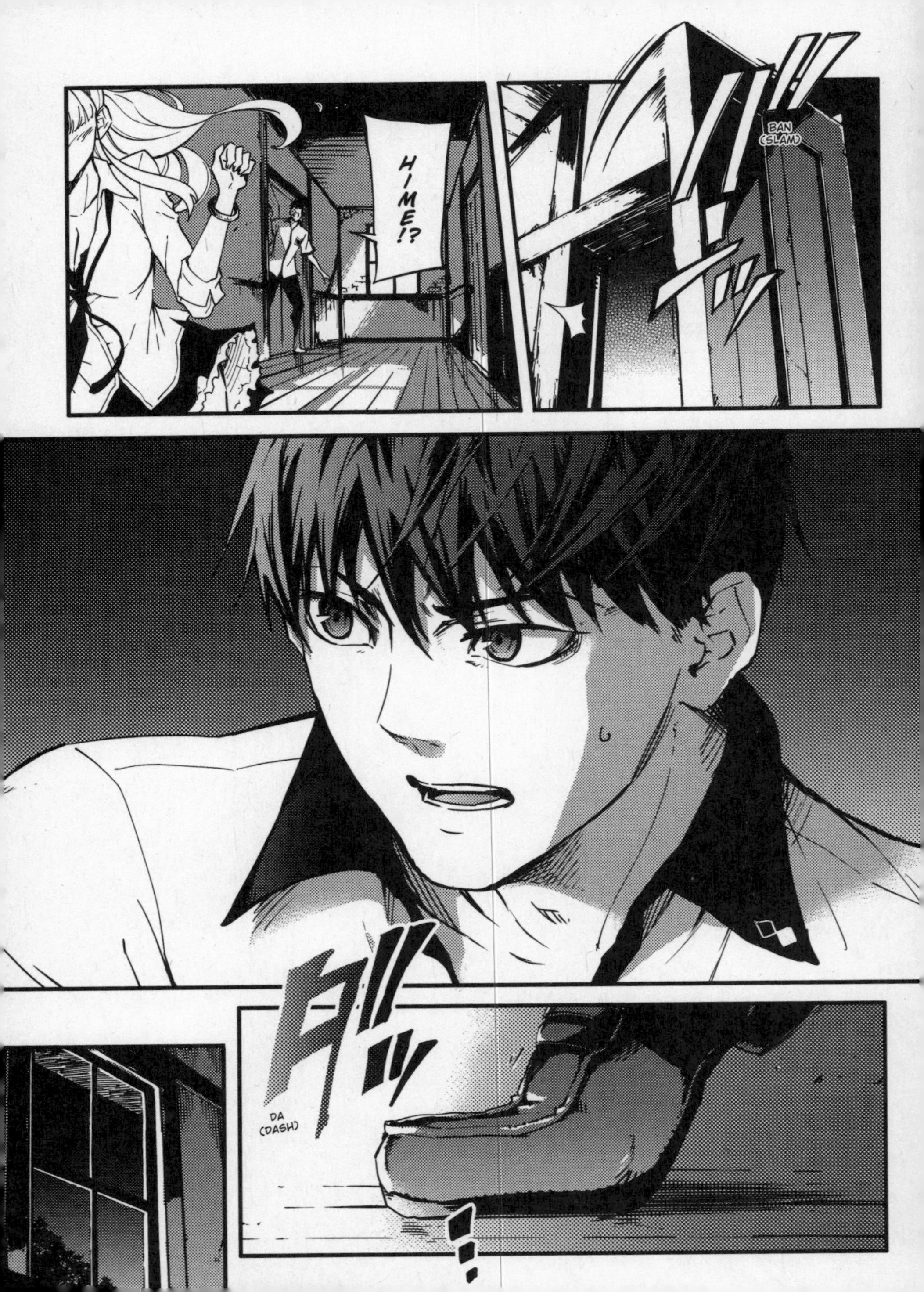
BAN
(SLAM)
HIME!?
DA
(DASH)

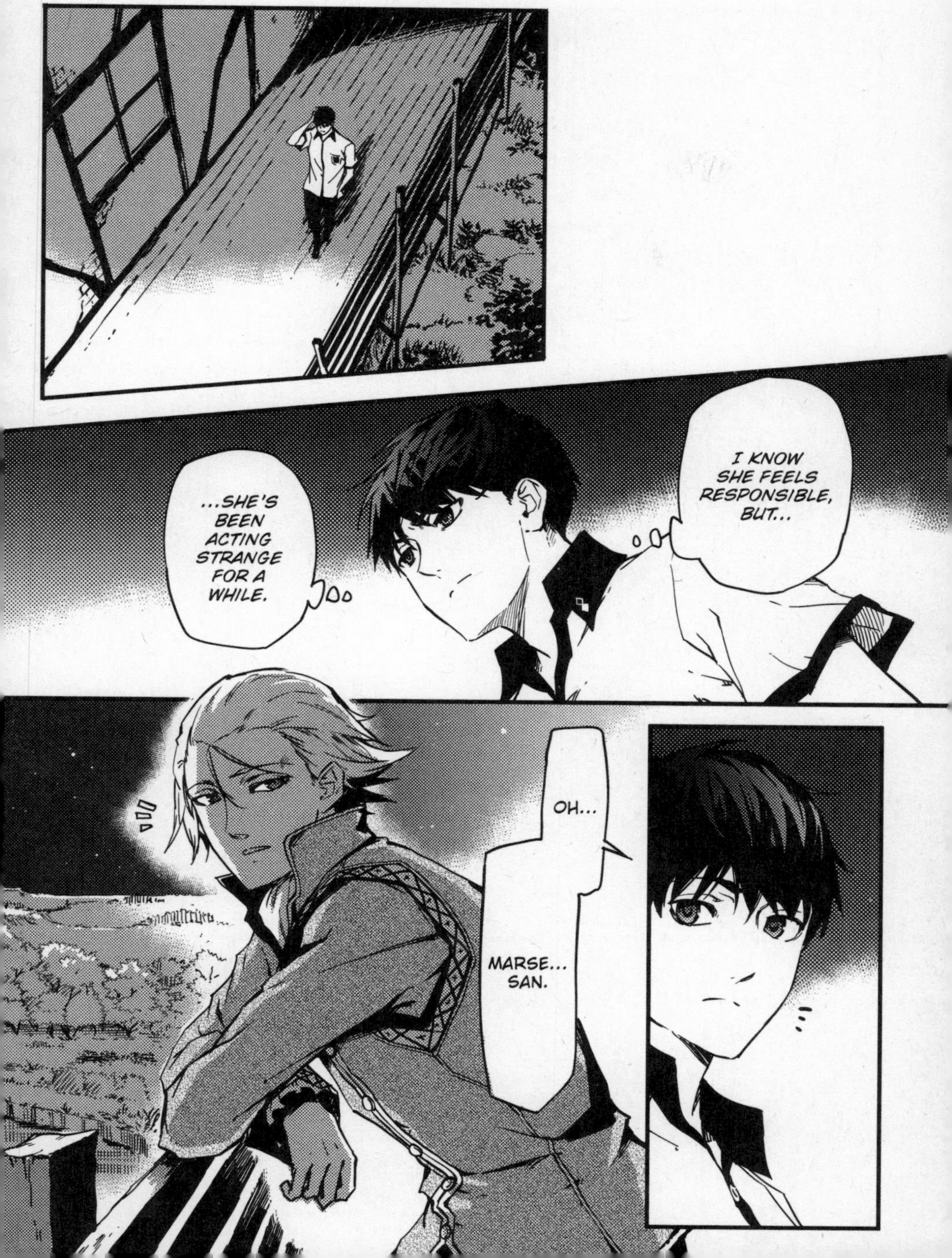
I KNOW SHE FEELS RESPONSIBLE, BUT...
...SHE'S BEEN ACTING STRANGE FOR A WHILE.
OH...
MARSE... SAN.

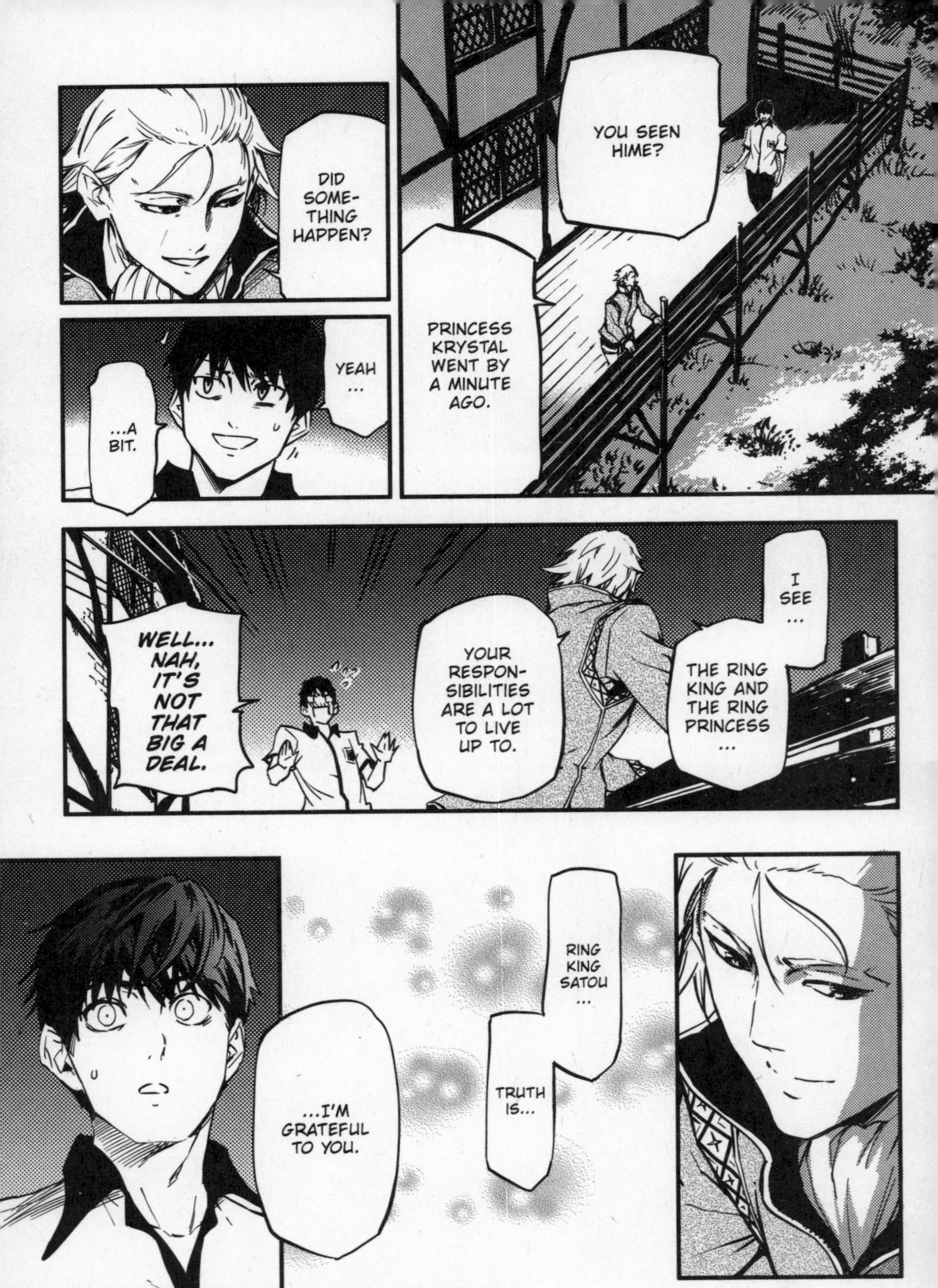
YOU SEEN HIME?
PRINCESS KRYSTAL WENT BY A MINUTE AGO.
DID SOME-THING HAPPEN?
YEAH...
...A BIT.
I SEE...
THE RING KING AND THE RING PRINCESS...
YOUR RESPON-SIBILITIES ARE A LOT TO LIVE UP TO.
WELL... NAH, IT'S NOT THAT BIG A DEAL.
RING KING SATOU...
TRUTH IS...
...I'M GRATEFUL TO YOU.

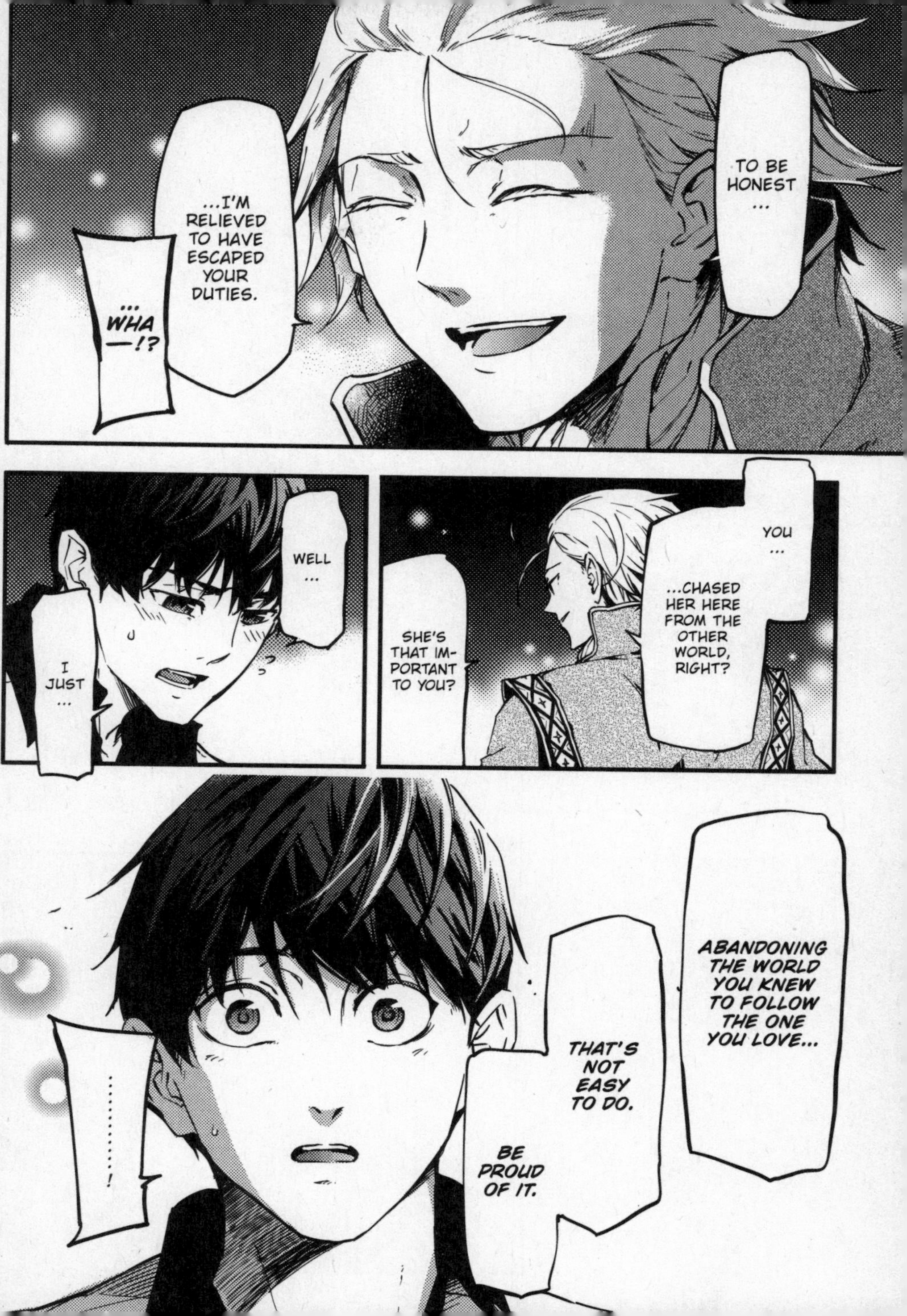
TO BE HONEST ...
...I'M RELIEVED TO HAVE ESCAPED YOUR DUTIES.
... WHA—!?
YOU ...
...CHASED HER HERE FROM THE OTHER WORLD, RIGHT?
SHE'S THAT IM-PORTANT TO YOU?
WELL ...
I JUST ...
ABANDONING THE WORLD YOU KNEW TO FOLLOW THE ONE YOU LOVE...
THAT'S NOT EASY TO DO.
BE PROUD OF IT.
......!

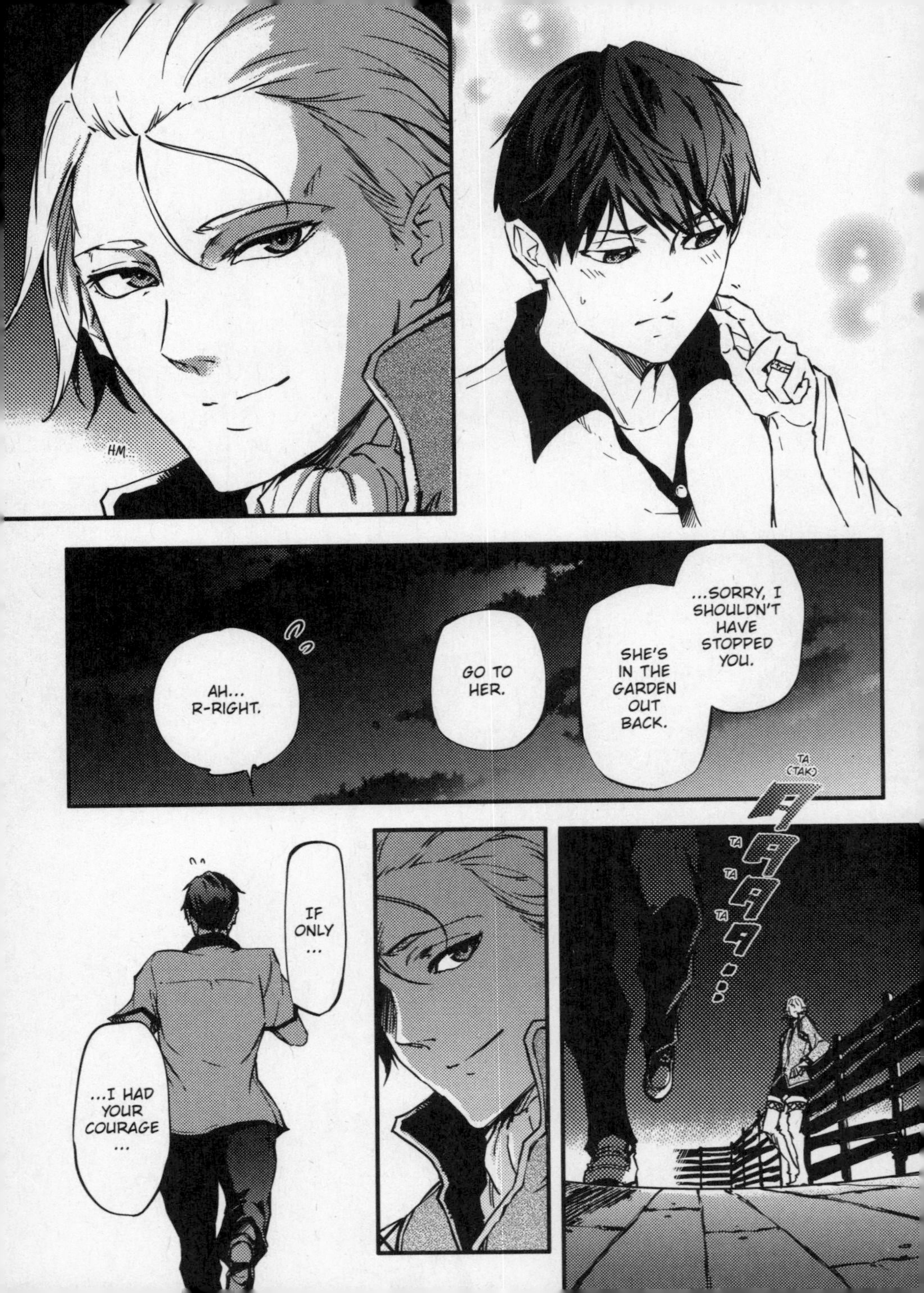
HM...
...SORRY, I SHOULDN'T HAVE STOPPED YOU.
SHE'S IN THE GARDEN OUT BACK.
GO TO HER.
AH... R-RIGHT.
TA (TAK)
TA
TA
TA
IF ONLY ...
...I HAD YOUR COURAGE ...

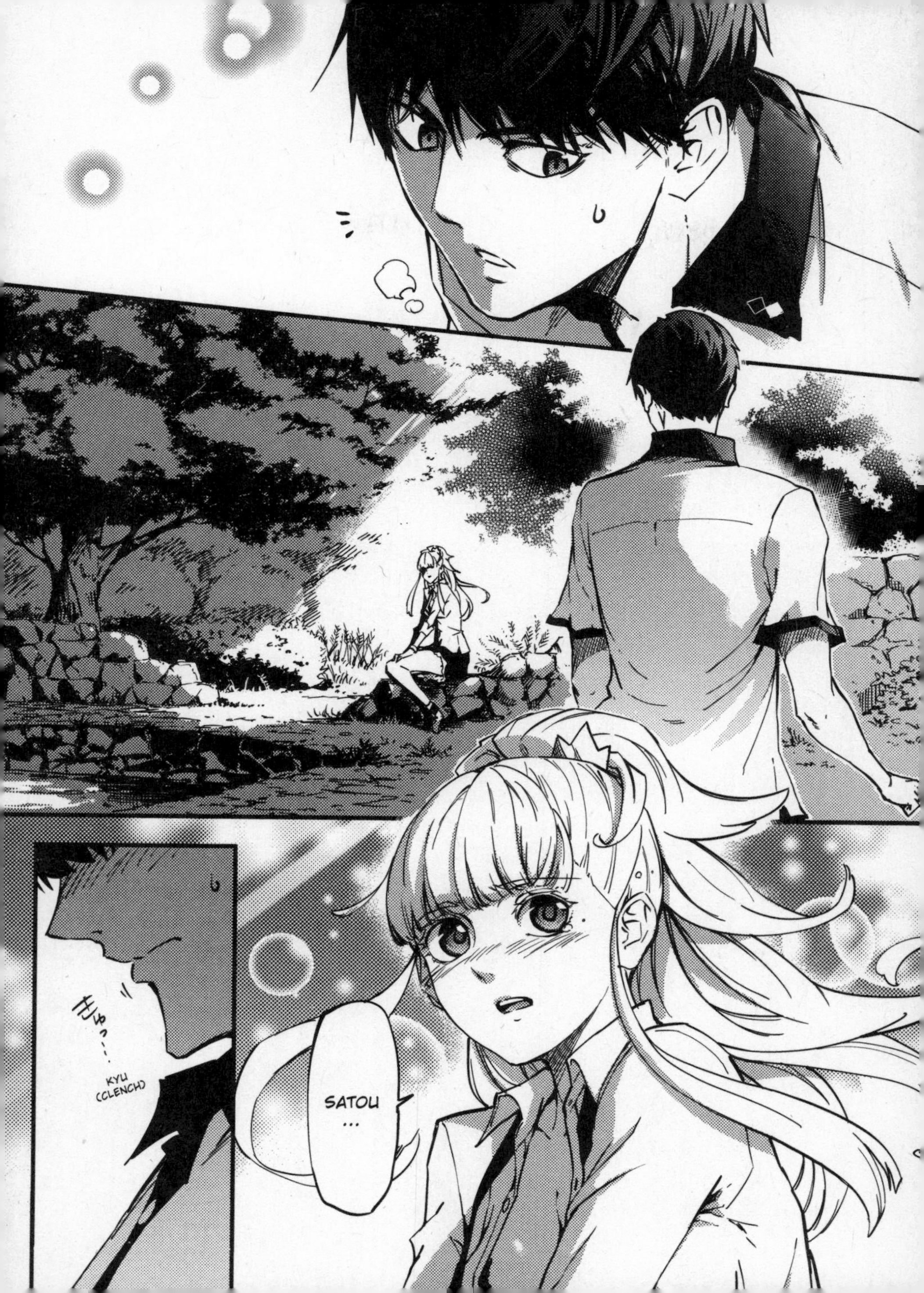
SATOU
...
きゅっ…
KYU
(CLENCH)

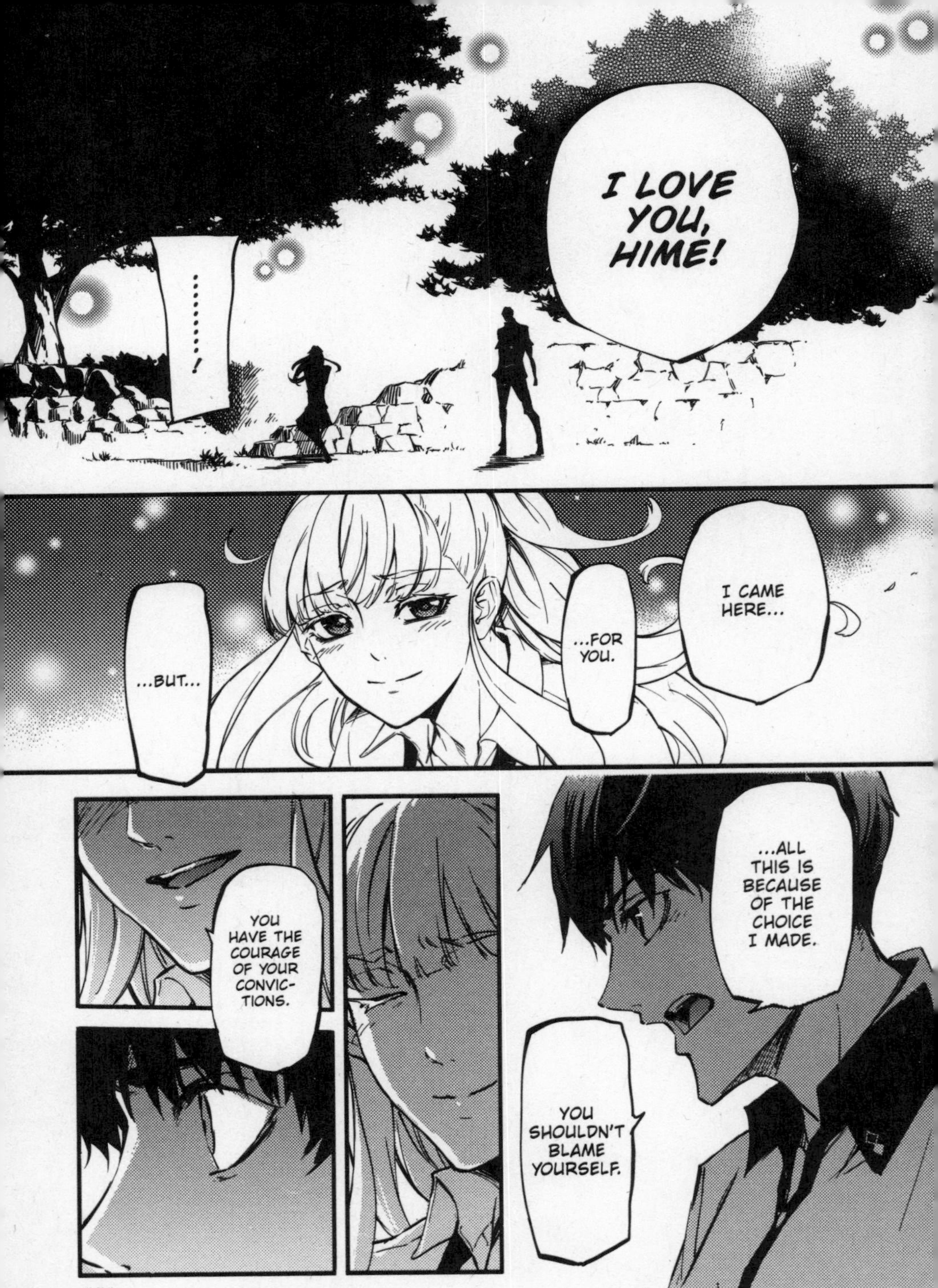
I LOVE YOU, HIME!
......!
I CAME HERE...
...FOR YOU.
...BUT...
...ALL THIS IS BECAUSE OF THE CHOICE I MADE.
YOU SHOULDN'T BLAME YOURSELF.
YOU HAVE THE COURAGE OF YOUR CONVIC- TIONS.

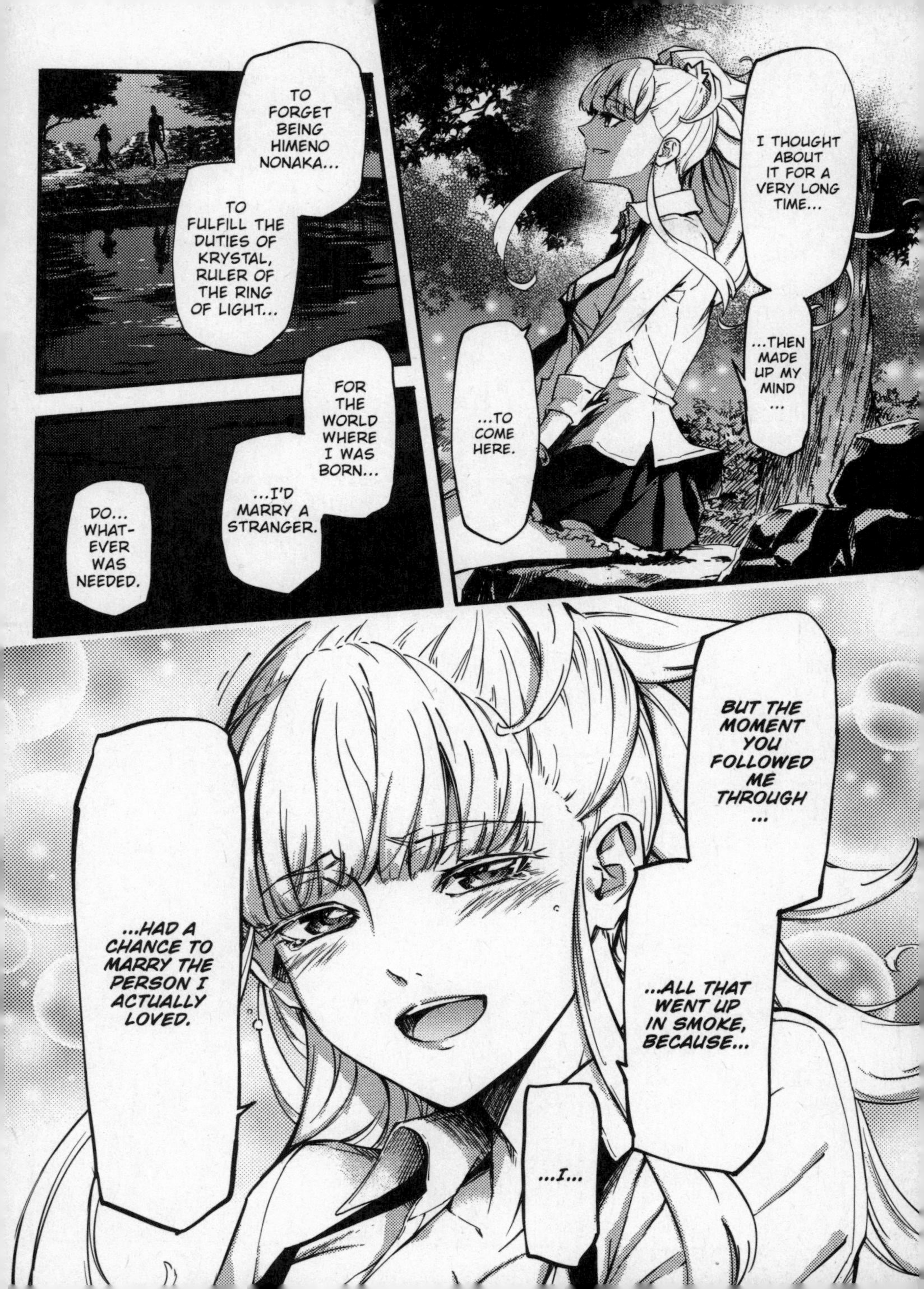
I THOUGHT ABOUT IT FOR A VERY LONG TIME...
...THEN MADE UP MY MIND...
...TO COME HERE.
TO FORGET BEING HIMENO NONAKA...
TO FULFILL THE DUTIES OF KRYSTAL, RULER OF THE RING OF LIGHT...
FOR THE WORLD WHERE I WAS BORN...
...I'D MARRY A STRANGER.
DO... WHATEVER WAS NEEDED.
BUT THE MOMENT YOU FOLLOWED ME THROUGH...
...ALL THAT WENT UP IN SMOKE, BECAUSE...
...I...
...HAD A CHANCE TO MARRY THE PERSON I ACTUALLY LOVED.

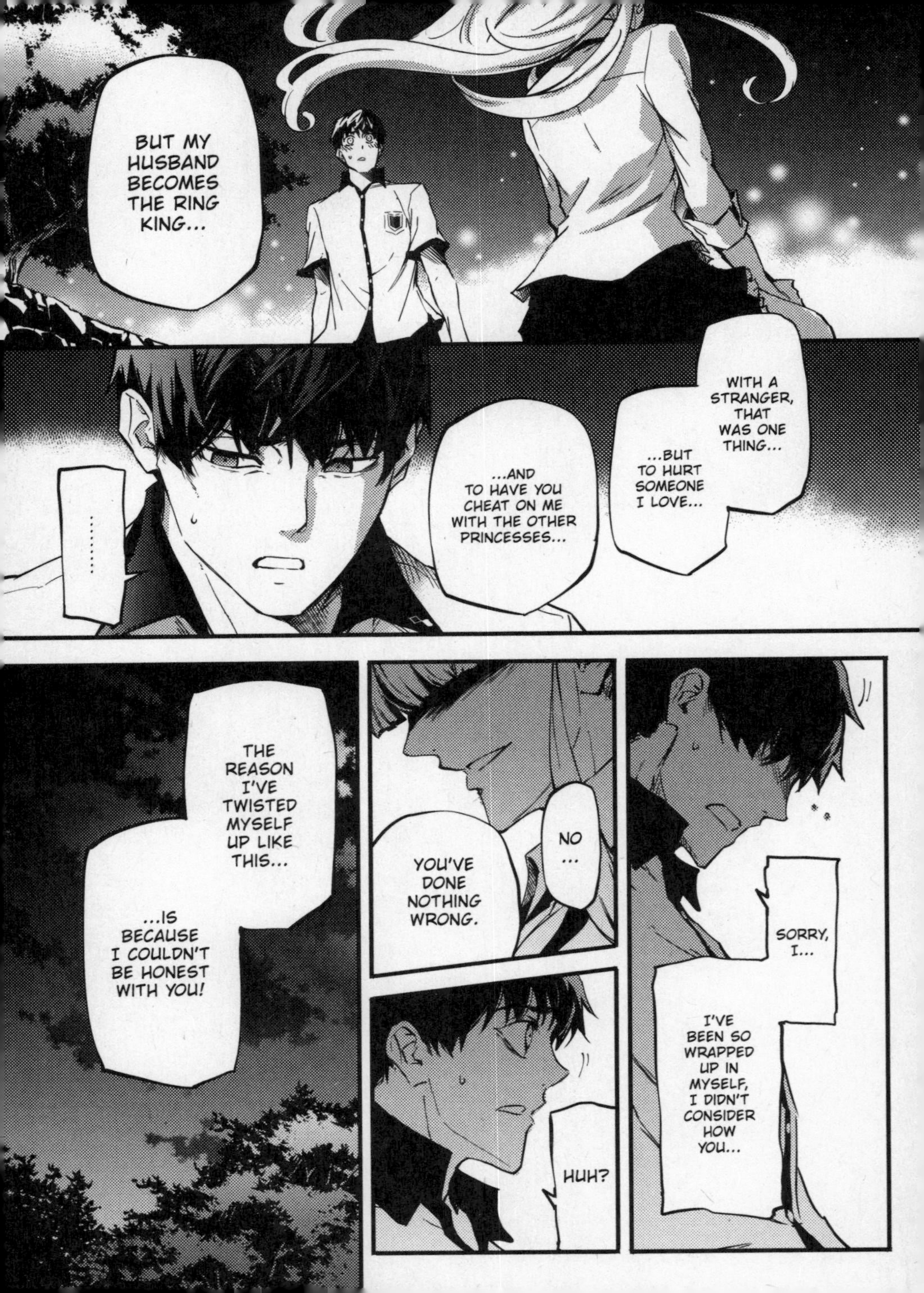
BUT MY HUSBAND BECOMES THE RING KING...
WITH A STRANGER, THAT WAS ONE THING...
...BUT TO HURT SOMEONE I LOVE...
...AND TO HAVE YOU CHEAT ON ME WITH THE OTHER PRINCESSES...
......
SORRY, I...
I'VE BEEN SO WRAPPED UP IN MYSELF, I DIDN'T CONSIDER HOW YOU...
NO...
YOU'VE DONE NOTHING WRONG.
HUH?
THE REASON I'VE TWISTED MYSELF UP LIKE THIS...
...IS BECAUSE I COULDN'T BE HONEST WITH YOU!

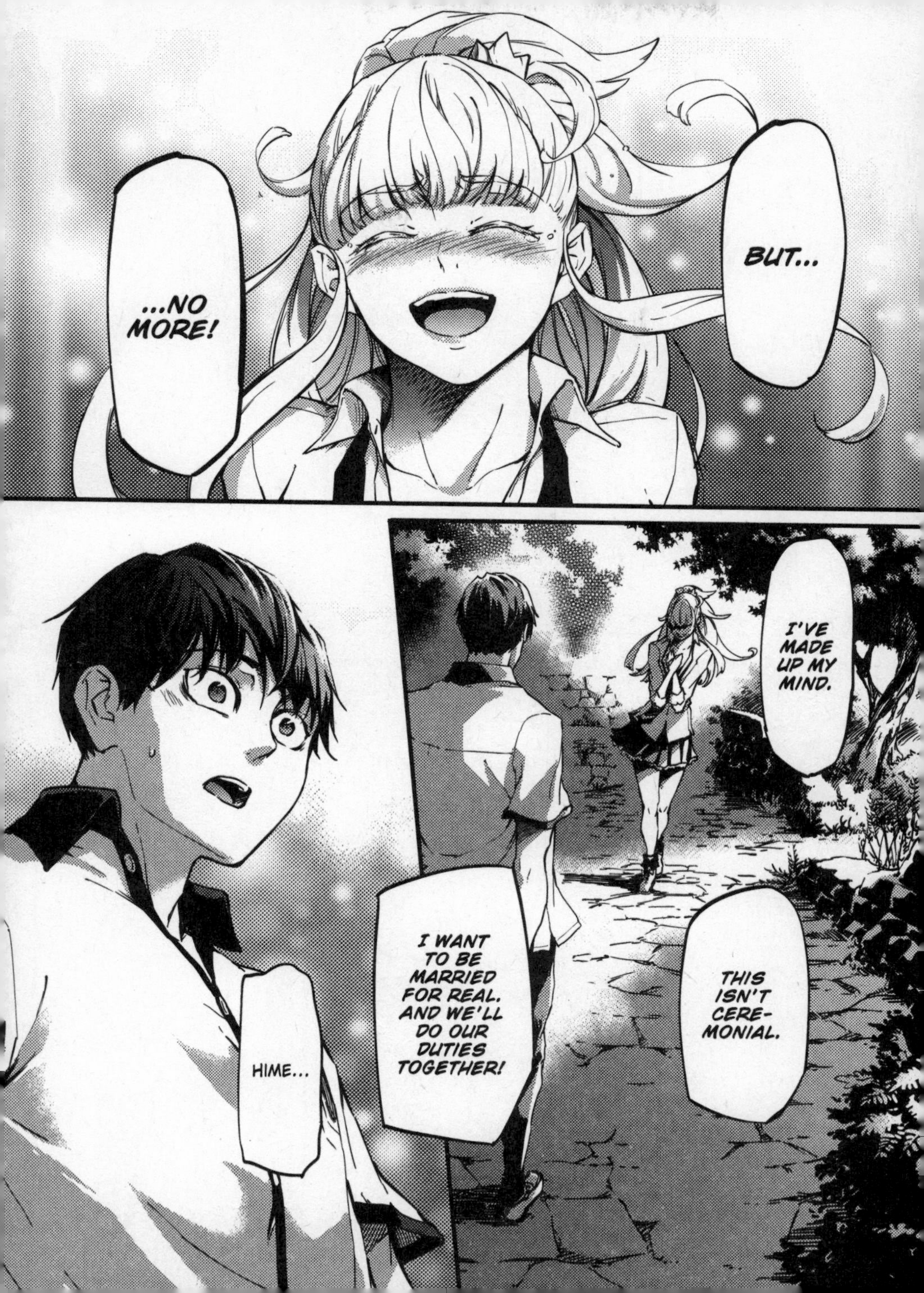
BUT...
...NO MORE!
I'VE MADE UP MY MIND.
THIS ISN'T CERE-MONIAL.
I WANT TO BE MARRIED FOR REAL. AND WE'LL DO OUR DUTIES TOGETHER!
HIME...

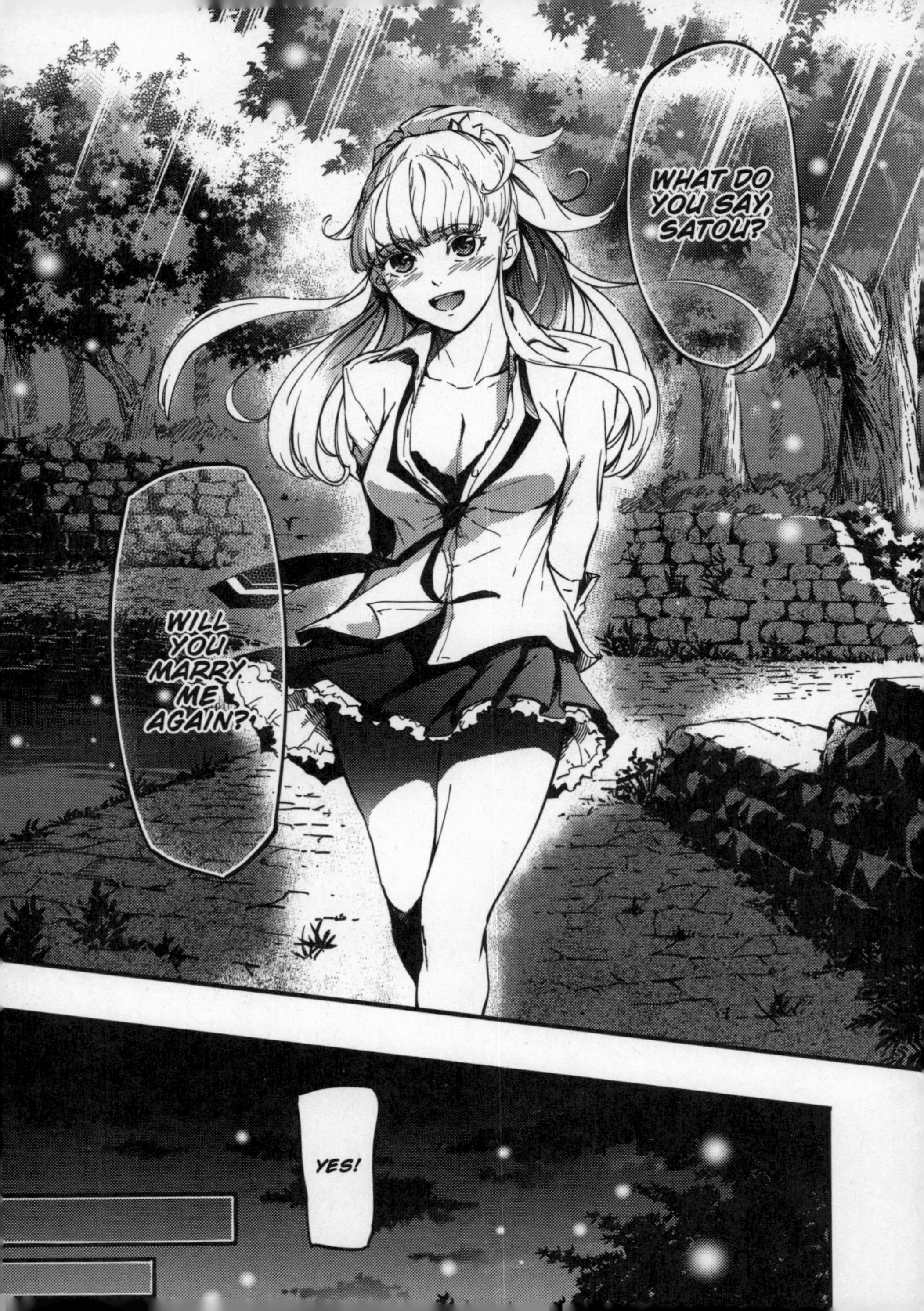
WHAT DO YOU SAY, SATOU?
WILL YOU MARRY ME AGAIN?
YES!

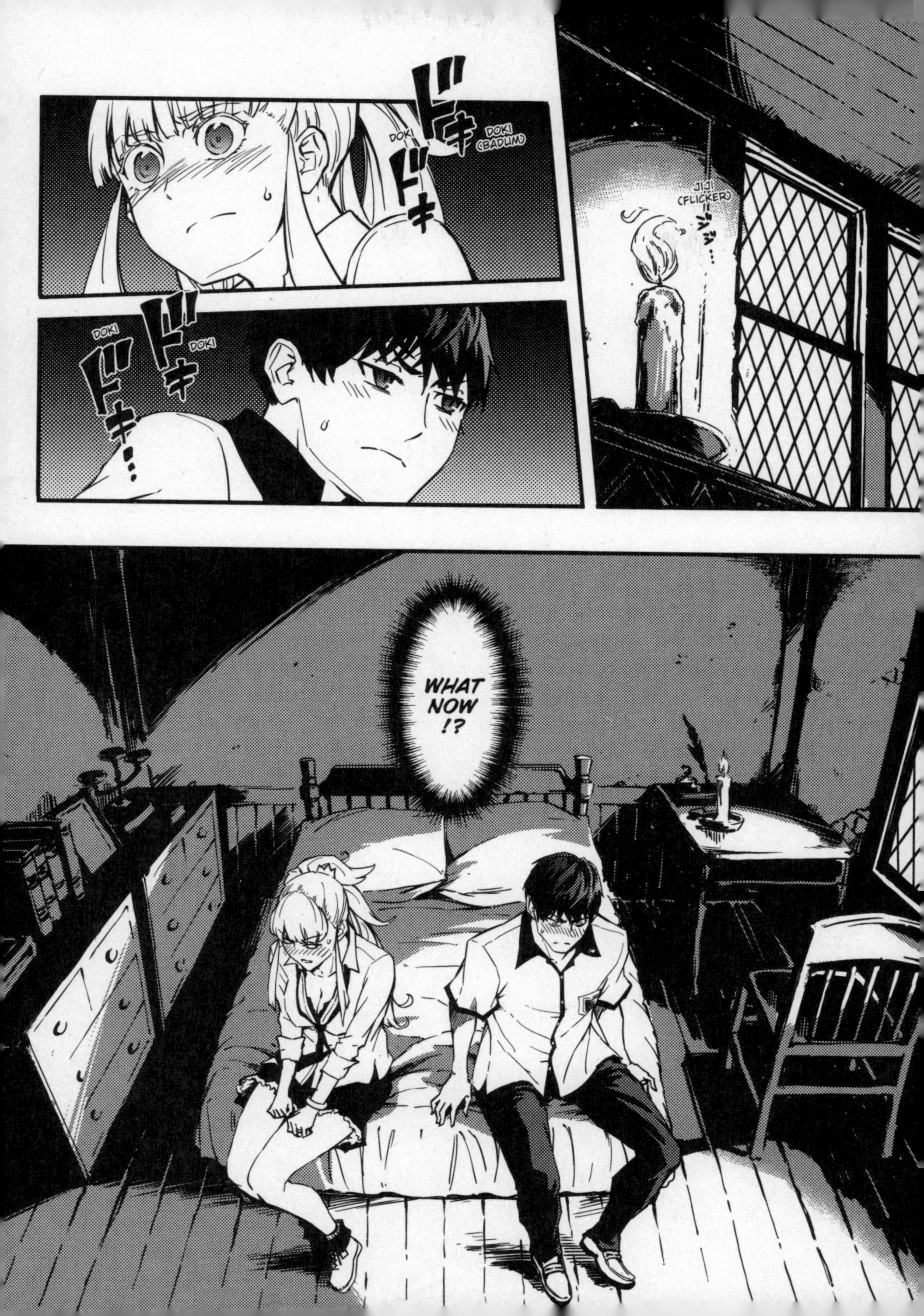
JIJI (FLICKER)
ジジ…
DOKI
ドキ
DOKI (BADUM)
ドキ
DOKI
ドキ
DOKI
ドキ…
WHAT NOW!?

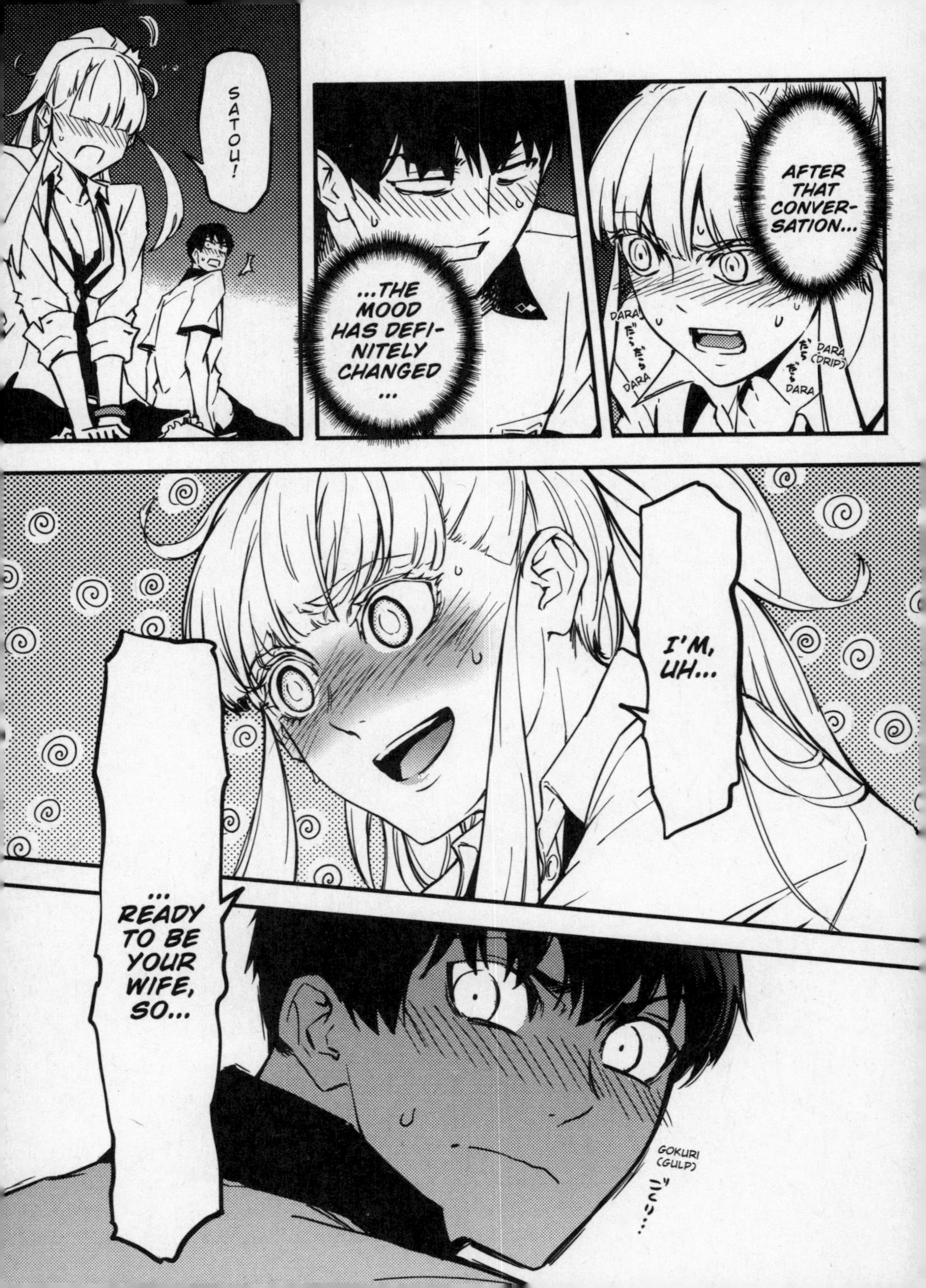
AFTER THAT CONVER-SATION...
DARA DARA
DARA (DRIP) DARA
...THE MOOD HAS DEFI-NITELY CHANGED ...
SATOU!
I'M, UH...
... READY TO BE YOUR WIFE, SO...
GOKURI (GULP)

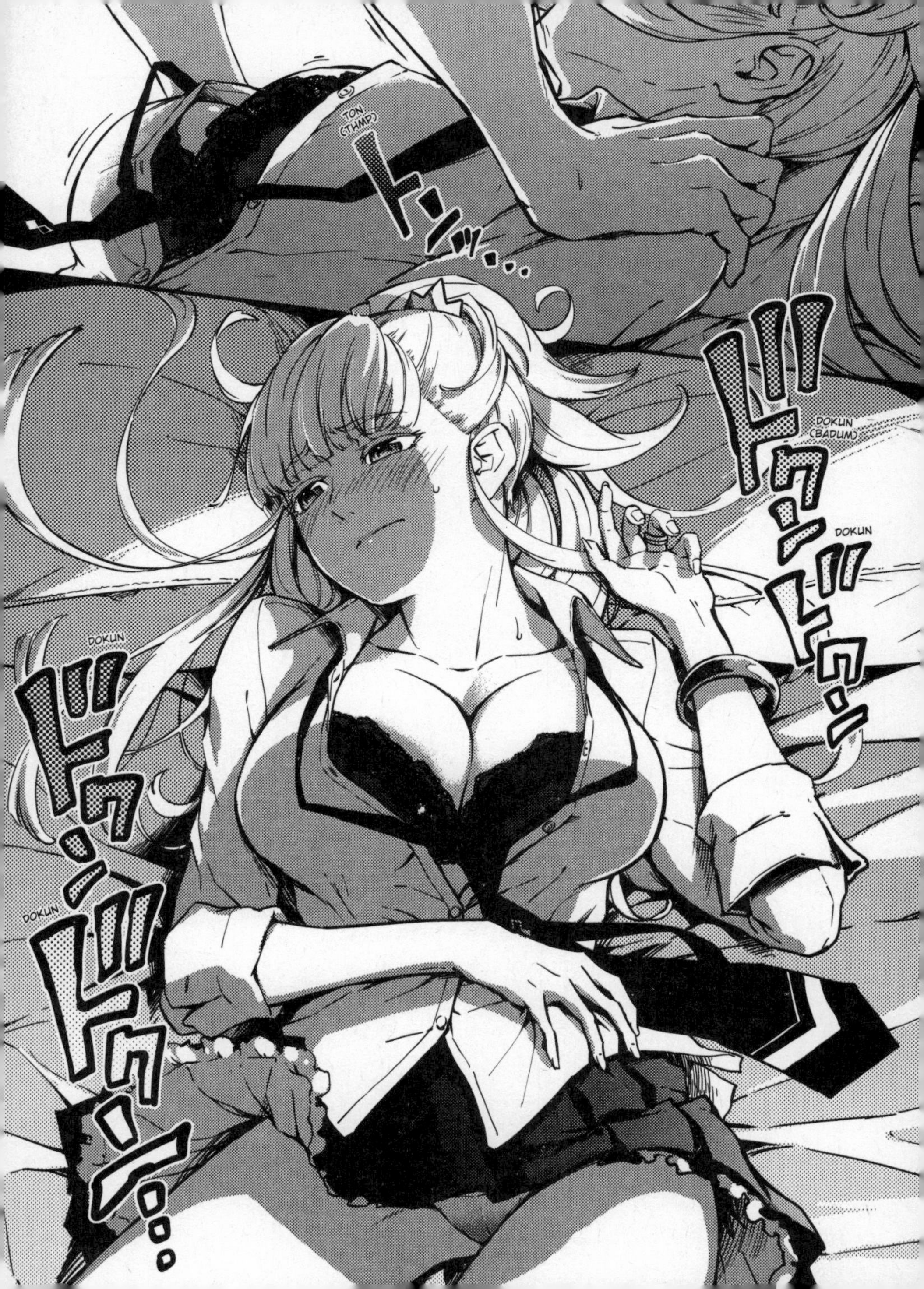
TON (THMP)
DOKUN (BADUM)
DOKUN
DOKUN
DOKUN

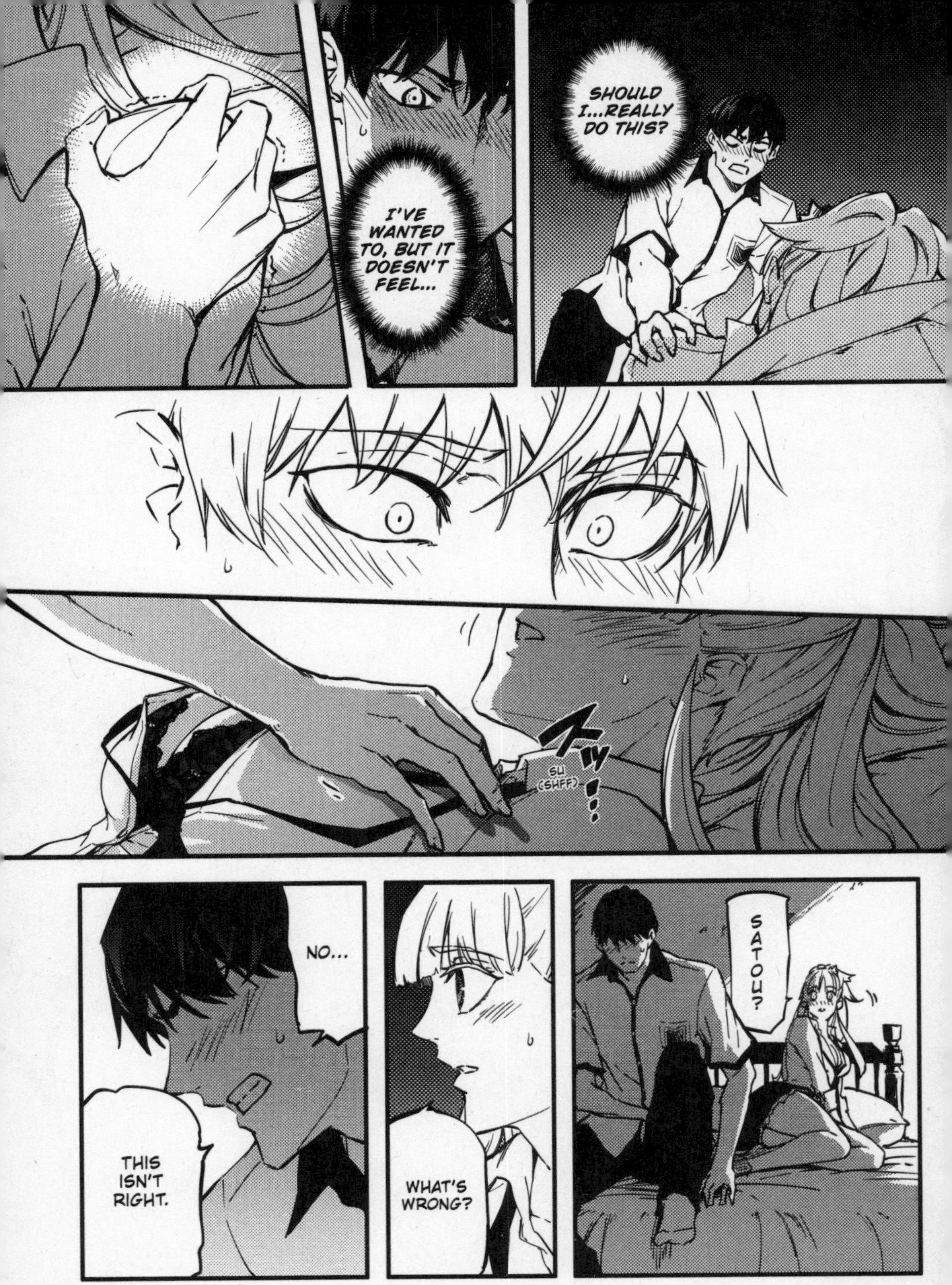
SHOULD I...REALLY DO THIS?
I'VE WANTED TO, BUT IT DOESN'T FEEL...
SU (SHFF)
SATOU?
WHAT'S WRONG?
NO...
THIS ISN'T RIGHT.

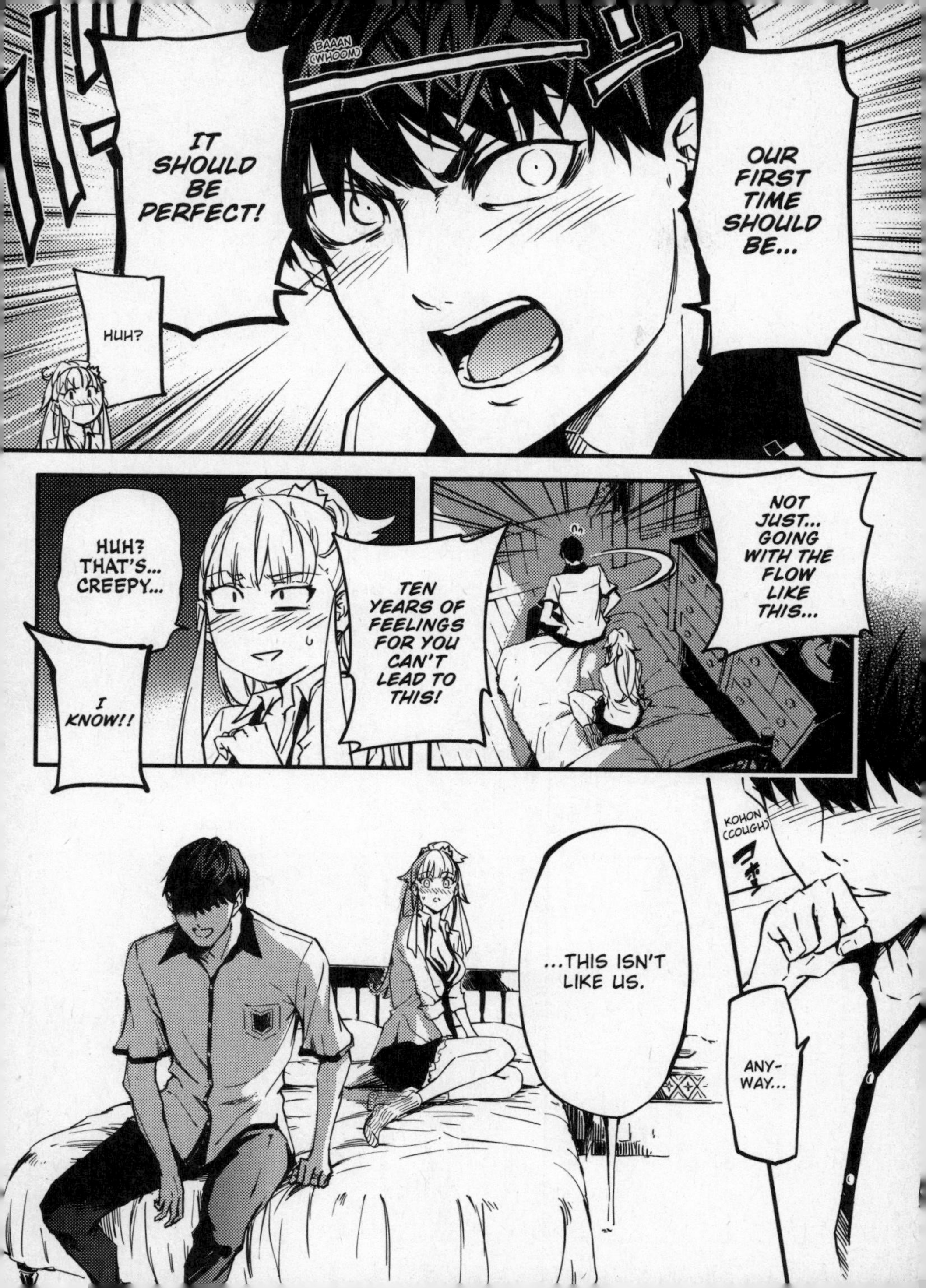
OUR FIRST TIME SHOULD BE...
BAAAN (WHOOM)
IT SHOULD BE PERFECT!
HUH?
NOT JUST... GOING WITH THE FLOW LIKE THIS...
TEN YEARS OF FEELINGS FOR YOU CAN'T LEAD TO THIS!
HUH? THAT'S... CREEPY...
I KNOW!!
KOHON (COUGH)
ANY-WAY...
...THIS ISN'T LIKE US.

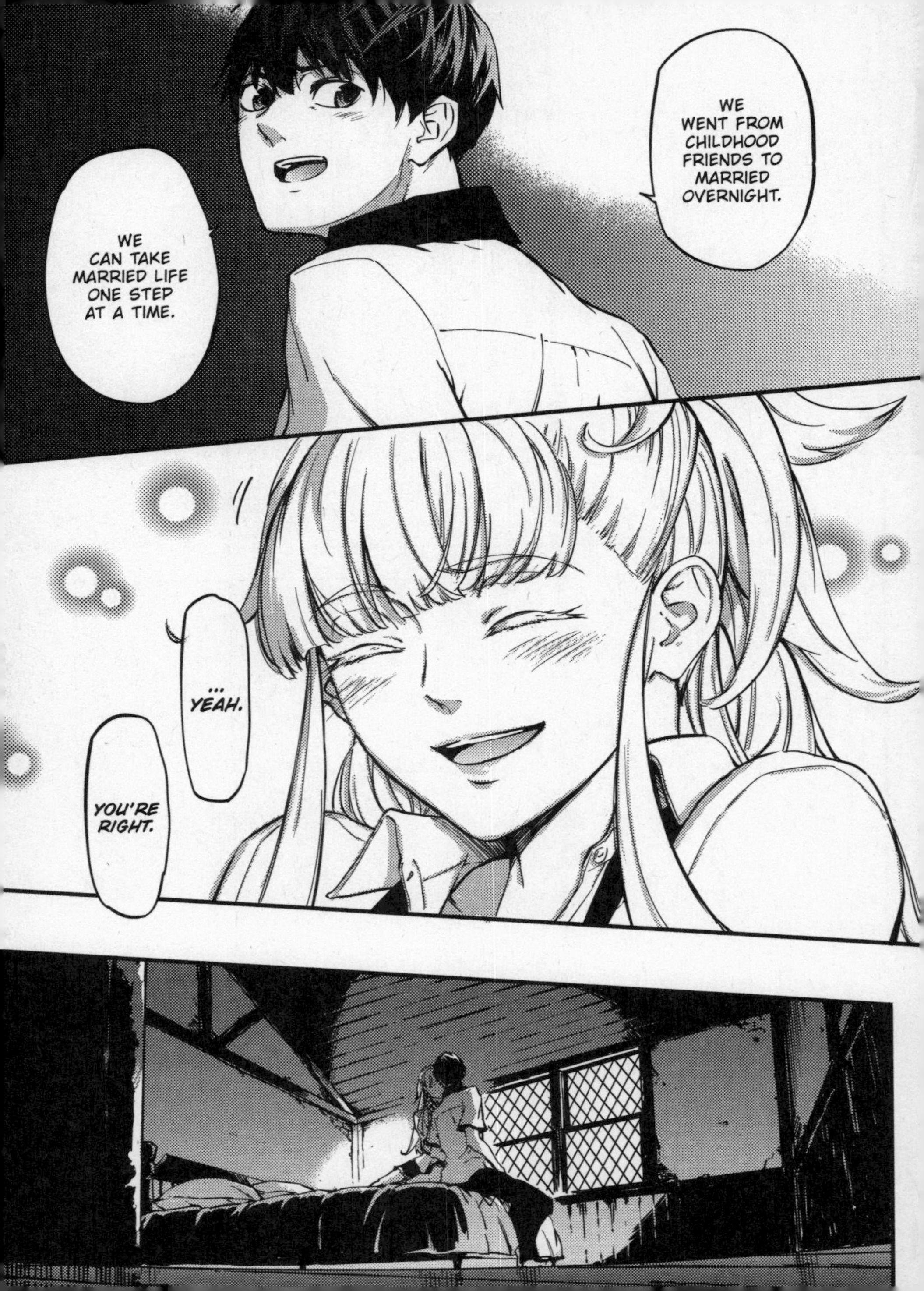
WE WENT FROM CHILDHOOD FRIENDS TO MARRIED OVERNIGHT.
WE CAN TAKE MARRIED LIFE ONE STEP AT A TIME.
...YEAH.
YOU'RE RIGHT.

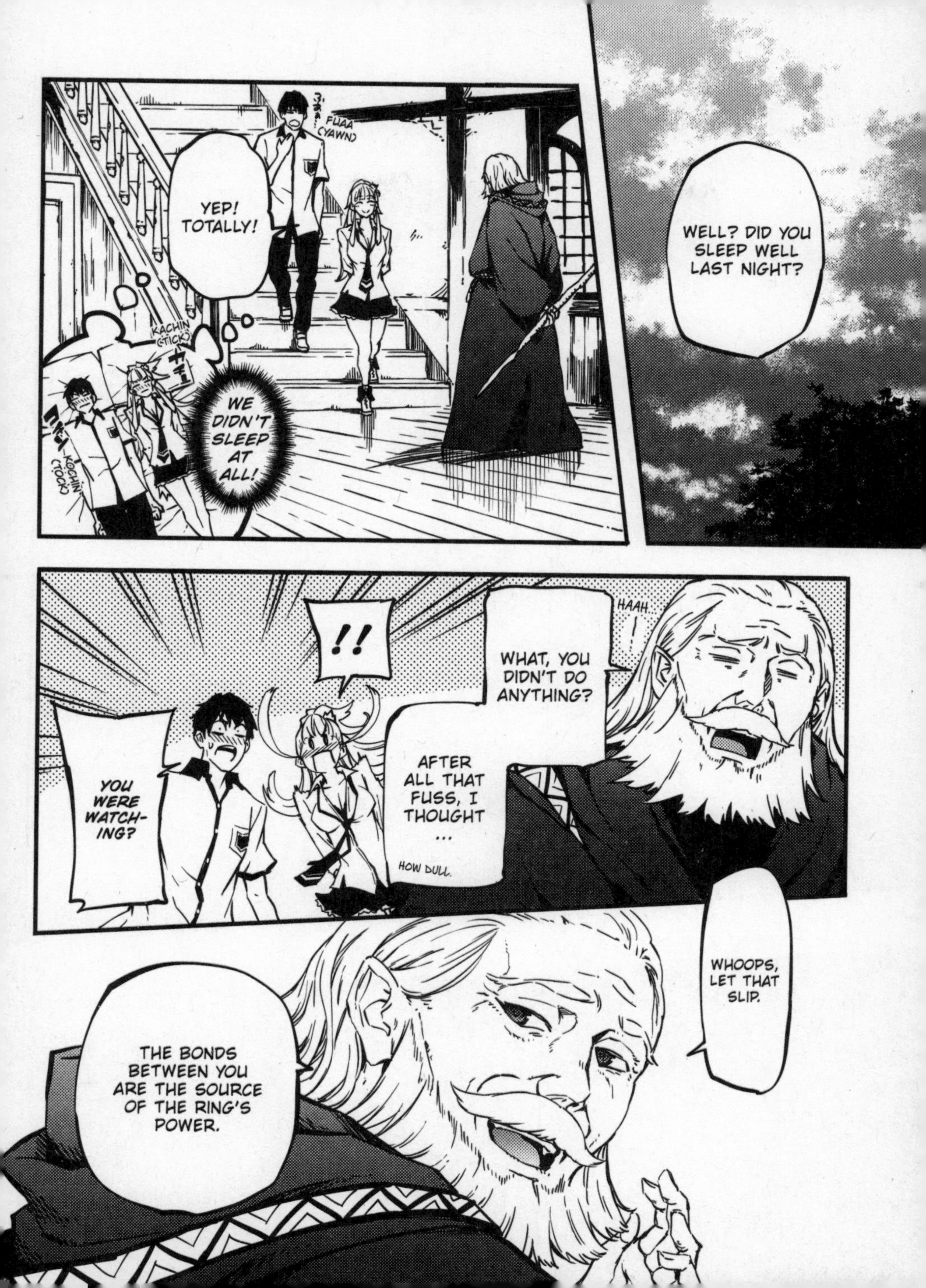
WELL? DID YOU SLEEP WELL LAST NIGHT?
FUAA (YAWN)
YEP! TOTALLY!
KACHIN (TICK)
WE DIDN'T SLEEP AT ALL!
KOCHIN (TOCK)
HAAH...
WHAT, YOU DIDN'T DO ANYTHING?
AFTER ALL THAT FUSS, I THOUGHT ...
HOW DULL.
!!
YOU WERE WATCHING?
WHOOPS, LET THAT SLIP.
THE BONDS BETWEEN YOU ARE THE SOURCE OF THE RING'S POWER.

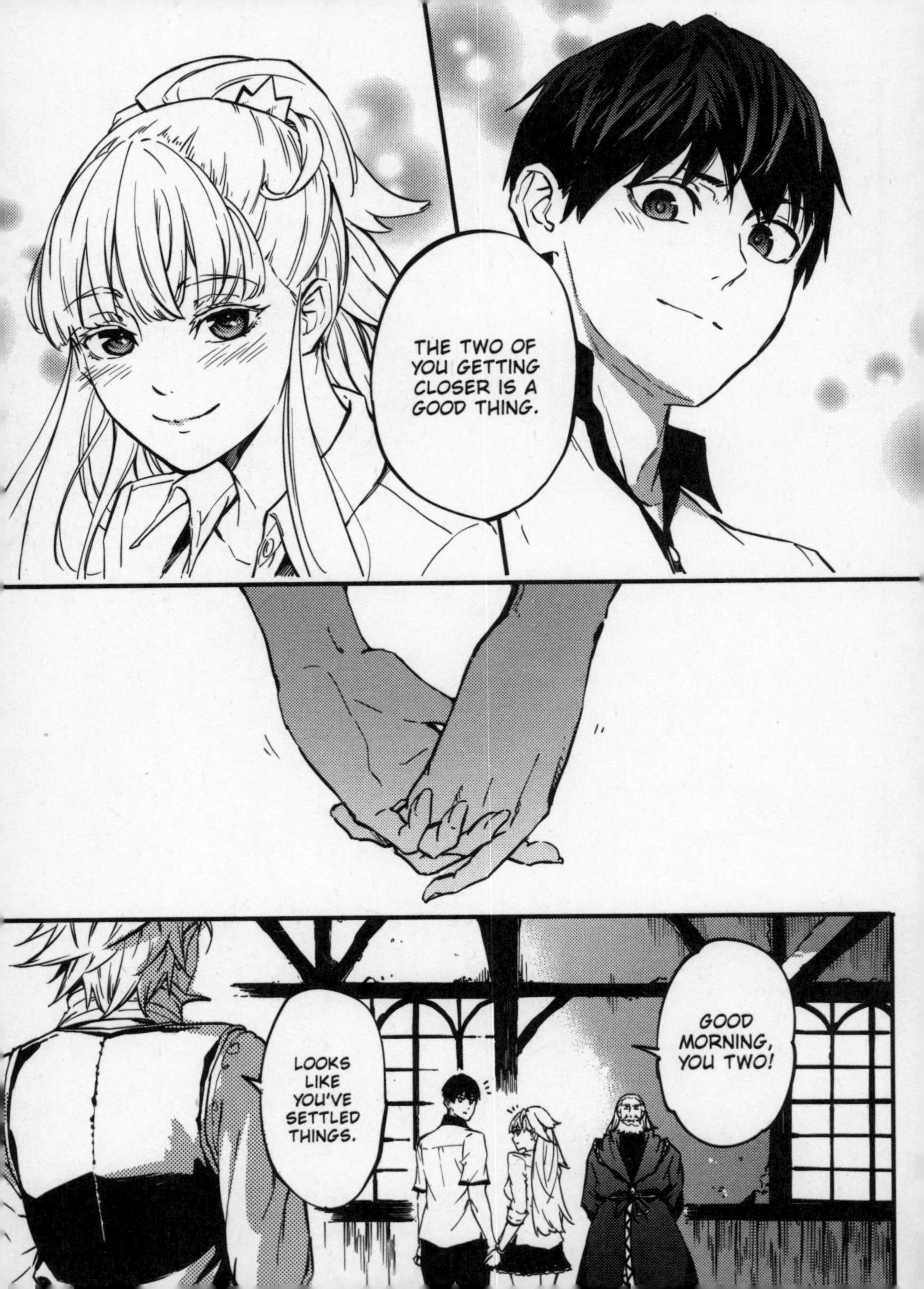
THE TWO OF YOU GETTING CLOSER IS A GOOD THING.
GOOD MORNING, YOU TWO!
LOOKS LIKE YOU'VE SETTLED THINGS.

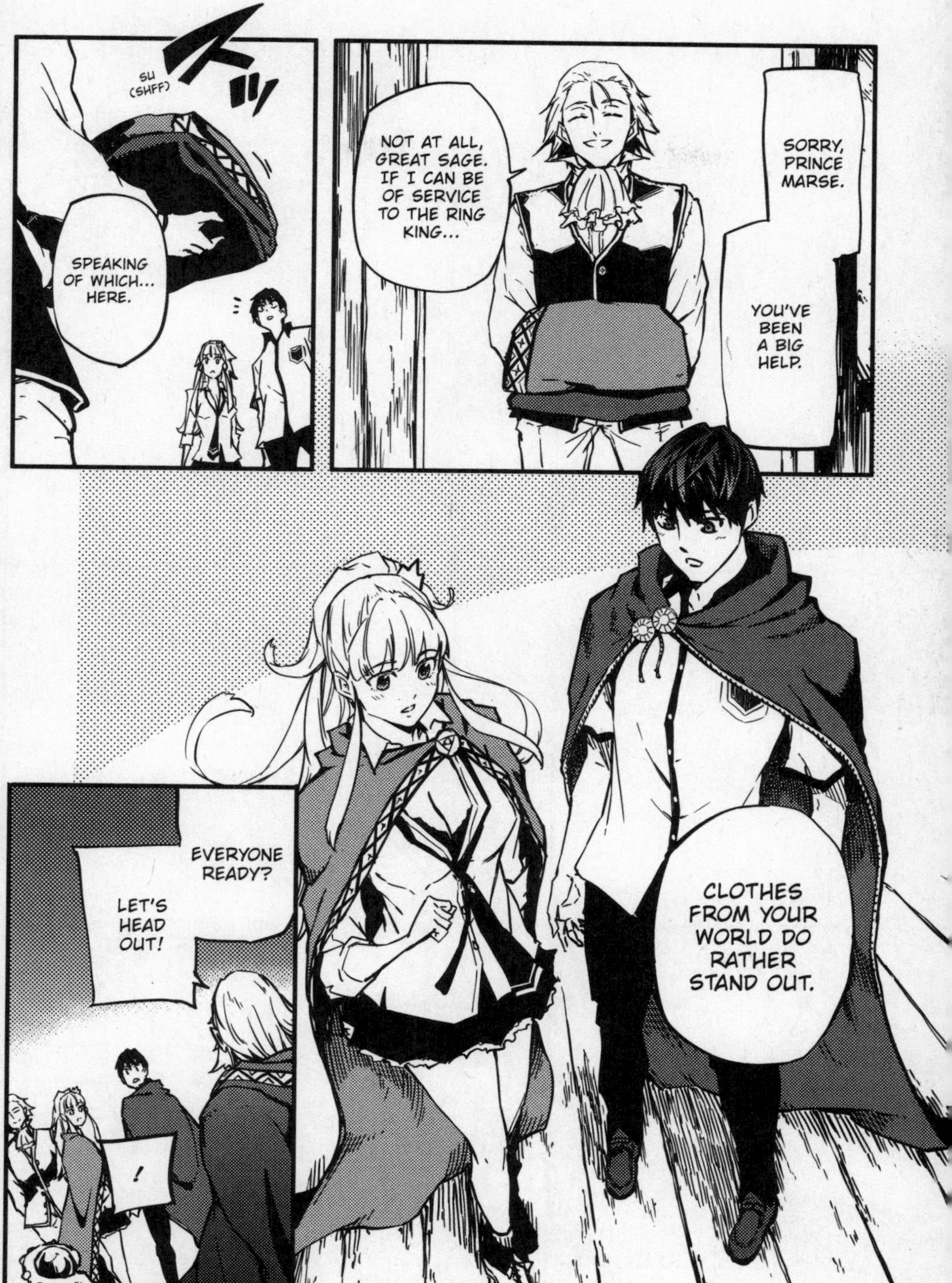
SORRY, PRINCE MARSE.
YOU'VE BEEN A BIG HELP.
NOT AT ALL, GREAT SAGE. IF I CAN BE OF SERVICE TO THE RING KING...
SU (SHFF)
SPEAKING OF WHICH... HERE.
CLOTHES FROM YOUR WORLD DO RATHER STAND OUT.
EVERYONE READY?
LET'S HEAD OUT!
!

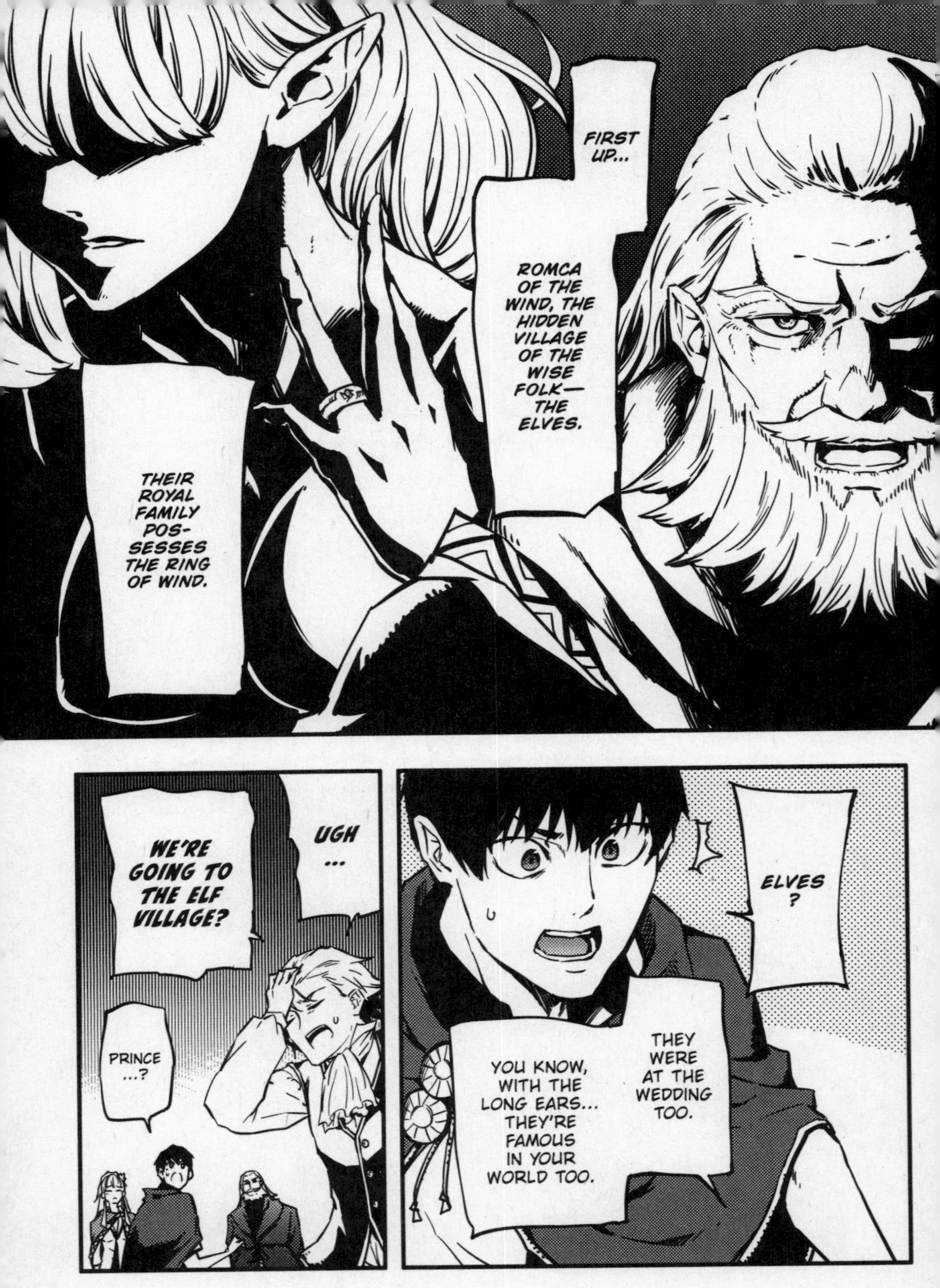
FIRST UP...
ROMCA OF THE WIND, THE HIDDEN VILLAGE OF THE WISE FOLK—THE ELVES.
THEIR ROYAL FAMILY POSSESSES THE RING OF WIND.
ELVES?
THEY WERE AT THE WEDDING TOO.
YOU KNOW, WITH THE LONG EARS... THEY'RE FAMOUS IN YOUR WORLD TOO.
UGH...
WE'RE GOING TO THE ELF VILLAGE?
PRINCE...?

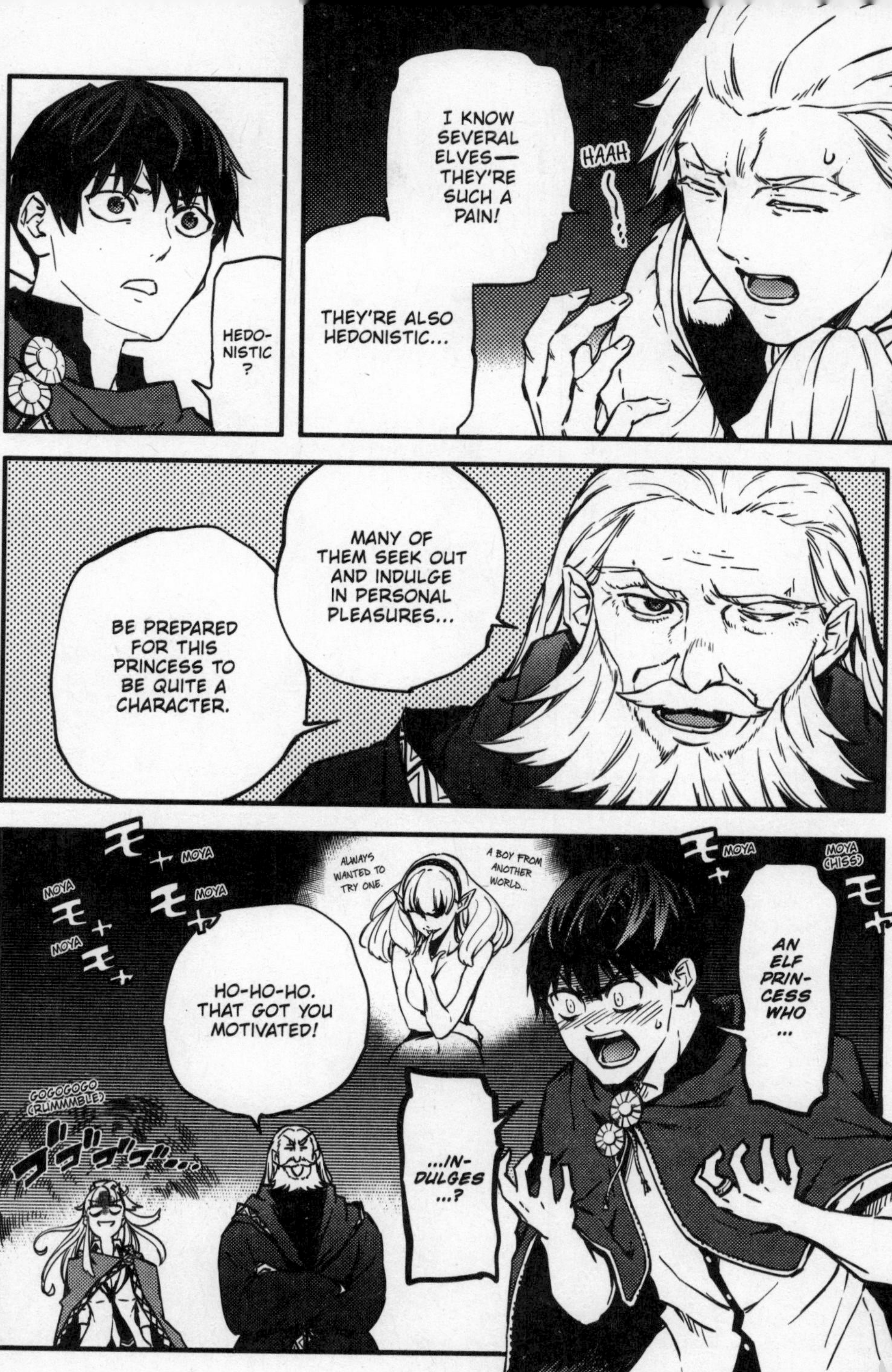

I KNOW SEVERAL ELVES— THEY'RE SUCH A PAIN!
HAAH
THEY'RE ALSO HEDONISTIC...
HEDO-NISTIC?
MANY OF THEM SEEK OUT AND INDULGE IN PERSONAL PLEASURES...
BE PREPARED FOR THIS PRINCESS TO BE QUITE A CHARACTER.
MOYA (HISS)
MOYA
AN ELF PRIN-CESS WHO...
...IN-DULGES...?
A BOY FROM ANOTHER WORLD...
ALWAYS WANTED TO TRY ONE.
HO-HO-HO. THAT GOT YOU MOTIVATED!
MOYA
MOYA
MOYA
MOYA
GOGOGOGO (RUMMMBLE)

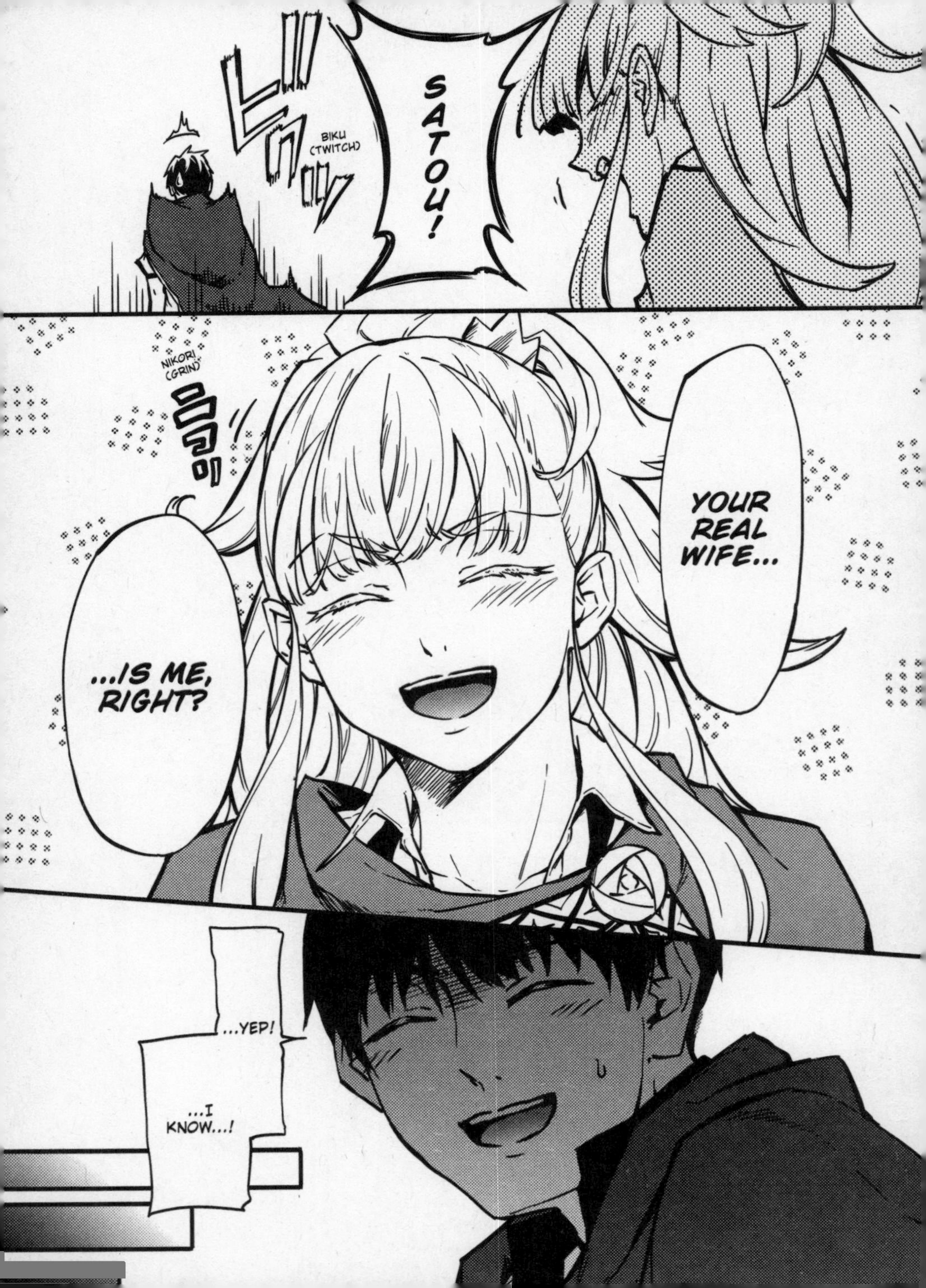
SATOU!
BIKU (TWITCH)
YOUR REAL WIFE...
NIKORI (GRIN)
...IS ME, RIGHT?
...YEP!
...I KNOW...!

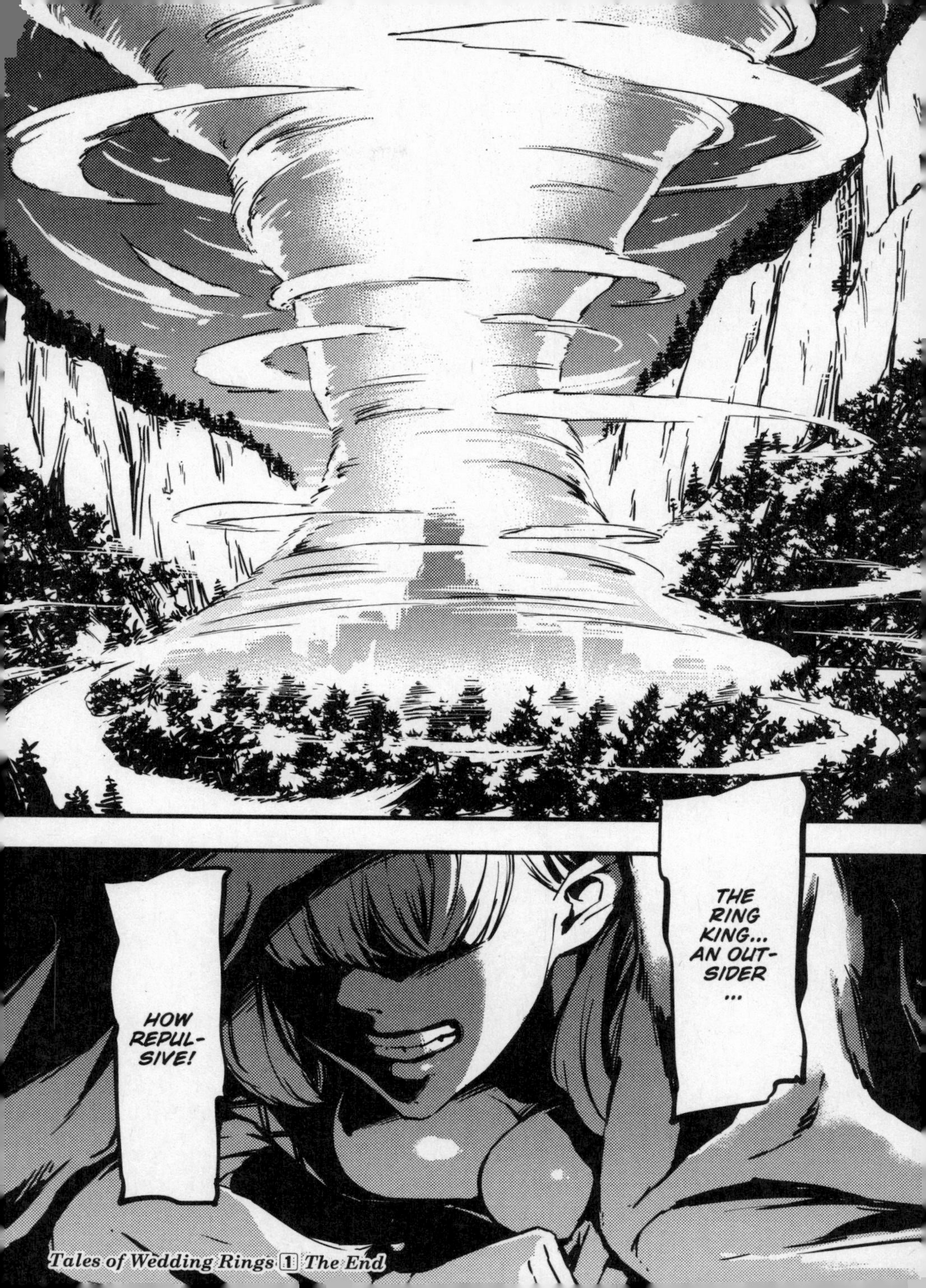
THE RING KING... AN OUTSIDER...
HOW REPULSIVE!
Tales of Wedding Rings 1 The End

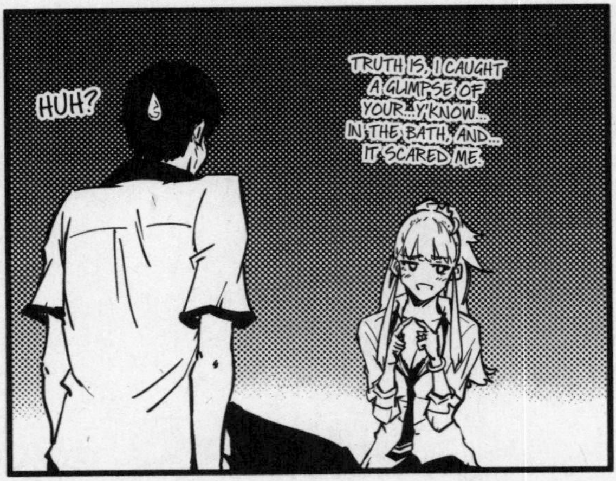
TRUTH IS, I CAUGHT A GLIMPSE OF YOUR...Y'KNOW... IN THE BATH, AND... IT SCARED ME.
HUH?

Tales of Wedding Rings

# AFTERWORD PAGE

I HONESTLY NEVER THOUGHT I'D DRAW A FANTASY MANGA...

MY LAST SERIES, DUSK MAIDEN OF AMNESIA, WAS SET IN THE CLOSED-OFF WORLD OF A SCHOOL, SO I FIGURED I SHOULD CHANGE THINGS UP A BIT, AND AFTER THINKING ABOUT IT AWHILE, I DECIDED TO TRY MY HAND AT FANTASY.

EARLY ON, I HAD A GIRL COMING FROM ANOTHER WORLD, PLUS THREE HIGH SCHOOL BOYS FLUNG INTO ANOTHER WORLD, EACH WITH THEIR OWN HEROINE, BUT A BUNCH OF STUFF HAPPENED, AND IT SETTLED ON THE SIMPLER STORY FOUND HERE. POSSIBLY, IT WOUND UP TOO SIMPLE, BUT THIS WAS MY FIRST STAB AT ANYTHING FANTASY-ISH, SO I'M NOT GONNA WORRY AND KEEP FEELING MY WAY THROUGH IT.

ADDITIONALLY, THE CONTENTS OF THIS VOLUME ARE NOT INTENDED AS A PARODY OF ANY FAMOUS WORKS. THE TITLE IS *TALES OF WEDDING RINGS*, BUT THAT IS SIMPLY A RESULT OF THE PLOT, A NATURAL COMBINATION OF PERFECTLY ORDINARY WORDS. PLEASE FORGIVE ME.

THE ILLUSTRATION HERE IS AN UNUSED ROUGH SKETCH OF AN AD FOR THE SERIALIZATION LAUNCH. A FEW DETAILS OF THE CHARACTER DESIGNS HAVE CHANGED! ALSO, SATOU'S FACE IS KINDA CREEPY.

MAYBE

properties make these beasts beloved and well looked after. They are called towelkets—the same name as a bed linen in another world—but what connection these two terms have remains a mystery.

A round the human territory of Nokanatika, faith in the Ring King has long been strong. Believers praise the Ring King and beg him to return to face the coming peril. However, the threat of the Abyss King has receded, and as peace has been maintained, the religious practices have grown somewhat abstract. Within Nokanatika alone, there are eighty-eight sites claiming to be the grave of the Ring Kings. No one is seriously attempting to investigate which, if any, are real; rather, they encourage pilgrims to make the rounds, visiting each of the graves. The annual Ring King Festival held in the Nokanatika commons is well attended, watched over by a large statue of the Ring King himself. At the end of the festival, the statue is burned, and a prayer is offered to protect all from sickness and misfortune—a tradition that has persisted for a hundred years.

K now the food, know the country. Below, I present an example of the Nokanatika family meal.

· Bread
Wheat flour, baking powder, and milk, kneaded and baked. Wheat is widely grown and eaten by peasant and noble alike.

· Vegetable-and-meat stew
The main vegetables are potatoes and beans. The meat is commonly towelket, with the royal family often presented with valuable, unsheared towelket. Truly a gift from God, towelket can provide both clothing and food.

· Fruit juice
Beverage made by squeezing a variety of fruits gathered in nearby orchards. Made to resemble the juices of the other world at the behest of the princess. However, the fruit of Nokanatika does not lend itself well to this treatment, and the Ring King has suffered greatly, forced to drink such odd concoctions.

Ugly but tasty, these vegetables' use is limited.

Adorable towelket turned into savory roast.

Vinegary

Bitter

No flavor

Tepid

# ARNULUS NATURAL HISTORY

**S**earch anywhere in the known world, and you'll find no writings that predate the legend of the Ring King and the Abyss King. Along with many countries, all writings and records of significance went up in flames. Once the Abyss King was sealed, people feared to even write his name. Yet fearing taboos, bereft of the light of knowledge, we cannot hope to illuminate the abyss. Just as our courageous ancestors left behind legends, I record here knowledge obtained when traveling the world as a young man.

—Sage Alabaster Getomik

**N**okanatika, the Kingdom of Light, is a country of "the true people"— humans—awaiting the return of the Ring King. The Nokanatika royal family bears the Ring of Light, are revered by the citizens who believe the legend of the Ring King, and have ruled in peace for many years. As such, in addition to agricultural businesses, the economy is primarily supported by tourism to the holy land of the Ring King legend. Folkcraft pennants, wooden replicas of the Ring King's weapons of light, and whittled images of the Ring King himself are popular souvenirs. Relations with neighboring countries are strong, with the biggest issue being regular complaints from pilgrims regarding restaurant prices. What could be more indicative of peace?

**B**eyond the ring faith, Nokanatika is also known for uniquely high-quality textiles. Cloth made from the fur of the herbivores grazing on the prairies is both absorbent and warm and is valued for many purposes. These beasts are extremely tall, their every inch so covered in fur that, while all have seen them, few have seen their faces. They have moderately curly hair that can easily be sheared and woven into cloth. Their gentle nature and beneficial

## Author's Note

I WANNA PLAY GAMES...
I'M BEAT...
STORY
ART

# Maybe

I watched all three *Lord of the Rings* movies in one day and nearly died. (And I didn't even get anything from them that I could use in this manga.)

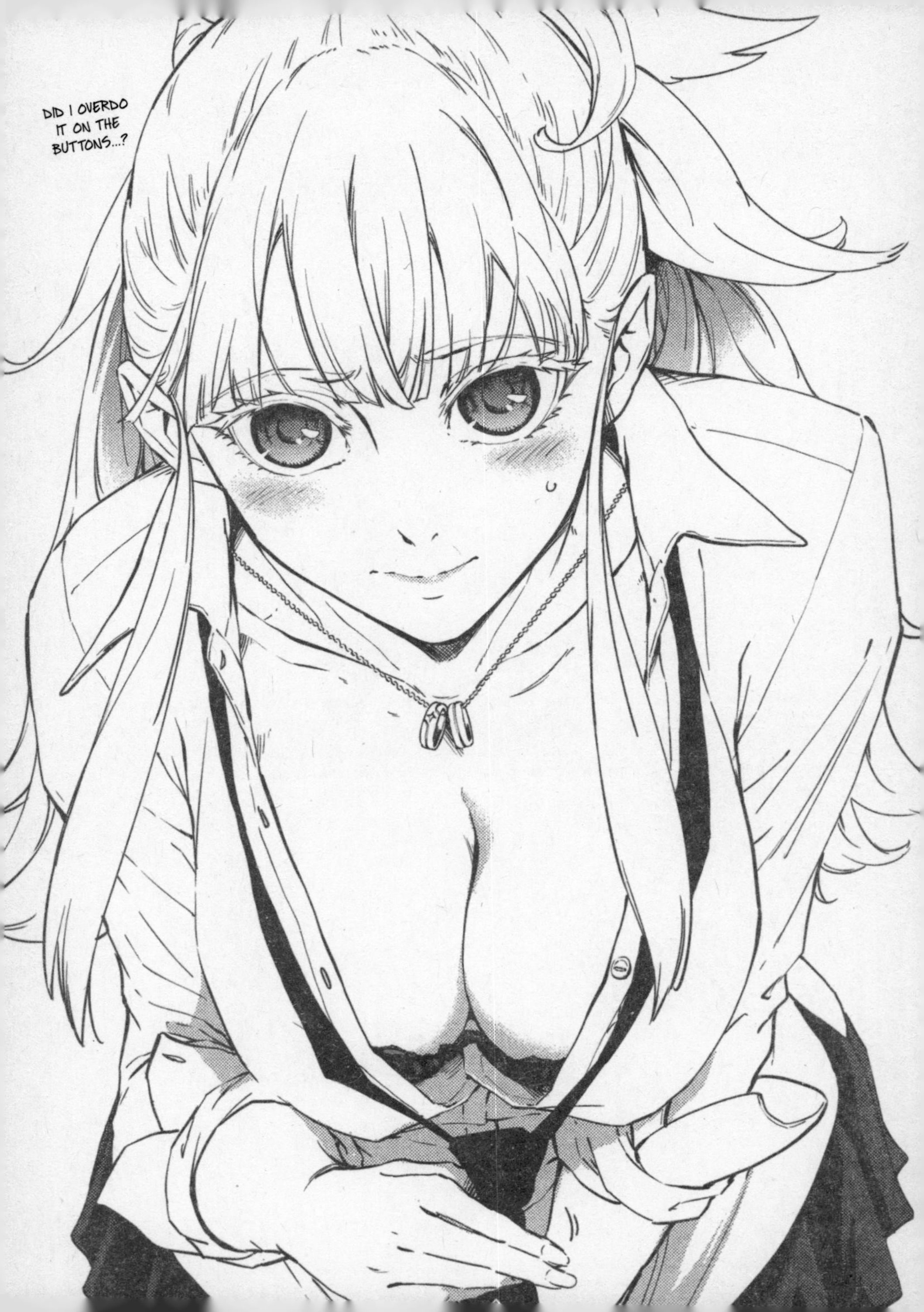
DID I OVERDO IT ON THE BUTTONS...?

# NEXT

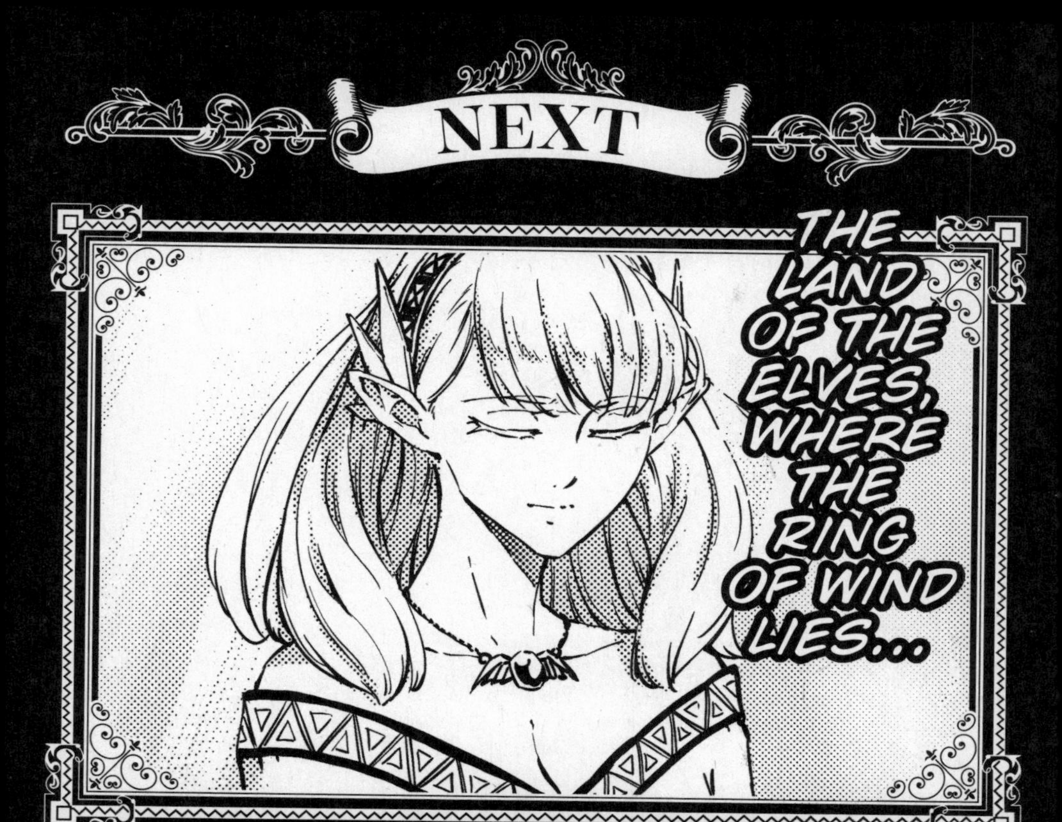
THE LAND OF THE ELVES, WHERE THE RING OF WIND LIES...

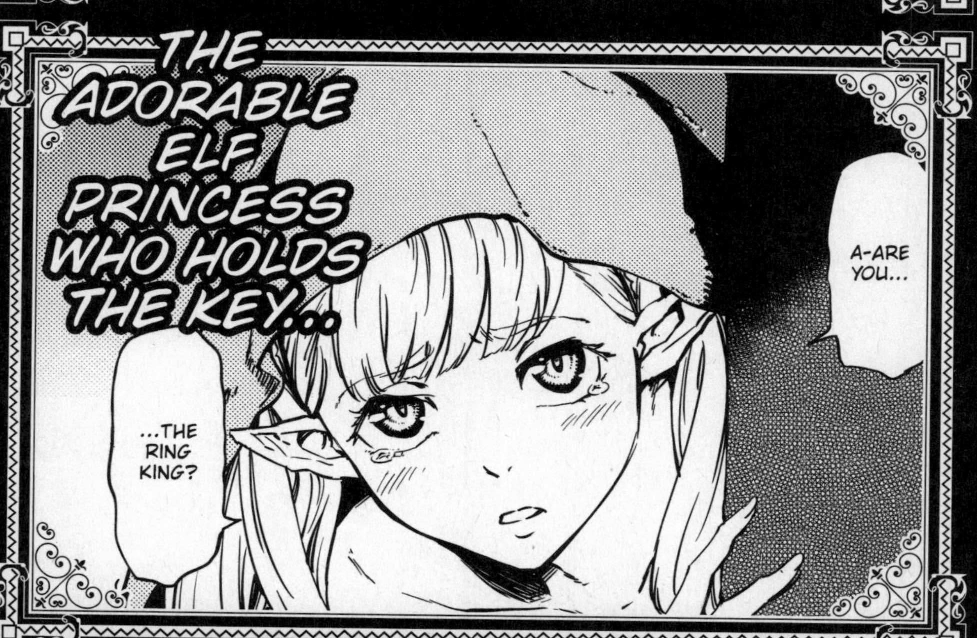
THE ADORABLE ELF PRINCESS WHO HOLDS THE KEY...
A-ARE YOU...
...THE RING KING?

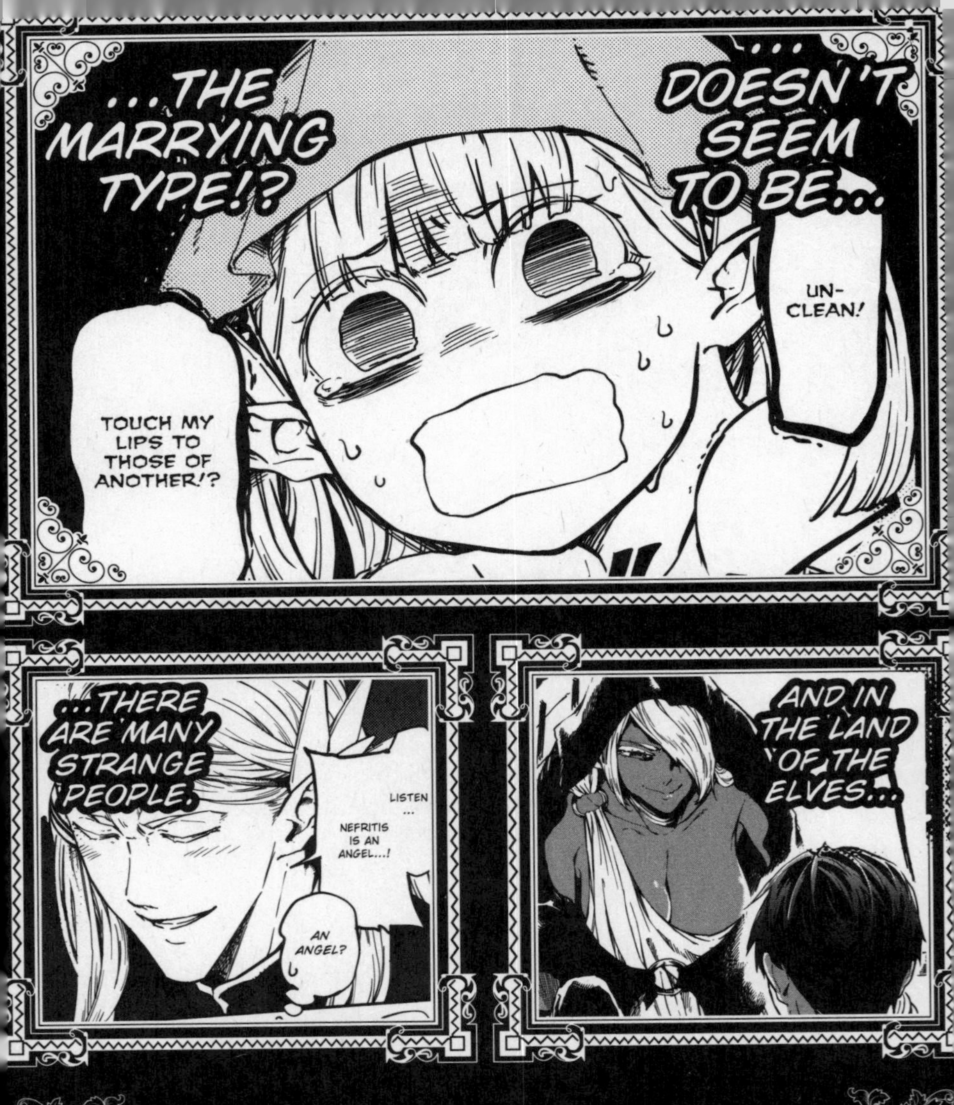

...DOESN'T SEEM TO BE...
UN-CLEAN!
...THE MARRYING TYPE!?
TOUCH MY LIPS TO THOSE OF ANOTHER!?
AND IN THE LAND OF THE ELVES...
...THERE ARE MANY STRANGE PEOPLE.
LISTEN...
NEFRITIS IS AN ANGEL...!
AN ANGEL?


What will befall Satou and Hime?

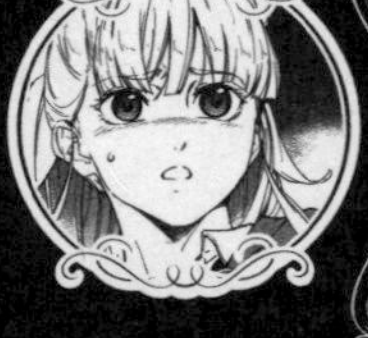

# Tales of Wedding Rings

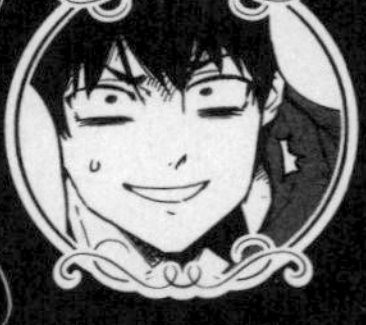

Maybe

◆ Look forward to Volume 2!

# MURDERER
## IN THE STREETS, KILLER
### IN THE SHEETS!

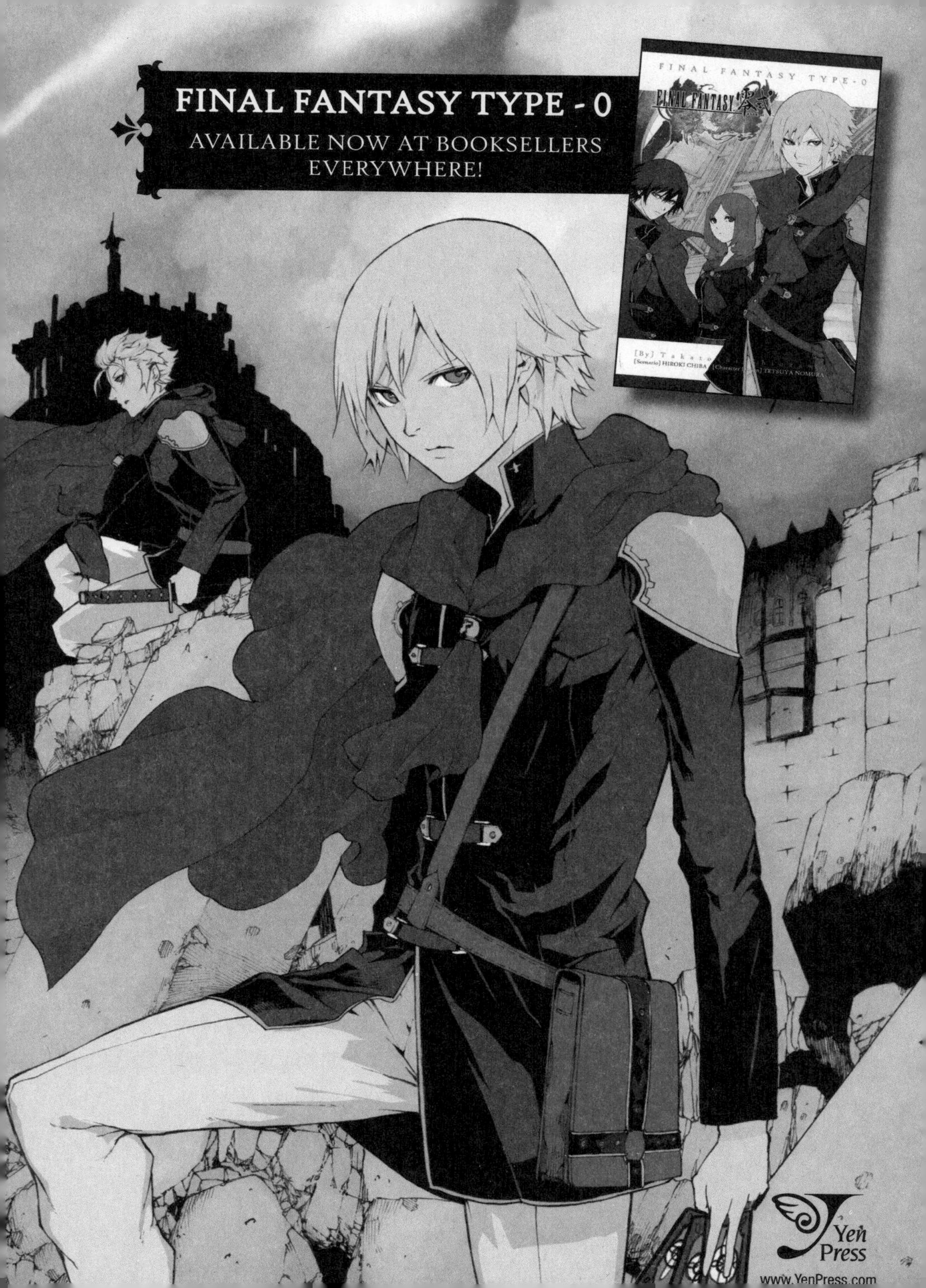

FINAL FANTASY TYPE - 0
AVAILABLE NOW AT BOOKSELLERS EVERYWHERE!
FINAL FANTASY TYPE-0
FINAL FANTASY 零式
[By] Takato
[Scenario] HIROKI CHIBA
TETSUYA NOMURA
Yen Press
www.YenPress.com

# FINAL FANTASY 零式 TYPE-0



Art: TAKATOSHI SHIOZAWA
Character Design: TETSUYA NOMURA
Scenario: HIROKI CHIBA

The cadets of Akademeia's Class Zero are legends, with strength and magic unrivaled, and crimson capes symbolizing the great Vermilion Bird of the Dominion. But will their elite training be enough to keep them alive when a war breaks out and the Class Zero cadets find themselves at the front and center of a bloody political battlefield?!

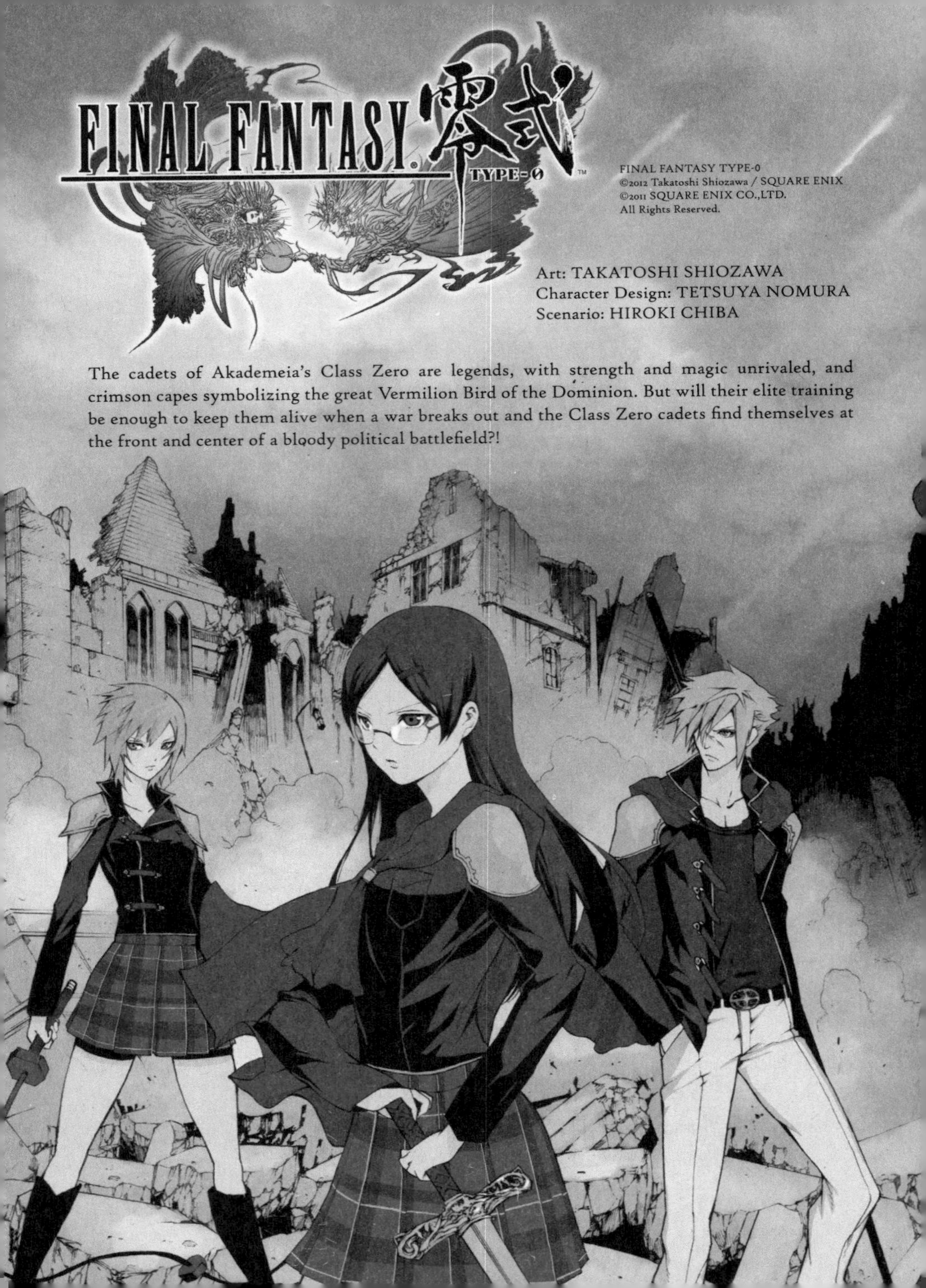

# Tales of Wedding Rings
## MAYBE
### 1

Translation: Andrew Cunningham ❦ Lettering: Phil Christie

This book is a work of fiction. Names, characters, places, and incidents are the product of the author's imag[...]s, locales, or

Fi[...]
Engl[...]
an[...]

Yen Press, LLC s[...] The purpose of copyright is to encourage writers and artists to produce the creative works that enrich our culture.

The scanning, uploading, and distribution of this book without permission is a theft of the author's intellectual property. If you would like permission to use material from the book (other than for review purposes), please contact the publisher. Thank you for your support of the author's rights.

Yen Press
1290 Avenue of the Americas
New York, NY 10104

Visit us at yenpress.com
facebook.com/yenpress
twitter.com/yenpress
yenpress.tumblr.com
instagram.com/yenpress

First Yen Press Edition: February 2018

Yen Press is an imprint of Yen Press, LLC.
The Yen Press name and logo are trademarks of Yen Press, LLC.

The publisher is not responsible for websites (or their content) that are not owned by the publisher.

ISBNs: 978-0-316-41616-0 (paperback)

D1291075